THE MAKING OF ZIMBABWE

THE MAKING OF

ZIMBABWE

Decolonization in Regional and International Politics

M. TAMARKIN

Tel Aviv University, Israel

FRANK CASS

First published 1990 in Great Britain by
FRANK CASS & CO. LTD.
Gainsborough House, 11 Gainsborough Road,
London, E11 1RS, England
in cooperation with the
Moshe Dayan Center for Middle Eastern and African Studies,
Tel Aviv University

and in the United States of America by
FRANK CASS
c/o Rowman & Littlefield Publishers, Inc.
8705 Bollman Place, Savage, MD 20763

British Library Cataloguing in Publication Data

Tamarkin, M.
   The making of Zimbabwe: decolonization in regional
and international politics
   1. Zimbabwe. decolonization, 1944–1980
   I. Title
   968.91'04

ISBN 0-7146-3355-0

Library of Congress Cataloging-in-Publication Data

Tamarkin, M.
      The making of Zimbabwe : decolonization in regional and
international politics / M. Tamarkin.
         p.   cm.
         Bibliography: p.
         Includes index.
         ISBN 0–7146–3355–0
         1. Zimbabwe—Politics and government—1965–1979.
      2. Decolonization—Zimbabwe.   I. Title.
      DT962.75.T36   1990
      968.91'04—dc20   89–31670
                                                                    CIP

Printed and bound in Great Britain by
BPCC Wheatons Ltd., Exeter

IN MEMORY OF MY LATE FATHER,
TO MY MOTHER
AND TO MY WIFE AVIVA

Contents

List of Abbreviations

ACCOR	Associated Chambers of Commerce of Rhodesia
AFM	Armed Forces Movement
ANC	African National Congress
BBC	British Broadcasting Corporation
CIO	Central Intelligence Organization
FLP	Front-Line Presidents
FROLIZI	Front for the Liberation of Zimbabwe
MNR	Mozambique National Resistance
MPLA	Movimento Popular de Liberacao de Angola
OAU	Organization of African Unity
OPEC	Organization of Oil Exporting Countries
PF	Patriotic Front
RAP	Rhodesian Action Party
RBC	Rhodesian Broadcasting Corporation
RF	Rhodesian Front
RLI	Rhodesian Light Infantry
RP	Rhodesian Party
SABC	South African Broadcasting Corporation
SAR	South African Railway
SAS	Special Air Service
SASCON	Southern African Solidarity Congress
SWA	South-West Africa
SWAPO	South-West African People's Organization
UANC	United African National Council
UDI	Unilateral Declaration of Independence
UNO	United Nations Organization
ZANU	Zimbabwe African National Union
ZANLA	Zimbabwe National Liberation Army
ZAPU	Zimbabwe African People's Union
ZDP	Zimbabwe Democratic Party
ZIPA	Zimbabwe People's Army
ZIPRA	Zimbabwe People's Revolutionary Army
ZLC	Zimbabwe Liberation Council
ZRBC	Zimbabwe Rhodesia Broadcasting Corporation
ZUPO	Zimbabwe United People Organization

INTRODUCTION

This is essentially a study in decolonization. Analytically, I approach the subject as a conflict resolution process. From this perspective 1974 was chosen as a point of departure because, following the decolonization of the Portuguese colonial empire, the uniqueness of the decolonization of Rhodesia became more apparent and the conflict began to realize its full potential. In order to capture the essential dimensions of the conflict resolution process and its dynamic qualities, I have employed three analytical concepts: (1) The goals' continuum; (2) The strategic options' continuum; (3) The interaction within and between the three levels of the conflict system. The concept of a continuum is being used because it facilitates capturing the dynamic quality of the conflict resolution process. Political phenomena, especially in such a context, are anything but static. Inherent in the continuum concept is the notion of a movement between its poles. Locating the different participants in the conflict resolution process on either continuum is vital to the understanding of the essence and evolution of the process. The interaction within the conflict system, which reflected the input of the different actors involved, provided the impetus, which in turn accounted for the intensity and the course of the process.

(1) *The goals' continuum.* At the root of the conflict lay the diametrically conflicting goals of the ruling white minority and the African nationalist movement. From the colonial perspective, Rhodesia, as part of the British colonial sphere, represents a unique case. After the Second World War, the goal of Britain's colonial policy in Africa was not the preservation of formal colonial rule. Britain, in fact, initiated the process of decolonization. The anti-colonialist struggle which ensued was rather about the modalities and pace of the decolonization process. Essentially Britain's goal was to implement its decolonization policy in a responsible and orderly manner, and in such a way as to socialize the emerging nation-states into an informal British sphere of influence. Consequently, at the level of the ultimate goals, the gap between the British and the African nationalists was not very wide. In Rhodesia, because of the unique nature of the settler-colonial state, the settler-colonial goal was the preservation of unmitigated white political supremacy and white economic and social privilege. The African

1

nationalist response to this unyielding position was the articulation of the goal of unqualified black majority rule. These were then the two poles of the goals' continuum. The dynamic quality of the conflict resolution process was manifested, as the process unfolded, in shifts along this continuum. The half-way point, which can assist in determining the extent of these shifts, was the concept of power-sharing on the basis of parity. Viewed from the vantage point of white supremacy, any solution which went beyond the half-way point was tantamount to black majority rule. Viewed from the opposite pole, any solution beyond the half-way point was essentially white minority rule. In fact, the insistence of the whites on supremacy shifted the goals of some nationalists even further. There were those who transformed the goal of the struggle from mere decolonization to 'de-imperialization', aspiring not only to capture the political kingdom but also to effect a radical, revolutionary transformation of the economy and the society. The settlement which was concluded at Lancaster House at the end of 1979 represented a compromise which can be located between the half-way point and the pole of unqualified black majority rule, albeit closer to the latter.

(2) *The strategic options' continuum.* The inherently wide gap in the goals' continuum, which characterized the colonial-settler situation in Rhodesia, is reflected on the strategic options' continuum. In the British colonies, with the exception of Kenya, the struggle for decolonization was essentially political and peaceful. Since the British themselves, after the Second World War, were intent on decolonization, they were responsive to moderate nationalist protest. This was certainly the case as regards their West African colonies. In Kenya, the British launched a full-scale war against the Mau Mau insurgents. The trauma of Mau Mau made the British more responsive to non-violent political pressures of the nationalist movements in the more problematic East and Central African colonial spheres. Indeed, the process of decolonization in these colonies was, on the whole, peaceful and constitutional.

The British tried in the late 1950s and the first half of the 1960s, to incorporate Rhodesia in this wave of peaceful decolonization. However, the settler-government, especially following the assumption of power by the Rhodesian Front (RF) in 1962, refused to cooperate. The African nationalists, who had been socialized into anti-colonialist politics within the broader context of decolonization in British Africa had also opted during the 1950s and early 1960s for the peaceful, constitutional struggle as the strategy of liberation. During the early 1960s, however, as the Rhodesian government persisted in suppressing .

their constitutional protest, banning their political parties and detaining their leaders, the African nationalists opted for an alternative strategic option – the armed struggle. In 1966, 1968 and 1970–71 the British tried to resuscitate the peaceful, constitutional option, but to no avail. Thus, from the mid-1960s to the mid-1970s, as the Rhodesian government demonstrated its determination to use state power to suppress the nationalists and to uphold white supremacy, the armed conflict between the nationalist guerillas and the security forces became the dominant feature of the Rhodesian decolonization process. In this respect Rhodesia formed part of the second wave of decolonization in white-dominated southern Africa. It was armed struggle which brought about the decolonization of the Portuguese colonies in 1974. By that time, however, the Rhodesian nationalist guerillas were nowhere near a military victory or even near to producing sufficient pressure to make the government shift its maximalist goal. From the end of 1974, with the launching of the so-called "southern African detente", a peaceful, constitutional settlement became a viable strategic option. Until the final settlement, the Rhodesian conflict shifted to and fro on the strategic continuum between the two poles of peaceful negotiations and armed struggle. From the perspective of conflict resolution, the armed struggle was as much part of the process as were the peaceful negotiations. In fact, the ultimate peaceful resolution of the conflict cannot be understood without reference to the impact of the military confrontation.

The reintroduction of the peaceful option in 1974 did not reflect the domestic balance of power between government and nationalists, or any narrowing of the gap between their diametrically opposing positions. Rather it resulted from the interaction between the actors involved within an expanding and intensifying conflict system.

(3) *The interaction within and between the different levels of the conflict system.* The re-emergence of the non-violent, constitutional option resulted from new impetus by external actors involved in the conflict system. "Conflict system" as an analytical concept is employed in order to focus on the decolonization crisis inside Rhodesia as the core of the conflict which also involved regional and global actors. In this respect, Rhodesia is not treated merely as part of a regional system or as a remote periphery of a global one. Rather, it forms the core of the system around which the roles of the external actors are dealt with and analysed. In the first phase of decolonization in Africa, in the 1950s and the 1960s, the conflict system was effectively composed of the metropolitan colonial power and the African nationalists. During the 1960s and the early 1970s as the nationalist guerilla struggle in southern

Africa and in Guinea Bissau, in West Africa, intensified, the decolonization process became more elaborate. Guerilla movements enjoyed asylum, training facilities, material assistance and operational bases in independent African states and also in those contiguous to their target countries. Thus, for example, Mozambique's FRELIMO was assisted by Tanzania, Angola's FNLA by Zaïre and Rhodesia's ZAPU by Zambia. African countries' assistance was directed almost exclusively to the war effort of their guerilla movements. They did so modestly, and without getting involved in a full-scale military confrontation with the guerillas' target countries. At that stage the communist powers, primarily the Soviet Union and China, began to extend military assistance on a sustained but limited basis to the various guerilla movements.

In Rhodesia, following the Portuguese revolution and the decolonization of Mozambique and Angola, the three levels of the conflict system – the domestic, the regional and the global – all became much more active. In particular, most external actors became more intensively and directly involved in the conflict, their roles becoming more varied. Their input became a major determinant in the evolution of the conflict resolution process. At the domestic level, the colonial factor was represented by the RF government which enjoyed an unchallenged position in the white settler community. The British were still formally the colonial rulers. However, Britain had never exercised effective control in Rhodesia. Since 1923 the white settlers had ruled the country subject to a very loose and remote metropolitan control. Having failed to assert their colonial authority during the 1960s and the early 1970s, the British faded into the background. Thus, to all intents and purposes, Rhodesia was a case of domestic colonialism. This characteristic goes a long way to account for the policies and behaviour of the RF government. On the African nationalist side, despite repeated attempts to secure unity, three main groups emerged. The Zimbabwe African National Union (ZANU) and the Zimbabwe African People's Union (ZAPU), the two exiled nationalist guerilla movements, represented the historical split which occurred in the early 1960s within the nationalist ranks. The African National Council (ANC), headed by Bishop Muzorewa, was essentially an internal political party whose origin was in the African popular resistance to the Smith–Home agreement in the early 1970s.

At the regional level stood, on the one side, South Africa, the bastion of white rule in southern Africa. South Africa, despite initial misgivings about the Rhodesian Unilateral Declaration of Independence (UDI) in 1965, soon became the regional patron of the Rhodesian regime.

Together with Portugal it enabled Rhodesia to survive the economic sanctions imposed by the UN. It also extended direct aid to its client. From 1968 South African troops were actively involved in the defence of the Rhodesian border on the Zambesi River. South Africa was governed by the Nationalist Party (NP) which ruled the country unchallenged by any formal opposition. On the other side, the African nationalists in Rhodesia had enjoyed, since about the mid-1960s, regional and broader African support. At the regional level ZANU was supported by Tanzania whereas ZAPU was supported by Zambia. ZANU cooperated with FRELIMO who fought for the liberation of Mozambique. FRELIMO supported ZANU and gave it access to Rhodesia through the liberated areas in Mozambique. Consequently ZANU was able to launch its guerilla campaign in 1972 in the north-east of Rhodesia. At the end of 1974, with the beginning of the southern African detente, the Front-Line Presidents (FLP) forum was established as a collective regional patron for the Rhodesian nationalists. This forum was originally composed of the presidents of Tanzania, Zambia and Botswana and Samora Machel, the president of FRELIMO who, in June 1975, became the president of independent Mozambique. In 1976, the FLP were joined by Agostinho Neto, the president of Angola.

Much of the dynamic of the conflict resolution process in Rhodesia in the subsequent years cannot be understood without reference to the interaction between the regional patrons and their Rhodesian clients. A cursory observation suffices to reveal the marked difference between the white and black patron–client networks. The white network was a uni-patron, uni-client one. Furthermore, the patron and the client represented strong governments which were also very stable within the context of their exclusively white political bases. In the case of white Rhodesia, not only was the ruling RF party supreme, but the regime was also highly personalized. Ian Smith was not only the symbol and father figure of the white community, he also had full control over his party and his government. The South African government, while being constrained by pressures within the ruling NP and Afrikanerdom more generally, was solidly in control, being led by John Vorster, a popular and assertive prime minister. This was a straightforward, manageable and relatively predictable patron–client network.

Because of the multi-patron, multi-client nature of the African regional and domestic network, the interaction between the collective patron and the clients was more complex and less predictable. The positions and actions of the collective patron and the collective client were themselves a reflection of the complex group dynamic within the

5

FLP and the nationalist camp. The three main components of the nationalist camp differed sharply on ideological, ethnic and personal grounds. The tireless efforts of the FLP to effect nationalist unity were designed to make their relations with their clients more manageable. The patrons themselves differed on ideological grounds and the Rhodesian conflict affected their national interests differently. In addition, some had their preferences among the nationalists. Thus, there developed sub-patron–client relations between Zambia and ZAPU, and Mozambique and ZANU. The diversity among the regional patrons accounts for inconsistencies and contradictions in their functioning as a collective patron. Moreover, the existence of alternative regional patronage reinforced the tendency toward disunity among the nationalist clients. By comparison, in the case of Mozambique, the functioning of Tanzania as a *de facto* uni-patron had enabled Nyerere to ensure FRELIMO's dominance. In Angola, on the other hand, the existence of alternative regional support and bases had exacerbated disunity.

The interaction between the regional and domestic levels of the conflict system was mostly vertical, the FLP interacting with the nationalists and South Africa with the Rhodesian government. There was also the occasional diagonal interaction. Thus on a few occasions, Zambia's president, Kaunda, and the FLP dealt directly with Ian Smith or his representatives.

The horizontal interactions at these two levels of the conflict were also very important in producing the impetus which determined the course and intensity of the conflict resolution process. At the domestic level, there was the violent interaction which was manifested in the guerilla war which began to escalate from early 1976. The domestic enemies were, however, also engaged in bilateral negotiations. Thus, in 1975 negotiations took place between the government and the formally united nationalist front. The climax of these futile negotiations was in the Victoria Falls bridge conference in August 1975. Subsequently, Joshua Nkomo, ZAPU's leader, was involved in separate negotiations with Smith which lasted some six months. In 1977–78, Muzorewa and others were engaged in negotiations with the government which culminated in the internal settlement in March 1978. Important horizontal interaction also took place at the regional level. In fact, such interaction in the second half of 1974 launched the Rhodesian conflict on a short course of negotiations. The horizontal understanding between South Africa and Zambia produced vertical pressures on the respective domestic clients to negotiate. This regional horizontal interaction persisted meaningfully until the Victoria Falls bridge conference. It reached a climax in the historical meeting between Vorster and Kaunda on Zambian soil. Subsequently, it faded away because of the failure of the conference and the South African military intervention in Angola.

With the loss of regional understanding, the impetus for a peaceful resolution of the conflict was lost. It was, indeed, at that point that the black regional patrons resumed their support for the armed struggle of their clients. A new impetus was needed if the peace option was to be kept alive. This was provided by a new global input. The Soviets continued to support ZAPU, their Rhodesian client movement. They did not become involved in the peace initiatives because their interests lay in a violent rather than peaceful resolution of the conflict. Neither did they seriously contemplate an Angola-type military intervention. However, the Soviet–Cuban intervention in Angola from late 1975 did have a considerable impact on the course of the Rhodesian conflict. The fear, or hope, of a similar intervention turned the Soviets into "hidden" but effective participants. It was the prospect of expanding Soviet aggression in southern Africa which prompted Henry Kissinger to become actively involved in the Rhodesian conflict. At the beginning of the southern African detente, there had been no active Western involvement. The British, remembering their bitter Rhodesian experience, were hesitant.

Following the launching of Kissinger's Rhodesian, or rather southern African, diplomatic offensive, active Western involvement became an important feature of the Rhodesian conflict resolution process. Kissinger's initiative, which achieved an apparent breakthrough in September 1976, was followed by an ineffectual British interlude at Geneva in late 1976 and early 1977. The new Anglo-American initiative launched by the Carter administration in 1977 was no more effective. Nevertheless, the global input kept the peace option alive. Indeed, from 1976 the impetus for a peaceful resolution of the conflict stemmed primarily from the global level of the conflict system. Kissinger used his influence among the regional patrons on both sides to put pressure on the domestic Rhodesian clients. During the years of the Carter administration, Britain and the U.S. operated concurrently through the regional patrons and directly with the domestic parties. Their failure to achieve what they considered to be a very important objective is indicative of the weakness of their position *vis à vis* the regional patrons. Because the regional patrons were not vitally dependent on them, the U.S. and Britain could rely only on the former's willing cooperation. Their failure stemmed from their inability to produce a compromise solution which would satisfy both

7

regional patrons. Indeed, the crucial levels determining the course of the conflict were the domestic and the regional. It was at these levels that the outcome of the conflict directly affected the vital interests of the participants concerned. It was also at these levels that the domestic clients, who constituted the hard core of the conflict, were ultimately totally dependent on their respective regional patrons. Thus, although Britain played an important role in the final act of the conflict resolution process, the success of the Lancaster House conference, at the end of 1979, can only be accounted for by reference to the horizontal interaction between the domestic parties and the vertical interaction between regional patrons and domestic clients.

In conclusion, in recounting and analysing the decolonization crisis in Rhodesia, I attempt to correlate and harmonize the shifts on the goals' continuum, the strategic option continuum and the impetus stemming from the elaborate interaction within and between the three levels of the conflict system.

CHAPTER ONE

From the Lisbon Coup to the Crossroad Speech: the Failure of Domestic Accommodation,

April–October 1974

On April 25, 1974 a military coup in Lisbon by the Armed Forces Movement (AFM) put an end to Salazar's New State. Caetano, the prime minister, was deposed and a Junta of National Salvation headed by the retired General Spinola was appointed to run the country. The coup, which originated in the colonial battlefields of Guinea Bissau, Mozambique and Angola, was to have a profound effect on the Rhodesian crisis. However, some six months had elapsed before it made a direct and substantial impact on the Rhodesian decolonization process.

There were some in Rhodesia who immediately grasped the implications of the coup. Muzorewa was jubilant: "The hand of God has been at work in Southern Africa bringing justice and true peace and the writing is on the wall for the enemies of freedom in this part of the world."[1] By late May 1974, a local newspaper commented that the promise of self-determination to the Portuguese colonies "could prove to be the biggest setback for Rhodesia since sanctions were imposed". The lesson for Rhodesia was that an agreement between Smith and Muzorewa "was not only important but vital to the survival of Europeans. . . ."[2]

Smith, following his principle of not believing what he read in newspapers,[3] was not unduly impressed by these gloomy forecasts. At the end of May he responded to the liberation "euphoria" which possessed Africa: "I can understand this kind of irrational thinking emanating from certain countries to our north. . . . I hope there are no Rhodesians quite so naive as to fall for anything so stupid."[4] Smith's own initial response betrayed total misperception of the unfolding events and the nature of the coup:

9

Rhodesia does not interfere in the internal affairs of the other countries and therefore the political changes in Portugal are essentially matters for the Portuguese. Rhodesia has always enjoyed the best relations with metropolitan Portugal and its provinces in Africa, and we believe these will continue.[5]

Such optimism may have been excusable at that early stage. A military regime headed by General Spinola, a colonial reformist, was not necessarily threatening. In fact there were those who entertained the hope that the new military government would more effectively carry out the anti-guerilla campaign.[6] The attitude of the new Portuguese regime towards the colonies was not yet clear. The more radical AFM which had engineered the coup crowned a Junta whose members were certainly not determined anti-colonialists. They broadly subscribed to Spinola's vision of autonomous colonies within the framework of a greater Lusitania.[7] On May 11 General Costa Gomes, a Junta member, stated in Lourenço Marques that the people of Mozambique would be given the opportunity to choose in a referendum between "one extreme of complete independence and another extreme of total integration". He himself favoured a compromise solution within "the great Portuguese community". He warned FRELIMO that if they rejected this plan, "the army will have no choice but to go on with the fight and possibly intensify it".[8] Immediately after the coup, even the experienced and sober Roy Welensky did not envisage Mozambique turning into a FRELIMO country.[9] One could hardly blame Smith and his colleagues for not espousing a more gloomy view of the future.

However, it soon became increasingly clear that Spinola's ideas were out of touch with the reality both in Mozambique and Lisbon. FRELIMO had not fought for years to submit itself to a democratic process under colonial auspices when total victory was within reach. On April 28 FRELIMO rejected the Junta's decolonization plan demanding full independence and transfer of power to them.[10] As the Junta refused to capitulate, FRELIMO rejected the former's cease-fire proposals and, in fact, expanded and intensified the war during May, June and July.[11] Spinola remained unyielding, insisting on June 11 that "democracy must precede independence".[12] He was definitely out of tune with the forces that had brought him to power. The AFM, representing the commanders in the battlefield, would not entertain the thought of having to fight on for the sake of the vague and unrealistic vision of Great Lusitanian democracy. Thus, in June, Otello Cravalho and Mario Soares, representing the AFM and the temporary Socialist–Communist alliance respectively, agreed to FRELIMO's demands. On

July 27 Spinola yielded to AFM pressure and promised independence to the colonies.[13] On September 7 representatives of the Portuguese government and FRELIMO signed an agreement for the transfer of power to the latter by June 25, 1975, and for the establishment of a joint transitional government.[14]

Smith should have been informed about trends in Lisbon and the chaotic conditions prevailing in Mozambique in the aftermath of the coup. He must have known FRELIMO's attitude towards white Rhodesia. In mid-June, Marcelino dos Santos, a prominent FRELIMO leader, said in London that a FRELIMO government would apply UN sanctions against Rhodesia and would assist in the struggle for the liberation of southern Africa.[15] Yet, white Rhodesian leaders continued to generate optimism and confidence. In a BBC interview in the first half of June, Smith said he was more confident than he was a year ago. He also said that he did not envisage bigger problems for Rhodesia in the event of a FRELIMO takeover, stating confidently that Rhodesia could defend all its borders.[16] On August 2, after Spinola had been forced to concede independence to the colonies, Smith made the following amazing statement regarding the situation in Mozambique:

> Things to a certain degree got out of hand. However, there are new developments and some of the messages I have had out of Lisbon have given me cause for a great amount of optimism. I have had a few encouraging messages and some of the things General Spinola has said and what he is trying to do are cause for satisfaction.[17]

This grossly undue expression of optimism cannot be dismissed as pure propaganda designed to cheer up domestic audiences. Smith shared with the majority of his white compatriots the "colonial blindness" which affected negatively their political judgement. This was captured by a prominent Africa observer: "The majority of whites in Rhodesia seem not to have begun to face up to the true implications of the coup in Portugal or the coming changes in Mozambique."[18]

Smith's government did take some actions in response to the changes in Lisbon and Mozambique. Towards the end of May 1974, the building of the Rutenga line designed to connect Rhodesia directly to the South African railway system was speeded up.[19] The difficulties caused to Rhodesia's exports in July by the uncertain conditions in Mozambique[20] further accelerated the pace of the work which was completed on September 10, 21 months ahead of schedule.[21] The hastening of the transfer in July of African peasants in the north-east to "protected villages" – an operation which had begun in early 1974 – was a response

11

to the increasing deterioration of the security situation along the Mozambique border.[22] The Rhodesian army was also preparing for the possibility of opening a new front along the eastern border.[23] The setting in motion of some economic and military contingency plans was well within the confines of a defensive strategy reflecting the siege mentality which had possessed white Rhodesia since UDI. It did not dawn on Rhodesian policy makers that the unfolding changes called at least for a re-evaluation of a siege strategy which had rested on the reality of an interdependent, mutually reinforcing white southern Africa. They certainly did not think that these changes warranted a more determined effort to resolve the domestic racial conflict by accommodating at least the moderate nationalists. In an interview in June, Smith reiterated his government's standard position that "while settlement is desirable, it has not been made essential by events in Mozambique." With his insatiable capacity for delusion, Smith told the viewers that in the aftermath of the Lisbon coup more Rhodesian Africans "are asking that Rhodesia should not go the same way as black African countries".[24] As a reflection of the general African mood, this was, of course, a colossal distortion.

In this frame of mind, Smith continued to conduct his talks, begun in March, with the ANC. On the day of the coup in Lisbon, he offered Bishop Muzorewa four additional African seats in Parliament. At a subsequent meeting on May 7 Smith was hardly more forthcoming, offering the Africans two additional seats, which would have given them 22 seats in a Parliament of 72.[25] This offer was to be considered by the ANC Central Committee on June 2. The details of the offer being unknown to the public, the government created an air of expectancy implying that agreement had been reached and that its approval by the Central Committee was almost a foregone conclusion.[26] As should have been expected, the Central Committee rejected unanimously this miserably inadequate offer on the basis of which the ANC calculated that it would take the Africans between 40 and 60 years to reach parity with the whites in Parliament.[27] It would not even have given them a blocking third to prevent changes in the constitution by the whites. Smith subsequently claimed that on May 7 Muzorewa accepted his proposals and promised to urge the Central Committee to endorse them.[28] Muzorewa's version differs in the extreme.[29] It is rather unlikely that Muzorewa accepted happily in May an offer of two additional seats compared to an offer he had rejected on April 25. It is at least as unlikely that he thought that there was a chance that the Central Committee would go along with it. Some suggest that it was part of a Smith exercise designed to discredit the ANC.[30]

The ANC rejected Smith's proposals as a basis for a constitutional settlement because his concessions were miserably inadequate. Smith, however, chose to put the blame on pressures from African countries and the influence of ZANU on members of the ANC Central Committee.[31] Undeniably, there were radicalizing pressures and influences on the ANC leadership and Smith should have realized this before June 2. Had he wanted a settlement, he should have made an offer enabling Muzorewa and his Central Committee to withstand pressures without losing their credibility as genuine nationalists. This Smith and his government were not prepared to do. He preferred to seek refuge in his dream of a viable alternative moderate black opinion. He indicated a shift in government settlement thinking from the ANC to "responsible" African leaders.[32] Smith referred, of course, to the politically insignificant pro-settlement groups representing a fraction of the modern African elite and the chiefs in government employment. Accordingly, he stated his intention to call a round-table conference with representatives from different African sectors. This was to be a substitute for his negotiations with the ANC.[33] The belief that at that juncture these collaborators, rather than the nationalist guerilla leaders, would be the alternative to the ANC was to say the least astonishing.

The climax of Smith's major policy statement of June 19 was the announcement of a fresh general election at the end of July 1974. The election was irrelevant from an African point of view. Few of them had the right to vote and only 6,938 bothered to register as voters.[34] Although the unfolding regional changes required the broadening of the political discourse, the Rhodesian government gave precedence to considerations pertaining to the circumscribed white politics. It seems that above all Smith wanted to settle the political account with the liberal opposition, and the Rhodesian Party (RP) in particular, which preached compromise and urged the government to offer more concessions to the Africans. They were certainly a major target in Smith's June 19 statement.[35] In fact, the RP, though more vocal than before, posed no challenge to RF domination. Thus, the RF electoral victory – 77 per cent of the voters and all the white seats – came as no surprise.

From the point of view of a prospective political settlement the election could only have a negative effect. It was, naturally, an occasion for the re-dedication of the RF to the goal of minority rule. Statements like "We will not sell out" and "Rhodesia speaks from a greater position of strength than ever before"[36] reflected the unreal, intoxicating election atmosphere. In such an atmosphere even an RP candidate had to plead not-guilty: "We are not a sell-out party. We are basically a European party." He also "boasted" that his party supported

13

segregation in schools, hospitals and residential areas.[37] Indeed, as the prospect of a radical nationalist option appeared on the Rhodesian horizon, the limits of white liberals' reformism became evident. Representing more enlightened and confident elements in the white society they saw the need for political concessions, for *sharing power* with well disposed, yet sufficiently credible, moderate African leadership.

Even this diluted reformism was anathema to the RF which represented mainly the interests and anxieties of those segments of white Rhodesian society which felt more threatened by African nationalism. Thus, even when the fate of Mozambique became increasingly clear, the RF insisted on total political control. Smith spelled it out in the RF Congress on September 20: "If it takes one year, five years, ten years, we are prepared to ride it out rather than give way on our standards, give way on our principles. . . . Our stand is clear and unambiguous. Settlement is desirable, but only on our terms."[38] Reg Cowper, a Rhodesian minister, indicated that the Rhodesian government was still riding a cloud, oblivious of terrestial reality: "In the context of racial strife elsewhere, Rhodesia was as utopian as that unattainable ideal could be."[39] Smith continued to radiate optimism regarding the security situation[40] and to toy with the idea of a round table conference or *indaba*,[41] despite the fact that his prospective partners, the pro-settlement groups, were routed in the elections[42] and that it was rejected by the ANC.

If a settlement between the government and the ANC was not achieved at that stage it was not because of the latter's extremism. The ANC represented essentially the aspirations of the moderate African nationalist elite. They were committed to a non-violent struggle and were prepared to pay an ideological and political price for their preference. Thus, they were prepared to compromise and accommodate white interests and anxieties within the context of a peaceful and evolutionary progress to majority rule. They had persisted in their moderate choice despite harassment, persecution and provocation by the government. Even the Portuguese coup and the imminent change in Mozambique did not significantly alter their positions. The coup, however, made them aware that the time for a peaceful compromise was running out. Dr Edson Sithole tried to convey this sense of urgency to the white ruling elite. He warned the whites that "the failure to reach an agreement with the ANC would bring about a situation in the near or distant future when the white man would have to negotiate his survival, a survival which would not offer the whites a position the ANC envisages".[43] These were prophetic words. In evaluating the implications of the Portuguese coup, the ANC leadership exhibited political astuteness and foresight unequalled by Smith's government.

Although the ANC leaders felt that in the aftermath of the Portuguese coup history was, at last, on the Rhodesian Africans' side, they did not significantly radicalize their demands. They ignored external leaders' attacks such as that of H. Chitepo, ZANU's chairman, who said that "the only use Muzorewa is serving is that of confusing the people by making many believe there is a solution outside the barrel of the gun".[44] The ANC preferred a peaceful solution and believed they could carry the majority of Africans behind them. They felt that a swift progress toward a settlement was vital to sustain the viability of their moderation. This was the clear message of Edson Sithole: "The ANC leadership has been patient and will continue to be patient. However, unless we are able to produce results soon our stand would lose meaning."[45] For a solution to be accepted by the ANC, it had to be, in the words of Muzorewa, "just and honourable".[46] Not backing up their positions with even a political campaign, they were hopelessly dependent on an enlightened attitude from the RF government. The proposals which the ANC Central Committee rejected on June 2 were neither just nor honourable. They were certainly a proof that the government was anything but enlightened in pursuing white interests.

While rejecting Smith's proposals on June 2, the Central Committee stated that it was willing to resume negotiations with Smith with an emphasis on parliamentary representation and the franchise.[47] Referring to the forthcoming election, G. Chavunduka, the ANC General Secretary, said: "Whichever Government comes to power . . . must attempt to reach a settlement with the ANC for the benefit of the country."[48] On June 10 Muzorewa was unequivocal about what the ANC considered a just and honourable settlement: "No solution short of parity in the Rhodesian parliament could now satisfy African opinion."[49] The determined tone notwithstanding, this was an astonishingly moderate position. Edson Sithole, an arch militant in the eyes of the government, repeated this demand, sounding another desperate warning to white Rhodesians: "White domination in Rhodesia is an anachronism. And if the white Rhodesians cannot negotiate with us to secure a place in the future, they will stand no chance with the likes of ZANU."[50] Towards the end of June there were signs that the ANC leadership was losing hope in the viability of an internal settlement with Smith. In replying to Smith's June 19 statement, in which he floated the idea of *indaba*, Muzorewa suggested a "fully representative constitutional conference in which the British Government and the detained African leaders will also participate".[51]

15

The ANC also sent a delegation to London to explore the possibility of a new political initiative.[52] On the eve of the general election Muzorewa appealed to the white electorate for a change of policy: "The present government, assuming they don't change their policies, will never, I repeat, never achieve a settlement, internal or otherwise."[53] His disappointment and pessimism regarding the election results were hardly surprising: "Rhodesians have voted for white supremacy. Many RF supporters said they voted for survival, but in fact, they have voted for speeding up a confrontation of the races."[54] The results had an immediate effect on the ANC policy. On August 4, the ANC formally announced its insistence on a constitutional conference "with all genuine leaders of political parties and including the detained leaders and the British Government."[55]

The Lusaka agreement between FRELIMO and the Portuguese government on September 7, and the setting up of a transitional government in Mozambique on September 20,[56] had a definite effect on Rhodesian Africans' opinion. A Rhodesian African journalist captured the prevailing mood among his fellow African compatriots: "As I see things, the time for a peaceful solution to Rhodesia's constitutional problems . . . is over. I have a strong feeling that the Rhodesian Front will be the last White Government in Rhodesia. With its rigid racial and even provocative policies, it left black Rhodesians, more especially the younger ones, with almost no choice but sacrifice their lives in an open confrontation with the authorities."[57] Muzorewa and his fellow ANC leaders, facing the repressive response of the government to the unfolding developments,[58] could ignore this rising tide only at the risk of becoming politically irrelevant. Thus, as Muzorewa continued to urge sobriety and responsibility in order to reach a settlement,[59] new themes began to emerge. In early October, a local white newspaper observed: "Muzorewa is now fast emerging as the key spokesman of the militant wing of the ANC in sharp contrast to his previous middle-of-the-road stand".[60] From the African point of view, the time for a domestic, internal settlement was definitely running out. On October 16 only a quarter of the hundred prominent Africans who had been invited by Smith to a tea party, a substitute for the abortive *indaba*, turned up.[61] The African half of the Rhodesian stage was being cleared to make room for a different cast and a different plot. The way was paved for militancy and for the carriers of the militant banner – the nationalist guerilla movements. These movements strongly objected to the Smith–ANC negotiations and to the idea of a moderate compromise.[62] At that stage, however, the guerilla movements were still playing a background role. They were still far from being in a position to exert effective pressure on Smith's government. Thus, as yet, neither the domestic nor the external African political forces were able to produce new inputs which could meaningfully change the white–black balance of power and set the Rhodesian crisis in motion.

There were also, at that stage, no external pressures which could cause the white government to be more accommodating. Britain, the colonial power, while not turning its back on its formal responsibility towards its rebel colony, was hardly in a position to make a significant impact. On the eve of the Portuguese coup, a Labour government was voted into office, with Harold Wilson as Prime Minister and James Callaghan as Foreign Secretary. A Labour government could be expected to adopt a more positive attitude towards the Africans' aspirations than its Conservative predecessor. However, Wilson had memories of the slippery Smith whom it was very difficult to nail down. Thus, favourable statements rather than political initiatives could be expected by the Africans from the Labour government. In June 1974 Miss Joan Lestor, the Under-Secretary at the Foreign Office, stated: "We have made it clear that any new settlement terms must enjoy the support of the African majority and that the Africans must play a major part in working them out."[63] However, when an ANC delegation came to London urging the Labour government to launch a new Rhodesian initiative they were cold-shouldered.[64] The government supported the ANC demand for a fully representative constitutional conference, but did nothing to bring it about.[65] On the eve of the regional breakthrough, in October 1974, the Labour government promised no fresh British action.[66]

South Africa was the only external actor involved which was in a position to force Rhodesia to make the concessions which could have facilitated a peaceful internal settlement. With the prospect of the rail link to Mozambique being cut, South Africa would have a total control over Rhodesia's life-line. Smith's government was in any case not in a position to reject a clear-cut message from their regional patron. Such a message, however, did not emanate from Pretoria. Until October 1974, the South African government re-evaluated the new regional situation and planned a new regional initiative. Until then no new coherent and determined policy toward Rhodesia had emerged. There were, however, indications of changing perceptions in South Africa regarding Rhodesia. In early June, Otto Krause, a prominent *verlig* Afrikaner journalist, wrote in the Nationalist daily, *Die Transvaler*: "Rhodesia is certainly the biggest obstacle in the way of South Africa's outward policy in Africa."[67] An editorial in the Johannesburg *Star* on

17

October 16 read: "He [Vorster] must spell out that the fantasy of indefinite White supremacy has a very limited tenure indeed. . . . If White Rhodesians cannot see for themselves, we must help them to do so. . . ."[68] Smith conveniently shrugged these messages off, attributing them to "left wing" elements which represented an insignificant minority in South Africa.[69] He could derive encouragement from another Nationalist daily, *Die Vaderland*, which dismissed *Die Transvaler* as not being representative of the government position: "South Africa will continue to support Rhodesia in every way in its struggle against terrorism. . . . Rhodesia is still a northern bulwark against the planned onslaught against South Africa."[70] Smith repeated this theme in Pretoria on August 23, saying that Rhodesia was an obstacle to the march of international terrorism against South Africa.[71] Smith claimed that the support for Rhodesia was growing rather than declining.[72]

Smith could persist in his optimism regarding South African policy because the messages emanating from Pretoria were confusing and contradictory. With the failure of the negotiations between Smith and Muzorewa in early June, South African policy-makers were concerned, but apparently did nothing.[73] On August 30 the Rhodesian diplomatic representative in Pretoria conveyed to the Rhodesian public the mood in South African government circles: "There is no doubt in my mind that they [South Africa] would welcome this – and internal accord more than anything else." He also warned Rhodesians not to take South Africa's help for granted.[74] On September 9 Hilgard Muller, South Africa's Foreign Minister, said himself that the decolonization of Angola and Mozambique would be followed by "a speedy and satisfactory solution of the Rhodesian problem".[75] On August 19 Smith met Vorster, the South African premier, in Cape Town to discuss the general situation in southern Africa.[76] Although no details of their discussion were released, it is very unlikely that Vorster did not give Smith at least a hint of South Africa's changing views on Rhodesia. There is some information that Vorster made use of Rhodesia's growing dependence on South Africa's railway lines to put pressure on Smith.[77] On the other hand, South African diplomatic sources in Salisbury, while confirming that Pretoria informed the Rhodesian government of its keen interest in an internal settlement, also claimed that no official pressure was applied.[78] In September, South Africa's Foreign Minister denied that South Africa was interfering in the internal affairs of Rhodesia. Vorster himself described as "nonsense" Harold Wilson's claim that he was applying pressure on Smith. In Salisbury, a government source confirmed that "at no time has Mr Vorster put the heat on us to settle".[79] The Rhodesian government's behaviour during the period leading up to the "crossroad" speech certainly indicated that they were not operating under effective pressure. Only some two weeks before the launching of South Africa's dramatic and consequential regional initiative Rhodesia's Minister of Defence could speak with a sense of elation: "The people of South Africa and Rhodesia stand united in their dedication to the over-throwing and total eradication of terrorism; to the preservation of our homes and the continuance of our ancient missions of maintaining civilization in southern Africa."[80]

Thus, despite the radical changes in southern Africa in the wake of the Portuguese coup, the Rhodesian conflict remained, for some six months, essentially a domestic Rhodesian affair. The Rhodesian government could have secured a settlement on the basis of immediate parity in Parliament with the ANC which enjoyed wide African support. In retrospect, such a settlement was very generous. At that time, however, the Rhodesian government regarded such a settlement as anathema. On the basis of their perception of the current white–black balance of power, they considered the concessions required of them as totally unwarranted. Indeed, with the guerilla war only at its initial stage and with the ANC unable or unwilling to translate its popular support into positive political action, the white minority government could continue to entertain the illusion of omnipotence. Very rarely will a group possessed by such self-perception relinquish or compromise its control. Only new inputs and pressures could salvage the Rhodesian problem from its state of immobility. These new pressures, regional in origin, were building up after the Portuguese coup. They matured and came to the fore six months after that event.

CHAPTER TWO

From Crossroad Speech to Lusaka: Regional Initiatives and Domestic Responses

October–December 1974

Vorster's "crossroad" speech on October 23, 1974, and the "voice of reason" reply by Kaunda, the Zambian president, had completed a process of reassessment of the changing conditions in southern Africa, of a redefinition of goals and of reformulation of policies at the regional level. These speeches ushered in a new phase in the evolution of the Rhodesian conflict. This phase was characterized by an intensive involvement of the regional patrons in an attempt to resolve peacefully the black–white confrontation in Rhodesia. The struggle of Rhodesian whites for the preservation of minority rule and of the Rhodesian African nationalists for majority rule remained the hard core of the conflict. However, with the failure of Smith to reach a settlement even with the moderate ANC and with the consequent prospect of an escalating violent struggle, the regional patrons, who had played in the past a secondary supportive role, decided to step in. From a conflict resolution perspective, this phase was characterized by extensive horizontal interaction at the regional level between South Africa and the African patrons and by vertical interaction between the regional patrons and their respective Rhodesian clients. The Portuguese coup, which radically altered the regional balance of power, threw the Rhodesian problem out of its domestic "deep freeze". The imminent changes in Mozambique, in particular, opened for the countries surrounding Rhodesia new threats as well as new hopes.

Although the South African government never had great admiration for the colonial exploits of the Portuguese, the coup and the resulting colonial abdication shocked the South African policy-makers. The realization that African liberation movements could, through long and sustained armed struggle, force a colonial power to decolonize, was in itself a shock. Moreover, the fall of the Portuguese colonial empire dramatically weakened South Africa's regional strategy. This strategy rested on a buffer zone, composed of Mozambique, Rhodesia and Angola, which shielded South Africa from emergent black Africa. This strategy had served South Africa well until the Portuguese coup. The buffer zone effectively prevented the penetration of nationalist guerillas into South Africa and South West Africa. With a token reinforcement of some 2,000 "policemen" in Rhodesia, South Africa made the Zambezi an effective and convenient defence line. Consequently, South Africa enjoyed a long spell of security and regional stability.

This came to an abrupt end in the wake of the Portuguese coup when Angola and Mozambique, at the two flanks of the *cordon sanitaire*, were to become black. In Angola, because of the intra-nationalist struggle for power, it was not yet clear what would be the nature of the emerging African regime. In Mozambique it was certain that South Africa was going to face a FRELIMO regime with its Marxist ideological leanings and communist connections. Black Africa was bouncing on South Africa with a vengeance. For the first time, there was a potential threat that neighbouring African countries would be used as launching pads for guerilla infiltration into South Africa and South West Africa. The prospect of a hostile regime in Mozambique was particularly unpleasant. Beyond the security threat, South Africa had cultivated very useful economic relations with colonial Mozambique. Some 25 per cent of the South African mines labour force came from Mozambique. The disruption of the flow of these migrant workers to the mines could have caused at least short term dislocation. Lourenço Marques port served South Africa as an import–export channel, the loss of which would have increased the pressures on the already highly congested South African harbours. South Africa also had a keen interest in purchasing electricity for its national grid from the Cabora Bassa hydro-electric plant which was nearing completion.[1] While the South African economic interests in Mozambique were far from constituting a vital South African dependence, they were also not ones which a government would lightly discard. Thus South Africa had very good security and economic reasons to establish a *modus vivendi* with its new unwelcome north-eastern neighbour.

The South African government responded to the challenge of the Portuguese abdication with a remarkable show of statesmanship. The fact that the Vorster government had been pursuing an outward policy towards black Africa since the 1960s made it easy for them to make the necessary mental and conceptual adjustments. In fact, the new South African policy towards Mozambique and southern Africa as a whole could be conceived as a dramatic application of an existing policy. At

21

the end of May 1974, just over a month after the Lisbon coup, Vorster said in reply to a question regarding the possibility of majority rule in Mozambique: "All we are interested in is that there should be good rule . . . but it is not for us to prescribe what sort of rule there should be." He also dismissed as "absolute nonsense" the speculation that South Africa was prepared to send troops to help the whites in Mozambique.[2] Speaking in Parliament on August 30, Vorster extended South Africa's hands to a future black government in Mozambique.[3] In September when it was clear that FRELIMO would form the government he said: "Whoever takes over in Mozambique has a tough task ahead of him. It will require exceptional leadership. They have my sympathy and I wish them well."[4] The fact that Mozambique had developed as an economic satellite of South Africa helped the South African government to respond to the prospective emergence of a FRELIMO government with apparent equanimity. Vorster referred to it candidly when he addressed Parliament on August 30: "But Mozambique is not a country which can stand on its own feet at the moment without co-operation from South Africa."[5] South Africa could certainly expect to deal with the new regime in Mozambique from a position of considerable strength.

However, South Africa could not isolate its relations with independent Mozambique from the broader regional context. A stable bilateral accommodation could only flourish in conditions of wider regional accommodation and stability. A search for a new regional accommodation with black Africa clearly became the highest South African foreign policy priority. This brought the Rhodesian problem to the fore. With the two flanks of the former buffer zone torn wide open, the usefulness of Rhodesia to South African defence was highly questionable. In fact, Rhodesia was becoming a major obstacle in South Africa's search for a new regional accommodation. It could be expected that with the decolonization of the Portuguese colonies the main thrust of the African liberation strategy would focus on Rhodesia, the most vulnerable of the remaining white regimes. With the possibility of Mozambique, in addition to Zambia, becoming a base for the Rhodesian liberation movements, the Smith regime was expected to be under increasingly heavy military and economic pressures. It was clear that under such adverse conditions Rhodesia could not defend itself and support itself economically. The burden of securing Rhodesia's survival would fall squarely on South Africa's shoulders. This would involve South Africa in a protracted guerilla struggle which could further radicalize and destabilize the whole sub-continent. This scenario was in total contradiction to the new regional strategy that

22

was emerging in Pretoria. Furthermore, exposing itself as the sole supporter of the rebel regime, South Africa could expect increasing international condemnation and pressure. On the other hand, a peaceful political settlement of the Rhodesian dispute under South African auspices, and in agreement with black Africa, could serve as a corner stone on which a new regional stability could be built. Thus, the role of white Rhodesia was being rapidly transformed from that of a vital defence outpost to that of a sacrificial lamb for a new regional order.

For the African countries involved in the struggle for liberation of southern Africa, the Portuguese coup and the consequent decolonization of Angola and Mozambique was a cause for celebration. The policy of concentrating their efforts in assisting the liberation movements in the Portuguese colonies had at last paid handsome dividends. Although it was not a case of a clear military victory, certainly not in Angola but also not in Mozambique, there was no doubt that the decolonization of the Portuguese colonies was a result of the increasing pressure of the nationalist guerillas. A major psychological barrier was broken by black Africa.

However, this glorious occasion also called for a re-evaluation of the liberation strategy. Most involved and active in this process was Kaunda. With the decolonization of Angola and Mozambique, the prospects and problems facing the strategists of liberation were of a totally different order. The front of liberation moved southward towards South Africa, the citadel of white southern Africa. Rhodesia, South West Africa and South Africa, itself, remained the last targets. South West Africa was ruled by South Africa as its fifth province. Rhodesia was economically and militarily supported by South Africa. In Mozambique, the liberation front ran along the borders of South Africa itself. An indiscriminate pursuance of the liberation struggle on the three fronts could precipitate a head on collision between the respective guerilla movements and their regional patrons and South Africa, the military and economic giant of the sub-continent. Such confrontation could have very severe consequences for the cause of liberation and for the independent African states in southern Africa. Kaunda was particularly concerned that in the event of such a confrontation, South Africa would prevent FRELIMO from consolidating its control over Mozambique. South Africa was also expected to continue to regard the Zambezi as its northern defence perimeter and to increase its direct military support for the Smith regime. This would have a considerable adverse effect on the prospect of liberating Rhodesia. Zambia itself would face a painful choice between supporting the Rhodesian nationalist guerillas and being engulfed in an escalating military confrontation against vastly superior forces and forgoing its traditional support for liberation.

The scenario of escalating military struggle for the liberation of Rhodesia seriously threatened the vulnerable Zambian economy which was in any case sliding into crisis. Zambia relied heavily on the export of copper as its main source of foreign exchange and of government income. As such its economy depended on the vicissitudes of the world metals market. After a short price boom in late 1973 and early 1974, the price of copper declined dramatically. From a record price of £1,400 per ton in April 1974, copper declined by September to only £600 per ton.[6] Moreover, in 1974 the considerable increase in the oil prices by OPEC began to have an adverse effect on the global economy and on the economies of the poor, under-developed countries in particular. Zambia's most immediately pressing economic problem in the wake of the Portuguese coup was its outlets to the sea. It was still suffering from the dislocations which resulted from the closure of its border with Rhodesia in 1973 which deprived it of its traditional rail route to the Mozambican ports. In the second half of 1974, the two alternative routes became increasingly problematic. In the east, Zambia's foreign trade suffered from congestion in Dar es Salaam port and from increased traffic charges. In the west, the atmosphere of insecurity and labour troubles in the port of Lobito after the Lisbon coup caused delays and congestion.[7] Furthermore, the unfolding civil war between the rival Angola guerilla movements did not augur well for the future usage of the Benguela railway line. Zambia thus faced the spectre of a devastating combination of economic and transport crisis. It had a vital interest in a speedy reopening of the Rhodesian route. The only way to expedite this eventuality was through a speedy political solution of the Rhodesian crisis. Zambia certainly had good reasons of its own to prefer a peaceful to a violent scenario.

Kaunda's preference for a political solution did not mean that Zambia was discarding its commitment to the liberation of southern Africa. A peaceful decolonization in Rhodesia in particular was perceived by Kaunda and his colleagues as serving the best interests of Zambia as well as those of black Rhodesians. A total confrontation involving South Africa on the side of white Rhodesia would certainly not have served the cause of the Rhodesian Africans. In principle, a violent solution for Kaunda, with his humanist philosophy, was a last resort. In the case of Rhodesia, terrestial interests and philosophy were mutually reinforcing. The Lusaka Manifesto of 1969, which laid down the liberation strategy for southern Africa, was very clear on that issue: "We have always preferred, and still prefer, to achieve it without physical violence . . . we would urge our brothers in the resistance movements to use peaceful methods of struggle even at the cost of some compromise on the timing of change."[8] While condemning apartheid and urging international sanctions against South Africa, the manifesto did not advocate a violent struggle against it.[9] Experience had shown that setting priorities and concentrating resources and effort on defined liberation targets were advantageous. Only an irresponsible leader would precipitate a general conflagration in southern Africa if it could be averted. It seems quite clear that Kaunda believed that it was possible to engage South Africa in a political process which would result in black majority rule in Rhodesia and perhaps also South West Africa. He was certainly encouraged by Vorster's attitude towards Mozambique.[10] In terms of Kaunda's liberation priorities, Rhodesia preceded South West Africa.[11] This was a Zambian national interest but it also made sense from a liberation strategy point of view because of the relative South African involvement in both territories. In the event of the peaceful initiative failing and the military option being adopted, it would be easier to disengage South Africa militarily from Rhodesia by engaging her politically in a search for regional accommodation. This could be a realistic and most advantageous secondary objective.

Kaunda could not carry the burden of negotiating with South Africa and with the Smith regime on his own. These were highly risky negotiations for an African leader to undertake. Firstly, Kaunda had to protect himself from criticism and attacks from black African quarters. Secondly, effective influence and pressure would have to be exerted on the Rhodesian liberation movements to guide them, willy nilly, along the path of a peaceful settlement. Thus, Kaunda approached President Seretse Khama of Botswana, President Julius Nyerere of Tanzania and Samora Machel, the leader of FRELIMO. Botswana and Mozambique were neighbours of both Zambia and Rhodesia, while Nyerere had established himself as the dean and patron of liberation. Kaunda had no problem with Khama. Botswana, an economic satellite of South Africa, had very good reasons to prefer a peaceful solution in Rhodesia. On the other hand, when Kaunda approached Nyerere and Machel in September 1974, they were sceptical about his initiative. They were, however, prepared to give it a chance.[12] These four men were to form the forum known as the Front Line Presidents (FLP) which functioned as a collective patron of the Rhodesian liberation movements. It was an impressive group, including two of the most credible and respected leaders in black Africa and the leader of an emerging radical regime. It also included all Rhodesia's black independent neighbours.

Thus there was a willingness on both sides of the regional dividing line to avert the escalation of violence and to explore the possibility of a peaceful solution to at least some of the problems between white and black in the sub-continent. There remained the problem of making the contact between the white and black regional patrons. Kaunda's unhappy experience of corresponding with Vorster in 1968,[13] could only discourage him from attempting to establish a new dialogue with him. On the other hand, the seriousness of the situation warranted a fresh endeavour. The initial link between Kaunda and Vorster was provided by Lonrho, the controversial multi-national corporation which had extensive economic interests throughout black and white southern Africa. Lonrho, which operated in many African independent countries, had no fear of majority rule. Indeed, Lonrho throve on African independence. In May 1974, "Tiny" Rowland, Lonrho's chief executive, spelled out his philosophy: "We believe in independent Africa. We will do anything we can to help independent African countries to achieve their full economic potential. We believe in partnership between Western technology, Arab oil money and African resources."[14] Lonrho's attitude to black Africa was hardly altruistic. Some 78 per cent of the corporation's turnover originated in black Africa as did 95 per cent of its total profit before tax.[15] In the same interview, Rowland said the following about the future of southern Africa: "I am convinced that South Africa will be governed by Africans 10 to 15 years from now, and in five years from now Rhodesia will be Zimbabwe."[16] Towards the end of the year, he predicted that "Rhodesia will be Zimbabwe by the end of next year" saying that Lonrho would "feel free and hopeful" to invest money in independent Zimbabwe.[17] Since a major military conflagration in southern Africa would be very detrimental to the corporation's interests, it had very good reasons to expedite the peaceful attainment of the inevitable. Lonrho's conribution to the peaceful resolution of the Rhodesian dispute was their transnational network of communication and contacts. By virtue of this, they were in a position to provide the "missing link" between Vorster and Kaunda. Dr Marquard de Villiers, a Pretoria physician and an associate of Rowland, who acted as the latter's contact in Pretoria, explained their role: "So Mr Rowland and I undertook to use our good offices to approach these two leaders and we had the advantage of not being connected to any particular political viewpoint or party."[18] What emerges clearly from de Villiers' account is Lonrho's self perception as being marginal in the context of regional, inter-state diplomacy. They could operate only on the basis of existing areas of agreements between the two parties. Furthermore, Lonrho could provide its contact service only as long as the two parties were interested in it. Thus, on October 26, at the request of Vorster, the role of Lonrho as a go-between was terminated.[19]

The initial contacts were made during June 1974, between de Villiers and Tom Mtina, the chairman of Lonrho Zambia and a close confidant of Kaunda. Soon, however, Mark Chona, Kaunda's Special Assistant took charge of the secret contacts with South Africa. In early July, de Villiers, Chona, and Hendrik van den Bergh, the powerful head of the South African Bureau of State Security (BOSS), held an exploratory meeting in Paris. Subsequently, Chona paid several secret visits to South Africa where he also met Vorster.[20] These secret contacts coincided with South Africa's renewed attempts to initiate dialogue with other African countries. In July 1974, the South African Foreign Minister visited a west African country, probably Ivory Coast, and met its president. Subsequently, emissaries from a west African country paid a visit to South Africa. These efforts culminated in September 1974 in Vorster's visit to the Ivory Coast and in his meeting with President Houphouet Boigny and Leopold Senghor, the President of Senegal.[21] These west African states were too remote, geographically and politically, to have a strong impact on the political dynamic of southern Africa. These contacts, however, contributed to creating in South Africa an air of great expectancy, a feeling of an imminent diplomatic breakthrough. This was definitely a conducive backdrop to the southern African peace initiative. The diplomatic thrust continued to hinge on the contacts between South Africa and Zambia. In September 1974, Hilgard Muller met, in New York, Vernon Mwaanga, his Zambian counterpart. Mwaanga, who wanted to find out if Chona's optimistic reports were justified, was told by Muller that South Africa was willing "to help in Rhodesia" provided there were "adequate guarantees for transition".[22]

On October 8, at State House, Lusaka, a final draft of a crucial document was typed. The document, also known as the "detente scenario" was entitled "Towards the Summit: An approach to Peaceful Change in Southern Africa". In the introduction to the document, Zambia pledged on behalf of itself and the governments of Tanzania, Botswana and Mozambique "to work for genuine peace which secures freedom and justice for all". Zambia and its fellow front line states agreed to a summit meeting between Vorster and Kaunda, on the request of the former, provided that its success was guaranteed. Thus, the "scenario' was to be unfolded within a defined period of six months. It also laid down principles and provisions relating to the main three issues on the regional agenda. It made provisions for normaliza-

27

tion of relations between South Africa and the new government in Mozambique. With regard to South West Africa, South Africa was not asked to make any major concession which could pave the road for African majority rule. Rhodesia was no doubt the prime objective of the "scenario'. South Africa did not undertake to declare its stand with regard to a settlement formula. All that was expected of Vorster was to advise Smith "that a political solution is most desirable and very urgent". He undertook not to interfere in Rhodesia's internal affairs and to declare the withdrawal of South Africa's forces and military equipment from Rhodesia. He was also expected to state that a negotiated settlement was in the best interest of Rhodesia and that he opposed any further escalation of the war in Mozambique or the growing tension in the region. All these undertakings Vorster was expected to fulfil by the end of November 1974. The South African government was to ensure that the Smith government proceeded quickly to a constitutional conference by doing the following:

a. Releasing all political detainees and prisoners since their voice is both credible and final in any negotiations;
b. Lifting the ban on ZAPU and ZANU and the restrictions of movements on leaders so that they participate fully and constructively in the search for a just political solution as an alternative to the current armed struggle;
c. Suspend political trials and revoke death sentences for political offenders;
d. Suspend all politically discriminatory legislation;
e. Gearing the SAG [South African Government] administration to help defuse racial tension and create a political climate for the acceptance of the proposal of the constitutional conference representing ZAPU and ZANU, the Rhodesian Front and other political parties in Rhodesia under British chairmanship. In these circumstances, the current armed struggle will be replaced by a new spirit of co-operation and racial harmony which is the foundation for political stability and therefore justifying withdrawal of the South African security forces;
f. SAG to make clear that they will support any legally constituted Government irrespective of its racial composition in Rhodesia.

Zambia "and friends" undertook to "use their influence to ensure that ZANU and ZAPU desist from armed struggle and engage in the mechanics for finding a political solution in Rhodesia". The "scenario" envisaged a meeting between Vorster and Kaunda in the second half of December 1974, assuming the programme outlined in it were applied by mid-December.[23] Martin and Johnson claim that the "scenario" was a collective effort of Chona, de Villiers and van den Bergh. A very well-placed South African source, which I cannot quote, denied the participation of van den Bergh in the endeavour. He also denied that the South African government, at any time, formally endorsed the content of this document. Indeed, the document is written from a Zambian point of view. Thus, the actual drafting of the "scenario" must have been the work of Chona and de Villiers. However, the role assigned to South Africa must have reflected the intensive negotiations between Zambia and South Africa, with van den Bergh playing a major role. According to this document, the commitments which South Africa undertook with respect to the future of both Rhodesia and South West Africa were broad enough and ambiguous enough, and should not have raised objections in Pretoria. The fact that the South Africa–Zambian initiative proceeded on this basis is a proof of that.

The secret contacts surfaced on October 23, 1974. On that day, Vorster delivered at the South African Senate his famous "crossroad" speech. The following passage represented the new spirit and the new era:

> Therefore, I believe that Southern Africa has come to the cross-roads. I think that Southern Africa has to make a choice. I think that the choice lies between peace on the one hand or an escalation of strife on the other. The consequences of an escalation are easily foreseeable. The toll of major confrontation will be high. I would go so far as to say that it will be too high for Southern Africa to pay . . . it is not necessary, for there is an alternative. . . . That way is the way of peace, the way of normal relations, the way of sound understanding and normal association. I believe that Southern Africa can take that way. I have reason to believe that it is prepared to prefer to take that way, and I believe that it will do so in the end. . . . I have never been more optimistic that the climate and the will to do so is there.[24]

Kaunda replied on October 26, in his "voice of reason" speech. Kaunda interpreted Vorster's speech as "the voice of reason for which Africa and the world have waited for many years". Like Vorster, Kaunda expressed his good intentions in general terms: "We do not desire to see an escalation of conflict in Southern Africa. The consequences of such an escalation are too grave in material and human sacrifice to be permitted either by design or default."[25] Vorster welcomed Kaunda's response saying that "it appears as if the President of Zambia is available for such action." Foreign Minister Dr Muller also sounded a hopeful note.[26] In a speech in his Nigel constituency, on November 5, Vorster further added to the verbal momentum: "Give South Africa six months' chance and do not make the road we are walking on more difficult than it already is, and if you give South Africa that chance, you will be amazed where South Africa will stand after that period."[27] In fact, the "crossroad" and the Nigel speeches generated such wild expectations that Vorster had to assure his supporters, in a subsequent speech in Zeerust on November 16, that whatever he had said did not apply to South Africa's domestic policies.[28]

This series of speeches fired the imagination of the Afrikaans Nationalist press. On the morning after the Nigel speech, *Die Vaderland* wrote that "it is also a message of hope and optimism that violence, confrontation and chaos do not await South Africa."[29] *Die Beeld* was impressed by Vorster's realism: "And it was not a rousing speech he made. It is optimism which clearly has a firm foundation." [30] In mid-December, *Die Beeld* praised Vorster:

> In totally unpromising circumstances, Mr John Vorster quietly went about doing the apparently impossible, to break down the walls of hostility, to establish greater understanding in southern Africa, to build for our children, the possibility of growing up in a relative peace and quiet, rather than under the clouds of war.[31]

A thorough examination of the "crossroad" and "voice of reason" speeches fails to justify this spate of optimism. Vorster began his speech by describing black Africa's underdevelopment and bleak economic future, generously declaring South Africa's willingness to "contribute its share towards bringing and giving order, development and technical and monetary aid, as far as this is within its means, to countries in Africa and particularly to those countries which are closer neighbours".[32] This was hardly a new vision. Besides being patronizing, it reflected the old style "outward policy", seeking to trade economic benefits for political recognition. Neither was there any great promise regarding the two main issues on the southern African agenda, namely South West Africa and Rhodesia. When the passage on South West Africa is decoded, it is essentially the territory's version of separate development.[33] Vorster's reference to Rhodesia held no greater promise:

> It must also be fully understood that I do not want to interfere in any way in the internal affairs of Rhodesia. . . . I believe that, with good will this matter can be settled, and I believe that an honourable solution can be found. . . . I know, and Hon. Senators know that attempts have recently been made by Mr Smith and his govern-

ment, but unfortunately these attempts, judging from reports, have failed. But I do know that as far as the Rhodesian Government is concerned, this matter is of the highest order of their priority list. . . . On the other hand, there are ZANU and ZAPU leaders outside Rhodesia who are suspected . . . of exerting influence on Black Rhodesians not to come to terms. I believe that now is the time for all who have influence to bring it to bear upon all parties concerned to find a durable, just and honourable solution, so that internal and external relations can be normalized.[34]

Besides general expression of good intentions, the only positive element in that passage was that South Africa would not stand in the way of a settlement arrived at in Rhodesia. The substance of the speech certainly did not justify Vorster's euphoric conclusion:

Therefore, I also believe it is not inappropriate that southern Africa can create its own, not U.N.O., but P.P.D., which will stand for peace, progress and development. Towards that end, I believe that South Africa is keen to co-operate, and to that objective I commit myself and my Government as far as the future is concerned.[35]

While committing his government to this noble vision, he undertook no commitment for any defined solution for South West Africa or Rhodesia. He certainly did not commit himself in public to majority rule in the two territories.

On the other hand, when deciphering Kaunda's "voice of reason" speech, it emerges clearly that majority rule in both territories was a *conditio sine qua non* for progress to peace. Kaunda expressed his determination not to compromise African goals.[36] From an African perspective, it had only one meaning – the attainment of majority rule. Even with regard to South Africa itself, Kaunda's moderate stance was more apparent than real. While accepting South Africa as a African country, his vision of South Africa was diametrically opposed to that of Vorster: "We do not question the rights of the whites in South Africa. What is at issue is their claim to have the right to dominate others on the basis of colour." While stating that black Africa would not take arms against South Africa, he implied that black South Africans could expect the same help that their brethren in Angola, Mozambique and Rhodesia had received and were receiving in their struggle for freedom.[37]

As it emerges clearly from the reading of the "detente scenario" and the public pronouncements of Kaunda and Vorster, there was no sound basis for the prevailing atmosphere of breakthrough. Agreement was reached regarding preliminary steps designed to facilitate the setting in motion of a conflict resolution process. However, regarding the terms for the settlement of the conflict, the gap between black and white remained almost as wide as before. How can one account for the gross discrepancy between the reality and the expectations? An explanation may be sought in the realm of political semantics, in distorted communication between leaders belonging to different political cultures. Indeed, the South African Nationalist leadership and the black African leaders involved in the liberation struggle were, in terms of ideology and politics, worlds apart. Years of isolation from one another not only exacerbated mutual hostility, but also adversely affected their ability to understand one another. In fact, the same words and terms carried different contents, different connotations. Thus, for example, self determination for the Afrikaner Nationalist was compatible with the policy of separate development. It was the very negation of this policy for African nationalists. Referring to Vorster's statement regarding South West Africa, Kaunda said in his "voice of reason" speech: "The South African Government's declaration that the future of Namibia should be decided by the people themselves is a welcome gesture."[38] However, Vorster, in saying that the "peoples of South West Africa would be allowed to decide their own future", was well within the framework of the existing policy of separate development, according to which each ethnic group (people) was allowed to decide its future in its homeland boundaries. Likewise, South Africans must have been pleased that Kaunda accepted South Africa as a legitimate African country. However, the term "African country" also implied the demand for a total transformation of South African society and the South African state. It is also possible that the leaders were aware of the chasm between them and chose to go through the motions, hoping to gain at least some lesser goals. As clearly indicated by Kaunda in his speech, his lesser goal was the military disengagement of South Africa from the struggle in Rhodesia.[39] Kaunda, it should be added, was less euphoric than his South African counterparts. As for the latter, it is possible that they believed that the mere dialogue would somehow improve their regional and international position. Among South African policy makers there was also a definite element of wishful thinking. After so many years of isolation and ostracism and of craving for recognition, they were carried away by the hope of a regional and continental breakthrough.

False hopes, wishful thinking and discrepancy between the basic position of the regional partners notwithstanding, there was an agreement between the respective regional patrons to set in motion a negotiating process. The regional patrons only set the stage and sketched the general outline of the plot. The respective domestic Rhodesian actors/clients were expected to fill the rest. However, a virtually unbridgeable gap between the positions and goals of the respective domestic actors exacerbated by deep mutual mistrust and animosity did not augur well for the negotiations. It was clear to the regional patrons that their clients would require guidance if they were to fulfil the role expected of them. It is doubtful that they imagined how difficult and frustrating their task would be. The agreement at the regional level set in motion a most interesting and complex interaction between regional patrons and domestic clients. This interaction was a dominant feature of the unfolding conflict resolution process leading up to independence in 1980. This set of interaction provided much of the dynamic, pace and direction of the process.

Vorster made the first move by reaching an agreement with Smith in October 1974, which set the conditions for the Rhodesian government's participation in a negotiating process. This promptness reflected the straightforward uncomplicated nature of this set of patron–client relationship. Firstly, this relationship was straightforward because it involved one patron and one client. In both countries, the ruling parties effectively controlled their respective white polities. The Nationalist Party in South Africa and the Rhodesian Front in Rhodesia were unchallenged. At the head of the respective governments stood two imposing personalities enjoying undisputed positions. Vorster was at the peak of his political career, his new regional venture greatly enhancing his stature and prestige. Smith held such sway over the small-scale white polity that one could speak of the "Smith regime". Additionally, no sensitive issue related to the ideological and existential core of either white regime had yet been touched upon. Last, but not least, in the aftermath of the demise of the Portuguese colonial empire, Rhodesia depended totally on South Africa for its very survival. Rhodesia was thus not in a position to oppose anything that South Africa wanted it to do. The content of the agreement reached in a meeting between Vorster and Smith was subsequently disclosed by the latter:

1. The Rhodesian Government would hold a constitutional conference on the Rhodesian settlement issue.
2. The detained Rhodesian African leaders and their followers would be released from detention and the leaders invited to participate in the conference.

33

3. As a quid pro quo for the release of these detainees, terrorism would cease immediately.
4. The released detainees would be permitted to engage in normal activities in terms of the laws applicable to all Rhodesians.
5. The South African Prime Minister had the support of the governments of Zambia, Tanzania and Botswana in these arrangements.[40]

The conditions of the agreement posed no serious problem to Smith because they did not commit his government to a specific solution. This left him, for the meantime, sufficient room to manoeuvre. Indeed, participating in constitutional talks without conceding white rule, was an old Smith tactic. He encountered resistance in the RF caucus to the release of the detainees.[41] To leaders of the besieged white community, this concession was conceived as a disturbing, unwarranted, show of weakness. Smith had little difficulty in convincing his colleagues. On November 1 he went further, pledging his government's support for the southern African detente: "As an integral part of southern Africa, Rhodesia will do everything in her power to bring about better understanding. Obviously, it will be to our mutual benefit if we work together in harmony. For this reason, Rhodesians will always support efforts to foster peaceful coexistence."[42] Although Smith must have been aware of the adverse implications for Rhodesia of the new diplomatic offensive, he knew that in a matter of such importance to his regional patron, he had to appear as cooperative as possible. His only hope could be that the initiative would fail to achieve its objective.

Once Smith agreed to play his part, the ball was in the African regional patrons' court. On November 3 the FLP met in Lusaka on the invitation of Kaunda. In this meeting, in which Kaunda reported on his contacts with Vorster, the FLP assumed their role of regional patrons.[43] The task of preparing the nationalist leadership for their role in the unfolding detente was much more difficult than that facing their South African counterparts. The difficulties reflected to a large extent the structure and nature of patron–client relationship on the African side. Unlike the pattern of white patron–client relationship, there were on the African side at the beginning of detente, four regional patrons and four African nationalist clients. This multiple patron–client relationship structure was inherently more difficult to manage and manipulate. The difficulty was aggravated by the heterogeneity of the patrons and clients. Among the patrons, there were potential differences stemming from consideration of national interests. Thus, Zambia, which bordered Rhodesia, and Botswana, which bordered both Rhodesia and South Africa, expected to be adversely affected by the escalation of violence in Rhodesia. Tanzania, on the other hand, was remote from Rhodesia and would not be directly threatened by an escalating war. Zambia and Botswana were moderate countries, while FRELIMO, which was to take over the government of Mozambique, was a Marxist-oriented party still imbued with revolutionary zeal. These differences had been reflected in Zambia's enthusiasm and Tanzania and Mozambique's scepticism during the stage of the preliminary secret contacts between Zambia and South Africa.[44] However, at the beginning of detente, all the regional patrons agreed to give it a chance.

Ideological, ethnic and personal factors divided the nationalist clients into competing, mutually hostile factions. There were three externally-based liberation guerilla movements – ZAPU, ZANU and FROLIZI – and the internally-based ANC. The most long-standing and bitter rivalry was that between ZAPU and ZANU. It dated back to 1963, to the split within ZAPU, which resulted in the formation of ZANU.[45] By 1974, ZAPU became a predominantly Ndebele/Kalanga movement, while ZANU was a predominantly Shona movement. ZAPU was supported by the Soviets and ZANU by the Chinese. There was also the rivalry between Nkomo claiming the position of leadership of the nationalist movement, and Ndabaningi Sithole, representing the ZANU challenge to this claim. FROLIZI, which was formed in 1971 as a nationalist unity movement, resigned itself to being a small faction of members of the Zezuru Shona tribe who had left both ZAPU and ZANU.[46] Within the ANC, there were pro-ZAPU and pro-ZANU factions and followers of the organization's president Bishop Muzorewa. This was then the African nationalist set-up with which the FLP had to deal. The FLP's most difficult and frustrating, yet most urgent, task was to unify the nationalist factions. They knew that Smith would thrive on the divisions within the nationalist camp.

The FLP must have been surprised to find that the initial obstacle to their unity effort was divisions within ZANU. When on November 5, 1974 Mark Chona came to Que Que prison delivering to ZANU's detained leaders an invitation to come to Lusaka, the latter refused. They responded positively when on November 8 Chona returned with Nyerere's private secretary handing a written invitation signed by the regional patrons. It was then that the FLP were astonished to discover that Sithole, whom they recognized as ZANU President, had been suspended on November 1 by fellow detained members of ZANU Central Committee. The committee sent to Lusaka instead, Robert Mugabe, ZANU's Secretary General and Morton Malianga. The FLP refused to recognize them as ZANU representatives and sent them back to Rhodesia. On November 12 Kaunda's private secretary came to the prison with a personal invitation to Sithole. The members of the Central Committee could not refuse and decided to send Maurice Nyagumbo with him. In Lusaka, the two prisoners met Chitepo and other members of Dare re Chimurenga, ZANU's external war council. These opposed the suspension of Sithole for fear that the Zimbabwe National Liberation Army (ZANLA), ZANU's military wing, would lose, as a result, its training and other facilities in Zambia and Tanzania. In a subsequent meeting in Dar es Salaam, on November 14–15, a ZANU delegation, which included Herbert Chitepo, the Dare Chairman, and Sithole, was warned by Machel, that he would arrest ZANU men in Mozambique unless the decision to suspend Sithole was rescinded. The detained members of the Central Committee had little option in the face of combined pressure from the FLP and the Dare.[47]

With the issue of ZANU presidency settled, the FLP could resume their efforts to forge a united nationalist movement. On December 4 they met in Lusaka with the leaders of the different nationalist factions. They soon discovered that their troubles with ZANU were not over. ZANU leadership was extremely unhappy with the regional initiative. Some two months later Mugabe recalled their mood saying that ZANU leaders "were very angry because we thought these heads of states were selling us out".[48] On December 4, on his way to the Lusaka meeting, Herbert Chitepo stated ZANU's militant position: "There will be no talks, no negotiations, no discussions, involving our movement until Mr Smith recognizes the right to immediate majority rule. . . . We are not going to be bound by whatever is decided in Lusaka."[49] ZANU's intransigence was also reflected in their opposition to FLP's attempt to merge the existing movements in a new nationalist organization. The fact that Kaunda and Nyerere wanted to install Nkomo as the president of the new party,[50] certainly did not endear the idea to them. Nyagumbo accused Kaunda of "stampeding ZANU into joining with ZAPU in an endeavour to save his useless friend Nkomo".[51] ZANU had little regard for ZAPU which had done little fighting since 1970. ZANU leadership viewed their movement as the only representative of the genuine nationalist spirit and aspirations. They had evolved political and military structures; they had evolved an appropriate guerilla strategy, instilled in their cadres dedication to the cause of liberation and had launched a sustained guerilla campaign. They believed that they possessed the keys to national salvation. A merger with ZAPU and the moderate reformist ANC would, they believed, dilute ZANU's essential qualities. Mugabe recalled shortly after: "We thought that ZANU was the only effective military machinery and political body and to bring us under one common umbrella would interfere with our military machine."[52] It also threatened, of course, to deprive the ZANU leadership of the commanding position in the nationalist movement and in the future Zimbabwe which, they believed, they were entitled to. In the face of a united position of the FLP, ZANU could not afford to reject the idea of unity outright. Their compromise was presented to the regional patrons by Sithole: "ZANU is for unity because we agree to a united front. All we object to is the form of unity now suggested."[53] ZANU's obduracy earned their leaders the wrath of their patrons. Nyerere accused ZANU of "being married to disunity" and labelled Chitepo a "black Napoleon".[54] Kaunda, according to Mugabe, called them "treacherous, criminal, selfish" and threatened that "if we did not comply, he would no longer entertain our military presence in Zambia."[55] Another source had it that Kaunda threatened that "if ZANU did not sign the unity agreement, he would immediately stop the supply of food, arms and ammunition to the guerilla fighters in Rhodesia."[56] After a few days of futile and frustrating discussions Nyerere and Khama flew back home. Left on their own, the Rhodesian nationalists realized that they faced a threat of losing their vital regional support. Meeting on their own on December 7, they agreed to sign a unity declaration which satisfied the demands of the FLP. According to article one of the agreement: "ZANU, ZAPU, FROLIZI and ANC hereby agree to unite in the ANC." Within four months, a Congress was to be held to elect "the leadership of the united people of Zimbabwe". Article 6 stipulated that "ZAPU, ZANU and FROLIZI will take steps to merge their respective organs and structures into the ANC before the Congress."[57] From ZANU's point of view, it was a compromise representing the lesser of two evils. While being committed by their signature to a nationalist merger, they were given a few months time to manoeuvre out of this undesirable commitment. According to Zvobgo: "they believed that by signing the agreement they would gain enough time to reorganize the army so as to break its dependence on Zambia."[58] The immediate leadership dispute was solved by the acceptance of Muzorewa as chairman. The Zimbabwe Declaration of Unity also committed the united ANC to participation in a conference "for the transfer of power to the majority".[59] The unity of the rival nationalist factions was a marriage of inconvenience forced by an overwhelming regional pressure. It did not reflect an urge for unity and held little hope for a genuine pursuit of it.

While the unity talks were nearing a climax in early December, white and black patrons combined efforts to keep the settlement initiative on course. Smith had been getting reports that the nationalist leaders expected to get much more out of the negotiations than he intended or had undertaken to give. Thus, on December 3, he sent the following message to Kaunda:

> The Prime Minister is concerned over reports said to be emanating from African leaders who went to Lusaka for discussions with the four Presidents. The reports indicate that these leaders are expecting majority rule to be attained within five years or the life of one Parliament. It will be recalled that the Prime Minister told Mr Chona that he would be prepared to consider variations of the present franchise, provided there was no lowering of standards.[60] In order that there should be no misunderstanding, the Prime Minister hopes that the Presidents will make this clear to the African leaders.[61]

This was one of the first cases of diagonal interaction between Kaunda and the Rhodesian government. The FLP apparently did not take seriously Smith's message and objections. In a meeting, held in Lusaka on December 6 between Rhodesian officials and the FLP, the former were told, according to Smith, that "there would be no cessation of terrorism unless it was agreed that a precondition of the constitutional conference was that it would be on the basis of immediate majority rule."[62] According to an African version, Nyerere told the Rhodesians: "Let us not waste time, gentlemen, we are here to discuss majority rule. Majority rule, not in the future, but now, before the holding of a summit conference."[63] Smith put much of the blame for what transpired at that meeting on the fact that Nyerere was in the chair.[64] As the regional initiative was getting off the ground, the FLP, aware of Smith's evasiveness, went beyond the terms of the "scenario" in an attempt to commit Smith to what was, for them, a *conditio sine qua non*. Smith was too experienced a negotiator to fall into the trap. He reacted promptly. At the end of an emergency cabinet meeting on December 7, he countered with his own preconditions for the holding of a constitutional conference: "Firstly, that there should be a cessation of terrorism. . . . Secondly, that any constitutional conference would have to accept that there would be no lowering of standards."[65]

Once Smith stated officially and publicly his preconditions, the whole regional initiative was seriously threatened. The regional patrons, and Vorster and Kaunda, in particular, could not allow the domestic clients to frustrate their efforts. Vorster, at the beginning, took his client's side. In a statement issued on December 8, he put on record South Africa's position. Referring to the controversial majority rule issue, Vorster made the following points:

5. As we see it, the discussions[66] foundered as the result of the new demand at the end of the proceedings. This demand was in total conflict with the spirit, intent and result of the agreement up to this point.
6. Rhodesia cannot therefore be blamed for the failure of the negotiations.
7. Unless the other parties return to the basis and method of approach which was agreed upon before the deadlock on December 6, it must be assumed that agreement cannot be reached.

However, while supporting his client on the issue of majority rule which arose on December 6, Vorster pledged to continue his efforts to revive the regional initiative because "the alternative is too ghastly to contemplate."[67] The thrust of the efforts of the regional patrons was now to get their clients to the negotiating table without preconditions. On December 9 Brand Fourie, from the South African Department for Foreign Affairs conferred in Lusaka with Kaunda about the crisis, and on the following day Vorster met Smith.[68] On December 11 Smith said the following in a nationwide broadcast:

> The exchanges continued this week and the difficulties I have mentioned have now been resolved. In particular, firstly, I have received assurances to the effect that terrorist activities in Rhodesia will cease immediately, and secondly, that the proposed constitutional conference will take place without any preconditions.

Smith, consequently, announced his agreement to release the detained nationalists allowing them "to engage in normal activity in terms of the laws applicable to all Rhodesians". However, while not specifying it as a precondition, Smith assured his fellow white Rhodesians that "we are not prepared to deviate from our standards of civilization."[69] The newly formed ANC responded on December 12 with a statement which was equally ambiguous: "Without preconditions on both sides, we are ready to enter into immediate and meaningful negotiations with the leaders of the Rhodesian Front on the steps to be taken to achieve independence on the basis of majority rule." With regard to the ceasefire, the ANC stated: "As a demonstration of sincerity, all Freedom Fighters will be instructed, as soon as the date for negotiations has been fixed, to suspend fighting."[70]

These two statements by the internal Rhodesian rivals paved the way for constitutional negotiations between them. A comparative examination of the statements clearly reveals that it was hardly a promising beginning. Although not stated as preconditions, the gap between "our standards of civilization" and "independence on the basis of majority rule" could not be expected to be easily bridged through mere negotiations. In view of the residue of hostility and suspicion, the variations regarding the cease-fire were also not as insignificant as they appear. The gap between cessation and suspension, between "immediate" and "as soon as the date for negotiations has been fixed" was potentially as wide as the negotiating parties wished it to be.

CHAPTER THREE

From Lusaka to Victoria Falls Bridge: the Limits of Regional Patronage

December 1974 – August 1975

The two statements made in December 1974 by the Rhodesian government and the ANC, known as the Lusaka agreement, ushered in a new phase in the evolution of the Rhodesian crisis which culminated in the Victoria Falls bridge conference at the end of August 1975. Until the Lusaka agreement, the process of conflict resolution was dominated by the regional patrons. During the period leading from the Lusaka agreement up to the Victoria Falls bridge conference, the domestic clients played a much more active role in the process. The regional patrons continued to be keenly interested in the process and its outcome. However, they chose to withdraw to the background and to act as crisis managers, keeping their clients on course, rather than dominating the negotiations. The manoeuvring space which allowed the Rhodesian clients to initiate, manipulate and ultimately determine the fate of the whole process was provided by the Lusaka agreement. Firstly, the Lusaka agreement failed to deal with the huge gap between the goals of the clients. Shortly after the conclusion of the Lusaka agreement, Kaunda addressed himself to this issue: "As far as I know, the discussions of constitutional changes are for Rhodesians themselves, both Black and White."[1] This approach was shared by Vorster. It required a great deal of optimism or naivity to expect that the huge gap between black majority rule and white supremacy would be bridged through negotiations between the concerned parties. Furthermore, the respective statements forming the Lusaka agreement were open to different interpretation on a crucial issue like the cease-fire. The comfortable manoeuvring space created for them by the regional patrons enabled the clients to wreck the whole initiative. Without

41

considerable pressures, the clients could hardly be expected to give up what they perceived as their vital interests.

Throughout the period leading up to the Victoria Falls bridge conference, the Rhodesian government exhibited publicly an unyielding attitude towards the nature of the settlement. Twice they refuted specific reports that there was an agreement between Vorster and Kaunda on the basis of majority rule within five years or that they had agreed to such a plan.[2] In mid-January 1975, Smith stated unequivocally: "We have no policy in Rhodesia to hand over to a black majority government."[3] In an interview with the BBC, Smith demonstrated his ability to play around with terminology: "Certainly, we have never ever said that majority rule isn't something which is inherent in the Rhodesian constitution. In fact, we have got majority rule today. I am the representative of the majority of the electors in Rhodesia. We don't object to majority rule; we have had it for the last 60 years – not quite so."[4] The concept of responsible majority rule as opposed to irresponsible majority rule[5] was Smith's contribution to political science. Speaking in Inyanga on May 26, he was more specific about what he objected to: "The idea of one-man-one-vote, or immediate parity is a non-starter."[6] In June, Smith stated his government's policy in positive terms: "Our policy . . . is based on a qualified franchise for all Rhodesians with standards of merit which ensure that government will be retained in responsible hands for all times."[7]

Thus the obsolete multi-racialism of the 1950s, which had failed elsewhere in central and east Africa, remained the policy of the RF government. There were some more sober and innovative voices. In retrospect, it is obvious that the leaders of the liberal opposition who saw doom in the failure to achieve a political settlement and in the prospect of intensifying armed conflict,[8] had the foresight and the courage to speak their minds. The liberal groups which continued to advocate concessions and political accommodation remained, however, marginal, divided and ineffectual. They had been routed in the 1974 general election and showed no signs of recovery.[9] The warnings of these prophets of doom went unheeded by the great majority of white Rhodesians. Smith reflected the mood of this majority when depicting the liberal leaders as "only a few opportunist politicians – who unfortunately are given a lot more prominence than they should get – who wanted us to lower our standards in order to settle this problem of ours".[10]

If Smith could shrug off his liberal critics he could hardly ignore the pressures from the far right. The far right parties which criticized Smith for his leniency[11] were, in themselves, politically marginal. However, their criticism had to be taken seriously because of its possible impact on the RF, itself a right-wing party. Indeed, there were far right elements within the RF who were increasingly unhappy with Smith's apparent flexibility and lack of resolve in defence of white supremacy. John Newington, the RF Deputy Speaker, was critical of Smith's handling of detente, saying that "no detente is worth economic and racial destruction."[12] Another RF MP, claiming that white Rhodesians had gone far enough, said that "the time has arrived for the Government to take the lead and demonstrate its determination to end this facade."[13] Furthermore, there were signs of the emergence of an ideological opposition to Smith's multi-racial approach. In May 1975, Wickus de Kock, a prominent Afrikaner minister in Smith's government, rejected multi-racialism and suggested that a solution might lie in the adoption of South Africa's policy of separate development.[14] This was, in fact, an elaboration on the policy of provincialization which had been adopted by the RF in 1972,[15] but left in abeyance by the government.

Thus, the balance of opinion within the white community was not particularly conducive to political moderation. The long life of isolation in the colonial frontier, particularly since UDI, turned the white settlers into a parochial, introvert community. The inevitable ideological and political inbreeding made the Rhodesian whites insensitive to global trends and even to regional changes, and to the implications for themselves thereof. This disposition was reinforced by the lack of African pressure inside Rhodesia. Because of reasons which will be discussed below, the military pressure of the nationalist guerillas hardly justified political accommodation.[16] Thus, basic disposition and domestic military and political balance of power combined to entrench white euphoria and intransigence. Towards the end of June 1975, Smith still expressed the view that time was on white Rhodesia's side.[17] Given such a state of mind, any suggestion of capitulation or even meaningful concessions were conceived as part of a political conspiracy rather than the exigencies of a rapidly changing situation. It was a storm that could and had to be weathered. Unmoved by the changes around them, white Rhodesians continued to draw inspiration and strength from their long historical experience as a dominant minority in colonial Africa. Wickus de Kock, referring to people misjudging Rhodesia's strength and determination articulated his compatriots' mood: "These people have disregarded Rhodesia's long history of being master in her own house, and that Rhodesia is different from every other former colony in Africa."[18]

The determination of the Rhodesian government to preserve effec-

43

tive white domination was also fed by the fate of the whites in Mozambique and Angola in the wake of the Portuguese abdication.[19] The scenes of white settlers fleeing Mozambique in haste to South Africa and Rhodesia cast a long shadow on the prospect of living in an African-dominated Zimbabwe. In this light, white survival, collective as well as individual, could be easily conceived as dependent on white control. The upheavals in Mozambique and Angola reinforced the white negative stereotype of African nationalist leaders. They were megalomaniacs or self-seeking opportunists who did not even have the interests of their own African brethren at heart.[20] The destiny of the white minority could certainly not be entrusted in their hands. White Rhodesians also had a comforting view of the needs and aspirations of the ordinary Africans. These were conceived as apolitical in the nationalist sense: "The real needs of Africa are food, jobs and education. . . . Ordinary people who have to do a day's work. . . . or who like to have a job would be more impressed if these people [the nationalist leaders] get down to sensible meaningful discussion."[21] This satisfying image of the African masses was certainly encouraging from the point of view of the respective prospect of African nationalism and white supremacy.

White determination was matched by an African nationalist one. White Rhodesians were facing a much more confident and steadfast African nationalist camp. Solutions based on "parity" or "blocking third", which may have been entertained by the ANC, disappeared even from the moderate nationalists' vocabulary. From an African nationalist perspective, majority rule, far from being a remote objective, became the starting point for any process leading to a political settlement. As seen earlier, in its December 12, 1974 statement, the ANC emphasized majority rule as the goal of the prospective negotiations.[22] Despite the agreement to negotiate without preconditions, even moderate Gabella made his position sharply clear: "The African stand for majority rule is clear and unequivocal. Both the British Government and the Ian Smith regime are in no doubt that our position on the principle is not negotiable."[23] Muzorewa, who less than a year earlier negotiated with Smith on the basis of a "blocking third", appealed to the whites in March 1975, from a different platform altogether: "The coming of majority rule is inevitable."[24] An ANC statement of March 23 put it on record that the concept of majority rule was "not negotiable".[25] The position of the newly-structured ANC was hardening not only on the principle of majority rule, but also on its application. In early January 1975 the moderate ANC secretary general, Gordon Chavunduka, still said that the ANC had not yet discussed a timetable for majority rule.[26] Later in January, even Ndabaningi Sithole, who was considered by the whites as a militant, conceded that there could be a compromise on the timing of majority rule. He said that if "Smith . . . was prepared to think in terms of majority rule in three to five years, it could put a different complexion on the settlement negotiations".[27] In early February, he agreed to a transitional period of one year, provided the Africans would be in control of the interim government.[28] In early May 1975, at the Commonwealth conference in Jamaica, he was even more specific and rigid: "I would say not more than 12 months. And in that interim there would be a black-dominated Government with a black Prime Minister and, of course, some white ministers."[29] Joshua Nkomo said his people wanted "majority rule now, not tomorrow".[30]

The hardening of attitudes in the African nationalist camp was in a way a reflection of the white regime's unyielding stance. The repeated rejection by Smith and his associates of the very principle of black majority rule pushed the nationalists to the other extreme. At an earlier stage of the negotiations following the Lusaka agreement, nationalist leaders condemned Smith for his statements regarding majority rule. In mid-January 1975, Edson Sithole said clearly that unless the white leaders ceased to proclaim their position in this regard, the African nationalists would have no choice but to adopt a similarly hard line.[31] The interaction between Rhodesian white and black nationalist leaders in the negotiating context generated a distinct radicalizing dynamic in the nationalist camp. This dynamic was reinforced by a euphoric sense of riding the wave of history. A journalist who had interviewed ANC leaders in August 1975, was impressed by their conviction that time was on their side.[32] Moderation is not habitually an attribute of those who ride the wave of history. The radicalizing dynamic within the nationalist camp acquired further momentum through the interplay between the conflicting nationalist factions. In such situations the group dynamic almost invariably pushes the moderate towards the extreme.

However, the radicalization among the nationalist leadership was limited to the issue of majority rule. Regarding the fate of the whites and the nature of independent Zimbabwe, moderation was the dominant trend. In early 1975 Eliot Gabella portrayed future Zimbabwe as a truly multi-racial country and not one totally dominated by black power.[33] Muzorewa himself declared in the Commonwealth conference that the "ANC policy was to encourage whites to stay with full rights."[34] Coming from known moderates, this was hardly surprising. Such attitudes were perhaps not expected of Ndabaningi Sithole, considered by the government as the arch militant nationalist villain.

On February 17, a fortnight before he was arrested by the government, in an attempt to get him out of the negotiating process, Sithole published an article in which he outlined his vision of independent Zimbabwe. He stated that in principle "African leaders, on all levels, accept the basic proposition that Zimbabwe is as much the White man's home as it is that of the Black man." In his conclusion, he exhibited the moderation and pragmatism which was at the root of his approach: "There can be no doubt that an independent Zimbabwe would be poorer without the many diversified skills, ideas and ideals of the White section of this country, and no progressive African is unaware of this."[35] Thus, even Sithole emerged as a "bourgeois" nationalist. He upheld ideals of the generation of anti-colonial nationalist leaders in British Africa who wished to inherit and Africanize the colonial state rather than radically transform its socio-economic structure.

There were, however, other divergent views on the nature of independent Zimbabwe. There were those, especially in ZANU, who were not satisfied with the mere transfer of power to black hands. There were those for whom the struggle was against the danger of "false decolonization" as much as it was for majority rule. For them neo-colonialism was anathema. In January 1975 Edison Zvobgo, a ZANU leader residing in the USA, stated clearly what was for him ZANU's position: "We do not want to just replace white faces with black faces. The system itself is unjust and needs to be changed." For him ZANU's Zimbabwe included a socialist government, dramatic land reform and other radical changes.[36] On July 8, 1975 a group of top ZANU political and military leaders, then in a Zambian prison, wrote in a letter that the goal of their struggle was "the transformation of the capitalist–racist edifice into a truly socialist state".[37] It was not surprising that such views and goals developed in ZANU which bore the main brunt of the guerilla war. The war itself and the ideological byproducts of the links with communist China had a profound effect on that movement. ZANU had been transforming from a "bourgeois" nationalist party to a revolutionary one, from a plain anti-colonialist to an anti-imperialist movement. It should be noted, however, that these revolutionary tunes, had not yet been played at the central arena of nationalist politics. At the level of public knowledge, they were still very marginal.

From the Rhodesian government's point of view, it was Ndabaningi Sithole, with his insistence on immediate majority rule and his moderate vision of Zimbabwe, who represented the wild nationalist extremism. It was his past reputation, his style, and his rhetoric, as well as white Rhodesians' political blindness which gave Sithole this image. For Smith and his government, of course, the gap between their

46

position and the moderate nationalists' demand for majority rule was too wide for them to worry about more extreme versions of African nationalism. Indeed, this huge gap had to be bridged before the questions related to the nature of independent Zimbabwe could be addressed.

It is astonishing that the regional patrons, and especially Kaunda and Vorster, who invested so much energy in, and pinned so many hopes on the resolution of the Rhodesian conflict, could believe that such huge gaps in perceived vital interests and goals could be bridged through negotiations between the domestic parties, namely the government and the nationals. The regional patrons soon discovered that vertical interaction between them and their respective clients was to be a permanent and vital feature of the negotiating process. It would be useful, before dealing with that process, to divert our attention to the evolution of the patrons' attitude towards the resolution of the Rhodesian conflict and of their relations with their clients in the period leading up to the Victoria Falls bridge conference.

Throughout this period, the regional patrons were, as a whole, interested in a peaceful settlement in Rhodesia. This was certainly true in the case of South Africa. Policy makers and public opinion makers continued to rave about the new era which was dawning on South Africa. In his New Year message Vorster elaborated on the forms and fields of cooperation between South Africa and its neighbours in southern Africa.[38] In February 1975 his publicized visit to Liberia[39] raised the expectations to a new level. Against this background and in relation to his detente policy, Vorster said: "My intention is . . . to normalize relations with all African countries, whether it be countries to the south, to the west or to the north."[40] In May, when at the end of the "six months' grace" the miracle failed to materialize and problems besetting the Rhodesian negotiations abounded, Vorster continued to radiate confidence and optimism.[41]

The Afrikaans Nationalist press provided Vorster with an appropriate background music. In early January 1975 *Die Vaderland* maintained: "For Mr Vorster, the present progress has been a personal triumph. This is acknowledged everywhere. He is a statesman of international stature and if peace comes to southern Africa, his name will be immortalized as the man who took the initiative."[42] Vorster's visit to Liberia sparked off a new outburst of expectations and admiration. *Die Transvaler* exclaimed, on February 19, that Vorster "deserves the honour and admiration he is receiving on all sides for his detente success in Africa".[43] On February 18 *Die Burger* stated that "the normalization of diplomatic, trade and technological relations were

47

the objectives of Vorster's African initiatives".[44] *Die Volksblad* surmised that the African countries swallowed South Africa's economic bait,[45] while *Die Beeld*, so impressed with the achievements so far, concluded that "even if detente should miscarry, there is already a lasting gain."[46] On April 4, while the Rhodesian negotiations were being dragged from one obstacle to another, *Die Burger* maintained that "Vorster's prediction of dramatic change in our international status 'within six months to a year' is coming true before our eyes",[47] and a month later *Die Transvaler* saw the walls of isolation around South Africa breaking down.[48] On August 22, a few days before the Victoria Falls bridge conference convened and failed, the *Oggendblad* said that "a bridge has been built between South Africa and Zambia – one that will make it possible to solve the problems of relationships more easily than before and for other contacts to be established that will benefit all the peoples of the sub-continent and increase the prospects of peace between the races."[49] On the day the conference opened, *Die Volksblad* believed that Vorster was "engaged in reaping the gains which are of permanent value to South Africa irrespective of the events in Rhodesia".[50]

Thus, the South African government and the Nationalist press actively instilled a sense of euphoria, a belief that South Africa had already achieved a regional and international breakthrough. Having experienced isolation and ostracism for so many years, and being possessed by a resultant craving for external recognition and legitimacy, South Africans were intoxicated by the mere fact that respected African countries and leaders were ready to deal with them directly and openly. The euphoria stemming therefrom, blurred their vision of the reality. In the real world, South Africa's hopes for a breakthrough depended totally on their ability to deliver Rhodesia to black Africa. The South African government was not unaware of the importance of the success of the negotiations between the Rhodesian government and the black nationalists. However, the euphoria which possessed them deprived them of an acute sense of urgency, which was essential for the success of detente. This lack of a sense of urgency was reflected in their dealings with their Rhodesian client in the period leading up to the Victoria Falls bridge conference.

Throughout this period, the South African government was faced with Smith's unequivocal public opposition even to the principle of majority rule. From their contacts with Zambians, the South Africans knew that this principle was non-negotiable. Thus, the Rhodesian position prevented any meaningful progress towards a peaceful settlement. This could not be accepted with equanimity by South Africa. For

48

domestic considerations (which will be discussed below), the South African government chose the Afrikaans press as a conduit for messages to the Rhodesian government and public. A veritable anti-Rhodesian press campaign was sparked off by a front page report in *Die Transvaler* on January 8, 1975. The report quoted an unnamed "informed source" who called on Smith to accept black majority rule in the near future. *Rapport*, another leading Afrikaans newspaper, implied that the report had been tacitly sanctioned by Dr Connie Mulder, who, in addition to being a prominent minister and a leader of the Nationalist party in the Transvaal, was also a director of *Die Transvaler*.[51] In an editorial of January 11, *Die Transvaler*'s message was still subtle and indirect. The editorial lamented South Africa's choices in Rhodesia, which it identified as being between "continued assistance to, and protection for, Rhodesia and the wrath of southern Africa and a large part of the rest of the world or total withdrawal from Rhodesia" and between "war and peaceful co-existence."[52] South Africa's favoured choice was so obvious that it required no spelling out. Two days later *Rapport* was more direct and blunt. After emphasizing the difference between South Africa's policy of "separate freedoms" and Rhodesia's policy of power sharing, the editorial questioned the logic of Rhodesia's position: "Therefore, we find Mr Ian Smith's view that majority rule will not come during his lifetime, peculiar. And we find the recent statements of other members of his government that it will never come, completely incomprehensible." It ended up by calling on Rhodesians to face squarely the implications of their own policy "painful though they may be".[53] On January 18, after stating South Africa's deep interest in the Rhodesian dispute, *Die Transvaler* followed a similar ideological argument. The editorial ended by refuting the claim that Rhodesia was still a useful buffer for South Africa and presenting detente as "the most realistic way to ensure White survival in the entire southern Africa".[54]

This editorial onslaught failed to have an impact on the Rhodesian government's policy because the messages emanating from South Africa were still indirect, unclear and conflicting. Soon after the Lusaka agreement, Vorster, commenting on reports that he had devised a plan that would lead to majority rule within three to five years, stated that South Africa would not interfere in the Rhodesian problem.[55] Referring to the solution to the Rhodesian problem in his New Year message, Vorster said that "this, however, remains a question for the Rhodesians alone to resolve."[56] Speaking at a press conference on January 20, he defined South Africa's role as being "to create the necessary climate for the different countries and the different people involved to meet. But South Africa has not tried to prescribe."[57] On February 11 he said in Cape Town that Rhodesia would not be sacrificed as a price for peace in southern Africa.[58] When worried Rhodesian officials hastened to inquire through diplomatic channels whether the original *Transvaler* report of January 8 represented official South African thinking, they were told officially that South Africa had not changed its policy of non-interference in Rhodesia's internal affairs. Subsequently, the RBC quoted unnamed government sources in Pretoria as stating that South Africa was not pressing for a black government in Salisbury.[59] Soon, there was a reaction to the press attacks on Rhodesia even from within the ranks of the Afrikaans press. On January 23 *Die Oosterlig* criticized "those – even a few Afrikaans papers in the north – who have tried to put pressure on Rhodesia to accept Black demands for majority rule for South Africa's sake also."[60] *Die Volksblad* spoke of the wrong impression that "South Africa is twisting Rhodesia's arms to force it into situations to which it did not move voluntarily."[61]

It soon became increasingly clear to South African policy makers that the Rhodesians were ignoring the veiled, unclear messages coming from South Africa. They realized that left to their own devices, Smith and his colleagues were never going to concede the crucial issue of majority rule. Rhodesian intransigence forced the South African government to focus more sharply on the question of majority rule in Rhodesia. Vorster had to look for new, more direct and clear methods of bringing the message to the attention of the Rhodesian government. Early in 1975 Vorster met Smith in Cape Town, but failed to make him admit that qualified franchise would ever result in black majority rule. This meeting caused a sharp deterioration in the relations between the two leaders.[62] Subsequently, the South African government sought to employ alternative channels of communication with the Rhodesian government. In early March 1975 Connie Mulder invited his Rhodesian counterpart and·fellow Afrikaner, Wickus de Kock, to come to Pretoria. With Smith's approval, Wickus de Kock took along with him, Mr Rowan Cronje, another Afrikaner minister. In the aftermath of the Portuguese coup, Smith increased the Afrikaner representation in his cabinet, hoping to strengthen his ties with South Africa. Now, the South Africans were using their fellow Rhodesian Afrikaners for their own purpose. In a long meeting in Pretoria, Vorster gave them a full presentation of South African policy towards Rhodesia. For the first time, as a result of that meeting, it dawned on Wickus de Kock that Rhodesia, as he had known it, was gone forever. The two Rhodesians learned how vital for South Africa was the success of detente. It was made clear to them that Vorster thought in terms of South Africa first, even if Rhodesia had to pay the price. Vorster even spoke of the withdrawal of the South African police force from Rhodesia and of cutting military supplies. With regard to the constitutional future of Rhodesia, Vorster said in no uncertain terms that, in his view, detente spelled out majority rule in Rhodesia. He spoke more concretely of majority within 15 years.[63] In his usual manner, Smith did not discuss the report on this meeting in his cabinet. He did arrange, as a result of this report, a conference between South African and Rhodesian delegations. This conference took place in Cape Town on March 16–17.[64] It should be noted that it was the first meeting of full delegations of the two white allies since the Portuguese coup. Characteristic of decision-making Rhodesia, the delegation had never met to discuss the forthcoming conference. As the conference opened, the Rhodesians found out that the South Africans were not interested at all in the military and intelligence briefings they had prepared. They were keenly interested, however, in the promotion of a constitutional settlement in Rhodesia. One of the main topics of discussion was the timetable for the progress to black majority rule. The South African delegation suggested majority rule within 15 years. After lengthy discussions, the Rhodesian delegation, including Smith, accepted it. This was the first time that Smith and an official Rhodesian delegation committed themselves to a definite date for majority rule. The Rhodesian delegation undertook, at South Africa's request, to work out the exact franchise qualifications which would lead to black rule within this time span.[65] The joint statement at the end of the conference had no trace of the agreement. It stated that "the future of Rhodesia is a matter for Rhodesians, Black and White to resolve among themselves."[66] Typical of the way Smith was running Rhodesia, the issue of 15 years transition was not pursued once the Rhodesian delegation was north of the Limpopo. It was never discussed in full cabinet and the franchise qualifications were not worked out. In fact, as seen earlier on, Smith continued to reject, in public, the very idea of handing over power. This time Smith was not taken to task by the Afrikaans press or by the South African government.

The African regional patrons were not more successful in preparing their nationalist clients for a peaceful settlement. As in the earlier initial regional contacts, Zambia continued to play a major role, both horizontally, *vis à vis* South Africa, and vertically in relation to the Rhodesian nationalists. This was so for very good reasons. As events in southern Africa were unfolding, it became increasingly clear that Zambia was going to be respectively the biggest loser or beneficiary of the failure or success of detente. It was the twin interlinked problems of slumping copper prices and outlet to the sea which clouded, more threateningly, the horizon of Zambia. On July 1, 1975 Kaunda referred to the illusion, fostered by the high copper prices in the last few years, that Zambia was a rich country: "We are not rich. We are a poor people and we have a long way to go in order to build a prosperous country."[67] So bad was Zambia's foreign exchange situation, that Kaunda suggested the imposition of petrol rationing. The economic difficulties stemming from low copper prices and high petrol prices were exacerbated by worsening transport problems. In January 1975, Kaunda could still count on the Benguella railway line.[68] However, as the civil war in Angola intensified in the following months, this route had to be counted out. Zambia's main economic lifeline was the newly completed Tanzam railway linking the Zambian copperbelt to the port of Dar es Salaam. However, teething problems combined with a badly congested Dar es Salaam port left Zambia with an urgent need to secure a reliable route for its export and import traffic. Thus, the reopening of its traditional routes to the Mozambican ports through Rhodesia became a matter of highest national priority for Zambia. Kaunda was badly torn between the vital interests of his country and his commitment to the cause of liberation. He was urgently seeking a solution which would satisfy both.

In his efforts to promote a peaceful settlement, Kaunda went beyond negotiating with South Africa and trying to influence the Rhodesian nationalists. He also attempted to foster the cause of a peaceful settlement among white Rhodesians. In mid-January 1975, he invited Sir Roy Welensky to attend the opening of the Zambian Parliament. Welensky told the Rhodesian public: "I am quite convinced that from the President of Zambia downwards, there is a genuine desire to try to bring about a peaceful solution of the problems."[69] On April 7 Kaunda met at State House in Lusaka two prominent white Rhodesian farmers. The two farmers gave a fairly positive impression of the position of white farmers in Zambia and of Kaunda's moderate disposition towards Rhodesia.[70] In June 1975, after months of futile negotiations between the Rhodesian government and the nationalists, Kaunda invited a high level RF delegation to come to Zambia. The delegation, which was headed by minister Wickus de Kock, included also five RF MPs.[71] It was the first such visit since UDI. During the visit, Kaunda and other Zambian officials and private citizens tried to impress upon their white Rhodesian guests that Zambia was a free, prosperous, harmonious and happy multi-racial country, and to persuade them to adopt this model in Rhodesia. Kaunda conveyed to his guests his desire for peace in southern Africa. During the visit, arrangements were made for regular telephone contacts between de Kock and Mark Chona. In regard to the solution of the Rhodesian problem, Kaunda was not specific. He did, however, tell his guests that there was no difference between his and Vorster's version of detente.[72] During his previous meeting with the two Rhodesian farmers, Kaunda was apparently more specific regarding a Rhodesian solution. He spoke, according to the report, in terms of qualified franchise and a transition to complete majority rule which might last more than 10 years.[73] Although Kaunda hastened to claim that the report was false, it sounds credible. It renders Vorster's belief that 15 years transition could serve as a basis for a settlement more comprehensible.

If Vorster viewed Kaunda's more compromising inclinations as representing the position of the African regional patrons, he was guilty of gross misunderstanding of the regional environment. Zambia was only one in a group of four African regional patrons. Zambia was the most interested among the African patrons in a speedy, peaceful solution. In the contacts and negotiations leading up to the Lusaka agreement in December 1974, Zambia was the initiator and the most active among the African patrons. Vorster apparently assumed that Kaunda represented a regional African consensus. However, after the Lusaka agreement, the FLP began to function as a veritable collective body. From that moment it was the group dynamic of the FLP, rather than the views of one member, which shaped the regional African position. The interaction within the FLP group produced a collective position which was different from that of Zambia. This was so, largely because the attitude of two important member-states was markedly different from that of Zambia. As seen earlier, Tanzania was remote from the focus of conflict and her particular national interests were unlikely to be affected by the escalation of the Rhodesian conflict. In fact, Tanzania could only benefit from a growing Zambian dependence on the Tanzam outlet to the sea. Thus Nyerere could pursue his traditional radical position regarding the liberation of southern Africa without reservations. Mozambique, on the other hand, could gain economically from a peaceful resolution of the Rhodesian conflict as it could suffer from its escalation. However, FRELIMO, which assumed full control over Mozambique only in June 1975, was still riding a revolutionary cloud, not giving due weight to mundane and selfish national interests. Botswana supported Zambia's moderation, but was hardly a political heavyweight.

Furthermore, the FLP were not free agents operating in a political vacuum. There had been a well-established tradition and practice of the liberation of southern Africa being the concern of Africa as a whole operating through the Organization of African Unity (OAU). There had been the OAU Liberation Committee which was charged with formulating strategy, channelling support to the liberation movements and supervising the progress of the struggle. Thus, Kaunda's views regarding a transitional period of more than ten years, or even five years, as Martin and Johnson suggested,[74] represented his inner thoughts rather than a FLP or OAU consensus. As such, they are significant only as reflecting Zambia's positions and preferences and as shedding light on positions adopted by South Africa. In fact, these moderate positions did not even represent Zambia's ultimate stand. The ultimate Zambian position, which counted at the level of regional politics, was not the views conveyed in confidential meetings, but rather those it was able to pronounce and defend in the councils of Africa.

In early January 1975, shortly after the Lusaka agreement, the OAU Liberation Committee, composed of representatives of 18 OAU members, convened in Dar es Salaam to reformulate liberation policies and strategies. In his opening address, Nyerere presented Smith with two political choices: "He can either accept immediate independence on the basis of majority rule with no interim steps to that majority rule. Or, he can renounce UDI of 1965, and be a participant with the nationalist leaders in negotiations with the British Government for independence on the basis of majority rule."[75] On February 2 Nyerere made his position even clearer: "Rhodesian blacks want independence yesterday."[76] In the Commonwealth conference, Nyerere reiterated his hard-line uncompromising position with regard to the African goals in Rhodesia: "We reject the idea that there should be an interim period between majority rule and something which is not majority rule for that country."[77] Soon it became clear that Nyerere, though perhaps more forceful in articulating African goals, represented a broad African consensus. In early April 1975, addressing the OAU Council of Ministers in Dar es Salaam, Vernon Mwaanga, the Zambian Foreign Minister, sounded as extreme as Nyerere: "Our objective in Zimbabwe has been and still is immediate majority rule."[78] The group dynamic within the FLP and within the OAU had a definite radicalizing effect.

The relevant OAU bodies also addressed themselves to the liberation strategy. The Liberation Committee, in its January 1975 meeting, adopted a dual liberation strategy for Rhodesia which was in tune with the Lusaka Manifesto of 1969, and with current inclinations of the FLP. The Liberation Committee also resolved to give maximum priority to the liberation of Rhodesia and Namibia.[79] The OAU Council of

Ministers meeting, convened in Addis Ababa on February 13, approved the priority given to Rhodesia and Namibia. In this broader body of African opinion, the FLP strategy of working with South Africa for the achievement of a peaceful solution came under attack. At the request of Lesotho, the Council resolved that members of the OAU should avoid contacts with South Africa as long as she refused to talk to its own liberation movements. Furthermore, the Algerian Foreign Minister persuaded his colleagues to call a special meeting in Dar es Salaam in April to discuss ways to check the South African diplomatic advance in Africa.[80] This thrust had the potential of disrupting the peaceful strategy adopted by the FLP. The Council also recommended substantial increase in the financial support for the ANC "in order to enable the people of Zimbabwe to intensify their armed struggle until total liberation was achieved".[81]

Thus, by the time the extraordinary meeting of the Council of Ministers opened on April 9, and as the Rhodesian peace moves failed to show signs of a meaningful progress, pressures from OAU militants were mounting. This was reflected at that meeting when representatives of hard-line states opposed contacts with South Africa and urged commitment to armed struggle.[82] It was in the face of this growing militancy that the Zambian Foreign Minister, Vernon Mwaanga, had to defend the peace initiative. Implicit in his speech was criticism of the militants who represented countries far away from the battlefield. In warding off the attack against contacts with South Africa, Mwaanga went as far as praising Vorster for his cooperation on the Rhodesian issue.[83] With regard to strategy, the offensive of the militants was checked. The meeting rejected Oliver Tambo's demand for the pursuit of a simultaneous war of liberation in Rhodesia, Namibia and South Africa.[84] The foreign ministers also reaffirmed the dual strategy for Rhodesia − i.e. that of negotiating while preparing for the intensification of the armed struggle.[85] While maintaining Africa's traditional hostility toward South Africa, the foreign ministers did not specifically veto the ongoing contacts between South Africa and Zambia.[86] Thus, after a series of deliberations in the Liberation Committee and the Council of Ministers of the OAU, the initiative and role of the FLP were endorsed.

As the southern African detente seemed to be getting off the ground, Britain, the formal colonial power, also came into the picture. Britain first learnt about the unfolding new regional initiative in a meeting between Callaghan and the Zambian Foreign Minister in Geneva on August 8, 1974.[87] With the memories of *Tiger* and *Fearless* still at the back of their mind, the Labour government had no inclination to get

55

involved. Reacting to the Lusaka agreement, Callaghan's intention was still to "let the black and white parties get on with the negotiations without British interference".[88] However, Rhodesian nationalists and their regional patrons wanted Britain to discharge its colonial responsibility. On the eve of the conclusion of the Lusaka agreement, representatives of the British government met counterparts from Zambia, Tanzania and Botswana, also members of the British Commonwealth.[89] By then Callaghan had already planned a ten-day African tour with an emphasis on southern Africa.[90] Arriving at Lusaka at the start of his tour on December 31, 1974, Callaghan announced his government's acceptance of her responsibility towards Rhodesia and its intention to discharge it in conjunction with her Commonwealth colleagues.

Callaghan described his visit to Lusaka as the high point in Anglo-Zambian relations. Britain and Zambia "agreed to work in close collaboration in determining the stages which should be followed in negotiations to bring about such a solution, including the holding of a constitutional conference". They also concurred that "it would become necessary for the British Government to enter into more direct and frequent contacts with the parties concerned in Rhodesia and elsewhere." Zambia on its part welcomed, and probably encouraged, Callaghan's decision to travel to South Africa to confer with Vorster.[91] Callaghan's meeting with Vorster in Port Elizabeth on January 5, 1975 did not appear particularly fruitful. "Businesslike", the adjective used by Callaghan to describe the meeting[92] is hardly a superlative in the diplomatic jargon. *Die Transvaler* blamed Callaghan for wanting to steal the show from Vorster.[93] In the press conference concluding the meeting, Vorster suggested to Britain, by implication, that she should keep her hands off Rhodesia.[94]

Thus, while African patrons and clients were eager that Britain should play an active role in the unfolding process of conflict resolution, the white patron and client were hostile to British meddling in the Rhodesian crisis. While not sounding too optimistic on his return to London, Callaghan accepted British involvement. He even contemplated the renewal of direct contact, on a non-diplomatic level, with the Rhodesian government.[95] Two days after he had reported to the House of Commons on his trip, Whitehall officials disclosed that Callaghan had sent messages to Muzorewa and Smith concerning possible steps towards a settlement.[96] Callaghan apparently offered to send British officials to Rhodesia to meet with the government and the ANC. In rejecting this offer, Smith told Callaghan that such a visit would at that stage be detrimental.[97] Undeterred, on February 25,

1975, Callaghan issued an invitation to the government and the ANC to send representatives to London, to explain their views. He added that the arrangements for a constitutional conference had to be agreed by Britain and the other parties concerned.[98]

In view of a determined South African and Rhodesian opposition to British involvement, Callaghan's declarations of intent were to little avail. Thus, in the aftermath of the Lusaka agreement, the Rhodesian conflict resolution process remained the domain of the regional patrons and their clients. The regional patrons, in fact, passed the bucket to their clients hoping that they would not spill the water.[99] It was highly unrealistic to expect the opposing domestic parties to negotiate in good faith when the gap between them was one between immediate majority rule and majority rule in 15 years, which Smith grudgingly accepted in principle, but never committed himself to publicly. In fact, the lengthy and frustrating negotiations between the nationalists and the Rhodesian government and the intensive involvement of the regional patrons in the period leading up to the Victoria Falls bridge conference, had nothing to do with the substance of a settlement. It was all about procedure. The negotiations on procedure turned into a major stumbling block, because the positions adopted by the domestic parties on these matters reflected the wide credibility gap between them as well as the chasm between their respective goals. Whereas the regional patrons regarded these negotiations as a prelude to a settlement, the domestic parties, or some of them at least, viewed them as a manoeuvring space to avert it. Essentially, the negotiating tactics of the domestic parties were geared to bring the process to a halt without being blamed for it by the respective patrons. Indeed, foremost in the eyes of the domestic negotiators was the need to ensure the support of the regional patrons in the struggle that lay ahead.

The so-called Lusaka agreement of December 1974, which set the framework and conditions for the prospective negotiations, provided the domestic parties with a comfortable manoeuvring space. There was no formal document to which the opposing parties subscribed. In January 1975, the ANC claimed that the Rhodesian government had made the following undertakings to the FLP:

1. That the Government would release all political detainees and restrictees (which included people in protected villages) immediately;
2. That the Government would release all political prisoners as soon as possible;

3. That the Government would revoke the death sentences on political prisoners and release them;
4. That the Government would grant a general amnesty to all those considered to have committed political crimes including those outside the country;
5. That the Government would lift the ban on ZAPU and ZANU;
6. That the Government would create conditions to allow free political activity and expression in the country;
7. That the Government would halt political trials;
8. That the Government would lift the state of Emergency.[100]

Smith's response was unequivocal: "There is no question of a written agreement. I know nothing about eight points and I think it is a fiction."[101] As Smith subsequently revealed, he was bound by the six points agreement, signed in October 1974 by Vorster and himself, which bore little resemblance to the ANC's eight points.[102] There was evidently a marked discrepancy between the terms of reference of the domestic negotiating parties. This did not augur well for the negotiations.

Under such circumstances, the regional patrons could not for long abstain from active involvement in the negotiations. Barely a week had passed since the conclusion of the Lusaka agreement, and Kaunda advised the negotiating parties: "They should speak less to the press galleries because if they continue, they will find that they have taken permanent stands and decisions in the eyes of the public which will be difficult to reverse."[103] This was only a foretaste. Throughout the period leading up to the Victoria Falls bridge conference, the regional patrons played a very active backstage role, without which the negotiations would never have got off the ground.

As soon as the bucket was passed on to the domestic parties, it became clear that they were not playing the role expected of them. Not only were they continually shouting from the tops of their voices their diametrically opposed conditions for a settlement, but very soon they began hotly to dispute the technical and procedural aspects of the so-called Lusaka agreement. The first major dispute which threatened to rock the negotiations concerned the nature, timing and conditions of the cease-fire between the Rhodesian security forces and the nationalist guerillas. The Rhodesian government insisted on immediate cease-fire, giving allowance for a reasonable time to transmit instructions to the guerillas in the bush. In leaflets dropped by the Rhodesian airforce in the operational areas, the guerillas were called to give themselves up or leave the country.[104] The position of the ANC was quite different. In announcing the ANC acceptance of the Lusaka agreement, Muzorewa linked the cease-fire, or rather the suspension of fighting, to the fixing of a date for negotiations.[105] On January 12, 1975, the ANC presented a more elaborate interpretation of the cease-fire. There was to be an informal cease-fire which would be officially announced only after the date for the constitutional conference had been finalized and meaningful negotiations commenced. The ANC also had a totally divergent view of the essence of the cease-fire. Branding the dropping of leaflets as a "flagrant violation of the cease-fire terms", they stated that "a cease-fire means no more than stopping to shoot and to advance beyond the lines where the respective forces are found."[106]

On the ground, however, there was no cease-fire, formal or informal. The bush war continued unabated and the Rhodesian authorities had a genuine cause for concern. The persistence of the guerilla war was due more to divergent views within the nationalist camp, than to misunderstanding between the ANC and the Rhodesian government. The guerilla operations in the north-east were a strictly ZANLA affair. The crux of the matter was that the leadership of the unified ANC, including Sithole, ZANU's formal head, had little influence on the guerillas and their command structure. The guerillas were controlled by the political and military leadership which had emerged in exile and which had conceived and executed the guerilla strategy since its inception. The guerilla war was controlled by the ZANU supreme council (DARE) and the military high command headed by ZANU's chairman, Herbert Chitepo and Josia Tongogara, respectively. The exiled leadership of ZANU led the movement's opposition to detente and to the unification of the nationalist factions. Their acceptance of unity and of the Lusaka agreement was purely tactical. They certainly had no intention of laying down their arms. Chitepo made his view on that matter very clear: "If we relax our effort in the front, we will guilelessly play into the hands of Smith."[107] In early January 1975 Chavunduka, an ANC leader, attributed the faltering of the cease-fire to problems of communication typical to a bush war.[108] However, a ZANU circular from December 27, 1974 stated clearly that "ZANU had not declared ceasefire" and in mid-January 1975, ZANLA infiltrated a group of 60 guerillas into Rhodesia.[109] Mugabe said that ZANU, in fact, urged the guerila forces inside Rhodesia "to intensify the war and ignore persistent calls for a cease-fire".[110] During January 1975, there was an average of six guerilla incidents a day in the north-east operational zone. From January 13 to January 22, 15 guerillas were killed. On the security force's side, four South African policemen were killed.[111]

Faced with persistent violations of the cease-fire, the Rhodesian government was reluctant to fulfil its part of the bargain. On December 18, Muzorewa expressed dissatisfaction at the government's failure to free some 200 detainees. The ANC stated that it would boycott the constitutional talks until all the detainees were released.[112] On January 10, 1975 a Rhodesian Minister officially announced that because of the cease-fire violations, the government had completely stopped the release of detainees.[113] A few days later a Rhodesian government source said that there would be no constitutional talks unless there were unmistakable signs that the fighting was coming to an end.[114]

The issues of the cease-fire and the release of detainees were the main stumbling blocks in the aftermath of the Lusaka agreement. However, other issues on which the government and the ANC were strongly divided, quickly surfaced. There was the question of British involvement in the negotiations. The Rhodesian government, for obvious reasons, wanted to exclude the British government altogether. The ANC, on the other hand, wanted Britain to convene and chair the prospective constitutional conference.[115] Another controversial issue concerned the venue of the conference. While Smith insisted on Rhodesia as the natural venue, the ANC stated categorically that it would not attend a conference inside Rhodesia. They wanted the conference to be held in London or in an African country.[116]

An observer of the Rhodesian scene wrote in early 1975, that "Smith no longer has any room to manoeuvre left."[117] In fact, Smith had, at that time, all the manoeuvring space he needed. Besides stating publicly his total opposition to majority rule, stopping the release of detainees and insisting on an effective cease-fire as a precondition for progress in the negotiations, he used additional obstructionist measures which irritated the African nationalists. Thus, he used technical arguments to prevent ANC leaders from travelling to Lusaka to meet Callaghan. Smith, who had little interest in seeing the negotiations through, could only be happy with the ANC's response: "The consequence of this unwise decision may wreck what were appearing to be moves towards a solution of the country's constitutional problems."[118] The Rhodesian government also placed restrictions on the political activities of the ANC inside Rhodesia in violation of the spirit of detente.[119]

Thus, if the regional patrons had hoped that the Lusaka agreement would provide a framework within which their clients would proceed smoothly towards a settlement, they were soon to be disappointed. In his New Year message, Kaunda already warned against over-optimism regarding a Rhodesian solution.[120] The regional patrons soon realized that their clients would have to be coached and urged on if they were to perform their assigned roles. On the African side, the divisions within the nationalist camp were the main source of concern for the FLP. The

ANC was a rather ineffectual umbrella organization and did not develop, as expected, as a unified nationalist movement.[121] The enforced organizational unity had failed to eliminate the deep-rooted causes of disunity. In early 1975 Kaunda sounded a warning: "I must say very, very seriously that unless our brothers and sisters in Zimbabwe hold on to this unity, they cannot expect real help from the rest of Africa."[122] In their efforts to strengthen the nationalist unity, the FLP enlisted the support of the OAU Liberation Committee. In its January 1975 meeting in Dar es Salaam, the committee recognized the ANC as Rhodesia's liberation movement, freezing the recognition of ZANU and ZAPU.[123] The turning of the ANC into the sole channel for OAU support to the Rhodesian nationalists was apparently expected to enhance its position as an effective unified movement.

Another major effort of the FLP was directed at the cease-fire violations. They were aware that these, as well, were playing into the hands of Smith. After a while it was impossible to attribute the violations to problems of communication between headquarters and the guerillas in the bush. Thus, on January 12, Meredith reported that Kaunda and Nyerere were applying strong pressures on the guerilla movements to suspend fighting.[124] On February 6, Muzorewa, Nkomo and Sithole were flown to Dar es Salaam for a meeting with the FLP. According to one source, Kaunda, in particular, was enraged with ZANU for its intransigence. The presidents impressed upon the ANC leaders the need for more flexibility.[125] Some ten days later, the OAU foreign ministers, meeting in Lusaka, endorsed a proposal by the ANC to suspend the guerilla war as long as the negotiations continued.[126] The regional patrons, however, were barking up the wrong tree and the ANC proposal carried little weight because the guerillas in the bush were still beyond the range of ANC control. Realizing that this was the case, the FLP had to adopt more direct measures. Thus, the Zambian government made it very difficult for ZANU to move arms and ammunition across their territory, while the transitional government in Mozambique disarmed ZANLA fighters who had withdrawn from Rhodesia.[127]

The South African government, on its part, while not happy with Smith's public utterances regarding majority rule, had few bones to pick with him about his conduct in terms of the Lusaka agreement. They singled out the ZANLA guerillas as responsible for the faltering of detente. In early January 1975, Vorster even paid a compliment to Smith: "I want to say emphatically, that as far as I know Mr Smith has honoured all his agreements."[128] However, as detente was increasingly threatened, it was necessary to do more than simply praise the conduct of the client. The success of detente being a supreme national interest, Vorster would not have it failing because of a few terrorist incidents. South Africa could not subscribe to Smith's refusal to negotiate before the cease-fire became effective. Thus, while the FLP were putting pressure on the nationalist leaders, South Africa was similarly engaged with the Rhodesians. The intended visit of Dr Connie Mulder in Salisbury, on January 21, 1975, was to be the culmination of this effort. The visit, however, was cancelled at the last moment. According to Mulder's Rhodesian counterpart, the visit was put off because of "wild speculations" that he intended putting pressure on Smith.[129] However, a press statement in Cape Town implied that that was, indeed, the purpose of the visit.[130]

Mulder's visit became superfluous because a day earlier, on January 20, the first formal meeting between the ANC delegation and Rhodesian government officials was held in Salisbury.[131] This marked the beginning of the "talks about talks". All that was known of this meeting was that it did not deal with substantive matters or with the date for the prospective constitutional conference.[132] Sithole gave a definite impression that the meeting gave the nationalist leaders no cause for optimism.[133] On February 5 a second meeting was held between the top ANC leadership and Smith. In this meeting issues concerning the timing of the conference, its venue and its chairmanship, as well as the release of detainees, were discussed.[134] The two sides stuck to their divergent views and no progress was made. Another unfruitful meeting between Smith and the nationalist leaders took place on February 12.[135] As the month of February drew to its close, it became increasingly clear that the negotiations wagon was deep in the mud. With a huge discrepancy in respective goals, the failure of the cease-fire and lack of progress even on procedural matters, there was little hope of a positive momentum emanating from the interaction between the domestic parties.[136]

All this time the respective regional patrons continued to maintain regular contacts between them. As before, Zambia had most of the direct contact with South Africa. Away from the public eye, representatives of Zambia and South Africa were exchanging visits.[137] The most dramatic contact at this level was the visit of Dr Muller to Lusaka in early February 1975. There he met with the foreign ministers of Zambia, Tanzania and Botswana to discuss the progress, or rather lack of it, of the negotiations between Smith and the nationalists. He also met the leaders of the ANC.[138] A concrete and significant result of this visit was a decision by South Africa to withdraw elements of the South African police from their forward positions on the Zambezi. This could be construed both as a gesture to the FLP and as a veiled threat to Smith to induce him to be more forthcoming. On their part, the Zambians gave undertakings to stop infiltrations across the river.[139]

Two dramatic events in March 1975, initiated by the Rhodesian government, precipitated a more vigorous intervention on the part of the regional patrons. On March 3 the domestic parties arranged another meeting for March 6.[140] This meeting never took place because on March 4 Ndabaningi Sithole was arrested by the Rhodesian authorities for an alleged plot to assassinate fellow ANC leaders.[141] There is no doubt that the allegation was groundless. Later in March, the prosecution, failing to bring concrete evidence on the alleged assassination plot, shifted the emphasis to Sithole's responsibility, as head of ZANU, for the continued guerilla attacks.[142] There is little doubt that in arresting Sithole, Smith wanted to provoke the ANC into breaking the talks.

Smith certainly provoked the African nationalists. The ANC leaders, divided as they were, unanimously condemned Sithole's arrest and decided to "stop forthwith any further talks with the Government . . . until the Rev. Sithole has been released". Kaunda condemned the arrest as an "unwarranted and deliberate act aimed at sabotaging ANC efforts to forge unity, mobilize the masses of Africans in Zimbabwe and form a united front in the independence negotiations".[143] Strong reaction to the arrest also emanated from OAU circles.[144] On March 17 Muzorewa flew to Lusaka for talks with Kaunda and other front-line leaders on the Rhodesian stalemate.[145] Departing from Salisbury, Muzorewa gave vent to his frustration: "We are sick and tired of being made scapegoats for further tactics which often turn out to be blunders and failure."[146]

If Smith was right in predicting the ANC response, he certainly failed to anticipate the reaction of South Africa. Had he bothered to consult his patron, he would have saved himself considerable embarrassment. The success of detente weighed much more heavily in South African thinking than dislike of Sithole. South Africa strongly objected to a blatant action which threatened their new regional strategy. The Afrikaans press again led the attack on the Rhodesian government for its ill-considered act.[147] On March 7, Dr Muller described Sithole's arrest as one of the obstacles to detente, and pledged his government's efforts to the removal of such obstacles.[148] On March 10 the South African Minister of Police announced a further step in the disengagement of the South African police forces from Rhodesia. All South African policemen in Rhodesia were confined to their camps and some 90, who had completed their term of duty, trekked back across the

63

Limpopo.[149] In the Cape Town meeting with the Rhodesians a week later, the South Africans insisted on an open trial and favoured Sithole's release by the court in a manner which would besmirch his reputation.[150] However, South African preference notwithstanding, the Rhodesian special court ruled on April 2, that Sithole be kept in detention for heading ZANU and ZANLA.[151] Sithole would have liked to have remained their head. South Africa's wish to see Sithole released was specifically linked to the prospective OAU Ministerial Council meeting which was convened to discuss the southern Africa strategy. South Africa and Zambia, in particular, wanted the moderates to prevail at that crucial African convocation. On the day the special court proclaimed its decision, Dr Muller flew to Salisbury and convinced a reluctant Smith to release Sithole and allow him to go to Dar es Salaam.[152] In a special broadcast to the nation, in which he announced the release, Smith all but admitted that his government obliged under duress and against its better judgement.[153] In a subsequent BBC interview, he openly admitted that he conceded to Muller's pressure.[154]

Before the Sithole crisis was sorted out, another dramatic event had occurred which was to have a considerable impact on the process of conflict resolution in Rhodesia. On March 18, 1975 Herbert Chitepo, ZANU chairman, was assassinated in Lusaka. It is clear by now, beyond any doubt, that the assassination was carried out by Rhodesian secret agents.[155] This single act was perhaps the greatest success of the Rhodesian security forces throughout their struggle against the nationalist liberation movements. The assassination of Chitepo incapacitated ZANU, the most formidable enemy of the Rhodesian regime, for about a year. The key to that success was in the fact that the perpetrators of the assassination left no traces whatsoever. There were those, such as Robert Mugabe, who immediately put the blame on the Rhodesian regime.[156] This, however, could not be proved at the time. As it was, there were enough people inside and outside ZANU who attributed the assassination of Chitepo to a struggle for power within ZANU. Such an interpretation could acquire credibility because it fitted in nicely with a power struggle within ZANU which had erupted in the so-called Nhari rebellion in December 1974.[157] This interpretation was particularly damaging to ZANU because it seems to have exacerbated ethnic divisions within the movement. Indeed, the power struggle was seen by some as a struggle between Manyika and Karanga, two Shona tribes. The Karanga, who were blamed for assassinating Chitepo who was a Manyika, strongly rejected this tribalist interpretation.[158] Martin and Johnson also strongly challenged the tribalist interpretation.[159] However, this interpretation was adopted by a "Special International

Commission on the Assassination of Herbert Wiltshire Chitepo" which was set up by Zambia, and which included representatives of 13 countries and the OAU Liberation Committee.[160] Worse still from ZANU's point of view, it was also adopted by conflicting factions within the movement. Thus, Ndabaningi Sithole fully endorsed the ethnic interpretation.[161] The group supporting the ZANU prisoners charged for the murder of Chitepo spoke about the "conservative Manyika group".[162] From reading Professor Zvobgo's report, it emerges clearly that many ZANU members involved saw ZANU factionalism in ethnic terms.[163] The assassination certainly exacerbated existing divisions within ZANU and weakened it.

This weakening of ZANU was not, however, the main benefit derived by the Rhodesian government from Chitepo's assassination. Left on its own, ZANU could have survived the assassination without too much damage. ZANU, with its collective leadership style, could have sorted out its internal divisions, ethnic and other. It was, however, not left on its own to solve its internal problems. It was the Zambian response to the Chitepo assassination which was most ruinous for ZANU and most beneficial for the Rhodesian government. Kaunda had no reason to like Chitepo or to mourn his death. Chitepo had been one of the bitterest opponents of his cherished detente. However, the assassination afforded Kaunda an opportunity to settle some scores with ZANU and to force that recalcitrant movement to toe his line. If faltering detente was to be given a fair chance, the hard line militants who controlled ZANU's political and military structures had to be neutralized. It was not easy to deal brutally with genuine leaders of a liberation movement whose only fault was an excess of anti-colonial zeal. It had to be justified in the eyes of Zambians, the FLP and Africa as a whole. This justification, or excuse, was provided by the Chitepo assassination. Whether Kaunda acted *bona fide* or not, there is little doubt that he acted with great single-mindedness and ruthlessness.

According to Martin and Johnson, there had been indications prior to the assassination that the Zambian authorities intended to act against ZANU. On the day of the assassination, ZANU leaders were warned by contacts that arrests of ZANU members would follow Chitepo's funeral. Indeed, on March 23 – a day after the funeral – some 50 leading ZANU members were arrested. Others who were not in the country were subsequently handed over by Mozambique.[164] On March 28 Aaron Milner, the Zambian Home Affairs Minister, hinted that the assassination might have been an inside job. On March 31 Kaunda condemned certain nationalist leaders who showed no concern about the assassination and who demanded that the investigation of it be stopped. It was in that broadcast that Kaunda announced the setting up of a special commission of inquiry. The *Times* of Zambia, reflecting the government's views, stated in an editorial that the commission's task should be not only to discover the culprits, but also to "sort out" the Rhodesian liberation movement.[165] Thus, one of the main thrusts of Kaunda's response to the assassination emerged clearly. By arresting the intransigent ZANU leaders, he wanted to promote unity in the ANC under a moderate and forthcoming leadership. It is hardly surprising that ANC leaders like Muzorewa, Sithole and Chikerema, who were to benefit from the removal of the militant ZANU leaders, supported Kaunda's measures.[166] In early April 1975, the Zambian government went further in their attempt to foster nationalist unity in the ANC when it banned ZANU, ZAPU and FROLIZI.[167] In reality, however, the banning order applied only to ZANU.[168] Tanzania followed Zambia and banned ZANU and ZAPU in May.[169] Kaunda went beyond arresting ZANU leaders. According to ZANU sources, between March 24 and 26, some 1,500 ZANU guerillas stationed in Zambia were detained. They and other ZANLA fighters were transferred to "ANC training camps" which were guarded by Zambian soldiers.[170] It appeared that Kaunda was trying to bring the ZANLA guerillas under the control of the moderate ANC leadership. This thrust received a further impetus in July 1975, when the ANC set up the Zimbabwe Liberation Council (ZLC) as its external wing.[171]

Smith, in arresting Sithole and in ordering the assassination of Chitepo, must have hoped to provoke the nationalists into obstructing the negotiations. Instead, he prompted the regional patrons into more direct and active intervention aimed at saving their peace process. At the level of their relations with their clients South Africa and Zambia, in particular, made special efforts to groom the Rhodesian government and the ANC respectively. At the regional level, it was at that juncture, in April 1975, that the FLP convinced the OAU Council of Ministers to endorse their peaceful initiative in Rhodesia.

In the wake of this meeting, the ball was back in the domestic court. Returning from Dar es Salaam on April 16, Muzorewa ostensibly played the role expected of him by calling for an immediate constitutional conference and by promising that the ANC would do its utmost to achieve independence by peaceful means. However, before a constitutional conference could be held, Smith would have to fulfil the obligations he undertook in the Lusaka agreement. He would have to stop hanging political prisoners, to release the remaining detainees and to refrain from detaining African nationalists. Muzorewa exhibited neither hope nor enthusiasm.[172] All African leaders still shared a deep suspicion of Smith. Smith did nothing to allay their suspicions. On the contrary, on April 28, he said again that "there is never going to be any hand-over in Rhodesia."[173]

Smith's response to Muzorewa's declaration reflected his negotiating tactics – rocking the negotiations without appearing too obstructionist. On the one hand, he invited Muzorewa to meet him the following week. On the other hand, his spokesman stated that the fulfilment of Muzorewa's demands was linked to the implementation of the cease-fire.[174] In reply to Muzorewa's specific inquiry about N. Sithole, Smith replied that Sithole would be redetained once he was back in Rhodesia.[175] To say the least, Smith made no contribution towards a conducive atmosphere for the prospective negotiations. On April 27 the ANC executive endorsed Muzorewa's earlier statement that it would resume negotiations only if the Rhodesian government fulfilled all the conditions of the Lusaka agreement.[176] The next day Smith was quick to exploit ANC "intransigence": "Let me once again reiterate how we have gone out of our way to assist in the detente exercise, and how inadequate has been the response of the ANC;. . . . how we have been provoked and in turn resisted counter-provocation." Smith had the audacity to say that, while almost in the same breath ruling out the prospect of African majority rule.[177] In a television interview on May 8, he again put the blame on the ANC: "They seem to be resorting to delaying tactics for some reason or other."[178] This was, of course, a gross misrepresentation of the reality. It was, however, an accurate reflection of his own tactics. Nkomo gave vent to the Africans' frustration: "Having had meetings with Mr Smith, the ANC executive was in no doubt that he was the type of man with whom no agreement could be reached."[179]

Yet, despite all this, Smith met with an ANC delegation on May 22, after the two sides had apparently been prevailed upon by their respective patrons to drop all preconditions.[180] However, no progress was made, the talks being adjourned for two weeks to allow the ANC to consider its position. Smith, in the meantime, had continued to provoke the ANC. In arresting Reverend Canaan Banana, former vice-president of the ANC, Smith may have been on safe legal ground but his motive was primarily political. Had it been his intention to provoke the ANC, Edson Sithole gave him full satisfaction: "This will certainly prove to be disastrous to detente and will also prove to be a blow to those who think the Rhodesian government has changed its vicious character."[181] On May 26 Smith threatened that if the next meeting failed to produce an agreement to hold a conference, the government "will then turn to other groups of Africans which have indicated a desire to talk".[182] Gordon Chavunduka, ANC Secretary General, agreed with Smith that the conference should be called off if the next meeting failed to produce an agreement, while Edson Sithole conditioned further negotiations on the Rhodesian government's fulfilling the provisions of the Lusaka agreement.[183] On June 1 the ANC executive adopted a resolution expressing its wish to hold preliminary talks leading to a constitutional conference based on majority rule now.[184] This was, of course, anathema to the Rhodesian government. The prospect of meaningful negotiations seemed bleak indeed. However, on June 3 the ANC Secretary General announced that both sides agreed to drop all preconditions and proceed with talks leading to a constitutional conference. This was confirmed by Smith the following day.[185] The regional patrons must have been active behind the scenes. Before the first meeting was held, it was reported from Cape Town, that Rhodesia was told that the South African railway system would not be able to handle all Rhodesian traffic if Mozambique closed its border with Rhodesia upon becoming fully independent later in the month.[186] In the meeting held on June 12, Smith and the ANC agreed to hold a constitutional conference, but failed to agree on its venue. While Smith insisted on Rhodesia, Muzorewa demanded that it be held anywhere but in Rhodesia. Smith "assisted" the ANC in rejecting Rhodesia by informing them that N. Sithole and other wanted nationalists would be arrested on entering the country.[187] The venue remained the last stumbling block. While the ANC remained adamant, Smith agreed to leave Rhodesia only for the ratification of the constitution.[188]

In the atmosphere of frustration and despair which set in as the deadlock persisted, attitudes on both sides were hardening. An ANC Congress, held in Dar es Salaam on July 8, resolved to "de-escalate talks and escalate the armed struggle". It appeared that two of the FLP, Nyerere and Machel, reached the conclusion that the talks were futile and that armed struggle was the only alternative liberation strategy.[189] In mid-July Nyerere said that "it begins to look to me that the need to resort to guerilla fighting is getting closer and closer."[190] It was now Muzorewa's turn to issue an ultimatum. On July 20 he gave Smith three months to hold a constitutional conference outside Rhodesia. Failing that, the ANC would unleash a greatly intensified guerilla war.[191] At the same time, the Rhodesian government, probably thinking that detente was coming to an end, were preparing for a big military drive against ZANLA guerillas operating in the north-east.[192] Politically, with his eyes set more firmly on the alternative internal settlement, Smith informed Parliament on July 8 that his government would appoint a commission to consider ways of removing "unnecessary and undesirable" racial discrimination. The ANC response was prompt and blunt: "We are not interested in racial discrimination as an issue. We are talking about power. We want the transfer of power."[193] Smith, however, had directed his new initiative against the nationalists rather than to them.

As the contending domestic parties were moving from talking to fighting, the regional patrons stepped in with greater determination. Vorster and Kaunda, in particular, were not prepared to be drawn into what could become a full-scale southern African conflagration because of their clients' intransigence. In July 1975 Brand Fourie made two secret visits to Lusaka to discuss ways to break the deadlock.[194] South Africa also announced the withdrawal of its forces from Rhodesia. In early August, Mark Chona and Vorster were busy in Pretoria on a plan to pave the way for the constitutional conference. Smith was then invited to come to Pretoria. He promptly arrived in Pretoria with a ministerial delegation with the intention of briefing Vorster on his plans to intensify his anti-guerilla campaign.[195] Arriving in Pretoria, Smith faced two surprises. Firstly, he was to confer not only with Vorster, but also with two Zambians, Mark Chona and P. Kasande.[196] Secondly, the topic of discussion was not the intensification of the war, but rather the convening of a constitutional conference. The outcome of the meeting was the Pretoria agreement, which was made public in Salisbury and Lusaka on August 12:

(a) The Rhodesian government, through their appointed representatives, and the ANC, through their appointed representatives, will meet not later than the 25th of August on the Victoria Falls bridge in coaches to be supplied by the South African Government for a formal conference without any preconditions;

(b) The object of the formal meeting is to give the parties the opportunity to publicly express their genuine desire to negotiate an acceptable settlement;

(c) After this, the conference will adjourn to enable the parties to discuss proposals for a settlement in committee or committees within Rhodesia;

(d) Thereafter, the parties will meet again in formal conference anywhere decided upon to ratify the committee proposals which have been agreed upon;

(e) The South African Government and the Governments of Botswana, Mozambique, Tanzania and Zambia, respectively, have expressed their willingness to ensure that this agreement is implemented by the two parties involved.[197]

69

In addition, the participants in the Pretoria meeting made a gentlemen's agreement that as long as the negotiations proceeded, there would be no terrorist infiltration into Rhodesia and no detention inside Rhodesia.[198]

The Pretoria agreement brought the so-called southern African detente to a climax. The meeting and the agreement shed light on the attitudes and role of the regional patrons with regard to the resolution of the Rhodesian conflict. Despite obstacles and frustrations, they still exhibited a keen interest in the peaceful resolution of the conflict. Among the African patrons, Zambia again appeared as the most keenly interested and deeply involved. Although Nyerere and Machel may have harboured doubts about a peaceful solution, they gave Kaunda a mandate to negotiate with South Africa, and endorsed the agreement. Between Kaunda and Vorster there appeared to have developed relations of mutual trust and cooperation. Having seen their efforts frustrated by the clients' inability to agree on the procedural terms leading to a constitutional conference, the regional patrons decided to involve themselves more directly and forcefully in determining those terms. Vorster and Chona had agreed on the terms which were then presented to the clients as a *fait accompli*. However, the patron–client relations on the two sides of the racial dividing line were not symmetrical. As in the case of the Lusaka agreement of December 1974, representatives of the Rhodesian government were directly involved in the negotiations. In both cases, the African clients were not even consulted. Bishop Muzorewa recalled:

> One evening Ndabaningi Sithole, Jason Moyo, James Chikerema and I received a summons to the Zambian State House. There Dr Kaunda told us of an "agreement" to have talks between Ian Smith and the Zimbabwean nationalists. . . . note that we of the ANC were not a party to this agreement. Dr Kaunda presented it to us as a *fait accompli*.[199]

As in the case of the Lusaka agreement, the ANC leadership, faced with the common and determined stand of their regional patrons, had little choice. In the case of the Pretoria agreement, there was in fact a Zambian–South African conspiracy against the ANC, to which even the Rhodesians were privy. Rhodesia was intentionally fixed as the venue for the committee stage of the conference in which the substance of the constitution was to be worked out. This was not done in response to Rhodesian insistence. All the participants at the Pretoria meeting felt that the presence of "extremists" like Sithole and Chikerema, who faced arrest in Rhodesia, would jeopardize the chances of the conference.[200]

If the regional patrons believed that they had laid the ground for a successful conference, they were soon to discover that they were still treading on the shifting sands of Rhodesian reality. The Victoria Falls bridge conference, which convened on August 25, was a colossal anticlimax. There had been bad omens even before the South African presidential coach reached the bridge. On August 14 Smith, informing his people of the Pretoria agreement, chose in his usual manner to emphasize the elements in it which could provoke his opponents. Thus, he belittled the conference at the bridge which would be a "formal" affair. He also chose to emphasize that there would be "no let-up in our operations in the north-eastern area". While speaking on the benefits of a settlement, Smith did not project much optimism. He gave the impression of a man forced to go through the motions, outlining the basic tactics which had guided him since the Lusaka agreement: "What is important is that if this particular exercise fails, the blame cannot be laid on our shoulders."[201] Muzorewa reacted vehemently to Smith's description of the nature of the conference at the bridge: "The African National Council has no intention whatsoever, to hold a serious constitutional conference for only 30 minutes as has been indicated by the Rhodesian leader." He also rejected the holding of the committee meetings inside Rhodesia.[202]

The Victoria Falls bridge conference which convened on August 25, was the zenith and nadir of the southern Africa detente. It started with an epoch-making meeting between Vorster and Kaunda on Zambian soil and ended in resounding failure within 24 hours. Wishing to crown their efforts and ensure the success of the conference, both heads of state offered their services as patrons of it. Their speeches formally opened the conference and their representatives and they themselves were deeply involved in the deliberations. In their opening speeches, Vorster and Kaunda set the tone praising the merits of peace and abhorring the violent alternative.[203] Their fine words, however, failed to inspire their Rhodesian clients. In his opening speech, Muzorewa proposed that the negotiations should result in a settlement that would "transfer power from the minority to the majority – that is majority rule now". Smith predictably rejected a declaration of intent of such a committing nature which was in clear contradiction with the terms of the Pretoria agreement. He offered a statement which was more in tune with the agreement: "Both parties took this opportunity expressing their genuine desire to negotiate a constitutional settlement. Both parties publicly expressed their commitment to work out immediately a constitutional settlement which will be acceptable to all the people of our country."[204] When the ANC agreed to that version, the conference proceeded to discuss the mechanism of the negotiations. It was in this relatively easy terrain that the conference got bogged down. As might have been expected, the ANC refused to take part in the committee stage inside Rhodesia. Before the conference their refusal had been categorical. During the conference, however, they indicated that they would be prepared to deliberate in Rhodesia, provided their representatives be granted immunity. This reasonable condition was included in a "Declaration of intent to negotiate a settlement", which was worked out by the ANC and, according to Muzorewa, signed by Vorster and Kaunda. Besides the immunity, the declaration included two deadlines: the committees would start deliberating within seven days, and would conclude a settlement by October 31, 1975.[205] This was a strait-jacket Smith was most reluctant to put on. His tactics were to stall the negotiations before they reached a substantive stage. Standing firmly on the ground provided by the written Pretoria agreement, he adamantly refused to grant the immunity. Thus, relying on a document signed by the regional patrons, Smith was able to derail detente. This was the ultimate victory of his tactics. The nationalists, for their part, could not, for very sound reasons, surrender their demand for immunity. Their demands were so reasonably based that they could even ignore Kaunda's threat that if they caused the breakdown of the conference they could expect little support or sympathy from Zambia.[206] Kaunda would not in fact have been able to justify in frontline and African councils retribution against the ANC on such an issue. Even the presence of Vorster and Kaunda and their top officials could not bridge the procedural gap between the domestic parties. It was a severe diplomatic failure for Kaunda and Vorster.

The regional patrons tried to maintain the diplomatic momentum. The South Africans were to send emissaries to Lusaka to sort out the deadlock.[207] Vorster said that he and Kaunda would continue their efforts to remove the obstacles which had arisen at the conference. He even said he was convinced that Smith was also trying to solve the present problems.[208] Kaunda sounded even more optimistic: "There are one or two points which need to be followed up. This will be done within ten days' time, but we are off to a good start and we will have a chance to settle the southern African problem peacefully."[209] A week after the failure of the conference, the Johannesburg *Star* was still raving: "Because John Vorster and Kenneth Kaunda were there, southern Africa will never be the same."[210] This optimism was unwarranted. The failure of the Victoria Falls bridge conference signified the demise of the southern African detente.

Smith was more realistic. Without waiting for the patrons' attempts to sort out the stumbling blocks, he informed a jubilant Parliament on August 26 of the failure, or rather "success", of the conference. To maximize his gains, he put the blame on the ANC while praising Vorster and Kaunda.[211] Predictably, Muzorewa blamed Smith for wrecking the conference. He also indicated that the ANC would not seek further talks.[212] A chapter in the Rhodesian saga came to an anti-climactic end.

The Victoria Falls bridge conference was a colossal failure for the regional patrons. Tremendous diplomatic efforts invested in securing vital national goals came to nothing. This abysmal failure was somewhat surprising because the conditions for achieving a peaceful settlement in Rhodesia at that historical juncture were not at all unfavourable. The regional patrons on both sides of the conflict gave the Rhodesian issue a high priority. From the point of view of patron–client relations, the situation was as favourable as could have been wished and hoped for. White Rhodesia was not in a position to refuse its patron's wish. The relations between patrons and clients on the African side, though more complex, were also conducive to the success of detente. The regional patrons, and Kaunda in particular, in forcing unity on the nationalist factions and more so in suppressing ZANU militants in the wake of Chitepo's assassination, demonstrated their resolve to guide and lead their clients. Within the ANC, there was considerable support for a peaceful settlement. At the same time, the military option of ZANU militants was hardly viable against a determined regional peace initiative. And yet, it was not to be.

The analysis of this grand failure is essential for the understanding of the structure and dynamics of the Rhodesian crisis. There were two failures which call for analysis. There was the micro-failure, namely the failure of the conference itself, and the macro-failure, namely the failure of detente. In a way, the micro-failure was the more severe and astonishing of the two, because it seemed much easier to ensure the success of the conference. The conflicting domestic parties were only expected to declare, on the basis of the Pretoria agreement, their willingness to negotiate and to proceed to the committee stage where the substance of a settlement was to be deliberated. The rock on which the conference foundered was the venue of the committee stage. As we have seen at the Pretoria meeting, it was agreed that the committees would convene inside Rhodesia, without proper arrangement of immunity for ANC members who would in that circumstance face arrest. The committee stage could still have gone ahead, had the Zambians convinced the ANC leadership or forced them to cooperate. However, more than 10 days before the conference it was clear that even the moderate Muzorewa rejected Rhodesia as venue for the committees.[213] The regional patrons thus had ample time to sort out this crucial procedural issue. And yet, it was left in abeyance. When this issue remained the last obstacle during the conference itself, one could have expected Kaunda and Vorster, who staked their respective personal prestige and national interest on the conference's success, to employ all their power to surmount this procedural obstacle. Evidently, what had seemed possible in the conspiratorial atmosphere in Pretoria, was impossible to uphold in the full light of the conference. It must have occurred to Kaunda that he could not "sell" to his front-line colleagues, and to Africa as a whole, the exclusion of top ANC leaders from the committee deliberations. Kaunda himself had to concede that the ANC insistence on immunity was reasonable and acceptable to him.[214] The only way left to save the conference was to convince Smith to grant immunity. Smith's argument that "it would involve people who are well-known terrorist leaders, the bearers of responsibility for murders and other atrocities",[215] while useful for domestic Rhodesian consumption, should not have unduly impressed Vorster. Yet, Vorster either accepted Smith's position or failed to change it. He exhibited either lack of statesmanship or lack of resolve.

The "original sin" of the southern Africa detente was that regional patrons launched the grand initiative without first agreeing on a model of solution to the Rhodesian problem. Seeing that the target of majority rule was subscribed to by all patrons, it is not inconceivable that an agreement could have also been reached on the duration and modality of the transition leading to it. The absence of such an agreement had an adverse effect on the prospect of a peaceful settlement. It could be construed by white and black Rhodesians opposing a peaceful transfer of power as reflecting lack of resolve on the part of their regional patrons. This provided them with manoeuvring space to pursue their divergent goals. Under these circumstances, procedural issues were not marginal. They were heavily loaded with the depths of emotions and the heights of conflicting aspirations of the contending domestic parties. The procedural controversies represented the most cherished goals for which blacks and whites had been struggling for so long. It was for this reason that the regional patrons found it so unexpectedly difficult to manipulate their clients and guide them along the tortuous procedural road. As the regional patrons were failing to demonstrate their resolve, the clients were increasingly reinforced in their belief that they could ignore the pressure and manipulate the patrons into supporting them through thick and thin.

How can one account for the failure of the regional patrons in a matter of such high national priority? Primarily, it was a case of gross miscalculation. The assumptions that the best way to secure a peaceful solution was to move from tactics to strategy and from procedure to substance, that the role of the patrons was to urge and encourage rather than to force and dictate, and that a settlement could be worked out by the clients themselves, were grossly unrealistic. This lack of realism on the part of the regional patrons can be at least in part accounted for by their lack of experience in regional diplomacy across the racial dividing line. Prior to the attempt to strike a peaceful coexistence, the relations between the black and white regional patrons had been characterized by intense conflict. South Africa and black Africa were, in fact, separated by a belt of conflict consisting of Angola, South West Africa, Rhodesia and Mozambique. The regional patrons had had the experience of assisting their respective clients in their armed struggle rather than of leading them along the road to peace. The combination of intense racial conflict and separation was a fertile ground for the breeding of prejudices, stereotypes, myths and misconceptions. These were hardly conducive to a realistic appreciation of the issues, factors and actors involved in a totally new situation.

In fairness, it should be stated that the blame for the failure of detente lay more heavily on the shoulders of South Africa. South Africa certainly suffered from lack of experience in the conduct of foreign relations. In early August 1975 *Die Burger* stated: "The South African public is not yet accustomed to foreign policy being conducted by its Government in recent times. It is, in fact, our first real experience of what foreign politics can entail."[216] The introvert Nationalist government was hardly attuned to understanding the complexities of black Africa's politics. The position of the FLP on the issue of majority rule was clear and unequivocal. Vorster knew that majority rule was the only basis for his detente. Yet, he failed to commit himself or Smith openly and clearly, even to the principle of majority rule in Rhodesia. Furthermore, he allowed Smith, throughout this period, to reiterate his rejection of the very idea of majority rule. This Smith continued to do even after Vorster brought him to accept majority rule in 15 years in the Cape Town meeting in March 1975. To Vorster, who was subjected to the same demand, it was difficult to be seen imposing majority rule on the loyal white minority in Rhodesia. Vorster seems to have had a psychological barrier which did not enable him to prevail on Smith. This may partly explain why Vorster did not apply effective pressure on the Rhodesians even in closed meetings.[217]

The psycho-political dilemma was reinforced by a very real domestic consideration, namely the fear of a white backlash. The South African government was beset by the fear of white, particularly Afrikaner, reaction to the selling of white Rhodesia down the Limpopo. This emotional issue could add fuel to the raging controversy between *verligte* and *verkrampte* within the ranks of the Nationalist Party. The HNP, the marginal extreme right wing opposition party, placed itself at the head of an organized pro-Rhodesian pressure group.[218] In mid-February leading *verkrampte* went to Salisbury to express their support for white Rhodesia. Their message was: "We either win together or hang separately."[219] Worse still, Andries Treurnicht, a leading NP *verkrampt*, was alleged to have offered his support to the pro-Rhodesian campaign.[220] There was a danger that the fate of Rhodesia would precipitate a split within the NP. Smith, with some understandable discretion, encouraged the pro-Rhodesian tide. On April 28 he warned South Africans of the "dangers inherent in the policy of appeasement" and reminded them of the communists' domino strategy.[221] A public opinion poll in June 1975, according to which 64 per cent of the Afrikaners opposed and only 18 per cent favoured the withdrawal of the South African Police from Rhodesia,[222] was an indication of the prevailing mood in Afrikanerdom. This was the nightmare of any Afrikaner leader; it was particularly so in the case of Vorster. Vorster's hypersensitivity with respect to Nationalist unity stemmed from his political biography. His rise in the party hierarchy was meteoric and in 1966 he was chosen to succeed Verwoerd as prime minister. However, the scars of earlier days[223] made him very sensitive to his position in the party. This sensitivity increased when, under his leadership, the HNP broke away and the Nationalist Party, which had steadily increased its parliamentary representation from 1938 to 1966, lost nine seats in the 1970 general election.[224] It was a shock which considerably affected his subsequent political behaviour. He used to say often: "A leader must be ahead of his people, but he cannot be that far ahead that they can't see him."[225] The fear of a split in the party had a debilitating effect on Vorster's performance in the regional arena.

This domestic constraint was exacerbated by another obsession, namely the principle of non-interference in the domestic affairs of other countries. This principle became enshrined in South African foreign policy making because South Africa itself was subjected to what it considered as such interference. Vorster and his foreign minister repeatedly declared in public that South Africa did not "dictate or prescribe" to Rhodesia or "meddle" in its internal affairs.[226] This was, according to Kaunda, also Vorster's message to the Zambians in private.[227] Smith would not have stated publicly that Vorster adhered to this principle[228] unless there was more than a grain of truth in it. The mutually reinforcing impact of the fear of white backlash and the non-interference principle had a disastrous effect on the course of detente and on South Africa's regional interests.

The diplomatic balance sheet of Zambia, as representative of the regional African collective patron was mixed. On the one hand, Zambia exhibited much more resolve in dealing with its clients. On the other hand, they shared with South Africa the fault of launching detente without having agreed on a definite settlement plan and of entertaining the unfounded optimism that the dynamic of the internal negotiations would produce the desired results. Even as late as April 1975, having experienced the delays and obstructions in the negotiations between the Rhodesian government and the ANC, the Zambian Foreign Minister said, referring to the prospect of achieving majority rule in Rhodesia and Namibia peacefully: "This is fact, not fiction."[229] The fact, however, was that the negotiations dynamic was counterproductive from the point of view of a settlement. The Zambians clung to their misplaced optimism, although they knew that Vorster had not committed himself to delivering Smith. They apparently believed that Vorster, being so keen on detente, would somehow convince the Rhodesian government to commit political suicide. They were proved wrong.

The failure of the regional patrons to work out a viable and effective strategy for the pursuit of their interests played into the hands of black and white Rhodesians who opposed, for obviously different reasons, the very idea of a peaceful settlement on the lines generally envisaged. The benefactors from the failure of detente were indeed those who wished it to fail, namely the Rhodesian government and ZANU militants.

CHAPTER FOUR

An Internal Interlude: the Failure of the Nkomo–Smith Negotiations

September 1975 – March 1976

In the aftermath of the Victoria Falls bridge conference, detente, as a comprehensive regional exercise, was virtually dead. There was, however, among participants at both domestic and regional levels, sufficient desire for a peaceful settlement. It was this desire which fed the negotiations between Nkomo and Smith.

These negotiations were pursued not only against the background of the failure of the peaceful efforts leading up to the conference, but also against the backdrop of a rapidly and radically changing regional environment. The phase of the Nkomo–Smith negotiations broadly coincided with the height of the Angolan decolonization crisis. This crisis culminated in an abortive South African incursion and in a massive Cuban-Soviet intervention which ensured by February 1976 the victory of the pro-Soviet MPLA.[1]

The military intervention in Angola was the very antithesis of the policy of detente pursued by the South African government. It was not a reflection of a carefully and thoroughly conceived alternative regional strategy. Detente was still the prevalent regional policy. The accommodating attitude of South Africa towards the FRELIMO Marxist regime in Mozambique was the true expression of the prevailing regional strategy. Had there been a similarly clear succession of the MPLA, South Africa most probably would have pursued the same policy towards Angola. The South African military intervention was an ill-conceived response to the unfolding Angolan Civil War. Inexperience in foreign and regional relations, the naive belief that they were operating on behalf of a determined Western block, including Zambia and Zaïre, lack of understanding of the political dynamic in post-Vietnam U.S., the perceived opportunity of turning Angola into a moderate and accommodating neighbour and a momentary ascendance of the military in the policy-making establishment, combined to produce an astounding regional policy blunder.

However, even while being engaged in an interventionist, aggressive policy in Angola, South Africa continued its vigorous pursuit of its African dialogue. In September 1975 the Minister of Information of the Ivory Coast paid an official visit to South Africa. *Die Transvaler* described the visit as "of great significance in the process of political detente". The *Natal Mercury* interpreted it as a "tangible evidence that the Prime Minister's diplomatic forays into black Africa are beginning to bring home the bacon".[2] South Africa was also successful in cultivating economic relations with the Central African Republic, Zaïre, Gabon and the Ivory Coast. The Central African Republic and the Ivory Coast agreed to grant landing rights to South African Airways.[3]

For obvious reasons, the regional detente was of far greater importance than the broader dialogue with black Africa. The unfolding crisis in the Atlantic flank of South Africa's regional parameter only served to emphasize the importance of a peaceful settlement in Rhodesia. As the Angolan crisis developed into a full-scale civil war, and as the Cuban-Soviet intervention brought the communist threat to their doorsteps, South African policy makers seriously considered the possibility that the failure of detente would result in the Angolization of their northern neighbour. All the ingredients were there: a white–black conflict, a bitterly divided nationalist movement and the Cubans around the corner. A guerilla war engulfing the whole sub-continent, coupled with communist military intervention would be a nightmare coming true. The end result could very well be that, instead of replacing the old buffer zone with a belt of peaceful coexistence, South Africa would find itself facing a chain of hostile, militant, pro-Soviet regimes. This threatening tide could be stemmed by a peaceful settlement in Rhodesia which would crown a moderate African regime. Detente in the region and Africa as a whole could be given a new lease of life.

For this reason, South Africa continued to view a Rhodesian settlement as a high national priority, and Vorster was not to be discouraged by the failure of the conference. Addressing a party congress on September 3, 1975, he maintained his optimism.[4] In a meeting in Pretoria on October 20, Smith was apparently told by South African leaders that the situation was grave and that a Rhodesian settlement was essential in order to strengthen the anti-communist block in the region. In a statement concluding the talks "both Prime Ministers have agreed that genuine attempts should be made to pursue policies leading to peace in southern Africa."[5] In November the South African Foreign Minister spoke clearly of the urgency with which South Africa viewed the Rhodesian question.[6]

The attitudes of the FLP to the resolution of the Rhodesian crisis in the wake of the failure of the conference were also influenced by the unfolding Angolan civil war. Kaunda continued to play a central role in the attempts to resolve the Rhodesian conflict peacefully. For Kaunda, from both regional and Zambian perspectives, the situation in the latter art of 1975 was more bleak and alarming than ever before. The anxieties of 1974 turned into a nightmare in late 1975. The thought of Rhodesia becoming a focus of a regional racial conflagration coupled with foreign military intervention was abhorrent to Kaunda as a man of principles and as a leader in charge of the destinies of his country and people. Zambia was facing a severe economic crisis whose intensity and consequences were closely linked to the prospects of a Rhodesian settlement. The persisting world economic slump continued to have a debilitating effect on Zambia. The price of copper, which accounted for Zambia's 90 per cent foreign exchange earnings and for over 50 per cent of the government revenue, plunged further during 1975, to reach the lowest price in real terms since the Second World War. Concurrently, the import bill continued to rise.[7] This had a devastating effect on Zambia's balance of payments. The government had to introduce severe import restrictions and to impose cuts on the remittance of profits and dividends by non-residents. It also introduced other foreign exchange restrictions.[8] In addition, the government had to take urgent action to prevent a national food crisis.[9] The economic crisis was exacerbated by the collapse of its transport system with the final closure of the Benguela railway line which had carried more than 60 per cent of the copper export. The alternative routes could not compensate for the loss of the Angolan route and Zambia's foreign trade suffered severe dislocations.[10] The prospect for 1976 was impending catastrophe.

Anglin and Shaw tend to minimize the weight of narrow economic interests in shaping Zambia's decision to pursue detente. To reinforce their argument, they cite Kaunda who said that Zambia "would not be cowed into doing wrong things because of routes".[11] This argument is carried to unrealistic lengths. While Kaunda was certainly not a traitor,[12] nor was he entirely altruistic in his motives. There is little doubt that broad and specific Zambian national interests, economic as well as others, played a predominant, rather than marginal, role in shaping Zambian policy in regional matters in general and with regard to the resolution of the Rhodesian crisis in particular. While Kaunda certainly had ideological "red lines" his regional policy can be attributed to Zambia's vital national interests at least as much as to his peaceful, humanitarian, Christian disposition. This was certainly true for the period following the Victoria Falls bridge conference, when considerations of national security and national economic interests were uppermost, quotations from Kaunda to the contrary notwithstanding. It was one thing to respond to Smith's challenge in early 1973 by closing the border between the two countries, before the energy crisis and when the copper price reached a peak of £1,400 per ton and having the use of two safe alternative outlets.[13] It was another thing to ignore the transportation crisis in the latter part of 1975 and early 1976, with the collapse of copper price and the devastating effects of the oil crunch. Under these circumstances, the Rhodesian rail route acquired tremendous importance. It is true that Kaunda declined to accept a Rhodesian public offer on the eve of the conference to resume Zambia's railway traffic through Rhodesia.[14] As the economic and transport situation worsened, a Zambian MP and former Finance Minister urged the government on November 16 to resume the usage of the Rhodesian route. In early December 1975, Kaunda, while saying that it would be unwise to reopen the border with Rhodesia at that moment, stated that the ruling party's Central Committee and the cabinet would keep the matter under review.[15] At least one source suggested that a decision to reopen the Rhodesian border was endorsed by the ruling party's Central Committee and the cabinet in December 1975, and that this option was ruled out when Mozambique closed its border with Rhodesia in March 1976.[16]

In declining the Rhodesian offer on the eve of the conference, Kaunda faced an unenviable choice. It was not, however, simply a choice between national economic interests and the cause of liberation, and his declining the offer was not a neat victory of principle over expediency. It could equally be conceived of as a tactical choice unrelated to high principles. Accepting the Rhodesian offer at that stage of the Rhodesian negotiations could have been construed as a show of African weakness. This could have hardened Smith's attitude and jeopardized the chances of securing a settlement which alone could guarantee Zambia's long term national interests. This consideration was valid later during the Nkomo–Smith negotiations. In giving legitimate national interests their rightful place in decision making, I do not mean to diminish the stature of Kaunda as an African leader. On the contrary, his prominence as an African statesman stemmed from his ability to reconcile higher principles and legitimate national interests, to combine idealism and pragmatism.

It is only against the background of this fusion of principles and interests, that Kaunda's approach to the Rhodesian crisis in the wake of the conference is comprehensible. Despite the difficulties and frustrations which culminated in the conference, Kaunda continued to have a clear preference for a peaceful solution. Appealing to white

81

Rhodesians in November 1975 to opt for a peaceful settlement, he gave expression to two basic goals which motivated him in his southern African policy. Firstly, he urged them to espouse peace because the consequences of black–white confrontation were "too ghastly to contemplate". Secondly, his immediate objective was to effect a breakthrough in the negotiations which would enable him to reopen the Rhodesian border. When asked about the possibility of reopening the border, he answered his Rhodesian interviewer: "When you have made some progress in terms of things that matter, it will make it easier for us."[17] Yet, despite Zambia's urgent need for a settlement, Kaunda insisted that only one which led to majority rule would be acceptable to him.[18] Majority rule was an ideological red line for him; it was also the only realistic basis for a lasting settlement which could stabilize the region. In the case of the failure of peace, the alternative to which he was committed was clear: "We will not support any settlement which falls short of majority rule. In this event, majority rule must be decided upon the battle field."[19]

Kaunda's approach of giving peace another chance was not fully shared by his front-line colleagues. Already in early July 1975 Nyerere and Machel exhibited increasing impatience with the negotiations and it was decided, between them and the ANC leaders, to "de-escalate talks and escalate the armed struggle".[20] After that meeting, Chissano, the Mozambican foreign minister said: "We are only waiting for our brothers in Rhodesia to tell us what they need from Mozambique for the liberation of their country, and we are prepared."[21] While not precipitating a new guerilla offensive, that decision highlighted the difference in inclination among the FLP. The failure of the conference could only reinforce the view of those who had already been sceptical about detente. In the wake of the conference, Nyerere came out more openly and forcefully in favour of armed struggle as the only viable liberation strategy. Speaking in London in November 1975, he explained why he was "very pessimistic": "I don't believe that Smith has at last accepted that he must have independence in Rhodesia on the basis of majority rule."[22] To students at Oxford he presented the alternative: "Unfortunately, but inevitably, the armed struggle in Rhodesia will have to be resumed until conditions are ripe for realistic negotiations."[23] It should be borne in mind that from the perspective of its national interests, Tanzania did not expect to be adversely affected by escalating violence in Rhodesia. It was conveniently remote from the battlefield. The Tanzam railway, linking the Copperbelt to Dar es Salaam port, which opened towards the end of 1975, could only benefit from the closure of Zambia's alternative routes. It is not suggested that

Nyerere precipitated a military confrontation in Rhodesia for national material gains. It does suggest, however, that Nyerere was not beset by the anxieties which were uppermost in Kaunda's troubled mind.

In the aftermath of the conference, Machel was also gravitating towards a military solution. However, unlike Tanzania, vital Mozambican national interests were involved. Unlike Tanzania, Mozambique's economy was deeply integrated in the southern African economic sphere dominated by the white regimes. It was mainly dependent on South Africa, the economic giant and the focus of the regional economy.[24] Mozambique also derived economic benefits from Rhodesia. In normal times, some 80 per cent of the Rhodesian foreign trade was conducted through Mozambique.[25] The economy of Mozambique, which had suffered from the protracted liberation war, faced a severe crisis as a result of the exodus of some 120,000 Portuguese whose services were essential.[26] This, in turn, increased Mozambique's dependence on available foreign, mainly regional, sources of income. On assuming power in June 1975, Samora Machel had little choice but to continue with the inherited regional patterns. Until March 1976, he adopted a policy of "business as usual" towards Rhodesia, including collaboration in sanction busting. This was not the role of which Machel had dreamt during his struggle for liberation. He could not even toy with the idea of confronting South Africa the regional military and economic power. On the other hand, active involvement in an isolated anti-Rhodesian guerilla campaign seemed to have its merits. True, there was an economic loss involved, but this did not seem at the time unduly heavy. It was estimated that the application of sanctions against Rhodesia would incur an annual loss of £12–20 million in revenue. This loss was expected to be offset by international aid from countries and bodies interested in turning the economic screw on Rhodesia. Already in May 1975, the Commonwealth conference decided to take "immediate practical steps to assist an independent Mozambique in applying sanctions".[27]

On October 6, 1975, the Mozambican Foreign Minister, appealing to the UN General Assembly to apply "a complete and total boycott against Rhodesia", said that "FRELIMO and the People's Republic of Mozambique are ready to assume all responsibility in conformity with their international duty."[28] Once the economic loss seemed to have been taken care of, active assistance to the armed struggle in Rhodesia had a definite attraction to FRELIMO and Machel. Resigning themselves to a neo-colonialist, dependent role dictated by the colonial heritage was abhorrent to FRELIMO leaders who were emerging from long years of struggle. Assisting the liberation of Rhodesia would

83

enhance the legitimacy of the FRELIMO regime in Mozambique and in broader African and international circles. It would also give the Mozambican leaders the satisfaction of living up to their own ideals and keeping alive the motto of their struggle – *la lutta continua*. As in the case of Nyerere, underlying the shift in FRELIMO's position was the deep-rooted belief, reinforced by their own experience, that settler-colonialists could not be expected to make the ultimate concession unless forced by armed struggle. Machel himself summed up his attitude on September 24:

> As was the case in our country, in the face of systematic refusal of the racist regime to accept a peaceful solution, in the face of its manoeuvres of hypocrisy, the people of Zimbabwe reached the decision to wage an armed struggle as demanded by the need to restore peace and justice to their country. The Mozambican People's Republic will not vacillate in the fulfilment of their duty and their fraternal solidarity.[29]

The unfolding victory of the anti-imperialist forces in Angola must have also had a radicalizing effect on Machel and Nyerere who supported the MPLA and the Cuban–Soviet intervention.

With Botswana siding with Zambia's approach, there emerged in the aftermath of the conference, a moderate and a radical orientation within the FLP. There was, however, no polarization. In principle, as well as in practice, the moderates did not rule out armed struggle, while the radicals did not totally reject a peaceful settlement. Each camp gave a different interpretation and emphasis to the accepted dual strategy. From this perspective, a strategic common denominator could still be worked out. It was worked out, because, above all, there was among the FLP the will to continue to operate in unison as the regional patrons of Rhodesia's liberation movement. In mid-September 1975 the FLP met in Lusaka to review their Rhodesian strategy. From available information,[30] as well as from subsequent developments, it is possible to reconstruct the strategy adopted by the presidents. Basically, the FLP continued to operate within the parameters of the dual strategy. There was, however, more emphasis on the military effort. No decision was taken to launch an immediate guerilla offensive. This would have been unwise, indeed foolhardy. The potential for a sustained and effective armed struggle lay in ZANU. ZANU, however, was at that juncture not in a position to launch an offensive. The suppression of ZANLA by Zambia in particular and the Rhodesian counter-insurgency efforts in the wake of the conference brought the guerilla war to a virtual standstill. By the end of 1975, most of the ZANLA guerillas in the north-east had been eliminated or had fled across the border.[31] Edgar Tekere recalled in August 1976, the condition of ZANU recruits in Mozambique in September 1975: "Here there were these young men and women out in the bush completely lost."[32] The commander of the Rhodesian Special Branch could thus inform senior officers in October: "As far as I am concerned Hurricane[33] had been won."[34] A credible guerilla option had to be cultivated before it could be unleashed.

This was decided upon by the FLP in their secret meeting in September. They resolved to remove the restrictions placed on the guerillas stationed in their countries and to transfer ZANLA guerillas from their camps in Tanzania and Zambia to bases in Mozambique in preparation for a guerilla offensive.[35] Samora Machel shed his previous inhibitions. Muzorewa recalled that part of the meeting: "Then President Samora Machel issued the magnanimous invitation: 'I now invite all of you Zimbabweans to come and live in Mozambique and operate from there.'"[36] Kaunda, accepting this shift of emphasis, came closer to the radicals' view that war was inevitable though not desirable. The radicals on their part also made a concession. Martin, having excellent access to guerilla and FLP sources wrote: "However, a rider was included in their agreement allowing the nationalists to try to reach a negotiated settlement."[37] This allowed Kaunda to continue to pursue the elusive peaceful settlement.

Thus, despite earlier frustrations, there was still a desire in both South Africa and Zambia to give peace another chance. There was, however, much less enthusiasm, determination and active involvement than before.

Ian Smith and his government would have liked the Victoria Falls bridge conference to be the graveyard of detente. Having adhered to the letter, though not necessarily to the spirit, of the Pretoria agreement, and having exposed the African nationalists as divided and unreliable, they must have hoped that their patron would drop detente and change course. They wished that the South Africans would draw the right conclusions from the unfolding communist onslaught in southern Africa and support them in their campaign against the communists' surrogates. Unfortunately for them, their patron still cherished the goal of a peaceful settlement. The Rhodesian government had no choice but to go along. This, however, did not mean that they were prepared to make the appropriate adjustment in their position on the nature of the settlement.

In his statement to Parliament on the conference in August 1975, Smith still toyed with his favourite plan of internal settlement, in which he wanted to involve "representatives of the Chiefs' Council" as well as "representatives of other organizations who have indicated a desire to participate".[38] After the conference, the security situation was steadily improving. The sharply deteriorating economic conditions in 1975[39] could be attributed to global economic slump, rather than to declining domestic and regional fortunes. The Rhodesians certainly saw no cause for abdication. The government felt confident enough in the future to select on September 24 a new national anthem for the Republic of Rhodesia.[40] The government, however, could not follow their inclinations and explore the internal option with the chiefs as a centrepiece. Thinking in terms of detente, the South African government wanted a settlement with credible nationalists who would bestow on it legitimacy and secure at least partial regional recognition. Smith could not afford to ignore his patron's desire. Addressing the RF Congress in late September, he referred to his followers' frustrations: "No matter how exasperated you may feel, no matter how disillusioned you are over this thing called detente, I believe we have no option other than to continue until we arrive at an answer one way or another."[41]

The choice fell on Joshua Nkomo. All of a sudden, in the wake of the conference, Nkomo became, as a South African journalist put it, the "new Great White Hope".[42] It seems that he earned his new title by default. Muzorewa was considered a political lightweight, while Sithole was perceived as a dangerous militant. Compared to them, Nkomo combined the virtues of nationalist legitimacy and relative moderation. He was also known to be the favourite of Kaunda, who could be expected to accord regional legitimacy to a Nkomo–Smith agreement. This, of course, holds water if Smith was genuinely interested in a settlement with Nkomo. It is not impossible that the Rhodesian government believed that a settlement with Nkomo on the basis of something less than majority rule could be reached.[43] Alternatively, it is arguable that the manipulative Smith wanted not a successful conclusion, but rather a credible failure. Having been forced by regional circumstances to continue to negotiate in the framework of detente, he needed a respectable nationalist partner to carry him safely through the motions. From this perspective, his tactics were still to bring the negotiations to a dead end while turning the blame on the nationalists. He chose Nkomo because he made himself available.

Before Smith could launch a new round of negotiations, he had to ward off a political–ideological challenge within the ranks of his own party. For the first time since the beginning of detente, he faced an organized and determined opposition from the right wing of the RF.

The challenge gathered momentum towards the party congress held in Umtali in late September 1975. Smith irritated the party hawks when he welcomed the idea of a multi-racial government, not even precluding a black prime minister.[44] For this he was taken to task by Des Frost, the RF Chairman in his report to the Congress.[45] The fear that the existing multi-racial policy might lead to majority rule, prompted the RF right wing to try to push through the Congress the policy of provincialization – the Rhodesian version of separate development. Those behind this thrust included the party chairman, two prominent ministers, a deputy minister and a few MPs.[46] Smith evaded the issue and received a mandate to continue negotiating for the best possible settlement without imposing on him any specific directives.[47] Smith was still invincible in his party. He personified white Rhodesia. He articulated in the face of the world their inner thoughts and feelings and propagated the justice of their cause. In the turbulent detente era, the bewildered whites had a particularly urgent need to trust their leader and be guided by him in the changing, collapsing world around them. Many rank and file and leaders in the party regarded Smith as a political *Midas*: "good old Smithy must have something up his sleeve."[48]

Having reasserted his authority in the party and having received a renewed mandate from its congress, Smith was in a position to spell out his intentions. Whereas on September 5 he spoke on negotiating with the chiefs and saw no moderates in the ANC,[49] on October 12 he indicated his willingness to negotiate with Nkomo: "Nkomo seems to be the only one who has standing in Rhodesia now. The others have disappeared from the scene and I believe that this is a very strong thing in favour of Mr Nkomo." In relation to a statement by Nkomo which, in normal times, Smith would have regarded as extreme, he said: "I don't think you must take too seriously what politicians say in public."[50]

Nkomo was ripe for the picking. Speculations that he was planning to negotiate with Smith were rife in early September 1975.[51] They were probably prompted by Nkomo being the only ANC leader who had gone back to Rhodesia after the conference. The suspicions of other ANC leaders were also fed by news and rumours of previous secret contacts between Nkomo and Smith.[52] Towards the end of September Nkomo made public his desire to resume negotiations with Smith.[53] According to Nkomo, it was Smith who renewed his approaches to him at the end of September.[54] What prompted Nkomo to pin his hopes on Smith despite his intransigence and obstructionism? Nkomo certainly took a gamble when defying the militant stance adopted by his co-leaders in the ANC in the wake of the conference. Sithole set the tone in early September when declaring: "We shall shoot our way into

Zimbabwe."[55] A militant stance was also adopted by the ANC official organ in its October 1975 issue.[56]

Nkomo would not have taken the risk of negotiating separately with Smith unless he believed that it could lead to the attainment of majority rule. The peaceful attainment of majority rule was his favoured solution. His Soviet connections notwithstanding, Nkomo did not espouse Marxism. He did not seek the total transformation of the colonial socio-economic structures. His goal was rather to inherit the colonial state and to gradually Africanize it. So-called neo-colonialism was certainly not an abomination to him. As victory became visible, the liberation struggle took an inward turn, acquiring an increasing dimension of a struggle for the inheritance of the colonial state between the different nationalist factions. From this new perspective, the Smith government and the white power structure could be perceived as potential allies as much as enemies. This complex situation called for an appropriate strategy which would guarantee the attainment of the dual goal of liberation and inheritance. In the case of Nkomo, there was a considerable discrepancy between his presumption to lead his people to and after independence, and the balance of power within the nationalist camp. It was this gap between pretence and reality that Nkomo's evolving strategy sought to close. Thus, Nkomo opted for a peaceful, negotiated settlement, not in response to an irresistible urge for peace, but rather because he realized that the alternative armed struggle option would play into the hands of his ZANU opponents. ZANU, despite the setbacks it had suffered in 1975, was better placed to pursue the armed struggle and to reap its fruits, not least because of its vast potential of ethnic mobilization. While ZAPU's leadership was truly multi-ethnic, its recruitment potential at the grass-roots was largely restricted to the Ndebele/Kalanga group, which accounted for less than 20 per cent of the African population. A peaceful settlement in the immediate post-Victoria Falls bridge conference would find ZANU in disarray and unable to realize its potential.

Even the peaceful option posed a problem to Nkomo. Within the ANC, which was set up as a vehicle for a peaceful settlement, Nkomo's position was precarious. Two of the four top leaders of the ANC, Sithole and Chikerema, were his bitter enemies. Bishop Muzorewa, the incumbent president, was hardly sympathetic to his leadership ambitions. Thus, the ANC, as constituted by the unity agreement of December 1974, was not a solid platform for the launching of Nkomo's peaceful option. Consequently, he worked out a strategy designed to maximize his political resources within the context of a peaceful settlement.

Elements of Nkomo's strategy had already emerged prior to the conference. Having concluded that the ANC collective leadership was not the medium through which he could promote his far-reaching ambitions, he sought to undermine and replace it. Already, before the conference, he planned to convene an ANC congress inside Rhodesia to elect a permanent leadership in lieu of the interim one instituted by the unity agreement. Nkomo was treading on sound constitutional ground, since the unity agreement stipulated that such a congress be held within four months. He must have believed that his chances were good to emerge as the ANC leader. ZANU, especially after Chitepo's assassination, was in disarray, Chikerema's FROLIZI was a spent political force and Muzorewa had not proved himself as an effective leader. In his political manoeuvres, Nkomo could also rely on the majority ZAPU apparently had in the ANC national executive as then constituted.[57] Nkomo hoped that once elected as leader he could mobilize the support of the broad masses as the father of African nationalism in Rhodesia. He moved in on June 1, 1975. In a stormy meeting of the ANC national executive, held in Salisbury, Nkomo managed to pass a resolution calling for a congress to be held on June 21–22.[58] Muzorewa stepped in on June 16, declaring that the congress would not convene.[59] This renewed leadership struggle was settled by an ANC leadership meeting held in Dar es Salaam on July 6. The meeting resolved to end the leadership struggle and to continue to operate within the existing leadership structures under Muzorewa's leadership.[60]

The lull in the leadership struggle did not survive the Victoria Falls bridge conference. Nkomo's departure to Rhodesia soon after the conference had dispersed, apparently under false pretences, aroused the suspicions of his rivals.[61] In fact, the anti-Nkomo elements had begun to hit back before the conference. On August 15 Nkomo's rivals convened a meeting which elected the officers of the Zimbabwe Liberation Council (ZLC), the external wing of the ANC. Nkomo was caught unprepared and the result was a virtual anti-Nkomo coup. Despite the protest of Nkomo's supporters, the meeting elected Sithole as chairman and Chikerema as secretary of the ZLC. Of the elected chairmen of the six committees, four were affiliated with ZANU and two with FROLIZI. For some reason, the plotters decided to announce the results of these elections only on September 1.[62] Four leading Nkomo supporters immediately denounced ZANU's and FROLIZI's "vicious campaign" and denied their right to take such action.[63] Nkomo's response to this challenge, which unfolded within a week, was to reactivate his internal option. On September 6 he convened a meeting of the ANC national executive which was attended by 37 of its 70 members. In a statement to the press, the meeting condemned the appointments to the ZLC "which were done by a clique, who by doing so attempted to usurp the power of the national executive committee". The statement also announced the holding of the ANC congress on September 27 and 28, 1975.[64] As expected, the congress elected Nkomo as the ANC president and a new set of Nkomo's men as officers.[65] In his autobiography, Nkomo refers to the congress as a purely ZAPU affair.[66] Muzorewa reacted to Nkomo's initiative, before the congress convened, by ousting him from the ANC. Nkomo responded by claiming that Muzorewa had no authority to do that and proceeded with his plans.[67] Nkomo's opponents rejected his congress and Eliot Gabella, the ANC vice-president, and a Muzorewa loyalist, announced a plan to hold a counter-executive meeting to decide on a counter-congress to be held on October 19 1975, which would be the "legal and constitutional congress".[68] This congress, eventually scheduled for October 26, failed to convene because of last-minute police intervention.[69]

The next stage in Nkomo's plan was separate negotiations with the Rhodesian government for a peaceful settlement which would satisfy both African aspirations and his own ambitions. This element in his strategy featured already in the June 1975 controversy over the convening of an ANC congress. Then it was used by Nkomo's opponents to delegitimize him as a nationalist leader. On June 18 Chikerema called on Nkomo to resign from the ANC for betraying the movement by making secret deals with Smith.[70] An ANC circular distributed in Salisbury, in fact, condemned Nkomo for striking a deal with Smith.[71] Rhodesian government sources confirmed that there had been contacts with Nkomo or his aides in June 1975.[72] Nkomo, understandably, vehemently denied the allegations.[73] While Nkomo's opponents probably exaggerated the extent of his dealing with Smith, available evidence and subsequent development suggest that Nkomo's vehemence was at least partly misplaced.

Nkomo's return to Rhodesia after the failure of the conference brought in its wake renewed speculation about possible talks between him and Smith.[74] A week before Nkomo held his congress, the ZLC issued a statement claiming that Nkomo and Smith had already made a secret deal involving Nkomo's heading a multi-racial government.[75] This was clearly unfounded. Nkomo himself did not expose his intentions before the congress.[76] Having been elected by the congress as president of the ANC, Nkomo was in a better position to state his intention. In his concluding speech, he said: "The people of Zimbabwe are prepared once again to realize their goal of MAJORITY RULE NOW by negotiations in accordance with the efforts of the four African Presidents."[77] Soon after the congress, Nkomo launched a drive to win the confidence of the Rhodesian whites, assuring them that they had nothing to fear from a black government.[78] He tried to create the impression that he was not going for a separate deal with Smith. On October 1 he insisted that the exiled nationalist leaders must be allowed to take part in the negotiations inside Rhodesia.[79]

Another thrust of Nkomo's strategy was directed at obtaining regional support. A separate internal settlement without regional support and legitimacy was not on his agenda. Such a settlement, a black version of UDI, was unacceptable to him. Nkomo's staunch supporter among the FLP was Kaunda. Kaunda and Nkomo belonged to the same generation of Central African nationalist leaders who came to prominence during the 1950s. Muzorewa noted that the "long-standing friendship of Dr Kaunda and Mr Nkomo was well known".[80] In his visit to Zambia before the conference, Wickus de Kock got a clear impression that the Zambians favoured Nkomo.[81] Indeed, at about the same time, Nkomo seems to have received Zambian support in his first bid, in June 1975, to convene an ANC Congress. On July 8 Lusaka Radio called on Rhodesia's Africans to exercise their right to elect their leadership as stipulated by the unity agreement in December 1974.[82] Radio Lusaka repeated its call some 10 days later accusing the ANC of operating under an illegal constitution.[83]

Thus, when Nkomo launched his new political initiative in September 1975, he believed he could get at least some regional support for a prospective settlement. Towards the end of September 1975, a journalist paraphrased the prevailing attitude in Zambia's official circles: "If Nkomo can bring about majority rule in Rhodesia and at the same time foster unity among his people, then he is as good a bet as anyone, probably better."[84] On October 26, on the eve of his preliminary talks with Smith, Nkomo met Kaunda in Lusaka. In a statement on the meeting a Zambian spokesman said that "the President told Mr Nkomo that Zambia would not support any settle-ment which falls short of majority rule."[85] On November 22 Kaunda told David Martin that "if Mr Nkomo clinches an agreement with Mr Smith on the basis of majority rule, then the Zimbabwe Liberation Council, led by Bishop Muzorewa would become irrelevant. And if he does not, then he will become irrelevant." This, according to Kaunda, was what he had told Nkomo.[86] It is clear that the Zambian government wanted to project an image of a detached uninvolved party.

The wish to project such an image is perfectly understandable. With the situation being so fluid and volatile, the Zambians chose to keep their options open as far as possible. They could not afford to further alienate ZANU, which was expected to become a dominant actor in the event of an intensified armed struggle. Unmitigated open support for Nkomo could also exacerbate divisions in the ranks of the FLP and weaken Kaunda's position in that forum. There is little doubt, however, that behind this public facade, Kaunda had a much more favourable attitude to Nkomo's initiative. It seems inconceivable that Nkomo would have adopted such a high-risk strategy without the connivance and encouragement of Kaunda. It could not have been a coincidence that Nkomo went to see Kaunda on October 26, on the eve of the "talks on talks". In fact, he flew to Lusaka on board a special aeroplane sent for him by Kaunda. The five-hour meeting between them was certainly more than a courtesy call. Nkomo's account of that meeting was most probably more reflective of its spirit, than that of the Zambian spokesman: "Dr Kaunda understands very clearly our problems and as always, he is ready to help and assist." He also said that they agreed on all the problems they had discussed.[87] Zambia's special relations with Nkomo also reflected on the relations between the Zambians and Nkomo's rivals. Thus, the Zambian government refused to endorse the expulsion of Nkomo from the ANC or even to announce it from Zambia.[88] On the day Nkomo was expelled, there was an armed clash between the Zambian army and ZANLA fighters stationed in Zambia.[89] Enos Nkala, an outspoken ZANU leader, hurled insults and abuses at Kaunda and the Zambians in general. In return, he was denounced by a Zambian spokesman as "a quisling" and "a running-dog of the rebels".[90] Kaunda also ordered Muzorewa and Sithole out of the presidential guesthouse.[91]

The full extent of Zambian involvement in and support for Nkomo's initiative was revealed subsequently when Kaunda sent a Zambian team of advisers to assist Nkomo in his talks with Smith.[92] Reacting to that, ZANU supporters in Salisbury carried posters attacking Kaunda and Zambia: "Kaunda is a political prostitute" and "Zambia get out of Zimbabwe". The Zambian government, on its part, insisted that its assistance to Nkomo did not indicate support for him.[93] However, earlier in December, Kaunda said in a major foreign policy speech that if the negotiations produced a settlement based on full majority rule the objective of Africa would be achieved. He stated that Zambia "would welcome and support such a settlement".[94]

Nkomo was not satisfied with only Zambian support. He sought broader regional support to legitimize his position as ANC President, his talks with Smith and a prospective settlement. Here, Nkomo, the international nationalist, was in his element, playing his favourite role as grand nationalist diplomat. At the beginning of October 1975, the secretary-general and chairman of Nkomo's ANC left for a regional tour to brief the presidents of Zambia, Malawi, Tanzania, Mozambique and Botswana on the Nkomo congress. Nkomo, himself, was also on the move. On November 7 he returned from Malawi where he met President Banda. Within a week, he was back on the regional trail meeting the four FLP.[95] The position of Nyerere was of particular importance to Nkomo. He had, however, little success in swaying him towards his side. In a press conference in London on November 21, Nyerere came closest to Kaunda's public stand: "I wish Joshua Nkomo well in his talks with Smith" adding that, in his view, the chances of the talks taking place were scant because Smith was not ready for change.[96] The thrust of Tanzania's policy was, from Nkomo's point of view, distinctly negative. Briefing the editors of government-controlled radio and newspapers in early October, top Tanzanian government officials said that Tanzania would not recognize any deal between Smith and Nkomo. They also instructed the editors to refer to Nkomo's congress as the "so-called" congress and to Nkomo's faction of the ANC as a minority group which negotiated a "sell-out" deal with Smith.[97] In early December, an editorial in the government-owned *Daily News* attacked the separate Nkomo–Smith talks and favoured the participation of all nationalist groups in any constitutional negotiations.[98]

This was then the regional background against which Nkomo pursued his strategy of negotiations. On October 31, 1975 teams headed by Nkomo and Smith began preliminary talks designed to clear the way for a full constitutional conference.[99] After the third meeting, held on November 12, a communique stated that the stage was set for such a conference. Subsequently, Nkomo went to brief the FLP,[100] while Smith went on holiday to South Africa where pressure was reported to have been exerted on him by Vorster.[101] On December 1 Smith and Nkomo signed a declaration of intent which formally paved the way for a constitutional conference.[102] With minor changes, this document was a reproduction of the declaration of intent which Smith refused to sign in the Victoria Falls bridge conference.[103] Smith also agreed to grant immunity to all African participants in the constitutional conference. Since those he wanted to exclude were not coming anyway, it was not a real sacrifice. All the same, a South African newspaper described Smith's concession as an "astonishing turnabout".[104] The large measure of identity between the two declarations of intent was not incidental. It could confer on Nkomo–Smith negotiations elements of continuity and legitimacy.

It was astonishing that an experienced nationalist leader such as Nkomo began negotiating with Smith without securing even a broad understanding regarding majority rule. According to Nkomo himself, all that he had asked for and got from Smith, prior to negotiating with him, was an undertaking to talk about majority rule.[105] This was particularly astonishing because throughout the period leading up to the negotiations, the gap between the two regarding the issue of majority rule was evidently very wide. Smith had not yet crossed the Rubicon to the territory of majority rule. Thus, the expressions of satisfaction, in Zambia and South Africa, over Smith's statement that he saw a possibility of a black prime minister in Rhodesia, were misplaced. On the same occasion, Smith also said the following: "We believe in quality as opposed to quantity. ... We think that the ideal is to be governed by the best people available in Rhodesia, irrespective of their colour."[106] It was the old concept of multi-racial meritocracy. Thus, when Smith said on the eve of the substantive constitutional talks that he categorically rejected a solution based on immediate majority rule,[107] he did not mean that he would accept it in the future.

This was, however, exactly the solution Nkomo had been adamantly insisting on. Responding, soon after his return to Rhodesia from the conference, to references to him as a moderate, he made his position clear: "If anyone thinks I am a moderate let me tell that man there is no such thing in the ANC. We want the same thing – majority rule now."[108] Nkomo spelled out this goal, and not only to his own African constituency. Addressing a white audience in late October, he said "The solution is majority rule now. I repeat: majority rule now."[109] He also threatened that unless his efforts to achieve majority rule "now not tomorrow" succeeded, he would turn back to the war path.[110] Towards the end of November, Nkomo clarified that majority rule now meant a transitional period of not more than 12 months which would itself reflect the principle of majority rule.[111]

It is doubtful that Smith was troubled by the width of the gap. Indeed, it guaranteed him the credible failure he sought since Nkomo demanded much more than he was asked to concede by South Africa. If Nkomo, who was interested in a credible success, did not take seriously Smith's public pronouncements, he was soon to discover his mistake.

The substantive constitutional talks, or what Nkomo termed as "the conference", began on December 15, 1975,[112] and were to last more than three months. This phase was a predominantly internal Rhodesian affair. South Africa and Zambia, which were still keenly interested in a peaceful settlement, withdrew to the background. This was a marked change from their vigorous involvement until the Victoria Falls bridge conference. Earlier frustrating experience made them more realistic about their ability to influence the process and to achieve their goals. Consequently, they were not inclined to stake their prestige and to pin high hopes on the Nkomo–Smith talks. The regional atmosphere was also changing for the worse. The substantive talks coincided with the victory march of the MPLA in Angola. The radicalizing impact of this development did not augur well for the peace efforts in Rhodesia. This also affected the degree of enthusiasm and conspicuousness these regional patrons were prepared to exhibit for the cause of peace.

The South African press continued to urge a peaceful settlement in Rhodesia. On November 20, on the eve of the substantive talks, *Die Burger* put forward a strong case for South Africa's interference in Rhodesia: "Rhodesia is a neighbouring state. Our vital interests are at stake with what happens there. If no interference means that we should sit with folded hands and let things slide, it would be sheer folly – in effect a sort of interference in favour of eventual violence and chaos."[113] Indeed, as the civil war in Angola was reaching its conclusion, South Africa became increasingly concerned about the future of Rhodesia. On February 8, 1976, referring to the Nkomo–Smith talks, the South African Foreign Minister said: "I think they must be realistic and realize that what happened in Angola could be repeated somewhere else."[114] Towards the end of February, *Die Transvaler* drew the Rhodesian lesson from the communist threat in the wake of Angola: "This all places an additional responsibility on Mr Smith and Mr Nkomo to show flexibility in their discussion on Rhodesia's constitutional future. A Rhodesian settlement will go a long way towards alleviating the situation in southern Africa as a whole."[115] On February 23 a political correspondent of the *Star* reported that "Rhodesia has suddenly ousted Angola as the crucial problem area of Southern Africa." He also claimed that "there are indications that the Government is still playing a major role behind the scenes in persuading ... Smith to face the realities of his country's situation in Africa."[116]

There is, however, no evidence that this was the case. In fact, in view of South African interest in a peaceful settlement, its involvement was astonishingly scant. It was even less than during the Nkomo–Smith preliminary talks. Then Smith went twice to South Africa for talks with Vorster. During the substantive talks, when what remained of detente was hanging in the balance, there was no such high level visit. The only visit was that of the Rhodesian Defence and Foreign Affairs Minister who came to seek more aid from South Africa.[117] In early March 1976 it seemed, for a very short time, that South Africa, at last, was prepared to exert real pressure to save its regional strategy. The opportunity presented itself when on March 3 Mozambique closed the border with Rhodesia. From that moment Rhodesia's dependence on South Africa for its economic survival became absolute. The *Johannesburg Financial Mail* made a passionate plea to force a settlement on Smith.[118] For a moment, it seemed that South Africa intended doing just that. Referring to the closure of the Mozambique border, the general manager of the South African Railways (SAR), Mr Loubser, told a South African journalist that the SAR would take the "regular Rhodesian quota and the Rhodesians will have to determine their own priorities". At the same time, he was more forthcoming with respect to the transport needs of Zambia and Zaïre.[119] This pressure was, however, very short-lived. The day after the report was published, Loubser "vehemently denied" what had been attributed to him. He added that "the SAR would and could accept increase in traffic from Rhodesia."[120] On March 9 the Minister of Transport rendered more weight to the denial saying in Parliament with regard to the same issue that "within the limits of physical capability we will continue to make our services available."[121] Later in March, at about the time the talks finally collapsed, Vorster told a British MP: "I will not twist Smith's arm. I have warned him; I have advised him. But, I am no more willing to use pressure on Rhodesia than I am willing to use pressure against any African state."[122] Thus, when asked on March 20 what would be the effect of the breakdown of the talks on Rhodesia's relations with South Africa, Smith sounded very optimistic: "I don't believe that this will in any way affect our relations with South Africa. South Africa has always gone out of their way to try to help and assist wherever they could. I believe that they will continue to do this."[123] In view of the available evidence, Smith does not seem to have exaggerated.

During the Nkomo–Smith talks, as in the earlier phase of detente, South Africa failed to produce the necessary pressure to secure the attainment of its regional goals. The Angolan debacle further aggravated the constraints affecting South African Rhodesian policy. South Africa, which had little experience in regional politics, was concurrently involved in a complex regional diplomatic exercise and in a high-risk military intervention with a heavy dose of aggressive international participation. This must have had a debilitating effect on South African policy makers. The Angolan fiasco, with a communist victory and American betrayal, must have shocked and bewildered them. The failure of the Angolan intervention also exacerbated the domestic constraint affecting regional policy making. The Nationalist government, which had succumbed to pressure in Angola, feared the domestic consequences of pressurizing white Rhodesia into submission. Vorster, being so sensitive about the unity of Afrikanerdom, could not ignore the mood of the party's rank and file. This mood had found expression earlier in the party Transvaal Congress at the end of August 1975. It was then reported that there was among the delegates "a vague uneasiness about the whole detente operation and about the ultra-conservative allegation that South Africa was selling Rhodesia down the river. ... Nationalists recognize that the situation is not an easy one and that their supporters must be delicately handled."[124] The Angolan affair could not have alleviated that uneasiness. Thus, the fear of Afrikaner backlash, magnified by Vorster's hypersensitivity still had a paralysing effect on South Africa's regional policy.

The duality which characterized the attitude of the FLP to the Nkomo–Smith preliminary talks persisted through much of the substantive negotiations. However, as the negotiations dragged on and as the MPLA victory was radiating radicalizing influence throughout southern Africa, there was a definite shift towards the armed struggle option. The Zambian legal team serving Nkomo's delegation, indicated an interest in the success of the talks. However, while giving occasional expression to his preference for a peaceful solution, Kaunda became increasingly pessimistic about its feasibility and increasingly inclined towards the violent alternative. Declaring a state of emergency in Zambia on January 28, 1976, Kaunda said that the Zambian nation must be prepared for an intensified armed struggle because "time and the tide of nationalism cannot wait until it suits Smith to accept majority rule."[125] In February, his change of heart appeared more definite: "Due to Smith's intransigence, Zambia has reached the end of the road regarding negotiations as an instrument for change."[126] On February 27, in response to a Rhodesian attack on Mozambique, Kaunda declared that an attack on Mozambique was an attack on Zambia. Radio Lusaka interpreted it as "virtually a declaration of state of war in our region with Mozambique and Zambia standing together as allies".[127] In early March, the *Times* of Zambia urged Botswana to join the war.[128]

Nyerere, who during the preliminary talks had been very sceptical about the prospect of a peaceful settlement, adopted a still more militant stance. On February 1, 1976 he told Zambian journalists that there was no alternative in Rhodesia but an intensified armed struggle.[129] Addressing students in Dar es Salaam on February 14, he stated that the peaceful option in Rhodesia had been ruled out.[130] In

97

early March, he said that "now the only course left was armed struggle".[131] On March 7 he indicated that any settlement which might result from the Nkomo–Smith negotiations would be rejected.[132] Machel continued his unwavering support for ZANLA guerillas who were preparing to launch guerilla offensive from Mozambique. The victory of the MPLA in Angola must have reinforced his revolutionary euphoria and his commitment to the armed struggle in Rhodesia. On January 19, 1976 he assured the members of the OAU Liberation Committee meeting in Lourenço Marques that "this is the epoch in which the final liquidation of imperialism from our continent had begun."[133] In early February he called on his countrymen to be on the alert and to join the Rhodesian liberation forces.[134] Machel demonstrated his ultimate commitment to the armed struggle on March 3, when announcing the closure of the border with Rhodesia. The significance of the border closure was that by eliminating all vestiges of normal relations with Rhodesia, Machel geared his country towards its role as a launching ground of the imminent guerilla war. In announcing his decision to close the border, Machel presented it as a fulfilment of "our internationalist duty towards Zimbabwe". However, in addressing his nation, he revealed that the decision was at least partly motivated by domestic considerations. He certainly made use of the occasion to whip up support for his struggling regime and to mobilize his people for the achievement of domestic goals.[135]

The growing regional radicalization was also reflected in the FLP collective attitude and actions. With the MPLA victory in the background, the group dynamic of the African collective patron added a further radicalizing impetus to the Rhodesian conflict. Although deeply divided on the Angolan Civil War, Africa in general, and the FLP in particular, were united in dealing with Rhodesia. Regarding the latter, the FLP were urged on by the OAU Liberation Committee. On January 19, 1976 the committee passed a resolution appealing to the Rhodesian ANC to intensify the armed struggle and calling on OAU members to support the "Zimbabwe struggle".[136] On February 6 the FLP met in Quelimane, Mozambique. At this meeting Machel reported that Mozambique had received Rhodesian guerillas who had been transferred from Zambia and Tanzania, as well as arms from China. He informed his colleagues that the guerilla war had actually been resumed on January 17.[137] The Quelimane meeting was most consequential. It underlined a definite shift of the FLP towards the armed struggle option to the exclusion of a peaceful settlement. This shift did not represent an inherent preference for violence. It was rather the result of the mutually reinforcing impact of a radicalizing regional environment and the apparent faltering of the peaceful option.

Nkomo, aware of the radicalizing tendencies among the FLP, which even his loyal patron could not resist, sought alternative sources of broad African and regional support. Immediately after the beginning of the substantive talks, he flew to Kampala to meet Idi Amin, the current OAU chairman. He apparently tried to convince him not to involve the OAU in the Rhodesian crisis.[138] Nkomo obviously feared that the OAU group dynamic would turn this organization against him and in favour of his rivals in the ANC. On his way back, Nkomo paid a visit to Kenyatta, the moderate African elder statesman.[139] Towards the end of January 1976, he visited Banda of Malawi, while two of his senior officials travelled to Lesotho and Swaziland to report to the governments of these countries on the progress of the talks with Smith.[140] These were largely wasted efforts since these states could hardly legitimate a Rhodesian settlement. The main arena where Nkomo strategy was to succeed or fail was the internal one. The crucial question was whether he would be able to wrest power from Smith through negotiations.

The substantive negotiations between the Rhodesian government and Nkomo's ANC opened on December 15, 1975. They finally collapsed on March 19, 1976. In view of the wide gap in the declared positions of the two sides with regard to the nature of the settlement, it is surprising that they lasted for so long. This gap showed no signs of narrowing down throughout the substantive talks. Smith continued to appear as intransigent as ever. He set the tone in his New Year message making it clear that "unless the agreement guarantees the retention of government in civilized and responsible hands, not short-term, not medium-term, but for all time, then it is unacceptable and I shall have no part in it."[141] On March 7 Smith reaffirmed his postition − "no majority rule in my life time".[142]

In view of this, it is even more surprising that the Nkomo camp radiated an air of optimism almost to the end. On January 4 Nkomo said: "I would not be talking with Mr Smith unless I believed it was worth the effort."[143] On February 17 Nkomo's vice-president told the BBC: "Mr Smith has indicated to us and from our own judgement we still feel that he intends to settle."[144] At about the same time, Nkomo said, at the end of a meeting with Smith's team, that the talks had been "very, very constructive".[145] Following another meeting, a "reliable source" around Nkomo said that there had been a "near break-through".[146] Nkomo's ANC national executive, convened on March 7, applauded the progress which had been achieved and gave the negotiating team "a further mandate to pursue the talks to their logical conclusion".[147] This euphoria was reinforced by an article in the *Zimbabwe Star*, a Nkomo mouthpiece: "There is a happy anticipation among the ANC delegation which suggests that a peaceful settlement of the Rhodesian constitutional problem is in the offing."[148]

It was only about a week before the final breakdown of the talks that the optimism subsided and gave way to a grim realism. On March 10 Smith denied having presented new far-reaching plans which warranted an ANC assessment of a "near breakthrough".[149] On March 11 it was reported that Nkomo had submitted a plan which guaranteed a marginal African majority rule within 12 months.[150] A few days later, Smith responded that if Nkomo didn't change his position on majority rule, there would be no settlement.[151] Nkomo was amazed: "Change what – majority rule? How can we change majority rule and make these talks meaningful?" He sounded despondent and resigned regarding the prospect of a settlement: "If it is hopeless, it is hopeless. I am not going to waste my time."[152] This, he said a day before the twelfth and last meeting between the negotiating teams was due to take place. The fate of the negotiations was sealed before this crucial meeting convened on March 17. On March 18 Nkomo flew to Lusaka to report to his patron. A day later, the breakdown of the talks was officially announced.[153]

In a lengthy statement, Nkomo's ANC revealed the extent of the differences between the two sides.[154] This most interesting document shows that Nkomo went a long way in his effort to secure a settlement. His team did not insist on a one-man-one-vote majority rule, the *sine qua non* of radical African nationalism. They devised a complex three-tiers electoral system which would have given the Africans a bare majority in the first election. However, the gap between this moderate proposal and the position of the Rhodesian government was still too wide to bridge. There were two issues on which the parties could not agree. The main issue was the timing of majority rule. Whereas Nkomo insisted on African parliamentary majority in the first election to be held within 12 months, Smith's team proposed voting qualifications which might have brought about that eventuality in 10–15 years. The secondary issue related to transitional arrangements. Whereas the Nkomo team demanded immediate parity in both government and Parliament the whites agreed only to parity in government. Smith was not even prepared to accept power-sharing on the basis of parity, the half-way point between the opposing goals of black majority rule and white supremacy. What was considered by Smith as "far-reaching proposals involving power-sharing and embodying considerable constitutional advance for the African people"[155] was viewed by Nkomo as grossly inadequate, as "racial and contemptuous".[156]

The length of the talks in view of the unbridgeable gap between them may be attributed to the negotiating tactics of both parties. Instead of tackling the main issue on the agenda, namely the firm commitment to majority rule, during the preliminary stage or at least at the beginning of the substantive talks, they placed it at the bottom of the agenda. This accounts both for the optimism throughout most of the negotiations which related to the less controversial issues and for the sudden, abrupt collapse coinciding with the negotiations over the crucial issues. Nkomo was optimistic that a settlement could be clinched probably because he believed that his offer was very generous. His concessions, which must have been endorsed by Kaunda, proved his sincerity and seriousness in his search for a settlement. This was certainly the best credible settlement the whites could secure in the context of majority rule. The Smith government, however, was not searching for the best majority rule settlement. They were rather seeking a credible failure which would avert majority rule. They must have known that Nkomo could not accept majority rule within 10–15 years. This time span was not incidental. It was related to the 15 years transition agreed upon by Smith at the urging of Vorster in March 1975. Smith, the political acrobat, was obviously playing for the South African gallery. The 15 years transition was his safety net.

Two days after the collapse of the talks, Smith made a surprising call to Britain to get more actively involved in the solution of the crisis.[157] This was a purely tactical move. While appealing to London, Smith was looking over his shoulder in the direction of Pretoria. With the collapse of the talks, he could expect the intensification of the guerilla war, a foretaste of which Rhodesia had already experienced, since January 1976. It was essential for Smith to secure as much support from South Africa as he could. South Africa, however, continued to prefer peaceful white surrender to an escalating guerilla war. Smith could not afford to appear as a warmonger blocking the progress towards regional peace. This would have been too costly in terms of his relations with his patrons. Hence the 15-year transition period, and the appeal to Britain.

While Smith was appealing to Britain in the name of peace, the frustrated Kaunda urged them to intervene militarily and take over the government of their rebel colony.[158] The British government, however, did not intend to respond to either call. They were not unconcerned about Rhodesia. They acknowledged their responsibility towards the colony they had never directly ruled. During the Nkomo–Smith negotiations, they kept in touch with the situation. On his visit to Lusaka in early December 1975, David Ennals, Minister of State in the Foreign and Commonwealth Office, said, after stating that his government would not be involved in negotiations inside Rhodesia: "but of course, we will be involved if they make any progress, and we will sit in the final constitutional conference."[159] In February 1976, as the talks seemed deadlocked, James Callaghan made a conditional offer to intervene.[160] Later in February, the British government sent Lord Greenhill, at the head of a small team, to Salisbury where they met both Nkomo and Smith.[161] These contacts and the final breakdown of the talks suggested caution. Thus, in the wake of the collapse of the negotiations, the British government indicated their willingness to "play a constructive role in any negotiations" provided the following preconditions were accepted: (1) acceptance of majority rule; (2) election leading to majority rule within 18–24 months; (3) agreement that there would be no independence before majority rule; (4) agreement that the negotiations would be short.[162] In other words, they wanted to guarantee the end result before joining the negotiating process. This was a very sensible negotiating tactic.

Because Britain had refused to become actively involved in salvaging the peaceful settlement, Rhodesia was inevitably heading for a guerilla war. After the failure of the Nkomo–Smith talks, there was no viable African political force which would have been prepared to engage in another attempt to negotiate a peaceful settlement. If Smith still seriously contemplated negotiations with "other responsible leaders",[163] he was totally out of touch with reality. He set his country on a course of intensified armed struggle without having secured the backing of his regional patron. Only active South African support could give white Rhodesians any hope of winning the war. Having announced on March 22 the total withdrawal of its forces from Angola, Vorster's government could not possibly contemplate another military intervention. South Africa was, in fact, still very keenly interested in a peaceful settlement in Rhodesia as a means of salvaging their detente.[164] South Africa, however, had not evolved a policy which could bring it about. Vorster, in fact, had no viable Rhodesian policy at all. Consequently, he was pulled by his nose, by his client. Kaunda was absolutely right when he put the blame for the collapse of the Nkomo–Smith talks on Vorster: "South Africa holds the keys to peace or bloodshed in Rhodesia. ... But, Mr Vorster and his colleagues made a big mistake in being very polite with the rebels."[165] Indeed, it was Vorster's incompetence, even more than Smith's intransigence, which tilted the strategic options pendulum towards the military pole. By late

March 1976, with the final withdrawal from Angola and the breakdown of the Rhodesian talks, South Africa's regional policy lay in ruins. Vorster's "crossroad" proved to be a cul-de-sac; his grand design turned into a grand debacle.

In the African camp there was, in the wake of the Nkomo–Smith talks, a large measure of agreement as to the strategic option to be adopted. The possibility of a peaceful settlement in the context of detente caused various African actors to vacillate. The Victoria Falls bridge conference and the Nkomo–Smith talks put an end to the vacillation. With a disappointed Nkomo back on the war trail, the Rhodesian nationalists were unanimous in favouring the armed struggle as a means to achieve their goal. On March 26 Muzorewa gave expression to this outlook: "Now that all peaceful efforts to settle the Rhodesian conflict have failed, we are united in approach."[166]

The FLP, which had suffered from strains in their ranks resulting from divergent positions on the Angolan Civil War and the Nkomo–Smith talks, were able to present a common front. The gap between moderates and militants was rapidly closing. The hard-liners were strengthened in their commitment to armed struggle. Nyerere was "very pleased" that the Nkomo–Smith talks broke down. He still envisaged an ultimate conference, but only after the armed struggle would prove its point.[167] Machel, riding a revolutionary wave, saw an opportunity for the re-enactment of the FRELIMO saga in Rhodesia.[168] For Kaunda, the admission that majority rule must irrevocably be decided on the battle field, was a painful one. It was for him a solution of despair, rather than of hope.[169] Even Khama of Botswana concluded that the liberation movements would have to intensify the armed struggle.[170] This newly discovered unanimity was reflected in the decision of the FLP summit in Lusaka in late March 1976 to support fully an intensified guerilla war against Rhodesia.[171] From Lusaka, December 1974 to Lusaka, March 1976, through Dar es Salaam, July 1975 and Quelimane, February 1976, the FLP moved all the way along the strategy continuum from peace to war.

The shift from a peaceful settlement to armed struggle was also reflected in the realignment of forces within the nationalist movement. This movement was changing and adjusting in preparation for the intensification of the liberation war. The collapse of the Nkomo–Smith talks gave impetus to an ongoing process which had its origins at the very beginnings of detente. The essence of the process was the confirmation of the nationalists' commitment to a militant struggle. This complex process was primarily fuelled by indigenous forces of African nationalism. It was only towards the end that the regional environment became conducive to its culmination. At the end of the process, the nationalist movement, while by no means united, was geared to take its destiny into its own hands. It was a process fraught with suffering and agony. At the end of it, there was a new military organization, the Zimbabwe People's Army (ZIPA), and there emerged a new leader of militant nationalism, Robert Mugabe.

At the beginning of detente, armed struggle was the very antithesis of the African regional patrons' approach. The nationalist leadership was too weak and divided, and the FLP too committed to detente to allow the emergence of a viable militant, violent option. Kaunda, in particular, in suppressing ZANU militants, demonstrated his resolve to deal with those who wanted to wreck his peaceful designs. Under these circumstances, most nationalist leaders joined the regional initiative. Restrictions and suppression brought the bush war to almost a halt by the end of 1975. It did not, however, extinguish the fire of rebellion. It was during this dark period in which they were persecuted by their own African brothers that ZANU militants proved their revolutionary worth. The shock, the dislocation and the confusion did not divert them from their course. The years of ceaseless and persistent efforts in organizing, training, indoctrinating and fighting were paying handsome dividends. The spirit and commitment of the ZANLA military command headed by Tongogara was not broken even under conditions of imprisonment and torture. In an open letter to the Chitepo Commission of Enquiry, dated July 28, 1975, they also issued a call to their comrades in arms:

> We urge our ZANU and ZANLA Comrades and Compatriates [sic] in Zimbabwe to intensify the armed class struggle which in the final analysis will not only liberate Zimbabwe, but will free us from the bondage of Zambian captivity. It is only through relentless struggle based on the mass line and revolutionary practice of ZANU and ZANLA that we can achieve the transformation of the capitalist–racist edifice into a truly socialist state, free from the unbridled terror and barbarism of the white settlers.[172]

The incarcerated leaders maintained contact with ZANLA commanders who remained loyal to them.[173] This loyalty was amply displayed in the Mgagao memorandum addressed in October 1975, to the OAU Liberation Committee and the Tanzanian and Mozambique governments by 43 ZANLA commanders in the main ZANLA training camp in Tanzania.[174] At the grass-roots, thousands of Africans responded to ZANU's recruitment campaign and crossed the border to Mozambique. Many of them joined ZANLA swelling its ranks.

As the peaceful initiative was faltering, particularly in the wake of the Victoria Falls bridge conference, it became increasingly clear that ZANLA would become the dominant actor as soon as the armed struggle would be intensified. Yet, ZANLA was only an army of a liberation movement which was itself, since December 1974, officially part of the united ANC. The relations between ZANLA and the political wing of the nationalist movement had to be sorted out before its forces could be effectively used in the battlefield. The political leaders must have realized that with the armed struggle looming large on the horizon, only leaders who could secure the support and loyalty of the guerilla forces would be relevant. Nkomo could rely, in the event of the failure of his talks with Smith, on his loyal ZIPRA forces. For the rest there was only ZANLA with its considerable military potential.

Thus, when the ANC leadership, headed by Muzorewa, Sithole and Chikerema, activated the ZLC in the aftermath of the Victoria Falls bridge conference, their target was not only, or even mainly, Nkomo. Primarily, the ZLC was to be the instrument through which they sought to secure control over the demoralized and supposedly leaderless ZANLA forces. They wished the latter to form the basis of the Zimbabwe Liberation Army (ZLA) under the political command of the ZLC. They were soon to discover, however, that ZANLA commanders and rank and file were not orphans searching for foster parents. The Mgagao memorandum was principally a denunciation of the leadership of Muzorewa, Sithole and Chikerema by ZANLA commanders. The text of this important document speaks for itself:

> These three have proved to be completely hopeless and ineffective as leaders of the Zimbabwe revolution. Ever since the Unity Accord ... these men have done nothing to promote the struggle for the liberation of Zimbabwe, but on the other hand, they have done everything to hamper the struggle through their power struggle. They have no interest of the revolution or the people at heart, but only their personal interest. They cherish insatiable lust for power.[175]

The behaviour of Sithole, still the formal leader of ZANU, in the wake of Chitepo's assassination earned him particular condemnation.[176]

Thus, the efforts of Muzorewa's ANC, through the ZLC, to assert control over ZANLA, were doomed to failure. ZANLA militants themselves were selecting the political leadership which would lead them in the struggle that lay ahead. In this process of selection, which eventually condemned leaders like Muzorewa, Sithole and Chikerema to political oblivion, Robert Mugabe was emerging as the political leader of ZANLA and ZANU. From the outset, Mugabe shared ZANU militants' hostility towards detente: "We have decided to accept detente purely as a tactic to buy the time we need to organize and intensify the armed struggle."[177] Back in Rhodesia, Mugabe, with like-minded ZANU leaders, preached the gospel of armed struggle and urged young Africans to join the ranks of ZANLA guerillas. On March 25, 1975, after the arrest of Sithole, a group of the original ZANU Central Committee, meeting in Salisbury, decided to send Mugabe and Edgar Tekere out of the country to Mozambique. Their task was to represent ZANU in the forthcoming OAU Council of Ministers in Dar es Salaam and to make contact with the ZANLA guerillas in Mozambique. This latter task was of particular importance because, with the death of Chitepo and the arrest of the ZANU leadership in Zambia, the movement had lost almost its entire external leadership. It was with the task of providing ZANU recruits guidance and leadership, that Mugabe and Tekere were involved after reaching Mozambique on April 5, 1975.[178] In August 1976 Tekere recounted their activity at that period: "Well, there we were then in Mozambique, sent by ZANU, to do a very important job. ... Here, there were these young men and women out in the bush completely. The burden was very heavy for our FRELIMO comrades in Mozambique." Until September 1975, Mugabe and Tekere lived with the guerillas in their camps, experiencing their hardships and providing them with political education. In September 1975 the FRELIMO government, being confused regarding the leadership squabbles in the nationalist movement, restricted Mugabe and Tekere to Quelimane, separating them from their followers.[179]

In a letter smuggled out of the Zambian prison, the imprisoned ZANU leaders noted that Mugabe was "indeed working all out for ZANU in Mozambique and that recruiting is quite high in the camps he had opened out".[180] In August 1975, Edison Zvobgo met members of ZANU's Lusaka District Council, and was told that "the leader of the Party is now Robert Mugabe and it is to him that all lower members of the Party should look." In his report, Zvobgo made a passionate call for the acceptance of Mugabe's leadership.[181] Of greater importance was the endorsement of Mugabe by ZANLA commanders in the Mgagao camp in October 1975 as their spokesman: "We will not accept any direct discussions with any of the three leading members we have described above. We can only talk through Robert Mugabe to them."[182]

In January 1976, Mugabe left Quelimane and went to London where he made public his views on the state of the liberation struggle. He presented himself as a staunch supporter of a ZANU struggle. But alas, the politicians betrayed the revolution: "We have a situation in which the ZANU leadership has abandoned the earlier ZANU stand to wage the war in as militant a way as possible and is now succumbing to the dictates of members who have come from lesser organizations." He praised the efforts of ZANLA people to intensify the armed struggle and called for a new kind of leadership: "The situation as it presents itself is a military one. It requires soldiers, and soldiers must be led by men with military knowledge. It therefore, behoves all of us who lack military knowledge to undergo military training immediately."[183] On January 21, 1976 Mugabe called for the dominance of ZANU and for the disbanding of the ZLC. He also delivered a scathing attack on Kaunda for his treatment of ZANU.[184] The detained leaders in Zambia listening to the programme were highly impressed by Mugabe. On January 24, 1976 Tongogara, Kangai and Gumbo, the leading detainees, sent Mugabe a letter congratulating him on his views, and calling on him to assume the leadership of the struggle. The three DARE leaders attached to their letter a "Declaration formally pledging support to Comrade Mugabe's leadership of the Zimbabwe African National Union (ZANU)" which was distributed in the guerilla camps and party branches.[185] This letter and declaration consummated the process of selection. ZANU would continue to play a dominant role in the liberation struggle under the leadership of Robert Mugabe.

A second development, away from the public eye, which was also indicative of the changing emphasis in the liberation strategy, was the formation of ZIPA as a unified command structure for ZANLA and ZIPRA. This unity was a result of a regional endeavour. The FLP being intimately involved in the attempts to resolve the Rhodesian crisis were frustrated by the divisiveness and power struggles within the ranks of the nationalist political leadership. In the wake of the Victoria Falls bridge conference, Nyerere and Machel were particularly involved in an attempt to resolve the sore problem of disunity among the Rhodesian nationalists. In view of the increasing emphasis on armed struggle, it is hardly surprising that they concentrated their efforts on the unity of the guerilla forces. Nyerere and Machel who were actively involved in the struggle for liberation in Mozambique must have had FRELIMO's experience in the back of their minds. Since Samora Machel, the military commander of FRELIMO's guerillas became, in the wake of the assassination of Mondlane, the president of the movement, FRELIMO demonstrated a remarkable unity coupled with the ability to pursue the armed struggle to a successful conclusion. The smooth and peaceful transition of power in Mozambique following the agreement with Portugal could also be directly attributed to the unity and effectiveness of FRELIMO. At the same time the dangers and horrors inherent in disunity and fraternal strife were unfolding in Angola in front of their very eyes. In Angola, unlike Mozambique, it was the nationalist politicians who occupied a dominant position in the nationalist camp. There is little doubt that Machel and Nyerere were determined to ensure that Rhodesia would follow the Mozambican rather than the Angolan decolonization pattern. They had in mind a united military force which would also become the political vanguard of the liberation. The wishes of the FLP, and Nyerere and Machel in particular, could hardly be ignored. They controlled much of the training facilities and the operational bases as well as the channels of supplies. The presidents were assisted in their endeavours by Colonel Mbita, who dealt with the Rhodesian liberation movements on behalf of the OAU Liberation Committee.

In explaining ZANLA's motives in agreeing to unity, Martin and Johnson quote from an interview with ZANLA commanders: "We knew ZAPU wasn't fighting, that ZAPU had no experience, but we felt they had reason to fight, that they had the desire to liberate the country through armed struggle and that therefore they should be brought in. We all agreed on this."[186] This idealistic interpretation is hardly convincing. This is particularly so because this sudden urge for unity was in contradiction not only with ZANU militants' past, but also current position. Since the unity talks in late 1974, ZANU militants persistently opposed unity. ZAPU and ZIPRA were held in contempt. ZANLA was viewed as the only viable guerilla force and ZANU as the only genuine revolutionary liberation movement. Unity, especially on the basis of parity could only be construed by the ZANU militants as an undesirable dilution of their revolutionary struggle. For their unbending attitude towards unity and detente, ZANU's militant leaders paid dearly after Chitepo's assassination. In the aftermath of the Victoria Falls bridge conference, there were no developments which could justify a change of heart. Edison Zvobgo, reflecting the views of ZANU militants was unequivocal: "ZANU should be preserved at all costs."[187] With Nkomo negotiating with Smith, there was certainly no new attraction in his loyal ZIPRA guerillas.

Thus, a sudden discovery of the virtues of unity is hardly a convincing explanation of the shift in the position of ZANU militants. Their motives are to be sought rather in the realm of revolutionary tactics. Just as they had done in December 1974, ZANU exclusivists in late 1975 bowed to the force of regional circumstances. In December 1974 there was a heavy direct pressure by the FLP. In late 1975, they responded to the wishes of their patrons and to the requisites of salvaging the liberation struggle. Towards the end of 1975, the fortunes of ZANU revolution were at a very low ebb. The guerilla thrust in the north-east came to a standstill, most members of ZANLA high command were in prison, more than a thousand ZANLA guerillas were under virtual detention in Zambia, and the guerillas in Mozambique and Tanzania were restricted. At one point during the renewed regional unity effort, Colonel Mbita, of the OAU Liberation Committee told ZANLA commanders that they would not be allowed to resume the war on their own, and that there had to be a joint guerilla force.[188] Unity was the price for saving the liberation struggle. In an article entitled "Facts about the reality of the Zimbabwe revolution: The necessity to recognize the Provisional Joint Military Command of ZANU and ZAPU", the militants of ZANU went to great lengths explaining the need for unity. While denouncing Nkomo's capitulation to Smith, the militants admitted that unity with ZAPU was essential: "Those of us who have been involved in the Zimbabwe liberation for several years know that the kind of unity that is acceptable to the OAU and the progressive international community at large must combine the genuine ZANU and ZAPU elements. Any other formula will run into a brick wall."[189]

ZAPU's motives in venturing unity with ZANLA forces were altogether different because its existential position was totally different. ZAPU and its military wing, ZIPRA, were not persecuted by the regional patrons. Its military effort had not been hampered because it was virtually non-existent. Its host country, Zambia, was very well disposed towards it. The movement itself, though at that stage not particularly active and dynamic, was well organized, disciplined and loyal to its leader, Joshua Nkomo. There were no signs that ZAPU was under heavy pressure from Kaunda to unite its guerilla force with ZANLA. How then can one account for the fact that ZAPU was engaged in negotiations for a military unity designed to intensify the guerilla war at the same time as it was involved in talks with Smith for a separate peaceful settlement? By the time ZIPA was formed in November 1975, the substantive negotiations had not yet started and the peaceful effort was definitely uppermost in Nkomo's thinking. The involvement of ZIPRA in the formation of ZIPA was certainly not pursued in defiance of Nkomo. It was not only ZIPRA that was loyal to Nkomo; the ZAPU leader most involved in the unity talks was Jason Moyo, Nkomo's right-hand man.[190] In fact, the military merger between ZIPRA and ZANLA was an integral part of ZAPU's post-conference strategy. ZIPA was ZAPU's second insurance policy, its safety net with view to a possible failure of the Nkomo–Smith negotiations. The military merger enabled

ZAPU and Nkomo to preserve their nationalist credibility, despite their collusion with Smith. Only Nkomo, being firmly in control of both political and military wings of his organization, could pursue such a dual strategy.

Thus, following a series of contacts in which ZAPU officials, ZIPRA commanders, ZANU officials, ZANLA commanders, Nyerere, Machel and Colonel Mbita were involved, ZIPA was formed on November 12, 1975, and the composition of its committee agreed upon. The army commander was Rex Nhongo of ZANLA, his deputy being John Dube of ZIPRA. The eight portfolios were equally divided between ZANLA and ZIPRA, each portfolio holder having a deputy from the other movement. Besides the command of the army, ZANLA controlled the two most important portfolios of operations and finance.[191] ZANLA, with its superior, better-trained and more active forces had to concede a near equality simply because they had little choice. Revolutionary tactics were the order of the day. The benefits of unity were immediate: guerillas were moved to Mozambique, supplies were reaching them and in January 1976, the guerila war resumed in earnest with the infiltration of a large number of guerillas from Mozambique to Rhodesia.[192]

The formation of ZIPA was unknown to Muzorewa, Sithole and Chikerema, who persisted in their efforts to make contact with ZANLA guerillas as part of their plan to assert the ZLC leadership over ZANU's military wing. In mid-November, at about the time that ZIPA was formed, Chikerema reached Mozambique at the head of some members of the Military High Command appointed by the ZLC. They had with them a convoy of five large trucks loaded with supplies. They never saw even one guerilla. They were arrested and detained by FRELIMO authorities.[193] Only at the Quelimane meeting in February 1976, Muzorewa, Sithole and Chikerema learnt about the formation of ZIPA, or the "Third Force" as it was also known. Muzorewa was bitter in his response to the FLP: "We cannot understand why a group of individual combatants would be given a hearing on matters concerning the liberation of millions of people whose direct representatives we are." Muzorewa reminded the presidents of the ANC's position: "it is the Party which commands the gun and not the gun, the party." In response, Nyerere gave vent to his frustration regarding the nationalist politicians: "You people seem to think that power comes from the barrel of the mouth instead of the barrel of the gun."[194] The ANC leaders failed to change the FLP decision. As the Rhodesian conflict entered a definite military phase a whole gallery of veteran nationalist leaders was on the way out. The stage and the new cast were ready for the opening of a new act.

CHAPTER FIVE

Rhodesia between Guerilla War and Super-power Diplomacy,

March–September 1976

From the point of view of conflict resolution process the breakdown of the Nkomo–Smith negotiations signified the final closure of a chapter which had opened with the beginning of the southern African detente. It was a failure of a comprehensive effort, initiated and orchestrated by the regional patrons, to effect a peaceful decolonization in Rhodesia. At the root of this failure lay the refusal of the Rhodesian government to abdicate. The ruling, privileged white oligarchy rejected majority rule even under the most favourable conditions. This introverted oligarchy lacked the foresight and the understanding of the dynamic of the unfolding regional changes. Only considerable pressures could have persuaded it to abdicate before having exhausted its resistance potential, and such pressures were not produced in the course of the short-lived detente, either regionally or internally. It is the purpose of this chapter to examine the gradual building up of such pressures. Internally, the failure of detente ushered in an intensifying and escalating guerilla war. Externally, the failure of South Africa to exert effective pressure on Smith precipitated a concerted American diplomatic intervention designed to avert a full-scale war and to set the conflict resolution process again on a peaceful course.

The collapse of the Nkomo–Smith talks gave impetus to the guerilla offensive which had been launched in January 1976. It completed the conversion of the African actors involved to the military option. At the regional level the regional patrons became fully committed to the guerilla war. On April 10, 1976 a Zambian official gave expression to the shift in his government position: "We were committed to the search for a negotiated solution in Rhodesia and we have travelled the road all the way down to Cape Town to honour the commitment. That search has finished and we shall now leave no stone unturned in aiding an armed struggle against Rhodesia."[1] In her search for peace Zambia had reached its red lines. Earlier, in late March, the FLP met in Lusaka to plan the escalation of the armed struggle.[2] The new guerilla strategy was fully endorsed by the OAU summit conference in Mauritius in July 1976.[3] Kaunda carried the message to the Non-Aligned Summit conference, meeting in Colombo in August 1976.

The commitment of Zambia and Mozambique, bordering Rhodesia on the north and the east, was of crucial importance. Their commitment went beyond the realm of declarations. Mozambique, as we have seen, allowed ZIPA forces freedom of operation from January 1976. In early April a high-ranking Zambian delegation, including the Chief of the Army as well as the commanders of the Airforce and the Police, visited Mozambique to coordinate the guerilla strategy. Significantly, the Soviet ambassador in Lusaka also participated in the deliberations.[4] Mozambique did not waver even in the face of escalating Rhodesian retaliations. Following a Rhodesian attack on Mapai at the end of June 1976, the Mozambican Defence Minister reaffirmed his government support for the liberation struggle in Rhodesia.[5] The reaction of the Mozambican government to the devastating Rhodesian attack on the guerilla refugees camp deep inside the country on August 9 was equally determined.[6] The Mozambican army not only rendered support to ZIPA guerillas but also took part in the fighting mainly in firing across the border.[7] Zambia also stood firm behind its declarations. On April 12 it was reported that Kaunda, "determined to show the world that his foreign policy is dictated by principle rather than pragmatism" had agreed to allow the opening of a guerilla front from his territory. Kaunda himself confirmed at the end of May that he would allow the guerillas to open a new front from Zambia.[8] Shortly after, the Rhodesian Defence Minister disclosed that this front had, in fact, been opened.[9] Blaming the Rhodesians for explosions in Lusaka on June 13, Kaunda declared that Zambians were prepared to fight.[10] Soon after, the ruling party's secretary-general threatened to go to war against Rhodesia.[11]

The militant posture of the African regional patrons offered the nationalists new opportunities. The way was paved for the long-awaited guerilla offensive. The main thrust of this offensive originated from Mozambique. It all began in January 1976, when Nkomo and Smith were still negotiating. On January 28 a Rhodesian government spokesman said that the guerillas had renewed their incursions into Rhodesia.[12] According to Rhodesian intelligence sources it started with the infiltration of 90 guerillas to Operation Hurricane zone in the north-east.[13] According to the same source, some 130 guerillas infiltrated the Melsetter area in the east in late February and a third wave of infiltration in the south-east area took place in mid-April.[14]

112

Martin and Johnson, relying on guerilla sources, claim that at the first stage, over 400 guerillas were deployed in the north-east, 150 in the east and 150 in the south.[15] On March 11, a Rhodesian deputy minister estimated that there were up to 1,000 guerillas inside the country.[16] In May the *Guardian* estimated that there were some 900 guerillas inside Rhodesia,[17] while Martin, relying on "reliable sources" in Dar es Salaam, claimed that their numbers were more than 3,000.[18] This figure would seem to be an exaggeration. In early June the Rhodesian Defence Minister said that there were about 1,300 guerillas inside the country.[19] Those inside Rhodesia were only the sharp edge of a fast growing number of guerillas who were undergoing military training in neighbouring countries. In March 1976 a Rhodesian deputy minister put their number at between 4,000 and 5,000.[20] In September Mugabe claimed that he had 15,000 troops in Mozambique.[21] Even if this figure was correct it could not have represented the number of fully-trained guerillas ready for action. To counter the expanding guerilla threat from Mozambique the Rhodesian government launched Operation Thrasher in the east in February 1976, and Operation Repulse in the south-east in April 1976.[22] In early June 1976 the Rhodesian government reported the infiltration of guerillas from Zambia. The report added that some 400 fully-trained guerillas were poised in Zambia ready to strike and that another 600 were heading for the border area.[23] This new front was launched by ZIPRA guerillas on June 5 with an attack on an airstrip in north western Rhodesia.[24] By August the situation on this front was serious enough to warrant the launching of the fourth Tangent operational zone.[25] In early June 1976 a Rhodesian military spokesman also reported guerilla activity in the south-west from bases in Botswana.[26]

While it is difficult to assess accurately the number of guerillas in action or in training, it is absolutely clear that within a few months the guerilla war scene had been dramatically transformed. Whereas at the end of 1975 there were barely a hundred guerillas in the north-east, within six months many hundreds of them had infiltrated along most of Rhodesia's borders with black Africa. This quantitative change was also reflected in the volume and nature of the guerilla war. Having gained the initiative the guerillas began to pursue a more comprehensive and determined strategy. This was aimed not merely at occasional harassment but rather at engulfing the whole of Rhodesia in a guerilla war geared to achieving the nationalist goals through the barrel of the gun. An analysis of the numerous guerilla actions reveals the new multi-faceted strategy. A major target of the guerilla thrust was the disruption of the Rhodesian transport system. After the closure of the Mozambique border the aim was primarily to hit Rhodesia's vital rail and road lifelines to the south.[27] The guerillas also concentrated their effort in disrupting the internal road communication system. This they achieved by laying ambushes and mines on roads in different parts of the country and in particular in the operational zones.[28] Another important target for the guerillas was the European farming sector. The aim was to disrupt agriculture, Rhodesia's main foreign exchange earner, and to scare the white farmers out of their farms.[29] The attacks on farms and farmers were also aimed at breaking the morale of the whites. The explosions in Salisbury in July and the mortar attack on Umtali in August[30] were similarly motivated.

Another thrust of ZANLA strategy was directed at the African collaborating structures.[31] By terrorizing African collaborators the guerillas disrupted the local administration and undermined government control in the African rural areas. This facilitated the guerilla penetration to the African reserves and the consolidation of their control therein. The killing of many African civilians by ZANLA guerillas[32] may have been similarly motivated. This was part of the struggle between the government and the guerillas for the control of the African rural population. For ZANLA guerillas this struggle was vitally important. Following Mao Tse-tung guerilla strategy, the support of the African population, especially in the rural areas, was a precondition for the success of their struggle. ZANLA went to great lengths in indoctrinating this vast human "sea". However, the attitude of the rural masses was determined not only by sympathy for and identification with the nationalist cause, but also by the balance of terror. Seeing that the government used liberally its coercive power to ensure the loyalty and cooperation of the rural population, the ZANLA guerillas reinforced their positive mobilization and educational drive with their own terror campaign.

The guerillas also directly challenged the security forces. In May 1976 they laid an ambush killing three soldiers. According to one report, the guerillas held their own in a fierce battle which lasted two and a half hours.[33] In June 1976 five Rhodesian soldiers were injured in an encounter with a guerilla group.[34] On August 8, guerillas launched a mortar attack on a security forces base killing four soldiers.[35]

While a ZIPA spokesman's claim that there existed "semi-liberated areas in Zimbabwe where the enemy has no control",[36] may have been somewhat exaggerated, the nationalist guerillas had definitely gone a long way. As indicated in September 1976 by a prominent ZANLA leader, ZANLA forces, operating as ZIPA, were implementing a well-defined overall strategy strongly influenced by Mao Tse-tung: "Our strategy has been that of fighting from the countryside encircling the cities."[37]

The intensification of the guerilla war was accompanied by an increasing leadership struggle in the nationalist camp. The transformation of the nationalist struggle from a primarily political to a primarily military one had a definite impact on the process of leadership selection. At one level the struggle for leadership between Nkomo and Muzorewa continued unabated. Muzorewa may have expected that the failure of the Nkomo–Smith negotiations would improve his position. However, he soon learnt that Kaunda's prediction, that in such eventuality Nkomo would become irrelevant, had not come true. In fact, Muzorewa faced, in the aftermath of the Nkomo–Smith talks, the severest challenge to his leadership. He was fighting a battle for political survival under increasingly deteriorating intranationalist and regional circumstances. His main weapon in this struggle was his quest for nationalist unity within the framework of his ANC.

Muzorewa made his first bid soon after the final collapse of the Nkomo–Smith talks. Emerging from the FLP summit meeting, held in Lusaka in late March 1976, he said: "There is a will for a united ANC. There will be a united ANC." He, in fact, said that it had been agreed "to unite for the purpose of fighting the enemy."[38] Repeating his call for unity on April 20,[39] he indicated that this latter presumption was unfounded. On the same occasion Muzorewa put forward his claim against Nkomo and his ANC: "There is no such thing as an 'internal' ANC and an 'external' ANC. There is only one ANC as constituted on 7 December, 1974 under the Zimbabwe Declaration of Unity and recognized by the Organization of African Unity." On May 31, addressing the OAU Liberation Committee he went further back to the formation of his ANC in December 1971. The 1974 Declaration of Unity only "reaffirmed the Unity and sovereignty" of this organization.[40] Realizing, however, that political reality was at least as potent as theoretical, historical claims, he renewed, in early July, his offer to Nkomo to reunite in the ANC.[41]

This offer by Muzorewa was rejected by Nkomo in July 1976, as it had been rejected in March. Back in March Nkomo explained his position: "As far as we are concerned there is unity. The ANC held its congress last year and elected office bearers, that is that."[42] Thus, at the level of political principle and rationalization Nkomo still premised his legitimacy on the sovereignty of the African people residing inside Rhodesia as against a mere agreement between political leaders. At the level of political reality unity still did not suit Nkomo's interests and ambitions. He was well aware that the considerations which had prompted him to break away were as valid as ever. Nkomo's anti-Muzorewa internal strategy was backed up by his military presence. It was not incidental that Jason Moyo, Nkomo's lieutenant, said in April 1976 that the guerilla operations were being carried out by a joint command and that the Muzorewa faction no longer had any loyal guerilla force.[43] Nkomo also reinforced his effort with an intensive international campaign. From early May to early September he visited 21 countries mobilizing support for his cause.[44]

Muzorewa soon realized that the main source of weakness *vis-à-vis* Nkomo, and in general, was his ANC being a purely political organization. Outwardly, Muzorewa tried to cover up his handicap. Thus, when asked to comment on Nkomo's spokesman's assertion that recent guerilla operations had been conducted by a joint ZIPA command, he said: "I don't think it is being honest for any one to say exactly who fired those bullets. What we know is that the forces of Zimbabwe are at work fighting."[45] Addressing a UN committee on behalf of Muzorewa's ANC, Sithole was even less inhibited: "Our freedom fighters are infiltrating into Zimbabwe along a border of 900 miles and they have gone deep inside the country."[46]

Face-saving notwithstanding, Muzorewa and his ANC colleagues were painfully aware of the reality. They knew that unless they regained access to the guerilla forces they were doomed to political oblivion. Their target was the ZANLA element in ZIPA. The choice of this target was dictated by ethnic affinity as well as by elimination; the only other available guerillas were Nkomo's loyal ZIPRA fighters. To make themselves ideologically more attractive to ZANLA militants the ZLC of the ANC adopted in April 1976 a hard-line, anti-American, anti-Imperialist stance.[47] Ideological cosmetics alone could not produce the desired effect. Having been barred, by FRELIMO authorities, from making contact with the ZANLA guerillas, the ANC directed their efforts to the regional patrons who had been behind the formation of ZIPA, or the "third force". In an interview on April 16, on the eve of a ZLC special meeting, Muzorewa gave vent to his deep sense of grievance regarding the attitude of the FLP.[48] On April 24, following the meeting, he sent a strongly-worded memorandum to Nyerere, the FLP chairman. He accused the FLP of taking over the liberation movement which was "a gross violation of the OAU principles of respect for the sovereignty and non-interference in the internal affairs of member-states and liberation movements recognized by it". After going to great lengths to account for all the cases of FLP illegitimate interference he demanded the recognition of ANC as "an independent sovereign liberation movement".[49] Muzorewa also went to Maputo where he had a "violent conversation" with Alberto Chipanda, the Mozambican Defence Minister, regarding the alleged torture and killing of guerillas loyal to him.[50]

Getting no redress from the FLP, Muzorewa's ANC decided to appeal to the OAU Liberation Committee. It had been, indeed, the OAU which had recognized the ANC as the sole Rhodesian liberation movement. Upon his departure to Dar es Salaam at the end of May 1976 to attend the Committee meeting, Muzorewa depicted the "third force" as a tribal organization, warning that its formation could lead to a civil war "worse than Angola".[51] In his address to the committee Muzorewa made a wild claim that more than 90 per cent of the guerillas in the camps were loyal to his ANC and that they were persecuted for that reason. After bitterly attacking the FLP and Colonel Mbita for interfering in the liberation struggle, he requested the OAU to recognize the sovereignty of his ANC, to grant it control over the armed forces and to channel all aid through it.[52] This earned Muzorewa severe criticism from Tanzania's vice-president and from the country's official *Daily News*.[53] The Liberation Committee gave full satisfaction to no one. The FLP failed to secure the recognition of the "third force" as the sole legitimate liberation movement in place of the ANC.[54] Muzorewa could, indeed, be satisfied with the reference to the guerillas as the "fighting cadres of the ANC of Zimbabwe" and with the call for the unity of the nationalist movement.[55] Thus, politically, the ANC still kept its head above the water. At the practical level, however, the committee resolved that the assistance to the liberation struggle would continue to be channelled through it. This was particularly painful to the ANC as it was coupled with an expression of appreciation for the "excellent work" done by Colonel Mbita, one of the main architects of ZIPA.[56] This decision condemned the ANC to continued isolation from the guerillas. It was a compromise which reflected the division between radicals and moderates in the committee.[57] In early July 1976 Muzorewa went to Mauritius to follow up his campaign for unity and leadership at the OAU summit conference. Again he achieved only verbal satisfaction. In essence, the OAU, in resolving to cut off direct funding to the different movements and to channel all aid for the guerilla war through the Liberation Committee and Mozambique, came close to giving full backing to the "third force".[58]

In early September 1976 the FLP, unexpectedly, made a last effort to unite all the nationalist factions. The special meeting which opened in Dar es Salaam on September 5, included the FLP, the top leadership of the different nationalist factions and four ZIPA leaders led by Rex Nhongo.[59] This attempt may have been partly prompted by the massacre of more than 600 black Rhodesians on August 9, in a camp in Mozambique, by Rhodesian troops.[60] As the war was sharply escalating, the quest for unity became again a matter of high priority. The FLP may have also turned again to the political leaders because the unity of the rival military structures and leaderships proved at least as elusive as that of the political factions.[61] They may have hoped that the leaders' visit at the camp might have softened their mutual hostility and resistance to unity. Unity of the political leadership was also of particular importance at a time when Kissinger's Rhodesian initiative was approaching a climax.[62] Four days of meetings behind closed doors failed to produce national unity. In fact they only served to further exacerbate disunity. According to Mugabe the efforts failed because Nkomo had refused to sign a new "unity paper".[63] Nkomo continued to view unity as detrimental to the position of his movement and to his own ambitions. He came to Dar es Salaam to deliver a *coup de grace* to Muzorewa and his ANC, rather than to assist in the search for unity. At the meeting he even objected to the very presence of Muzorewa.[64] Emerging after the collapse of the talks Nkomo declared, rather jubilantly, that the meeting had been the burial ground of the old ANC. He also announced his intention to hold an ANC congress inside Rhodesia in October 1976.[65] This was a clear manifestation of the persisting internal dimension of his overall strategy.

Nkomo's assessment of the prospect of the "old ANC" was accurate. The Dar es Salaam meeting in failing to achieve unity, sealed the fate of those who had no guerilla forces under their command. These were pushed to the periphery of the increasingly militant nationalist politics. Aware of the fate awaiting Muzorewa's ANC, Ndabaningi Sithole, the chairman of the ZLC, announced that he had reformed the old ZANU and was taking it out of the ANC.[66] Sithole must have hoped, through his reformed ZANU, to attract old loyalties. He was, however, at least as objectionable to ZANU militants as was Muzorewa.

The Dar es Salaam unity talks were, from an FLP perspective, totally counter-productive. Not only did they fail to forge unity between the political leaders and between the political and military wings of the nationalist movement, but also the process of disintegration of ZIPA, on which so many hopes had been pinned, was completed. After the talks Mugabe said plainly that unity was not essential to the pursuit of liberation "because it is ZIPA which is doing the fighting anyway". What he really meant was that the ZANLA element of ZIPA were carrying the burden of the guerilla war. Nkomo was more forthright, saying that black Rhodesians had to choose between ZAPU and ZANU. He claimed that his ANC – ZAPU – was the only liberation movement officially recognized by the OAU.[67] The rather early divorce resulted from the fact that the marriage had been in the first place one of convenience. In fact the cohabitation was extremely inconvenient to both parties.

Mugabe, who was emerging as the leader of ZANU and the ZANLA guerillas, was a staunch supporter of ZANU's independence. The functioning of ZIPA certainly did not inspire him and his colleagues to stake the future of the liberation struggle on unity. The cohabitation only served to exacerbate old animosities and suspicions between the two components of ZIPA. ZIPRA guerillas were clearly loyal to Nkomo who was still involved, after the beginning of the new guerilla offensive in early 1976, in "sell-out" negotiations with Smith. ZANLA leaders claimed that ZIPRA guerillas made little contribution to the guerilla effort. Furthermore, in training camps in Tanzania there were bloody clashes between ZANLA and ZIPRA recruits in which many of the latter were killed.[68]

Mugabe made his views clear in a memorandum which he sent to ZANLA guerillas on April 15, 1976 and signed as Secretary General of ZANU. The opening sentence was revealing: "Dear Comrades, Congratulations! ZANU is once again in its full revolutionary stride." He expressed his deep objection to Nkomo and "his counter-revolutionary approach" saying of ZIPA: "There is therefore, a joint military front between ZANU and ZAPU but only at the fighting level and no other."[69] In fact, as we have seen, there was hardly that either. The U.S. Congressman, Solarz, who met Mugabe at that time was impressed by his single-mindedness on this issue: "He was very candid and it was clear there had been divisions among his people. But he said again and again that he put the integrity of ZANU above everything else."[70] Indeed during 1976 Mugabe emerged as the champion and reorganizer of ZANU. His task was not easy. As late as August 1976 Edgar Tekere said: "ZANU has more than recovered, but only in the military sense ... ZANU has not yet recovered administratively as a political party ... we indeed were politically dead ..."[71] In a meeting with Machel in late August 1976 Mugabe presented himself as Secretary General of ZANU. Martin and Johnson describe it as the first public re-emergence of ZANU.[72] Mugabe was the focus around which a new ZANU political leadership crystallized. In the Dar es Salaam unity summit in early September 1976, the ZIPA/ZANLA commanders submitted the following list of acceptable political leaders to the FLP: Robert Mugabe, Edgar Tekere, Enos Nkala, Maurice Nyagumbo, Muzenda, Hamadziripi, Mudzi, Tongogara, Kangai, Gumbo and Chrispen Mandizvidza. At that meeting Nkomo refused to sign a document on which the members of the ZIPA delegation were signed, claiming that their leader, Mugabe, must sign on their behalf.[73] Indeed, by then, as ZANU/ZANLA were being reunited, ZIPA was becoming synonymous with ZANLA. The revived *Zimbabwe News*, ZANU's organ, wrote that "after many months of hammering and battering by the enemies of the Zimbabwe's Revolution, ZANU became of its own again in September 1976."[74]

Nkomo and his loyal political organization also never saw ZIPA or the "third force" as a vehicle for the attainment of nationalist unity, political or military. As ZIPA was becoming increasingly predominantly ZANLA in composition, Nkomo must have feared that it would be used by ZANU to dominate radical nationalist politics. Thus in its March/April 1976 edition Nkomo's organ came out strongly against the "third force".[75] Clearly Nkomo feared that the externally-based "third force", if espoused by the FLP, would pose a serious challenge to his internally-oriented strategy. At the OAU conference in early July 1976, Nkomo joined Muzorewa in denouncing the "third force" and in charging that it had been imposed on the nationalists by the neighbouring states. Both strongly opposed the proposals to cut off all direct funding to the different movements and to channel all aid through the OAU Liberation Committee and Mozambique. They argued that it meant that the "third force" would become the sole recipient of such aid.[76] Nkomo's strong objections to the channelling of all aid to the military organization of which his loyal guerillas were still formally part were hardly surprising. By early September almost all ZIPRA guerillas and members of the joint military command of ZIPA had left Mozambique and returned to their more solid regional base in Zambia.[77] Thus, when Nkomo said in Dar es Salaam in September that black Rhodesians had to choose between ZANU and ZAPU, he reflected the reality. By the end of September ZANU and ZAPU (rather than ANC factions) featured prominently in press reports.[78] On September 26 the *Observer* (London) featured an article on the two nationalist movements: "ZAPU and ZANU".[79]

Thus, by the time the U.S. Rhodesian initiative reached a climax in September 1976 the nationalist movement was badly divided, politically and militarily. However, the military and political revival of ZANU/ZANLA was sufficient to introduce a new nationalist military input which began radically to change the white–black power equation and the nature and dynamic of the Rhodesian conflict as a whole.

The expansion and intensification of the guerilla war in 1976 drastically changed the reality of life in Rhodesia. For the 270,000 whites a new era had dawned. The success story of UDI was coming to an end at the beginning of its second decade. The twin blessings of security and prosperity, which had enabled the whites to pursue their somewhat unrealistically comfortable colonial way of life, were being seriously undermined.

The most dramatic change was in the security situation. From the beginning of detente the threat was diplomatic rather than military. From early 1976, when the threat of detente subsided, white Rhodesians began to experience the foretaste of a fully-fledged guerilla war. By August 1976, with the launching of the fourth Tangent operational zone on the Zambian border, Rhodesia was facing a guerilla threat along much of its perimeter. For the small Rhodesian white community, the rising number of security forces casualties was becoming alarming. The formation of the War Widows Association in June 1976 "to extend companionship and help the widows of men killed in the country's anti-terrorist operations"[80] reflected a grim reality. White civilians, too, soon became victims of guerilla attacks on farms and road traffic. In one day, June 7, 1976, the death of five whites – including a mother and her two children – was announced.[81] This was a heightened instance of what was becoming a new reality for white Rhodesians.[82]

The almost daily human toll, military and civilian, introduced an air of gloom and depression to the previously carefree and confident white Rhodesia. A white woman gave expression to this new mood in May 1976: "Things seem to be getting worse and worse, and the awful thing about it is that we don't appear to be achieving the military breakthrough that we all want."[83] Because of the deteriorating security situation, new safety measures were introduced which restricted the freedom of movement of whites in many areas.[84] The expansion of the war imposed new and heavy demands on the very limited white manpower.[85] According to the *Rhodesian Herald*, for many young men it meant "a full-time commitment to fighting the war".[86]

The guerilla war in 1976 was beginning to take an economic toll as well. The escalating war imposed heavier financial burdens on the government. On April 15, the Finance Minister was forced to introduce an interim budget designed to raise an additional R 60 million to meet the rising cost of the war effort.[87] The budget presented on July 15, for 1976/77 included an increase of 40 per cent and 23 per cent in the defence and police vote respectively.[88] The additional financial burden had to be shouldered by an economy which had begun to falter. An official economic survey for 1975, published in early May 1976, revealed a definite economic decline.[89] The mildly optimistic forecast of the survey for 1976 failed to materialize. 1976 was also the worst year for tourism – an important foreign exchange earner since UDI.[90]

The acceleration of the economic decline in 1976 was related to the expansion and intensification of the guerilla war. The tourism industry was certainly a direct victim of the war. The over-exploitation of white manpower for military purposes also began to have an adverse effect on the economy. Many skilled men served in the army for increasingly long periods instead of fulfilling their vital economic roles. In the Associated Chamber of Commerce Congress in May 1976 delegates complained about dislocations resulting from the military call-ups of white personnel.[91] A big nickel producer said that he was more worried about the shortage of skilled manpower than about any other difficulties.[92] Another war-related difficulty was in the sphere of transport. While the Rhodesian government averted a collapse of its transport system by hastily completing the Rutenga line linking Rhodesia to the Transvaal railway system, the closure of the Mozambique border in March 1976 was having an impact on the flow of goods in and out of the country. Shortage of wagons (expropriated by Mozambique) and congested South African railway system and harbours caused hardships to Rhodesian producers and businessmen.[93]

The deteriorating security and economic situations were also reflected in the figures of white emigration. In 1976 14,000 whites left Rhodesia. For the first time since UDI there was a net loss of whites (5,914). Official statistics showed that the loss was not only quantitative but also qualitative. Almost half of those leaving were in their twenties and thirties, many being highly skilled.[94] The "chicken-run" had begun.

While the deteriorating security and economic situations were having an adverse effect on the quality of life of many white Rhodesians, the external circumstances were no brighter. The FLP were committed to the military overthrow of the Rhodesian regime while Rhodesia's regional patron was not in the least inclined to come to its rescue. Furthermore, Kissinger was roaming around Africa peddling Callaghan's formula of majority rule within two years. One might have expected that the ominous signs on the domestic and external fronts would have shaken the Rhodesian government into re-evaluating its positions and working out an appropriate positive response. This, however, did not occur.

There were critical voices on the left. The dominant theme of the RP congress at the end of May was the failure of the government to produce a viable political initiative to support its military effort.[95] Yet, the positive response of the party to the deepening Rhodesian crisis was grossly unrealistic and inadequate. In late April 1976, Tim Gibbs, the party president, said that Kissinger was out of touch with reality because he thought in terms of majority rule within two years.[96] The party's congress demands amounted to the scrapping of discriminatory legislation and a return to a common roll based on a qualified franchise.[97] So much for the foresight and political innovation of white Rhodesian liberals.

The opposition parties to the left of the government had little impact on decision making in Rhodesia, thus their views are of somewhat academic interest. Neither did Smith have to take seriously his noisy critics from the marginal far-right. He did, however, have to contend with the right-wing hard-liners within his own party. These were well represented in the RF parliamentary caucus, mainly on the back bench, and their leader was Des Frost the party chairman. The hard-liners were still committed to provincialization, or confederation, the Rhodesian version of separate development, with Shona, Ndebele and white homelands under the control of a central government.[98] The supporters of this policy, by no means discouraged by their defeat in the previous party congress in 1975, were preparing to try again in September 1976.[99] On July 20, the prospects of confederation were discussed at a discreet dinner party attended by some 20 MPs, including the party chairman. According to one report (which was subsequently denied), the group also plotted the replacement of Smith.[100] At the party congress in September, Des Frost urged white Rhodesians not to be brainwashed into believing that black majority rule was inevitable and that all was lost. He argued that provincialization, which was the party's declared policy, would enable Rhodesians of all ethnic groups to control their own areas and preserve their own identities, cultures, traditions and way of life.[101] It was indicative of the unreal world in which they were living that these apostles of Rhodesian apartheid believed that the implementation of this policy would guarantee the support of mother apartheid.[102] It was equally amazing that they believed that this policy, so late in the day, would be their salvation. In Frost's own words: "We have the men of vision and ability; we have the people. We have Rhodesia, and with God's guidance we can win through."[103] It was opponents such as these that Smith had to take into account in shaping his policy.

Smith himself had hardly become an apostle of appeasement. At the end of April 1976 he said that neither he nor his colleagues were in the mood for appeasement.[104] In June he rejected the idea of majority rule out of hand: "We don't believe we should have majority rule based on colour in Rhodesia, not at any time."[105] In late August, addressing a local audience, Smith vowed not to deviate from "the most sacred and fundamental principle of the party – the retention of government in responsible hands".[106] Speaking in an NBC programme Smith stated unequivocally his objection to the extension of the vote, claiming that one-man-one-vote would lead to chaos. He repeated the cliché that Rhodesia already had majority rule, one based on qualified franchise.[107] Clearly, the mounting economic and guerilla war pressure had not produced a radical change in the political thinking of the Rhodesian government and of most white Rhodesians. Black majority rule was as absent as ever from their political agenda. A government which had viewed Nkomo's moderate compromising position as extreme had a great deal of progress to make, ideologically and psychologically, before it could engage in meaningful negotiations for a settlement.

Having excluded the option of the negotiating table, the battle-field was the only arena in which the white regime intended to meet the nationalist challenge. Indeed, in May 1976 Smith maintained that military superiority was essential for the securing of an acceptable political solution.[108] In public, Rhodesian leaders expressed confidence that military superiority was attainable. In early May Lieutenant-General Walls said that "a fairly quick success" in the war could be achieved, adding arrogantly that he would not bet "a rouble, or even a kopek" on the guerillas' chances.[109] Equally confident, and arrogant, was Defence and Foreign Minister van der Byl, answering a question on the ability of the Rhodesian army to wipe out the guerillas inside Rhodesia: "It is just a matter of hunting them down and getting your hands on them."[110] By August, when the guerilla attacks had increased considerably, he still expressed confidence that the guerilla threat could be checked for quite a long time.[111] In early August, Smith himself, while acknowledging some setbacks, also projected confidence.[112] It may be argued that these expressions of confidence and optimism were purely for morale-boosting purposes, and that they did not truly reflect the views of the government. However, the total rejection of political accommodation with the nationalists is incomprehensible, unless the white leadership believed that the guerilla offensive could be at least contained.

The leaders of white Rhodesia knew that military superiority could not be taken for granted. The intensifying guerilla war required the maximization of the regime's military potential. Thus military service was extended for conscripts as well as for those called up for service in the territorial units. The Africans also shouldered the heavier military burden with the foundation of a third infantry batallion composed of volunteers. The army laid special emphasis on special, elite counter-insurgency units. The three Special Air Service (SAS), all white, commando units and the equally famous racially mixed Selous Scouts, whose numbers increased considerably, were playing an increasingly important role in the counter-insurgency effort.[113] The anti-guerilla campaign involved a variety of defensive measures, including mine-sweeping and convoy systems to protect military and civilian vehicles in operational areas, and improvement of the defence capability of isolated farms. In the African areas the government sped up the resettlement of Africans in protected villages. By 1976 some 250,000 rural Africans were herded in such villages.[114] It was a policy designed to improve the control over the native population and isolate them from the guerillas, thus making it more difficult for the latter to survive in the countryside.

Counter-insurgency also involved an offensive thrust. This included an effort to track guerilla groups, to engage and eliminate them. The Selous Scouts used ingenious pseudo-gang tactics to locate and destroy guerilla groups, with devastating effect.[115] White Rhodesians could derive some satisfaction from the dramatic rise in guerilla casualties.[116] However, from a strictly military point of view, there was no cause for celebration. Except for the activity of the Selous Scouts, whose scope of operation had definite limits in a vast country infested with guerillas, the army operated inside Rhodesia mainly on a reactive basis leaving the initiative to the guerillas. In such a war the army could not make full use of its air and ground superiority. There was little point in chasing the guerillas operating inside Rhodesia, when thousands of them were being trained and infiltrated mainly through Mozambique. In June 1976, following an incident in which a white mother and her two daughters were killed, a municipal councillor from the border town of Chipinga gave vent to his frustration regarding the passive, reactive nature of the military strategy.[117] On July 2 General Walls found it necessary to respond to the "unfounded, destructive criticism of the army" saying that wherever there was a need for it the army crossed the borders.[118]

Carrying the war into neighbouring countries which served as launching pads for the guerillas had clear advantages for the Rhodesians. One manifestation of this strategy was "hot pursuit". On June 6 van der Byl spelled out the government's position regarding that practice: "It's a part of international law, the doctrine of hot pursuit. ... And this is something we have always believed in in Rhodesia, and we have always practised it and will continue to practise it because it is a normal practice and an effective way of dealing with these people who come across the border and then go back to take shelter under FRELIMO."[119] Later in June Smith himself warned Zambia and Mozambique that they would lay themselves open to hot pursuits if they encouraged guerillas to operate from their territory.[120] However, the effectiveness of strict hot pursuit was very limited because of its reactive nature and because it involved mostly small guerilla groups.

Of far greater military potential were the pre-emptive operations across the border against staging posts, transit camps, arms and ammunition depots and training bases of the guerillas. Such operations could enable Rhodesian security forces to seize the initiative and maximize their advantages over the guerillas' army. They could choose the target, the time and the tactic, inflicting heavy blows and disrupting the implementation of the guerillas' strategic plans. Ron Reid Daly recalled his views on this issue in June 1976: "My personal report was that the current overall strategy being employed against the terrorists [internal operations] seemed akin to trying to empty a bath with a small can, while both taps were turned on full. 'Surely' I argued, 'it must be better to turn off the taps [through operations in Mozambique] while still using the bucket to bail'."[121] Such small-scale operations had been in fact carried out by the Selous Scouts since January 1976.[122] In May a mini-flying column of the Scouts raided ZANLA camps around the town of Chigamane some 180 kilometres inside Mozambique.[123]

These small-scale operations, which had little impact on the guerilla war, were not made public by either side. On June 26 a Selous Scouts flying column raided a ZANLA transit camp in the town of Mapai in Gaza Province, some 90 kilometres from the Rhodesian border.[124] This time the Mozambican Ministry of National Defence issued a special communique disclosing the details of the attack.[125] Significantly the Rhodesian government repeatedly denied having raided Mapai.[126] These denials highlighted the dilemma the Rhodesian government was facing with regard to pre-emptive strikes across the border. On the one hand, militarily, as the guerilla war escalated, such operations became essential. In August Smith himself put forward this argument.[127] He also had to take into account the mood of his white constituency. Spectacular raids across the border could boost sagging morale and deflect criticism of the government handling of the military situation.[128] On the other hand the government had to consider the potentially negative implications of such escalation of the war. Speaking in August, both van der Byl and Smith emphasized the danger of further alienating world opinion.[129] This consideration was of particular importance at a time when Kissinger was taking a keen interest in the Rhodesian crisis. Smith had also to take into account his regional patron's reaction. South Africa having been bent on a political solution could hardly have been expected to be indifferent to a transformation of an internal military confrontation into a regional conflagration.[130]

There was also the danger that a regional military escalation would precipitate an Angola-type, or an OAU, military intervention.[131]

Clearly, by early July 1976 the Rhodesian government had not solved this dilemma. They opted for a compromise – launching pre-emptive raids into Mozambique while denying responsibility for them. This compromise could not have a considerable impact on the course of the war because to remain anonymous the raids had to be limited in scale. Furthermore, with a cloud of secrecy around them such operations could hardly produce the desired effect on the morale and confidence of the whites. This compromise did not last long. The deteriorating security situation and increasing domestic pressures were pushing the government into adopting a more decisive stand. By late July preference was being given to military and domestic considerations. On August 10, 1976 Defence Headquarters in Salisbury announced: "Following an increased tempo of terrorist attacks in the eastern border operational area, in which the Mozambique armed forces are known to have participated, Rhodesian security forces became involved in hot-pursuit operations on Sunday, August 8th against terrorists who were based and supplied from Mozambique." The communique stated that more than 300 guerillas and 30 Mozambican troops were killed.[132] The reference to hot pursuit was more an indication of the government sensitivities and anxieties than a reflection of the reality. The raid on the Nyadzonia base on the Pungwe river deep inside Mozambique was hardly a hot pursuit. It was a large-scale pre-emptive strike. The plan for the operation was submitted to General Walls by the Selous Scouts on July 23, and was approved, though not without hesitation, by the Special Operations Committee a few days later. According to a ZANLA report captured subsequently by the Scouts the casualty list included 639 men, 21 women and 15 children dead.[133] The Nyadzonia raid was definitely a turning point in the guerilla war. The Rhodesians had crossed the Rubicon signalling their determination to give preference to military and domestic considerations. This successful raid gave them greater confidence that the guerilla threat could be at least contained. It also boosted the morale of the whites.

Although the military effort was perceived as vital it was by no means the only sphere in which the government was labouring in its attempt to guarantee the survival of the regime. The military command itself impressed on Smith that the guerilla challenge could by no means be successfully met only on the battlefield.[134] When Kissinger entered the arena, Rhodesia could ignore the avenue of political solution only at its own peril. In May Smith himself said: "We have embarked on this new military offensive in order to re-establish our military superiority and at the same time we have embarked upon a political initiative."[135]

At the diplomatic level it had always been Smith's tactics to generate activity and create the impression that some progress was being made. Thus in May 1976 he told a British journalist that he was in contact with "a number of foreign governments" in a fresh effort to achieve a negotiated settlement.[136] In June he called on the British government to send to Rhodesia a "commission of wise men" to work out a political settlement.[137] Adjusting himself to the American taste he argued that it was time for the U.S., as the leader of the free world, to play a greater role in southern Africa in order to prevent the region from falling into communist hands.[138] Smith and his government knew, however, that the days when mere diplomatic platitudes could get their country out of trouble were long gone. At a time when majority rule in two years was the formula adopted by the British and the Americans, they had to offer a viable alternative if they were to get a hearing at all. It was a historical irony that Smith assumed the role of an apostle of change. Smith's vision of change did not include, however, the accommodation of the nationalists' aspirations. It rested on the naive and fallacious assumption that there was a substantial alternative African constituency and a viable alternative African leadership which could be enticed and co-opted into a system of effective white domination under the guise of power-sharing.

This then was the worn-out concept of internal settlement which was once more dusted down and taken off the bare shelves of the Rhodesian library of political ideas. It was the gravity of the situation which shifted it from the realm of threats to the realm of implementation. On March 20, 1976, with the collapse of his talks with Nkomo, Smith restated his preference for an internal settlement.[139] On April 28 four Africans were sworn as ministers. The ministers were prominent chiefs who sat in the Rhodesian Senate.[140] This was not coincidental as the chiefs were the core of Smith's alternative. He appeared still to believe in the viability of this source of leadership: "It is well known that chiefs are the traditional leaders of the African people – leaders in every sphere."[141] Recognizing that there were modernized Africans as well, Smith considered it desirable "to bring Africans other than chiefs".[142] The fact that the three representatives of the non-traditional sector were appointed deputy-ministers was indicative of the government's perception of the relative weight of tradition and modernity in African society. Smith expected that this marginal co-optation would convince the world that the majority of Africans supported his government.[143] A white minister expressed the belief that the inclusion of Africans in the government would go a long way towards meeting "the aspirations of the country's responsible black citizens".[144] These were clearly manifestations of self-delusion. There was one senior civil servant who was candid as well as apologetic about this "bold initiative": "It's all very well for outsiders to say this is window dressing. For us, though, it is a significant step forward."[145] This was certainly true. As late as September 1976, a short while before Kissinger's initiative reached its climax, Smith was still thinking in terms of co-opting more Africans to his government provided they were "the right sort of Black people".[146]

A second major thrust of the government's domestic initiative was in the sphere of racial discrimination. As late as September 1976 Smith viewed petty racial discrimination as a major stumbling block on the way to a viable internal settlement.[147] Earlier, in April 1976 Smith received the report of the Quenet commission, which had been appointed in 1975 to investigate racial discrimination. The content of the report remained secret until June 14, while Smith had been studying it.[148] Smith described the report as "balanced and reasonable",[149] whereas Des Frost, reflecting the view of the RF right wing, claimed that many of its recommendations were contrary to the party principles.[150] Summing up the debate on the report in Parliament on July 23, Smith made a noble appeal against racism. With the same breath he informed Parliament of the government's opposition to three major recommendations: the opening of white lands to African farmers; the return to a common voters' roll; and giving the courts the authority to decide whether any law contravened the declaration of rights.[151]

Clearly, the response of the Rhodesian government to the deteriorating security situation resulting from the escalating guerilla war, was grossly inadequate even in terms of their own political preferences. They must have believed that the guerilla war was at least containable and that they had sufficient time and manoeuvring space to implement an internal settlement which would preserve both white privileges and power.

From the internal perspective of the Rhodesian crisis in the wake of the failure of the Nkomo–Smith negotiations, the further intensification of the guerilla war seemed the only realistic scenario. However, the withdrawal of the regional patrons from active pursuit of a peaceful solution and the escalation of the guerilla war attracted new actors to the Rhodesian stage. In the wake of the failure of the Nkomo–Smith negotiations the Rhodesian crisis attracted, for the first time, active super-power involvement.

If Smith was serious about inviting the British government, in the aftermath of his talks with Nkomo, to assume an active role in the resolution of the Rhodesian constitutional dispute, he could not have liked their response. In a statement in the Commons in March 1976 the prime minister, James Callaghan, put forward four conditions for Britain's participation: (1) acceptance of the principle of majority rule; (2) the holding of an election for majority rule in 18–24 months; (3) agreement that there would be no independence before majority rule; (4) agreement that negotiations would not be long.[152] On this basis Smith could easily have settled with Nkomo without British meddling. It was hardly surprising that Smith rejected these conditions out of hand claiming that Callaghan "did not offer any hope of making real progress towards the constitutional settlement which we all desire."[153] Britain, as before, had no means to compel Smith to accept their proposals. Responding to a call by Kaunda for direct intervention, the British government restated its opposition to coercing white Rhodesia by military means. The British contribution was restricted to formulating the terms for a settlement which served as a basis for the diplomatic offensive launched by Henry Kissinger. The British proposals needed for their implementation a more powerful and determined agent.

Kissinger's Rhodesian diplomatic offensive followed, indeed resulted from, his Angolan failure. The collapse of the Caetano regime in Portugal, and the subsequent disintegration of the Portuguese colonial empire, flew in the face of U.S. southern African policy. The famous "tar baby" option, for which Kissinger was responsible and which was premised on the stability and durability of the white regimes in southern Africa, served as a basis for a policy which regarded the white citadel as a regional mini-power protecting and promoting American and Western interests in the region.[154] The liberation of Angola and Mozambique not only proved the flimsiness of the premise and the futility of the policy; it also posed new threats to the U.S. position in the whole region. The overriding concern of Kissinger's global policy was still the containment of the Soviets. Yet, in southern Africa, in the wake of the Portuguese colonial abdication, the Americans were clearly losing ground to the Soviets. In Mozambique, Marxist FRELIMO was the inheritor of the colonial state. In Angola, Marxist MPLA, a Soviet protégé, was a strong contender for the colonial spoils. The spectre of a domino scenario for the rest of southern Africa was real. This danger had to be averted. The American initial response to this challenge was almost instinctive. They sought to contain the Soviets through covert military assistance to the anti-MPLA liberation movements and through the encouragement of regional support for them.[155]

The American administration, however, underestimated the

intensity of public aversion for far-away military adventures – an aversion which was mirrored, if not magnified, in Congress. Given such a prevailing mood, a limited covert assistance to local proxies was too reminiscent of the modest beginnings of U.S. involvement in Vietnam. The administration also misjudged the balance of power between the White House and Capitol Hill in the post-Vietnam and post-Watergate era. A crippled presidency, particularly with Ford as a non-elected president, could not force such a controversial policy on a determined and assertive Congress.[156] Ford and Kissinger's urgings and assertions that vital American interests were involved were to no avail. By December 1975, a month after Angola became independent and when the civil war was approaching its peak, the Congress refused to allocate any funds for covert assistance to the pro-Western movements.[157] This signalled the total collapse of the U.S. Angolan policy. The American involvement, coupled with South Africa's intervention, only served to precipitate and legitimize the massive Soviet–Cuban intervention which installed the MPLA in power. U.S. credibility suffered a heavy blow while the Soviets enhanced their prestige as dependable allies of the cause of African liberation. They could be expected to continue to ride the wave of liberation on the way to Rhodesia, Namibia and eventually to the ultimate prize – South Africa.

This was a bleak prospect the U.S. could not have allowed to materialize. Kissinger, at the helm of U.S. global policy making, was not the man to throw in the towel. The question was how to check or divert what seemed to be a wave of history. U.S. policy in Angola had been reactive, manipulative and unimaginative. In the face of changes of historical magnitude its policy had lacked both insight and vision. It had been a crude application of the force against force recipe. This recipe produced a most distasteful Angolan dish. Clearly a new southern African strategy had to be formulated if the U.S. was to take part in reshaping the region. Elements of the traditional reactive containment strategy persisted. Asked on May 2, 1976 about the possibility of a large-scale Cuban intervention in Rhodesia, President Ford said: "We have diplomatic, we have economic and we have military options and whatever they do we will exercise the necessary option to make sure that they are not successful."[158] Yet, a more imaginative policy designed to recover the losses incurred in Angola had already been launched.

An alternative viable policy had to rest on a broader view of the historical process and on a deeper understanding of the regional political forces and trends. Previously, Kissinger, the architect of the new policy, had shown little sympathy for the African cause. When, during his visit to Washington in April 1975, Kaunda called on the U.S. to desist from assisting the minority white regimes and to lend support to the cause of freedom and justice, Kissinger was said to be furious.[159] In the aftermath of Angola Kissinger realized that the forces of freedom and justice were the forces of the future and that they were the forerunners of Soviet influence. The direct Soviet involvement in Rhodesia at that time was minimal. They supported ZAPU, their Rhodesian protégé, the lesser of the two guerilla movements. However, through their large-scale intervention in Angola, the Soviets became powerful absentee actors on the Rhodesian stage. Their potential, rather than actual, involvement was the major factor which precipitated the formulation of a new U.S. southern African policy, focusing on Rhodesia. The goal of the new policy remained the same as before: arresting Soviet expansion and influence in that region. The strategy, however, changed radically. In Angola the Soviets proved again that they excelled in and thrived on regional conflicts. As in the Middle East after the 1973 war, Kissinger sought to tilt the regional super-power balance in America's favour by playing the peace-maker. He would fight the fire not with fire but rather with water. He would do that by harnessing the liberation energy and forces and utilize them for the enhancement of U.S. influence in southern Africa. He would do that by facilitating the attainment of the liberation goals through a peaceful process of conflict resolution under U.S. auspices. As in the Middle East Kissinger would exploit the only advantage which the U.S. had over the Soviets, namely accessibility to both sides of the conflict equation.

This was the background for Kissinger's Rhodesian, or rather southern African, diplomatic initiative which was launched in April 1976. Significantly, on the eve of his first grand African tour Kissinger met Anthony Crosland, the new British Foreign Secretary.[160] This was indicative of his intention to supplement, rather than supplant, the British in their decolonizing responsibility. It gave Kissinger a convenient umbrella of international legitimacy, an insurance against accusations of American meddling in a regional conflict for the pursuit of its narrow national interests. It was in Lusaka that Kissinger unfolded the new American southern African policy. In his "message of commitment and cooperation" on April 27, he gave a clear verbal expression to the radical shift in U.S. policy. He opened by subtly addressing the issue of Soviet intervention. While calling for common action to achieve "the great goals of national independence, economic development and racial justice" he emphasized that "Africa's destiny must remain in Africa's hands." He assured Africa that the U.S. did not wish to establish a pro-American bloc or to interfere in intra-African conflicts. He added, however, that "neither should any country pursue hegemonial aspirations or block policies." The main thrust of his speech was a ten-point plan designed to expedite the achievement of majority rule in Rhodesia. The first point emphasized that the tour represented an Anglo-American, rather than a strictly American, initiative: "The U.S. declares its support in the strongest terms for the proposals made on March 22, by the British that independence must be preceded by majority rule achieved within two years." Most of the other points gave expression to American commitment to put pressure on the Rhodesian government and to offer material help to African countries which suffered as a result of the struggle against Rhodesia. Kissinger also offered a programme of economic, technical and educational assistance to an independent Zimbabwe. To the whites he offered civil rights under majority rule. He also addressed himself to the other outstanding southern African issues in the African agenda, namely Namibia and South Africa.[161]

Kissinger was well aware that his African tour was only a first hesitant step in a long and arduous march. His main objective at that stage was to establish a measure of American and personal credibility among the African regional patrons. In view of his record as the spiritual father of the "tar baby" option and as the architect of U.S. Angolan policy his task was not easy. For this reason his tour was restricted to black African states, and he went out of his way to satisfy black Africa's sensitivities and aspirations. However, even Kissinger's Lusaka manifesto did not eliminate African scepticism and suspicion towards U.S. intentions. Mozambique, in particular, remained unconvinced. Radio Maputo interpreted Kissinger's initiative as a neo-colonialist plot designed to protect the long-term interests of monopoly capital.[162]

Clearly Kissinger urgently needed to deliver at least some goods if his plan to improve U.S. fortunes in southern Africa was to succeed. Rhodesia, the most explosive issue, was on the top of the agenda. He soon concluded that the keys to the success of his new strategy were not in the hands of the black regional patrons but rather in those of white South Africa. His hope of a breakthrough depended on his ability to convince the Rhodesian government to accept majority rule within two years. However, America had no direct means to deliver Rhodesia. South Africa alone could bring the Rhodesian sacrificial lamb to the altar of the high priest of U.S. diplomacy. As he told the Senate Foreign Relations Committee the FLP made it clear to him that no solution to the problems of southern Africa was possible without the active cooperation of South Africa.[163]

Already in his Lusaka speech Kissinger displayed some awareness of South Africa's centrality. While identifying with African aspirations, his plan for South Africa was not spelled out in specific terms, as in the case of Rhodesia and Namibia. His contrasting attitude towards South Africa during his African tour was noted with satisfaction by the Afrikaans press.[164] There was, however, also some disappointment with Kissinger's "ignorance about the true state of affairs in South Africa". *Die Transvaler* concluded its editorial with the suggestion that Kissinger might also have a credibility problem in South Africa as well.[165] Vorster himself expressed his disappointment when telling *Newsweek* that it was difficult to assess U.S. policy because its pronouncements and solutions had not been subjected to consultation with all concerned parties including South Africa.[166] This should be viewed in the light of the credibility crisis among South African policy makers resulting from the perceived U.S. betrayal of South Africa in Angola. South Africa was definitely signalling to Kissinger that their cooperation could not be taken for granted.

Thus in the wake of his African tour Kissinger concentrated his efforts in mobilizing South Africa's cooperation. He, in fact, did it almost to the total neglect of the FLP. Approaching South Africa Kissinger found a willing partner. The same Angolan débâcle, which caused resentment in South Africa towards the U.S., also created the conditions for South Africa's eagerness to join Kissinger in his peace initiative. In the wake of its Angolan adventure, South Africa's regional and international position was at a low ebb. Detente, on which so many hopes had been pinned, was dead and buried. South Africa was regionally isolated and condemned. In Angola a Marxist regime was emerging from the ashes of the civil war. As the guerilla war north of the Limpopo was escalating, the danger of an Angola-type situation increased alarmingly. This would complete the transformation of the former *cordon sanitaire* into a Marxist, pro-Soviet belt poised against South Africa. Beset as they were by communist paranoia, policy makers in Pretoria could well visualize communist hordes marching on South Africa. Internationally the Angolan disaster only exacerbated South Africa's position. On April 1, 1976, even the U.S. did not oppose a Security Council resolution condemning South Africa as the aggressor in Angola.[167] In southern Africa the objectives of South Africa and the U.S. were identical – the stemming of the communist tide. Furthermore, Kissinger's initiative also held the promise of resurrecting detente. The collaboration with the U.S. could also be expected to improve South Africa's international standing.

Shortly after returning from his African tour Kissinger met Pik

Botha, the South African ambassador to the UN. President Ford even spoke of a possibility of meeting Vorster. Vorster's response was enthusiastic. He said that such a meeting would be to the advantage, not only of southern Africa, but of the free world as a whole. He declared that he would always be willing to play a positive role in furthering understanding and peace in the sub-continent. The SABC commentator was jubilant: "Suddenly South Africa has acquired a new standing in international affairs." [168] In a speech in the Senate in Cape Town on May 17, Hilgard Muller urged the West to join in a new peace initiative in Rhodesia. This the West was called to do before Russia and the Cubans were given the chance to create a bloodbath.[169]

Domestically as well the stage was set for purposeful contacts between the U.S. and South Africa. On June 16, 1976, a week before Kissinger and Vorster met in the Bavarian village of Grafenau, South Africa was shattered by the eruption of riots in Soweto, the black satellite of Johannesburg. The riots which subsequently spread like bush fire throughout the country were the worst outburst of violent protest South Africa had ever experienced. South Africa was in a state of shock. The government realized that South Africa could not be an island of peace and stability in the midst of an unstable, rapidly changing and transforming region. The stabilization of the region became a matter of the highest domestic priority. Furthermore, the brutal suppression of the riots earned South Africa world-wide condemnation. The UN Security Council unanimously passed a resolution condemning South Africa and calling for urgent steps to eliminate apartheid and racial discrimination.[170] The message was clear: the wave of African liberation reached South Africa in full force and the government would have to concentrate much of its attention and energy on the erupting domestic front. This would be at best a long, arduous and painful process of change and adjustment. The only immediate relevant action the government could take was to ease regional tension and to try to deflect world attention.

Thus, when Vorster met Kissinger on July 23, he was well disposed towards the American initiative. Indeed, what Kissinger apparently had to offer Vorster had a clear appeal. On the eve of the meeting Kissinger told the House of Representatives Foreign Relations Committee: "The question which I would like to explore with Prime Minister Vorster is whether South Africa is prepared to separate its own future from that of Rhodesia and Namibia."[171] In other words, if South Africa would assist in solving the latter problems, the U.S. would not put pressure on it regarding its domestic regime. This was in the best tradition of Kissinger's diplomatic strategy of achieving the achieve-able. It was also clear that, in accordance with his step-by-step diplomacy, Kissinger was at that time mainly concerned with the resolution of the Rhodesian crisis. In the light of his main objective – checking Soviet expansion – this priority made sense. While the guerilla war in Rhodesia was escalating, the security situation in Namibia was well under control. In view of the forthcoming U.S. presidential election it is doubtful whether Kissinger was really concerned with a concrete solution to the situation in Namibia. The centrality of Rhodesia in Kissinger's thinking was also reflected in the role allocated Britain. It was not a coincidence that he conferred with the British prime minister immediately after his meeting with Vorster.[172]

Kissinger must have discussed with Vorster the role South Africa was expected to play within the framework of his strategy, namely that of pressurizing Smith into accepting majority rule on the basis of the British plan. This South Africa had in the past declined to do because of the overriding "white backlash" constraint. As late as May 1976, while announcing his government's intention to join the initiative to resolve the Rhodesian crisis, Muller added South Africa's holy dictum: "provided it did not mean interfering in Rhodesia's affairs".[173] However, in the aftermath of the Kissinger–Vorster meeting it was clear that South Africa could not any longer hide behind diplomatic niceties. The Callaghan–Kissinger plan was on the agenda and South Africa was expected to make a definite stand. The first indication that South Africa was shedding its past inhibitions was given by Foreign Minister Muller on August 13 in a speech in the Natal congress of the Nationalist Party. In this solemn party forum he indicated that the government would lend support to Kissinger's initiative. Being sensitive to the mood of his audience, Muller was vague and ambiguous enough to allow for conflicting interpretations. Even Dr Mulder, a fellow minister, attacked newspapers for deducing from the speech South Africa's support for the Callaghan–Kissinger plan. However, in a preamble to the speech, released at the UN, the South African position was given a more positive twist: "A solution to the Rhodesian issue on the basis of majority rule with adequate protection for minority rights, is acceptable to the South African government."[174] While not specifying the term of two years it was clear that the preamble was related to the Anglo-American plan.

While Kissinger was concentrating his efforts on South Africa, he also maintained indirect contacts with black Africa. After his meeting with Vorster he sent William Schaufele, the Assistant Secretary of State for African Affairs, for a tour of seven African countries, in order to report on the meeting.[175] The FLP had to be kept in the right frame of mind. To prevent the development of a negative African momentum Kissinger relayed sympathetic messages to black Africa. In two major speeches at the beginning and at the end of August 1976, in Boston and Philadelphia respectively, he referred to the problems of southern Africa. In Boston, he appealed for a quick, peaceful settlement of the Rhodesian dispute. While not ignoring Namibia he insisted that Rhodesia was the most burning issue in southern Africa. The speech was well received in Zambia being praised by the *Times* of Zambia as the most revolutionary speech on U.S. policy towards Africa since Kissinger visited Lusaka.[176] In Philadelphia he spoke not only on majority rule in Rhodesia and Namibia. Against the background of continuing unrest in South Africa he said: "And in South Africa itself, the recent outbreaks of racial violence have underscored the inevitable instability of a system that institutionalized human inequality in a way repugnant to the world's conscience."[177] In his speeches Kissinger also spelled out what he expected of South Africa. In Boston he said: "South Africa must demonstrate its commitment to Africa by assisting a negotiated outcome."[178] Vorster had not yet given Kissinger a firm commitment.

It must have been to secure such commitment that Kissinger met Vorster in Zurich for three days, from September 4 to September 6. This meeting seems to have been more successful than the former. Emerging from the talks Kissinger sounded confident and optimistic.[179] He would not have planned a dramatic and crucial shuttle trip to southern Africa within a week[180] unless his optimism had some basis. Back in South Africa Vorster contributed to the air of optimism. Addressing the Free State Nationalist Party congress on September 8, he prepared his people for what was to come. He said that the extent to which South Africa would fall under the communist yoke depended on the outcome of the American effort. He stated that he would stand by the U.S. because they were anti-communist.[181] However, Kissinger himself admitted on his way to Africa that he had not yet had a South African commitment to work towards majority rule in Rhodesia on the basis of the Anglo-American plan.[182]

On September 12, on the eve of his departure to southern Africa, Kissinger gave a dramatic account of his task: "At issue is not only the future of the two states in Southern Africa but the potential evolution of all of Africa with its potential impact on Europe and the Middle East."[183] The reception on Kissinger's arrival at Dar es Salaam, the first leg in his second southern African shuttle, on September 14, 1976, did not augur well for his mission. Students demonstrated at the airport

137

against Kissinger and his southern African shuttle diplomacy.[184] A Tanzanian government statement issued on the day of his arrival challenged him to declare that, if his mission failed, the U.S. "will be on the side of those who fight for freedom". The statement was also critical of some of U.S. positions with regard to southern Africa.[185] So disturbed was Kissinger that he responded with an unusual statement designed to pave the way for a better start: "Every step that brought us here we have carefully discussed with the African leaders ... Every step in the future will be coordinated with the front line presidents. The United States wants nothing for itself except in the interest of peace and economic and social progress."[186] At the end of a day of deliberations Nyerere said that he had learnt nothing new and that he was not particularly optimistic about the outcome of Kissinger's mission.[187] He must have been disappointed that Kissinger still ignored his advice to give priority to the Namibian problem. His pessimism was also reflected in what he told Kissinger before leaving Dar es Salaam: "If you are saying that you can convert Smith, the chances are nil."[188]

Arriving at Lusaka on September 16, Kissinger encountered a sense of urgency, but there was less pessimism. This more positive attitude was reflected in a *Zambian Daily Mail* editorial: "Dr Kissinger's task is formidable, though this must not be given as the reason for exaggerated pessimism."[189] Kaunda placed on Kissinger's agenda the immediate independence of Namibia and Rhodesia and the eradication of apartheid in South Africa.[190] He did not however, object to the Rhodesian question being given priority. Kaunda still preferred a peaceful solution because, borrowing Vorster's famous warning, "the alternative was too ghastly to contemplate". He pinned his hopes on Kissinger's ability to persuade Vorster to cooperate. He also issued a veiled threat that if Kissinger failed the Africans would turn to the Soviets for military support. Noting that "time was running out" Kissinger indicated that he had internalized the message of urgency relayed to him by Nyerere and Kaunda.[191] It was perhaps his meetings with these leaders that prompted Kissinger, on his way to Pretoria on September 17, to cast some doubt about the chances of his current shuttle: "If I didn't think that it was possible that Smith would yield at some relatively early stage, I wouldn't be here. But I never said it was possible on this trip."[192]

Saying this, Kissinger revealed again the main thrust of his strategy – to bring Smith to accept majority rule on the basis of the British plan. Smith himself did not seem to be disturbed by the approaching storm. On September 12, before flying to meet Vorster to be briefed on the Zurich talks with Kissinger, Smith was his old self. While admitting that some changes were necessary he sounded as obstinate and determined as ever.[193] He was full of fighting spirit: "We will resort to the well-known free world tradition of being prepared to stand and fight for freedom."[194] Smith still had to be delivered. From this perspective, Kissinger, in coming to Pretoria, was approaching the climax of his mission.

The task that Kissinger expected Vorster to perform was a difficult and painful one. Emerging from the Zurich meeting Vorster was vague about South Africa's prospective role: "to create the climate that will make peace possible and that will bring people together to discuss their affairs and to talk it out rather than shooting it out". He, in fact, ruled out pressure on Rhodesia.[195] This he repeated on September 13, on the eve of his meeting with Smith.[196] It did not, however, represent the actual South African position. On his way to Africa Kissinger told journalists: "Vorster would not have gone that far if he did not want to make a major effort. He knows what the U.S. needs in terms of concessions. We have to assume he is doing it in good faith. We have evidence that South Africa is putting the screws on Rhodesia."[197] The combination of overriding regional and international considerations overruled the domestic constraint. To minimize the danger of a white backlash the pressure had to be subtle and undetectable. In fact, while making the noble pronouncements regarding non-interference, Vorster had already been putting significant pressure on Rhodesia. Rhodesian goods, to and from South Africa, failed to reach their destination due to congestion, real or contrived, vital military supplies were held up and direct military support was withdrawn.[198]

On September 14, the day Kissinger landed in Dar es Salaam, Smith and Vorster met in Pretoria for four and a half hours. Smith did not sound as confident after the meeting as he had before it: "Obviously southern Africa is going through a crucial period in its history, and I do not have to tell you these matters are highly sensitive, and much is in the melting pot at the moment because of Dr Kissinger's pending visit."[199] The drop in his mood barometer was justified in view of the optimism expressed by Dr Hilgard Muller less than 24 hours after taking part in the Vorster–Smith meeting: "If we and the other African states are also prepared to throw in our full weight – and South Africa is prepared to do it – then I believe that the peace offensive can succeed."[200] This was a clear indication of South Africa's commitment to deliver Smith to Kissinger. If Vorster did not force Smith to accept the Kissinger plan at that meeting there is little doubt that he prepared him for the ultimate surrender. Smith went straight from the Pretoria meeting to the RF congress in Umtali to seek a mandate to negotiate the future of Rhodesia. Despite serious challenge from the right wing he got his mandate.[201] He was still master in his own house.

All the ingredients for a peaceful settlement seem to have been ready. On September 17, 1976 the American chef arrived in Pretoria to give the dish the final touch. Kissinger went from the airport straight to Libertas, the prime minister's official residence, where he held talks with Vorster.[202] The presence of Kissinger in Pretoria provided Vorster with a convenient smoke screen to deal with Smith when he arrived on September 18. There is no doubt that at the meeting he had with Smith, which Meredith described as brutal, [203] Vorster used all the cards in his hand. Previously, in Dar es Salaam, Kissinger had told Nyerere: "If you hear that I have seen Smith it is because Vorster has assured me that Smith accepts the thing."[204] In the early morning of September 19, Kissinger told journalists that "Vorster has gone along on the whole with the basic approach we follow. The likelihood is that Smith is on the brink of making some decisions."[205] On his way back to Dar es Salaam, on September 21, Kissinger told journalists that "the key to breaking Smith was Vorster".[206] On September 23 an "informed source" in Salisbury said: "When you are presented with a situation in which you get no more logistical support you have no more options."[207] The following day Smith himself publicly admitted that "the alternative to acceptance of the proposals was explained to us in the clearest terms which left no room for misunderstanding."[208] Smith met Kissinger for four hours on the morning of September 19. In this meeting the Anglo-American plan was formally submitted to the Rhodesian delegation headed by Smith. At 2 p.m. the Rhodesians withdrew for consultations. There were hardly any consultations. According to one participant Smith withdrew to his room for a few hours for rest and reflection. When he re-emerged he simply told his colleagues that they had to accept the plan.[209] This was typical of decision making in white Rhodesia which reflected the guru–disciples relations between Smith and his colleagues. At 6 p.m. the Rhodesian delegation went to a second meeting with Kissinger at Libertas, with Vorster in attendance. Being aware of Smith's slippery record, Kissinger must have deemed it necessary that the final act should be witnessed by the powerful regional patron. Kissinger wanted Smith to announce publicly his acceptance of the plan there and then. Smith, however, insisted on first getting it approved by his cabinet and parliamentary caucus.[210] Smith himself, while accepting the plan asked for three modifications to be made. One was semantic and symbolic. Originally Smith wanted to accept responsible majority rule rather than black majority rule, but he accepted Kissinger's compromise–majority rule without a qualifying adjective.[211] Kissinger's approval of the two other modifications, regarding the chairmanship of the State Council and the ministries of Defence and Law and Order, was received according to Smith in Salisbury through the South African government on September 22.[212]

The plan in its final shape, as announced by Smith on September 24, and having been approved by his cabinet and caucus, was as follows:

(1) Rhodesia agrees to majority rule within two years.
(2) Representatives of the Rhodesian Government will meet immediately at a mutually agreed place with African leaders to organize an interim government to function until majority rule is implemented.
(3) The interim government should consist of a Council of State half of whose members will be blacks and half whites, with a white chairman without a special vote. The European and African sides would nominate their representatives. Its functions will include legislation, general supervisory responsibilities, and supervising the process of drafting the Constitution. The interim government should also have a Council of Ministers. For the period of the interim government the Ministers of Defence and Law and Order would be white. Decisions of the Council of Ministers to be taken by two-thirds majority. Its functions should include delegated legislative authority to executive responsibility.
(4) The United Kingdom Government will enact enabling legislation for the process of majority rule. Upon enactment of that legislation Rhodesia will also enact such legislation as may be necessary to the process.
(5) Upon establishment of the interim government, sanctions will be lifted and all acts of war, including guerilla warfare, will cease.

The lengthy final clause was about "substantial economic support ... by the international community to provide assurance to Rhodesians about the economic future of the country".[213]

Referring to the analysis of the Anglo-American plan by the Rhodesian delegation after receiving it, Meredith emphasizes the manipulative element in the acceptance of it: "Yet, on examination, the five points offered considerable scope for manoeuvre."[214] This was certainly not the essence of Smith's capitulation. From a white Rhodesian perspective the surrender in Pretoria was a breaking point, a historic watershed, a turning point from which there was no return. According to Meredith himself, Smith said to Kissinger upon reading the plan: "You want me to sign my own suicide note."[215] Of course, the

Smith record could give credence to the suspicion that he was up to his old tricks. To this Kissinger gave a succint and convincing answer when he departed from South Africa: "It would not be costless for Smith to double cross me or con me in the presence of the South African Prime Minister who got us to talk in the first place."[216] In the aftermath of the capitulation in Pretoria, a whole array of political slogans and axioms, like "majority rule not in a thousand years" or "responsible majority rule" were thrown in the dustbin of history. There was, of course, a manipulative element in Smith's response to the Anglo-American plan which he also used to convince his cabinet and his caucus to accept it.[217] He could count, as before, on the divisions in the African nationalist camp. It is also possible that at the back of his mind he believed, or hoped, that the plan would be rejected by the nationalists. The twist he gave the plan in his surrender speech on September 24, certainly did not make it easier for them to come forward. However, having said that, it must be emphasized that Smith was now playing for far lower stakes than before. He was now fighting a rearguard battle to secure the survival and prosperity of his white community in an African-ruled Zimbabwe rather than to maintain white domination in Rhodesia.

Until Smith delivered his September 24 speech there was an air of optimism regarding the prospect of a settlement. U.S. officials suggested that an interim government could be established in four to six weeks.[218] Anthony Crosland, the British Foreign Secretary, said that "it is by far the best chance we've ever had of a breakthrough on the whole Southern African question."[219] Vorster also sounded a note of cautious hope.[220] Kaunda, after meeting Kissinger, was non-commital only saying that he saw no reason why the American shuttle diplomacy should not continue.[221] The *Zambian Daily Mail* editorial, however, reflected a much more hopeful mood: "there is a ray of hope piercing through what has been ... impenetrable darkness."[222] Even the sceptical Nyerere was apparently optimistic. Colin Legum described him as "almost jubilant", speaking in terms of a "breakthrough" and suggesting that the Rhodesian question was "drawing to an end".[223] There were, however, also some dissenting voices. Nkomo, who was apparently aware of the details of the plan, said that it had "very serious flaws".[224] ZIPA's deputy political commissar was unequivocal in condemning it as being designed "to sabotage our struggle".[225] Since Kissinger's strategy was to work through the regional patron these rumblings among the nationalist clients may not have been particularly disturbing. There was, however, an indication that Mozambique, a crucial patron, also did not think much of the plan.[226]

Following Smith's speech on September 24, these dissenting voices became the dominant theme in the African response to the plan. The front-line consensus regarding the plan as outlined by Smith was expressed in a statement issued at the conclusion of a summit meeting held in Lusaka on September 25–26: "The Presidents have carefully studied the proposals as outlined by the illegal and racist regime which, if accepted, would be tantamount to legalising the colonialist and racist structures of power." The presidents reaffirmed their commitment to the armed struggle. The only element of the plan acceptable to the FLP was majority rule in two years. They flatly rejected the clauses relating to the transitional arrangements. They called on Britain, as the colonial power, to convene a constitutional conference outside Rhodesia for the following purposes:

(1) To discuss the structure and functions of the transitional government.
(2) To establish the transitional government.
(3) To discuss the modalities of convening a full constitutional conference to work out the independence constitution.
(4) To establish the basis upon which peace and normalcy can be restored in the territory.[227]

This response contrasted sharply with the optimism which had emanated from the U.S., Britain and South Africa in the wake of Smith's speech. The South African government expressed great satisfaction.[228] In London the British government paid tribute to Kissinger,[229] and a Foreign Office statement reflected optimism about the follow-up: "With good faith on all sides, it should now be possible for Africans and Europeans, working together, to lay the foundations for independent Zimbabwe, in peace and prosperity."[230] President Ford hailed Kissinger's southern African diplomacy and sounded a hopeful note about the prospects for Rhodesia.[231]

The FLP statement on September 26, which was tantamount to a rejection of the Kissinger plan, served as a cold shower on the heads of the enthusiasts. Judging by their initial reactions, the U.S. and Britain did not expect a flat rejection of essential elements in the plan. A salvage operation was urgently needed if Kissinger's effort was to have an impact on the Rhodesian crisis. In Washington it was pretended that the FLP response was essentially positive. The State Department argued that the presidents accepted the basis of Kissinger's plan and that the only point of difference was that they wanted the details for the transitional period to be left to the constitutional conference. The State Department did not consider that this would constitute a serious problem.[232] Kissinger and William Rogers cheered themselves up by claiming that they had received messages from some of the presidents indicating that they had not rejected the proposals. Rogers said that those presidents agreed to take part in a conference with Rhodesian representatives without preconditions.[233] If the presidents were prepared to proceed to a constitutional conference it was not on the basis of the Kissinger plan. Indeed, if peace in Rhodesia and southern Africa was to be given a chance, a constitutional conference on a basis acceptable to the FLP was essential. Thus on September 29, 1976 the British Foreign Secretary announced his government's decision to call an immediate conference on the formation of an interim government in Rhodesia.[234] This announcement marked the effective end of Kissinger's Rhodesian adventure. Kissinger had handed over the responsibility to the British. In the U.S. presidential elections which were held shortly after, President Ford was defeated, and Kissinger was out of office.

In terms of what it set out to achieve, the Kissinger initiative was clearly a diplomatic blunder. It did not avert the escalation of violence, nor did it check Soviet influence. It did not launch Rhodesia and southern Africa on the road to peace, stability, prosperity and a pro-Western orientation. Smith could not be blamed for Kissinger's failure. He may have given, in his interpretation, a certain twist to the plan. However, the FLP rejected not only the twist but also the plan itself. With regard to the essence of the plan Smith did not play any tricks. A British Foreign Office spokesman confirmed that Smith's version "was an accurate playback ... of the Anglo-American plan".[235] Martin and Johnson quote one of Callaghan's aides who put the blame on Kissinger's assumption that the FLP could dictate to their nationalist clients.[236] The argument would have been valid had the regional patrons accepted the plan and failed to impose it on the nationalists. This was clearly not the case, as the FLP themselves rejected it. Kissinger's tactics of operating through the regional patrons was not inherently wrong. Had the FLP accepted the plan unanimously and wholeheartedly there is little doubt that they could deliver the nationalists. It was in his dealings with the FLP that Kissinger badly miscalculated.

Kissinger's initiative failed primarily because he had not secured the prior agreement of the FLP to the plan accepted by Smith. During his second African shuttle he gave the impression that the presidents were behind the plan. The Rhodesian government claimed that in a message which they received from Kissinger on September 22, he had indicated that the presidents agreed to the modifications in the plan asked for by Smith.[237] The journalists on Kissinger's plane were also under the impression that there had been prior agreement by the FLP to the plan as announced by Smith. However, cornered by well-informed journalists, William Rogers, who had accompanied Kissinger, was forced to concede that the plan had never been accepted by the FLP. He admitted that the latter accepted only three points: (1) the fundamental principle of majority rule in two years; (2) negotiations for an interim government and a meeting for that purpose; (3) negotiations on how to arrange a constitutional conference to draw up a constitution for independence. He also admitted that the six-point plan was drawn up by the American team on the plane on the way from Lusaka to Pretoria.[238] Kaunda subsequently revealed that Kissinger never discussed with him the details of his plan.[239]

How can one account for such a blunder by an international diplomat of such standing? Primarily it was a case of miscalculation. Analysing the Rhodesian conflict Kissinger must have concluded that the refusal of the Rhodesian government to concede black majority rule was the main stumbling block on the way to a peaceful settlement. Hence the main thrust of his strategy and his second shuttle was to bring Smith to accept majority rule within a time-span put forward by the British and accepted by the FLP. To achieve this objective he was prepared to make concessions to the whites which, he must have known, would make the plan more objectionable to the FLP. In order to close the obvious gap between what was acceptable to whites and blacks Kissinger employed what William Rogers termed "tactical ambiguity"[240] – a euphemism for deception. To make Vorster and Smith accept the plan he had to come to Pretoria equipped with African consent. To secure the impression of African consent to his plan, he discussed with Nyerere and Kaunda only the broad principles acceptable to them. He probably believed that once Smith had accepted majority rule, in two years the gulf between the positions of blacks and whites could be narrowed by eroding the concessions given to the latter. Thus, when Rogers had to concede that the plan had not been approved by the FLP, he said that the six-point plan was merely Smith's "negotiating position".[241] If this was the case, then Kissinger had failed to grasp Smith's crisis management tactics. It had been standard Smith tactics to use regionally accepted agreements as firm bases from which he manoeuvred and manipulated to prevent the conflict resolution process from proceeding in an undesirable direction. He did this with the Lusaka agreement of December 1974 and the Pretoria agreement of August 1975. Smith may have been playing for lower stakes following his surrender to Kissinger, but he did not lose his manipulating genius. Expressing surprise at Rogers' reference to the six points as negotiating positions, a spokesman for Smith was quick to point out that the plan was presented to the latter as "a package deal which would have to be accepted or rejected in its entirety".[242] Kissinger, in fact, provided Smith with another solid base from which he could conduct his rearguard action. The involvement of Vorster in witnessing the final meeting between Smith and Kissinger only made it worse from the latter's point of view. Vorster, without hesitation, gave credence to Smith's version.[243] Vorster, against the background of the perceived American betrayal in Angola, could construe Rogers' twist as another treachery on the part of perfidious Uncle Sam.

Kissinger's consideration for Rhodesian whites' sensitivities and anxieties may also have been partly related to the settlement model he had in mind. He was not interested simply in the transfer of power to the black majority. He wanted to usher in a stable, moderate, pro-Western regime, resting on a prosperous, free-market economy. The last clause in his plan, which dealt with economic assistance, was aimed not only at maintaining but also at expanding the capitalist base of the country. In this scheme the whites, being the backbone of the economy, had a vital role to play. The Western financial assistance was designed not to buy the settlers out, but rather to create the conditions which would induce them to stay. However, financial inducement was clearly not sufficient. In the radical change from white domination to black majority rule security and political guarantees were at least as important. From this perspective the modifications demanded by Smith were not unreasonable. Kissinger himself subsequently told Nyerere that he conceded to Smith's demands partly to prevent a white exodus.[244]

In his eagerness to entice the whites Kissinger badly neglected the African side of his Rhodesian equation. He showed little regard for African sensitivities and scant appreciation of the complexity and diversity of the regional African collective patron. He should have known that by shaping and adjusting his plan to the taste of the whites he made it objectionable to the FLP who alone could deliver the Rhodesian nationalists. He should have known that with the incorporation of Neto, the president of Angola, the group dynamic of that collective regional patron was pushing it to a more militant posture. Even Nyerere and Kaunda, who approved of Kissinger's involvement, were not committed to a peaceful settlement at any price. Kissinger should have taken this more seriously into consideration, particularly because he had no leverage to use in his dealings with the FLP. On the other hand, the white segment of the conflict system was much easier to manage and manipulate. This was so, not only because of the simple, one patron–one client structure of the white component, but also because Vorster was ripe for the picking and could force Smith to accept a less favourable settlement. Thus if Kissinger had wanted to effect a real, rather than merely a psychological, breakthrough, he should have made sure that his plan was acceptable to the FLP. Having failed to do that he handed over to his British counterpart not a viable plan but rather a "mission impossible". Kissinger himself might have been able to pick up the pieces. However, Britain was not America, and Crosland was not Kissinger.

CHAPTER SIX

The Lion's Peep: Britain's Geneva Interlude,

October 1976 – January 1977

On October 8, 1976 Crosland, the British Foreign Secretary, announced that a conference, to follow up the Kissinger initiative, would assemble in Geneva on October 21.[1] This was a culmination of a hectic British diplomatic effort to ascertain the feasibility and desirability of taking over from Kissinger. Soon after Smith's surrender speech, Callaghan made an appeal to the FLP not to give the Rhodesian leader the opportunity to get off the hook. He offered to send a British official to clear the way for a conference. Perturbed by the FLP response to Smith's speech, Crosland urged the presidents to "latch on to what is the essential part of Mr Smith's offer and to go ahead from there".[2] On September 27 Ted Rowlands, the Minister of State in the Foreign Office responsible for African Affairs, flew to southern Africa "to discuss the strategy of the conference".[3] In Gaberone, Rowlands joined William Schaufele, Kissinger's top Africa hand, for an "extremely good" meeting with Kaunda and Khama.[4] This mini-Anglo-American shuttle which proceeded to Maputo, Dar es Salaam and Pretoria culminated in a meeting with Smith in Salisbury on October 4. A joint communique at the end of the meeting stated that "it was in the interest of all that the conference should take place as soon as the practical arrangements can be made."[5] In Washington, the American administration had already been engaged in a diplomatic rearguard action designed to launch the British-led conference and to extricate themselves from the Rhodesian mess.[6] It was after meeting Rowlands and Schaufele on their return from southern Africa that Crosland announced the plan to convene the Geneva conference.

It was surprising that a Labour government which, since the beginning of the southern African detente, had studiously avoided direct active involvement, decided to play a major decolonizing role in a full constitutional conference under hopeless circumstances. It may be accounted for by the astonishing optimism projected by the British during the short period leading up to the conference. This unwarranted optimism seems to have stemmed from the assumption that Smith's acceptance of Kissinger's plan amounted to unconditional capitulation. This was reflected by Rowlands upon departing for his southern African tour: "The proposals are a major breakthrough. This is the most important development in 11 years in Rhodesia and we hope to push it forward."[7] Only on the basis of this assumption did Callaghan's suggestion that an interim government would be established in four to six weeks[8] make sense. Ivor Richard, the British ambassador to the UN, said on October 11 that calling the conference under his chairmanship was realistic and worthwhile, and that it had "a good chance of success".[9] On the eve of the opening of the conference, he sounded equally optimistic: "I perceive the components of a settlement here."[10] Speaking in Parliament on October 20, Crosland, while being cautious, expressed confidence that "we shall not fail."[11] Possibly the British government was misled by the progress made by Rowlands and Schaufele in paving the way for the conference.[12] These, however, dealt with procedure rather than substance. In the realm of substance, one fails to come across evidence which could justify British optimism. On the contrary, as the opening of the conference was approaching, the gap between the contending parties seemed increasingly unbridgeable.

Nationalist attitudes in the period leading up to the Geneva conference were influenced by the continuing realignments and internal strifes in the nationalist camp As seen earlier, the FLP in September 1976 made another abortive attempt to unify all the nationalist factions. This failure did not put an end to the search for unity and political alliances. Paradoxically, at the centre of this search was Nkomo, who played a major role in frustrating the September unity effort. Nkomo was plainly aware of his weakness in the face of future military and political challenges. Clearly he had to expand his political base if he and his party were to survive the struggle for the leadership of the nationalist movement and of independent Zimbabwe. Nkomo exhibited his usual opportunism in his search for a broader political base.

Despite bitter traditional hostility and rivalry, Nkomo sought an alliance with Mugabe's ZANU. In view of the expanding guerilla war, an alliance, distinct from unity, with ZANU was a sound investment in the future. As a member of such a powerful alliance, Nkomo could hope to undermine Muzorewa's domestic base and transform his own ANC into the dominant domestic nationalist organization. With his solid regional base in Zambia and the international support which he continued to court and cultivate both in the East and the West,[13]

Nkomo's political horizon looked sufficiently bright. While Kissinger was shuttling, Nkomo plotted his new alliance. In Lusaka, while describing Muzorewa's ANC as a spent force, Nkomo said that he was engaged in talks about a "working arrangement" with ZANU.[14] Back in Salisbury on September 25, he said he had a list of names of ZANU leaders who were "potential talking partners", implying that Mugabe was one of them.[15] On September 27 Mugabe said that talks between ZANU and ZAPU had actually started on that day, implying that it was the former's initiative.[16] From ZANU's side, as well, the initiative was primarily tactical. An alliance could at least enable ZANU to keep a watchful eye on the scheming and volatile Nkomo. Thus, on September 29 ZAPU and ZANU delegations flew from Lusaka to Maputo for unity talks.[17]

While negotiating with ZANU, Nkomo also sounded out Muzorewa for a possible alliance. This search for reinsurance was indicative of Nkomo's perception of his own political weakness. Although he had been engaged in a bitter struggle with Muzorewa over the legitimacy of their respective, competing ANCs, an alliance with him was not without merit. Ideologically, Muzorewa's ANC was more appealing to Nkomo than ZANU militants. Together they could hope to monopolize the African domestic political scene. This could compensate for his military weakness. With his additional regional and international support, he could hope to be well placed for any eventuality. In fact, it seemed that Nkomo preferred a union with Muzorewa to one with ZANU. On September 30, in Gaberone, Nkomo offered Muzorewa unity.[18] This offer should have appealed to Muzorewa who lacked regional and international support and whose position within the nationalist camp had been seriously eroded. However, political acumen not being among his qualities, Muzorewa deferred his reply pending his forthcoming meeting with his executive. On October 3 he returned to Salisbury after a long absence from the country and was enthusiastically welcomed by more than 100,000 people.[19] This was a considerable boost to Muzorewa and his ANC. In a fit of euphoria, the ANC executive failed to decide in favour of unity with Nkomo. Nkomo, who was waiting in Gaberone for a reply, was insultingly told on October 4 that Muzorewa had "more important issues to discuss at the moment".[20] This was a fateful response which had a considerable impact on the turn of events in Rhodesia. On October 6 Nkomo left for Maputo, and by October 9 Nkomo and Mugabe had resolved to form the Patriotic Front (PF) as an alliance between ZANU and ZAPU.[21]

The alliance between ZANU and ZAPU considerably strengthened the militant wing of the nationalist movement. Militancy was further reinforced on the eve of the Geneva conference by the attitude of ZIPA. According to Ranger, by December 1976 ZANU's authority over ZIPA was well established.[22] However, as Martin and Johnson convincingly argue, this was clearly not the case. It was certainly not the case on the eve of the Geneva conference. In fact a crisis within ZIPA and between it and ZANU was nearing a climax. It was successfully resolved, from ZANU's and Mugabe's point of view, only in the early months of 1977.[23] Within the ranks of the new ZIPA leadership, which had been carrying the burden of the guerilla war since the arrest by Zambia of the old ZANU/ZANLA leadership in March 1975, there had developed a political and ideological dynamic which stemmed from the experience of the escalating war. In a movement which had known so much political strife and bloody fraternal conflicts, the newly discovered unity, purposefulness, effectiveness and success must have had an intoxicating effect. Not having been linked to an effective political leadership, it was hardly surprising that a growing number of ZIPA leaders began to perceive themselves and their army not merely as a military instrument, but rather as a veritable political and ideological vanguard of a popular revolutionary war. This trend was developing on the eve of the Geneva conference into a proper movement which began to assert itself politically. At the centre of this movement was Dzinashe Machingura, ZIPA's deputy political commissar, a young man with strong Marxist convictions. On September 22, 1976 he spoke about the role of ZIPA:

> ZIPA is a unique and revolutionary army in the sense that it has a strategic role of transforming itself into a political movement ... And moves to do so are already well under way, moves to transform this organization into a revolutionary vanguard of the people's struggle.[24]

A ZIPA commentary, broadcast from Mozambique, spoke thus: "The Zimbabweans, under the vanguard leadership of their party, the ZIPA ..."[25] In a press conference on September 30 Machingura stated that ZIPA did not identify with any of the factions "that are now fighting politically".[26] By mid-October he openly rejected Mugabe's political leadership.[27] ZIPA military commanders defied members of the ZANLA high command released from Zambian prison on the eve of the Geneva conference. In a ZANU consultative conference in Lusaka, Machingura refused to submit to ZANU's authority and to include ZIPA in the ZANU delegation to Geneva. ZIPA, in fact, elected its own eight-member delegation which failed to go to Geneva only because they believed that

Nyerere, whom they had met, did not want them to go. Only one ZIPA commander responded to Mugabe's call and joined the ZANU delegation. Rex Nhongo, ZIPA supreme commander, who personally recognized Mugabe's leadership, was well aware of the defiance of his men.[28]

The group dynamic of a radicalized and divided nationalist camp did not augur well for the Geneva conference. The tone was set by ZIPA's militant leadership. In a press conference on September 30, Machingura made ZIPA's attitude towards the Kissinger proposals crystal clear: "We reject them outright without reservation."[29] On October 4 ZIPA broadcast a memorandum submitted to the FLP and the OAU which stated its official position. It repeated ZIPA's total rejection of "Kissinger's vicious scheme" aimed at "sabotaging the Zimbabwe struggle and simultaneously preserving Western interests in Zimbabwe". In their eyes, Kissinger's initiative was no more than a neo-colonialist conspiracy precipitated by the perceived military defeat of the white regime and designed to install a puppet regime which would preserve the capitalist economy.[30] For them armed struggle was not a necessary evil. Rather, it was a desirable means to "destroy the repressive apparatus of the Rhodesian state" which defended "the interests of the exploiters",[31] and to build on the ruins of Rhodesian capitalism a progressive socialist Zimbabwe.

Even if Mugabe wished to respond more positively to the Kissinger plan and to the prospective Geneva conference, he could have hardly afforded it. Mugabe himself was militant enough, though perhaps not as hot-headed as the young ZIPA zealots. Towards the end of September 1976 he spoke of his plan, which bore little resemblance to that of Kissinger: "On our part we want a transitional government of 12 months during which the vital instruments of power could be handed over to the majority in order to take full control of law and order."[32] Arriving in Geneva on October 24, Mugabe was even more extreme in his demands: "The theme of the conference must be the transference of power and the achievement of independence within the next few months."[33] A senior legal adviser in Mugabe's delegation said on the eve of the conference that the conference was a waste of time and that his party preferred a military solution.[34] Mugabe's vision of Zimbabwe, as expressed on the eve of the conference, was identical to that of ZIPA militants. Nkomo could not be expected to lag much behind his new militant ally. In a statement on October 9, 1976 the PF demanded total and immediate transfer of power from Britain to the people of Zimbabwe. The PF refused to negotiate with a separate white delegation and insisted on a transitional period of one year at the most.[35]

Sithole and Muzorewa, leaders of the two other factions to be represented at the conference, could not but follow suit.[36]

Unlike the Rhodesian negotiations of 1974–1975, the FLP did not exert a moderating influence on their clients. They themselves had already expressed their opposition to Kissinger's plan. Angola, in particular, had no reason to rave about an initiative whose prime mover was Kissinger. Thus, the Angolan Premier, Lopo do Nascimento, denounced the Anglo-American plan as a bid to create a neo-colonialist buffer for South Africa.[37] In Mozambique, *Noticias*, a government mouthpiece, depicted Britain as the enemy of the people of Rhodesia, denouncing it also for inviting Smith to the conference.[38] The Tanzanian government also demanded that the Rhodesian government be excluded from the conference.[39] Nyerere demanded majority rule within four to six weeks.[40] Kaunda also became increasingly belligerent. On October 8 he said that only if the people of Rhodesia were satisfied with the outcome of the conference would the armed struggle come to an end.[41] As a token of his commitment to the armed struggle he released Tongogara and his fellow ZANLA commanders on the eve of the Geneva conference.[42] On October 17 the FLP convened to discuss the forthcoming conference. They reiterated their rejection of the Kissinger plan and called on Britain to assume the role of an effective decolonizer. They also agreed that ZIPA should continue to wage a relentless guerilla war until power was transferred.[43] The mood of the FLP was also reflected in their solid support for the PF and ZIPA, the political and military manifestations of militant nationalism. It should be noted, however, that the FLP had not yet formally accorded exclusive recognition to any nationalist group. They did not object to Muzorewa's participation in the conference and even decided not to exclude obsolete Sithole.[44]

Faced with such an adamant and united African position regarding the very basis of the conference, the British adopted the American attitude, namely that the Kissinger proposals were nothing but a basis for negotiations.[45] If the British inherited the American view that, having crossed his Rubicon Smith had lost his manoeuvring space, they were in for a big surprise.

Smith was still his old self. On the one hand, he projected good will and even a measure of optimism. Thus, on the eve of his departure to Geneva, he released two of Muzorewa's men from detention to allow them to join the latter's delegation.[46] On leaving for Geneva, he also expressed his government's good intentions with regard to the conference.[47] Arriving in Geneva, he said that he had come in a positive frame of mind and that he would bend over backwards to make it

153

succeed.[48] After meeting the British chairman he even sounded an optimistic note regarding the prospects of the conference.[49] However, Smith's expressions of goodwill sounded hollow and his optimism unwarranted in view of the other side of his double message. On the substance of the prospective negotiations Smith stuck firmly to his guns, insisting that Kissinger's plan was a non-negotiable package deal.[50] Smith viewed the role of the conference as one of elaborating on rather than renegotiating it. He even warned that if the package was opened to renegotiation, so would be his acceptance of majority rule in two years.[51] If this was not enough to provoke the nationalists, he declared that he intended to play a leading part in the future of his country.[52]

The Rhodesian government was firmly supported by its regional patron. On October 13, 1976 Vorster told a National Party gathering in Ladybrand that the Geneva conference would succeed only if all the sides adhered to the Kissinger plan.[53] About a week later, he positively supported Smith's position.[54] On the eve of the conference, Dr Connie Mulder also lent support to Smith's version regarding his agreement with Kissinger.[55]

Thus, when the Geneva conference was formally opened on October 28, the diametrically opposed positions of the Rhodesian government and the African nationalists were solidly backed by their respective regional patrons. Ivor Richard, the British chairman, faced the ominous task of reconciling the seemingly irreconcilables. At the opening session the delegations reaffirmed their respective positions. Smith stated that he came to discuss the implementation of the "Anglo-American proposals",[56] while the nationalists, with different nuances, argued against this premise and exhibited a rigid attitude about transfer of power.[57] And yet, the British chairman, naive, euphoric, or simply out of touch, was encouraged: "I was extremely impressed with the tone of the speeches, with the moderation of the statements, with the constructive nature of what they had to say and with the atmosphere."[58]

Richard's optimism notwithstanding, the conference got bogged down as soon as it began to discuss substance. The first issue on the conference's agenda was the independence date. To Smith, the timing, as such, was "a matter of little consequence".[59] The date of independence was merely the result of translating the desirable transitional process into time span. Two years were simply essential for the implementation of the transitional arrangements envisaged by the Kissinger plan.[60] The most the white delegation was prepared to concede was a transitional period of 23 months.[61] To prove its point, the

Rhodesian government released, on November 24, an eight-point transitional plan which necessitated a 25-month timetable.[62]

The time-scale issue should not have presented a problem at all since it was the only element in the Kissinger proposals accepted by the FLP. The nationalists, however, insisted that this issue be renegotiated and agreed upon before the conference proceeded. It became such a stumbling block because of the deep mistrust shared by the nationalists towards Smith. Two days after the official opening of the conference, a spokesman for Nkomo distributed an alleged official government document stating its intention to use the two-year transition to boost the economy and to build up arms supplies and military force. A comment by a Nkomo aide reflected the nationalists' mood: "Now ... we realize just what Smith had in mind when he accepted majority rule."[63] Thus, from the nationalists' point of view it was vital to shorten the transitional period as much as possible. Furthermore, the PF, and ZIPA and ZANU in particular, were suspicious of the British motives as well. They suspected that they intended to pre-empt their victory and the establishment in Rhodesia of a truly socialist state. Crosland, stating on the eve of the conference that his government would do everything within its power to ensure the success of the conference which "will bring within our grasp a great prize, a free, prosperous and multi racial Zimbabwe",[64] could only confirm their worst suspicions and fears.[65] The severity of the controversy over the timing of independence, an issue regarded by Richard as "almost ... a technical argument",[66] also reflected the nature of the radicalizing group dynamic of a divided nationalist camp. Once the one-year term was in the air, no nationalist leader could appear more compromising. Thus even Muzorewa, who had an interest in the success of the conference and in a political rather than military solution, had to join the chorus. In fact Muzorewa, according to his own account, was the one who demanded a nine-month transition.[67]

The controversy over the date of independence dragged on. On November 4 the conference faced its first crisis. Smith, tired of the futility of the negotiations, returned to Salisbury. He attributed the lack of progress to the British government's appeasement policy. For the record, and the gallery, he said that he was cautiously optimistic.[68] Mugabe, on the other extreme, delivered an ultimatum: "It has to be 12 months – or we go." Richard's compromise of 15 months was unacceptable to all sides.[69] On November 15 Richard put forward another compromise designed to meet the nationalists' demand: 12 months if it was technically possible, and 15 months at the latest.

Nkomo and Mugabe insisted on December 1, 1977 as a definite date for independence.[70] On November 23, 1976 the British proposed March 1, 1978 as the latest date. On November 26, 1976 the PF accepted this compromise while stating that the British had accepted their amendments. The nature of their amendments came to light in a PF statement on November 29 in which, while accepting the date set by the British, they reiterated "our stand that independence shall come strictly within the 12-month period". They were prepared to postpone further discussions on the date "to facilitate the business of the conference".[71] The agreement of the PF to proceed with the conference was facilitated through the efforts and pressures of the FLP operating through their observers in Geneva.[72] Not being really agreed upon by either the nationalists or the Rhodesian government, the issue of the independence date was deferred rather than resolved.

The conference then moved on to the more substantive issue of the interim government. The removal of the first obstacle only revealed that the second one was even more insurmountable. As promised, Smith returned to Geneva on December 7, for the second stage of the negotiations. Upon departing for Geneva, he deemed it necessary to restate his position: "The Kissinger plan, or the Anglo-American plan, is an agreement, a contract. Any attempt to change the plan would be a breach of contract which would necessitate a review of the whole situation."[73]

The nationalist camp was reinforced at that stage by a ZIPA delegation which included leading dissidents who were forced to attend the conference by Samora Machel.[74] Their self declared task was "to prevent the racists and their imperialist allies and the apologists of monopoly capitalism from neo-colonizing Zimbabwe". They still preferred the armed struggle. They also stressed that "ZIPA will be in Geneva as ZIPA and not as part of any political faction now at Geneva". At the same time, they were prepared to support those in Geneva "who are prepared to protect, safeguard and guarantee the genuine independence and freedom of the masses of Zimbabwe".[75] This was certainly not an infusion of moderation.

The nationalists, who were united in their opposition to the Kissinger transitional arrangements, were anything but united on the question of the desirable transitional government. Muzorewa insisted on one-man-one-vote elections for the interim government. His insistence was reinforced by an enthusiastic welcome by some 200,000 Africans who came to greet him on his return from Geneva on December 12, 1976.[76] The PF expressed its commitment to one-man-one-vote elections but not "under the canopy of the Smith regime". Such elections could be held under an interim government controlled by the "liberation movement",[77] namely the PF itself. With the ZIPA delegation breathing down his neck, Mugabe sounded increasingly militant: "The emphasis should be on the armed struggle, not on the constitutional conference ... It is war that brings independence and elections and not empty words."[78] The elections controversy mirrored the underlying intra-nationalist struggle for the colonial spoils. Muzorewa, confident of his internal support, wanted the elections to determine the composition of the transitional government. The PF, whose strength was in their guerilla armies and who were yet unsure of their domestic constituency, wanted control before elections.

Rejecting the Kissinger interim arrangements, the PF submitted on December 2 alternative proposals which envisaged a direct British role in the transitional period. Britain was to be represented by a Resident Commissioner charged with "ensuring that the Geneva Agreement will be fully and properly implemented, and that independence will be achieved in the manner and within the time planned, and that in the interim period there will be good and orderly government". A Prime Minister and a Council of Ministers were to form the interim government. The Prime Minister and four-fifths of the ministers were to be from the "Liberation Movement",[79] alias the PF, Already on October 17, emerging from the FLP summit meeting, Nyerere said that the presidents expected Britain to assume its responsibilities as the colonial power at the forthcoming conference and "during the Black majority transitional government".[80] On December 2 the *Zambian Daily Mail* argued that a "strong transitional government with the British assuming their full responsibility" was essential to the success of the conference.[81]

Replying to a question in Parliament on December 2, Crosland said that Britain was ready to assume a direct role in an interim government.[82] On December 11 it was reported that Crosland, Kissinger and Richard had worked out a new initiative. On December 12 British and American officials confirmed that they were devising a compromise which would meet nationalist opposition to white control of the ministries of Defence and Law and Order during the transitional period.[83] On the same day, the *Observer* reported on proposals which included "a substantial British involvement" during the interim period in both the administration and the security forces.[84] The British were, however, flogging a dead horse. In fact, the conference had already begun to disperse. Smith and Muzorewa had gone back to Rhodesia and Nkomo was in London.[85] On December 14 Richard adjourned the conference until January 17, 1977.[86] The statements of the PF leaders

157

upon departing from Geneva did not augur well for British future efforts. Nkomo said that he was interested in nothing less than the total surrender of the RF government and the hand-over of power to the guerilla forces. Mugabe demanded much the same.[87] They also condemned the British and the Americans for wanting to establish a puppet reactionary regime in Rhodesia.[88]

At the end of December 1976 Ivor Richard began his tour in southern Africa which lasted about a month. Emulating Kissinger's shuttle diplomacy, the British must have believed that they had a fair chance of succeeding where they had failed in Geneva. Away from the floodlights of the city of international conferences, and from the negative dynamic of a full constitutional conference, they probably hoped that the gap between the opposing parties could be bridged.

While Richard's shuttle was in progress, the nationalist camp was undergoing important changes in the shaping of which the FLP took an active part. The process of selection and consolidation which had gained momentum on the eve of the Geneva conference was reaching its climax once the nationalist leaders were back in their southern African bases. These changes had a considerable effect on the outcome of Richard's mission and on the subsequent evolution of the Rhodesian crisis. While favouring and encouraging the formation of the PF, on the eve of the Geneva conference, the FLP did not withdraw their recognition from the other nationalist factions. However, the deep divisions among the nationalists which were manifested again in Geneva, and the prospect of a failure of the diplomatic initiative and of a consequent intensification of the armed struggle, prompted the FLP to define their position towards the different nationalist factions more sharply. Already, during the Geneva conference, the relations between Zambia and the Muzorewa ANC had come under increasing strain.[89] In their Luanda meeting on January 9, 1977 the FLP resolved "to give full political, material and diplomatic support to the Patriotic Front to enable the Front to achieve its objectives in the struggle in Zimbabwe".[90] This amounted to an exclusive recognition of the PF. Both Muzorewa and Sithole denounced the FLP decision. Muzorewa linked it to Kaunda's plot to crown Nkomo and accused the presidents of trying to impose a leadership on Rhodesia's Africans.[91] The exclusive recognition of the PF was a heavy blow to both Sithole and Muzorewa. In a highly regionalized and internationalized decolonization crisis, regional support was an essential political asset. Sithole, having no loyal guerillas and little domestic support, became politically irrelevant. Muzorewa, who commanded no guerilla force, could at least claim an internal political organization and popular support.

However, with no regional support and without a political solution in the offing, his potential electoral support remained an unexploitable resource. As it was, Muzorewa's domestic position was being challenged. Already in Geneva, two members of his delegation had defected to join Mugabe's ZANU, calling on his supporters to follow them.[92] On January 1, 1977 a group of 12 defectors from Muzorewa's ANC national executive formed the People's Party, an internal party supporting Mugabe.[93] To uphold his nationalist credentials, he joined the militant chorus calling for the unconditional surrender of the Smith regime.[94]

The exclusive recognition by the FLP gave the PF a clear advantage. They were now well poised for both political and military solutions. The recess in the conference was used to strengthen this problematic alliance. On December 26, 1976 Mugabe said that the leadership of ZANU and ZAPU had been discussing the forging of a stronger fighting force to complement the political alliance between them. The Zambian Foreign Minister welcomed the prospect of reunification of the liberation armies.[95] On January 15–17 leaders of ZANU and ZAPU, headed by Mugabe and Jason Moyo, met in Maputo to discuss the objectives and strategy of the liberation struggle. They resolved to set up a 10-member coordinating committee[96] which served to enhance and further institutionalize the ZANU–ZAPU alliance.

The recess of the Geneva conference and Richard's shuttle also coincided with the culmination and resolution of the conflict between ZANU political leadership, reinforced by the ex-ZANLA command, and the ultra-militant ZIPA leadership with their strong leftist leanings. The challenge of ZIPA ultra-militants had been nearing a climax during the Geneva conference. The dissidents' threat reached such proportions that Tongogara, together with Hamadziripi and Kangai, fellow members in the ex-ZANLA high command, were sent from Geneva back to Mozambique to deal with it. These, and other ex-ZANLA leaders, were denounced by the dissidents as "reactionary and bourgeois who were not fit to lead an army which had been transformed, which had attained a certain ideological platform".[97] In a memorandum from November 20, 1976 addressed to ZANU detainees released from Zambian jail, ZIPA dissidents attacked the ZANU central committee led by Mugabe. They condemned the practice of co-optation to the committee as a deliberate attempt to reinforce "the bourgeois ranks within the party", thus giving rise to "rightist opportunism" which would lead to defeating the people's struggle. They again rejected the identification of ZIPA with ZANU.[98] This was one of a few similar documents produced by the dissidents. They singled out Mugabe,

Tekere and Muzenda for condemnation, denounced the Geneva conference and declared their intention to transform ZIPA into a political party. The Mozambican government must have been particularly horrified at the prospect of an intra-ZANU struggle being fought on their territory. They clearly took Mugabe's side. When Mugabe was still in Geneva they kept Tongogara informed about the dissidents' plans and manoeuvres. Machel himself convened the whole ZIPA military committee and condemned their actions. It was he who made them send a message of solidarity to Mugabe and prevailed on them to send six representatives to Geneva to join the ZANU delegation.[99] On January 18, 1977 the Mozambicans played a leading role in eliminating the ZIPA challenge and in entrenching the position of ZANU and of Mugabe vis-à-vis ZIPA.[100] The growing unity within ZANU enhanced the unity between ZANU and ZAPU. This, in turn, had a radicalizing effect on the stand of the PF. Thus, one of the four objectives set by the PF in mid-January was "to eliminate all forms of capitalist exploitation and thus create conditions for a full-scale social revolution". The PF also restated its commitment to the intensification of the armed struggle.[101]

Thus, Richard had to deal with a radicalizing nationalist camp and a white government which gave no evidence of capitulation. Before leaving for southern Africa, Richard went to Washington where he held discussions with Kissinger and with Cyrus Vance, Carter's prospective Secretary of State. With the changing of the guards in the White House, it was essential to reconfirm U.S. support for the British effort. The main topic of discussion in Washington was the nature of British involvement in the interim government. According to Richard, a British resident commissioner, who would not be responsible for the day-to-day running of the country but who would be more than merely a "surrogate monarch", was an essential component of the crystallizing plan. He also presented four options to resolve the controversy over the control of the ministries of Defence and Law and Order.[102]

On December 30, 1976 Richard began his shuttle in Lusaka. The Zambian Foreign Minister stressed his country's interest in peace and stability while Kaunda pointed to the grim alternative.[103] His next stop was Salisbury where he met Smith who had made public his view on the prospects of Richard's mission in a very vivid and uncomplimentary manner a fortnight earlier: "I would say that my enthusiasm for this exercise is much the same as it would be if I were asked to the premiere performance ... of Swan Lake and I was told that Mr Richard was to play the leading part in the show."[104] Referring to his meeting with Smith, Richard said that the former had "not slammed the door and locked it".[105] As much as it sounded uninspiring, Richard may have been over-optimistic. Smith himself was to describe that meeting as "a good verbal punch up".[106] His next meeting with Vorster was described by Richard as useful and constructive,[107] which, in diplomatic jargon, does not indicate a large measure of agreement. Yet Richard still expressed optimism and a belief that there was a basis for a settlement.[108] From South Africa Richard went to Botswana where on January 5 he met Seretse Khama, the only president who had previously supported the British proposals.[109] In Maputo he held talks with Machel on January 6. Saying that the meeting went "extremely well", Richard stated that Mozambique and Britain shared similar approaches to the Rhodesian issue.[110] Richard could only be pleased with Machel's new accommodating mood.[111] By then, indeed, Mozambique was beginning to pay a heavy toll in economic destruction for its commitment to the liberation of Rhodesia, and the British proposals must have seemed adequate for ensuring genuine decolonization. Richard was at least equally pleased with his meeting with Nyerere on January 7, running "out of adjectives" to describe its success.[112] Nyerere gave him assurances, on behalf of the FLP, that the guerilla war would stop once the interim government was set up.[113] Completing his first round, Richard went to Nairobi for "rest and reflection".[114]

Richard began the second round of his shuttle on January 18, 1977, flying to Cape Town for a meeting with Vorster to whom he presented Britain's latest proposals for a Rhodesian settlement. Richard was reported to have been in a confident mood, describing the meeting as "very useful". One fails to trace a sound justification for this mood seeing that Richard himself said that he did not even ask Vorster's assistance in persuading Smith.[115] The shuttle reached its climax in two meetings with Smith in Salisbury. In their first meeting on January 21 they studied together the latest British proposals. The interim government was to be headed by a British-appointed interim commissioner with residual responsibility in the spheres of external affairs, defence, internal security and the implementation of the programme for independence. The interim government was to have three principal organs:

(1) *A Council of Ministers.* The Council, with "full executive and legislative competence for the Government of Rhodesia, subject only to the Interim Commissioner's reserve powers", was to be composed of an equal number of members representing each of the groups represented at Geneva and a similar proportion of whites

nominated by the Commissioner. The Council also had the responsibility of working out the independence constitution and implementing the "programme for independence".

(2) *An Advisory Council of Senior Ministers.* This Council, composed of the leaders of the delegations at Geneva, was to form the inner cabinet and to act "in a general advisory capacity to the Interim Commissioner".

(3) *A National Security Council,* responsible for defence and internal security, was to consist of the Interim Commissioner, the leading members of the Council of Ministers, the two chiefs of staff and the Commissioner of Police. The Interim Commissioner could appoint and remove these officers who would be responsible to the National Security Council.[116]

Speaking to journalists after the meeting, Smith, while denying that there was at that stage a prospect of a breakdown, could hardly disguise the disagreement between him and Richard. Saying that they had had a good frank discussion, a diplomatic euphemism for serious disagreement, he stated that the British proposals were further away from Kissinger's plan than he had expected.[117] Indeed, the proposals amounted to immediate surrender of power, entrusting the future and safety of white Rhodesians in the hands of the nationalists and "perfidious Albion". For tactical considerations, Smith deferred his reply until after he had discussed the proposals with his cabinet. On January 24, after meeting Richard and exactly four months after accepting Kissinger's plan, Smith, in another major address to the nation, rejected the British proposals, even as a framework for negotiations, while offering to continue negotiating on the basis of the original Kissinger plan.[118] Richard, in his own words, was "extremely sad and disappointed".[119] If he was disappointed, it was only because his analysis of the situation was unsound, his optimism unwarranted and his expectations unrealistic. Already on January 13 the RF national executive had unanimously rejected the idea of a British presence during the transitional period because of their past record.[120] He should have known that the Rhodesian government would not accept a settlement amounting to surrender and abdication unless under conditions of *force majeure* which Kissinger had been able to produce.

A military defeat and South African pressure could produce the conditions for another surrender. Military defeat, or near defeat, in the guerilla war could have brought Smith to his knees. However, this was clearly not the case in early 1977. The guerillas, mainly ZIPA, did make a sustained effort to tip the military balance in their favour. Following the dictum of their mentor, Mao, that "you cannot win at the conference table what you have not won at the battlefield", ZIPA stepped up the infiltration of guerillas fom Mozambique. During the conference and Richard's shuttle, the RBC reported almost daily encounters between the security forces and guerillas.[121] In retrospect, from the point of view of the military balance, the guerilla infiltration which gathered momentum in late 1976 and early 1977 was the beginning of the end for white Rhodesia. Policy makers, however, act on the basis of prospect rather than retrospect, of self-delusion as much as of naked realities. There were those in the white establishment whose projection rested on a realistic assessment of the situation. Thus, the commander of the Selous Scouts wrote the following to the army commander in the wake of the Nyadzonia raid of August 1976: "We firmly believe that as long as the enemy has the capability to reinforce and in turn to receive large numbers of recruits at will, we are fighting a losing battle."[122] With his troops in the forefront of internal and external operations, he was in a position to assess the military situation more realistically than staff officers and politicians in Salisbury. However, it was Deputy Minister Sutton-Pryce, categorically ruling out a nationalist military victory, who represented the official mind.[123] The commander of the Repulse operational zone was even more optimistic: "We are on top."[124] Even the more realistic commander of the Selous Scouts believed that with a change of strategy the guerilla offensive could be contained.[125] The white public and politicians could take comfort in the successes of the security forces. The Selous Scouts, in particular, had perfected their internal pseudo-guerilla operations.[126] In November 1976, 245 guerillas were killed inside Rhodesia and the figure for the whole year was 1,852.[127] In addition, the Rhodesian army stepped up its external operation. In October 1976, and throughout the "British phase", the Rhodesian elite units carried out devastating attacks inside Mozambique.[128] The Rhodesian army was certainly coming out of its defensive shell. These external operations not only served to boost the morale of the security forces and the public at large; they also encouraged the government into believing that they could contain the guerilla thrust. The cost of the war, human and economic, was not yet one which could bring white Rhodesia to submission. Clearly ZIPA's claim that its offensive brought the Rhodesian government to the conference table had little to support it.

With the military balance unable to break the political deadlock, the crucial variable, as in the case of the Kissinger shuttle, was a regional one. In September 1976 the South African pressure forced Smith to succumb to Kissinger; in January 1977 the lack thereof enabled Smith to reject Richard's proposals. The pressure exerted in September 1976 was neither unconditional nor irrevocable. It was applied under mental and political duress and was justified by the prevailing regional and international circumstances and by the prospects of regional peace and stability within the framework of a defined settlement plan. Applying further pressure was not made easier by the fact that it had been once applied. The domestic constraints inhibiting the exertion of further pressure on the neighbouring white regime were still considerable. In fact, Smith's surrender in September 1976 made it more difficult to keep up the pressure. Smith, after all, had done what had been expected of him by Vorster. He had acted honourably by remaining obstinately faithful to his original commitment. Not having been privy to Kissinger's "tactical ambiguity", Vorster could not but endorse Smith's position and insist that a settlement was possible only within the framework of Kissinger's proposals.[129] In this position, Vorster was firmly supported by the Afrikaans press.[130]

South Africa's support for Smith's position also rested on wider regional and international considerations. In this respect, there was a large measure of convergence between South Africa's and Rhodesia's interests and objectives. It should be recalled that Vorster concurred with Kissinger on the understanding that a peaceful, moderate settlement in Rhodesia was an essential part of a determined U.S. anticommunist strategy. Those who might have forgotten it were reminded by a South African radio commentator that "the whole point of Dr Kissinger's original venture into southern Africa was to prevent an Angolan-style take-over in Rhodesia."[131] In early January 1977, SABC commentary restated South Africa's condition for its cooperation: "If, in its own interests, the West shows that it has the will and honesty to resist the march of militant Marxism in southern Africa, it can rely on South Africa's full support."[132]

To the paranoid South Africans, the communist threat in southern Africa in the wake of Kissinger's shuttle was imminent and overwhelming. There was increasing evidence which could only confirm their worst fears. In October 1976 the Soviets signed a treaty of military cooperation with Angola.[133] During November 19–25, a delegation of the Central Committee of the Cuban Communist Party visited Mozambique. A joint communique at the end of the visit expressed solidarity with the people still struggling for national liberation.[134] Back in August 1976 the Soviets had appointed Dr Vasiili Solodovnikov, the foremost Kremlin Africanist, as ambassador to Zambia.[135] In November 1976 Solodovnikov offered military aid to moderate

Botswana and admitted that Russia was training southern African guerillas.[136] On December 30, the same day Richard began his shuttle, it was announced that Nicolai Podgorny, the President of the Soviet Union, would visit southern Africa early in 1977. It was hardly surprising that SABC commentary saw "a danger that President Podgorny's visit is part of a well-laid Kremlin plan to convert the conference into a booby-trap for the West".[137] Throughout the conference and the subsequent Richard shuttle, the Soviet threat and the Soviet plan to subvert peace and stability and to undermine the position of the West in southern Africa featured prominently in South African newspapers and radio broadcasts.[138] The Soviet threat seemed particularly ominous because they had faithful surrogates at the regional and the domestic Rhodesian levels. At the regional level, Angola and Mozambique were considered by South African policy makers as loyal Soviet pawns. Machel's reference to the setting up of "the bases for support ... for extending the socialist camp from the Indian Ocean to the Atlantic Ocean"[139] could only confirm their worst nightmares. The exclusive recognition granted on January 9, 1977 by the FLP to the PF further aggravated South Africa's suspicions and anxieties. *Die Transvaler* and *Die Burger* saw it as part of the Soviet design.[140]

Thus, the kind of solution envisaged and desired by the South African government in September 1976 seemed to be vanishing as Richard's mission progressed. Without firm American stand and commitment, there was little hope of stemming the Soviet tide. In fact the British plan, fundamentally altering the original Anglo-American plan, and Richard's attitude, both at the conference and during his shuttle, strongly suggested a bias in favour of the Soviet clients. At a time when South Africa was facing increasing international pressure and the prospect of a guerilla front in Namibia,[141] it could have hardly been expected, for sound domestic reasons as well as for reasons related to perceived vital national interests, to be instrumental in ushering in what they viewed as a Soviet proxy regime in Rhodesia.

The U.S. presidential elections in November 1976, resulting in a new man in the White House, also influenced South Africa's policy towards Rhodesia. Kissinger's Rhodesian finale became irrelevant as South Africans were eagerly waiting for the prelude of the new administration. It would have been politically unsound to commit the future of Rhodesia and the region before the policy of the new administration became clear. This was all the more appropriate in view of some new and unpleasant tunes emanating from Carter's camp. In a pre-election interview, Carter himself said that he strongly favoured majority rule, not only in Rhodesia but also in South Africa. Andrew Young, Carter's

165

chief black supporter, said in the wake of the election that he expected Carter "to follow a most sensitive but most aggressive policy in southern Africa". A South African newspaper predicted growing pressure on South Africa by the Carter administration.[142] The new unpleasant sounds became increasingly alarming as the assumption of power by Carter was getting nearer. In mid-January 1977 Andrew Young, who was rewarded with the position of U.S. representative to the UN, said that "there should be a plan, right now, to train leadership to be able to run South Africa once majority rule comes." It was also reported that he would tour southern Africa in the first week of February, meeting, amongst others, Sam Nujoma, SWAPO's leader.[143]

It was, indeed, hardly surprising that South Africa was not prepared to put pressure on Rhodesia to accept the Richard plan. The Rhodesians were well aware of the warmer winds blowing pleasantly across the Limpopo. They were delighted with South African support for their position on the Kissinger plan. They were enchanted with the changing tunes of the Afrikaans press. They may have been over-optimistic in their interpretation of the depth of the change in South Africa's attitude,[144] but it was their perception thereof which largely shaped their policy and behaviour. Their assessment in January 1977, which ruled out pressure from their regional patron,[145] was certainly correct. The change in South African policy manifested itself not only in statements. After Smith's acceptance of Kissinger's proposals, the pressures which had been applied were removed. In mid-October 1976, the Rhodesian Minister for Transport and Power reported that the flow of Rhodesian exports to South African harbours had improved.[146] This was also true for the flow of military supplies into Rhodesia which had been previously held up.[147]

Thus, far from being defeated militarily and freed from regional pressure, the Rhodesian government did not have to settle at any price. When in December Smith called on the nationalists to realize "that the hand of friendship which has been extended is not and never will be the hand of a surrender",[148] he reflected the prevailing mood in government circles. Smith's rejection of Richard's plan could only confirm the suspicions of those who had viewed Smith's surrender to Kissinger as manipulative. To those holding such a view Smith gave a direct reply in his address to the nation on January 24, 1977, in which he rejected Richard's proposals:

> To those of you who still doubt the Government's sincerity in accepting the Anglo-American agreement, I ask them to analyse this contention. If this Government, or any Rhodesian govern-

ment, attempted to renege on such a solemn undertaking, not only their enemies, but their friends, as well, would turn on them. There could be no surer way of Rhodesia committing suicide.[149]

This, however, did not mean total surrender and abdication. Not all was lost. In this respect it should be noted that Rhodesian whites did not constitute a nation in the full sense of the word. They were few in numbers and many were only first generation in the country. Until UDI, and perhaps also afterwards, many of them regarded themselves as British as much as Rhodesians. Unlike the Afrikaners in South Africa, white Rhodesians did not share a deep sense of collective historical ties with the African land; neither did they possess a genuine commitment to a collective national destiny. While lacking the zeal, the fervour and the commitment of a vibrant nationalist movement, they were also spared from the depth of despair of a nationalist movement which had lost its cause. This made it easier for them to adjust to even radically changing circumstances. Essentially, they were fighting for economic and social privilege, for their colonial way of life, for a place under the African sun. Until Kissinger came, white political supremacy was viewed as a prerequisite for the preservation of the white community and its way of life. After September 1976, a new strategy was required to safeguard the essence of white Rhodesia without political domination. On December 6, 1976 Rowan Cronje, a Rhodesian minister, spelled out the new vision of Rhodesia that the government was fighting for:

> And I wish to assure you that this Government, while doing everything it possibly can to make the conference succeed, and to seek a just and peaceful solution to our problems, will not accept a solution which will jeopardize the stability, the economic resilience, the way of life, the peace and security of our country.[150]

In other words, they were striving for a neo-colonial Zimbabwe in which the whites' way of life and future would be securely entrenched.

The Richard plan was rejected out of hand because it did not provide the necessary guarantees. While Kissinger's strategy was originally aimed at neutralizing the militants and at ushering in a moderate, pro-Western regime, the Richard proposals were perceived as promoting the emergence of a militant, Marxist, pro-Soviet regime. Such a regime was the very antithesis of the whites' neo-colonialist vision. In the words of David Smith, the Deputy Prime Minister, on December 23, 1976: "Their aim is to destroy the Rhodesian way of life and replace it with a system alien to the nature, traditions and institutions of all Rhodesians − black and white."[151] Rhodesian whites needed not trouble their imagination. For them, neighbouring Angola and Mozambique were horrifying examples of Marxist regimes African style. During the Geneva conference and Richard's shuttle, there were increasing and ominous signs of the approaching communist menace. The emergence of the PF deprived the whites of Nkomo, a promising candidate for a moderate settlement. The anti-imperialist, anti-capitalist verbal barrage stemming almost daily from ZIPA's broadcasts was a cause for grave anxiety. Mugabe, the "blood-thirsty Marxist puppet",[152] who was rising to prominence, did nothing to allay white fears. In one interview for British television at the end of November 1976 he earned all his notoriety among Rhodesia's whites. He demanded the demobilization of the Rhodesian forces and spoke of confiscating farms without compensation. He also said that "certain people, including Mr Ian Smith, who constituted the illegal regime, will have to answer for their crimes in open courts."[153] It was with this in mind that van der Byl rejected the British ideas: "If this new proposal was to be imposed on us, it is better to fight to the last man and the last cartridge and anyway die with some honour than die in front of one of Mugabe's people's courts."[154] The increasing regional support for the militants exacerbated white anxieties. On January 15, 1977 Smith said that the exclusive recognition of the PF by the FLP put an end to the hope of reaching a settlement within the framework of the Geneva conference.[155] It was indicative of white perception of the implications of the British initiative that even the National Unifying Forum, a liberal pressure group, lent support to Smith in his rejection of the Richard plan.[156]

The Rhodesian government's alternative to the Richard plan was not a return to white political domination, but rather a settlement on the basis of the Kissinger plan with representatives of moderate African opinion. This was a variant of the internal settlement with which the government had toyed in the past. The temptation for the Africans was, however, much greater. The last time they had negotiated such a settlement they had not even been prepared to offer Nkomo parity in Parliament. A year later they were offering majority rule in two years, a prize Nkomo would have grabbed in March 1976. On January 24, 1977, after rejecting Richard's plan and reaffirming his commitment to Kissinger's, Smith appealed to his potential partners: "The alternative is that Rhodesians come together within their own country and solve the problem among themselves."[157] The only question was, who would these internal partners be?

The obvious ones were the chiefs who operated within the structure of white domination. However, at a time of such radical changes they required a more legitimate political appearance. It was with this in mind that, at the end of December 1976, a new party, the Zimbabwe United People's Organization (ZUPO), headed by senior chiefs Chirau and Ndiweni, was formed. Reflecting the winds of change blowing across Rhodesia, ZUPO denied being connected to the RF and sought to achieve majority rule within the shortest possible time. They wished, however, to achieve it peacefully through negotiations with the government.[158] Claiming that they were the natural leaders of Rhodesia, they wanted the British to invite them to Geneva.[159] Although the government much overstated the potential strength of ZUPO, they knew that a party based on the chiefs could not give substance, credence and legitimacy to a moderate internal settlement. Muzorewa and Sithole were the obvious targets for the government's overtures. Muzorewa, who was considered as leading the biggest nationalist constituency inside the country,[160] was a particularly appealing partner. Already on November 16, 1976 Smith had linked the prospect of a moderate solution to the readiness of some of the participants in the conference to pursue negotiations inside the country.[161] On his way back from Geneva on December 13, he said he was willing to meet Muzorewa during the Christmas recess.[162] The following day the RBC praised Muzorewa and Sithole as the only "truly willing parties to the conference", adding that "Smith is liable to concentrate his efforts on these elements in the hope of sorting something out before the next conference begins".[163]

With a view to creating a conducive atmosphere for a moderate settlement, the RF parliamentary caucus decided, before the end of Richard's shuttle, to repeal discriminatory legislation, including the crucial Land Tenure Act.[164] However, the prospective nationalist partners did not respond favourably to the suggestions and inducements emanating from the Rhodesian government. They had fully to internalize the radical changes in the nationalist camp and in their own position before they could give these suggestions serious consideration. They were still very sensitive to possible effects on their nationalist credentials. They had to seem as militant as anybody else. Thus on January 16, 1977 Muzorewa called for the "unconditional surrender of whites".[165]

Faced with Smith's rejection of his plan, even as a basis for further negotiations, Richard knew that his mission had come to an end. His immediate reaction was to blame Smith for his failure and to state that there was no point in reconvening the conference.[166] The British government, not yet being prepared to concede defeat, instructed Richard to stay on in southern Africa and try to salvage something from the wreckage. Richard obliged, announcing that the conference was, after all, still in recess and that he would stay on in the region. His mission came finally to a dead end on January 30, 1977, when he was rebuffed by the PF whose leaders refused to meet him in Lusaka because of their annoyance at his unilateral termination of the talks. The naked truth was that the British government did not possess the necessary diplomatic resources to close the wide gap between the Rhodesian government and the nationalists. The Geneva conference and Richard's shuttle joined the long list of Rhodesia's missed opportunities.

CHAPTER SEVEN

From International to Internal Settlement,

February 1977 – March 1978

Kissinger, despite the failure of his initiative, left a deep imprint on the process of decolonization in Rhodesia. His vital contribution was that at the level of the objectives, majority rule within a time-span broadly acceptable to most participants, at all levels of the conflict, became a new frame of reference. This was a breakthrough which proved irreversible. This was achieved, however, at the cost of maintaining confusion with regard to the nature of independent Zimbabwe and the transition period leading thereto. Because these crucial issues were left unresolved, the two strategic options – peaceful settlement and military struggle – remained open. But even at that level, Kissinger proved that through the skilful use of diplomatic resources and skills the conflict could be advanced towards a peaceful resolution. It was undoubtedly partly as a result of this lesson that the initiative in the conflict resolution effort throughout much of 1977 remained in the hands of the international actors. The international effort, which bore no fruits, gave way in November 1977 to negotiations between the Rhodesian government and internally-based moderate African groups. These negotiations culminated, in early March 1978, in an internal settlement. The internal settlement was favoured by very few. It was vehemently opposed by the PF and the FLP. The international actors laboured hard against it. South Africa clearly preferred an internationally recognized settlement. At least some of the signatories to the internal settlement would rather have been involved in negotiating an internationally recognized one. The internal settlement came to pass because its opponents did not produce sufficient energy – military, political or diplomatic – to effect their favoured solution. Furthermore, their actions and abstentions contributed to the ripening of the conditions in which the internal option emerged.

The concept of internal settlement was not, as we have seen, a new one. It was not merely a threat used by Smith whenever faced with

171

"extreme" demands. It was, in fact, inherent to the political philosophy of white Rhodesia. The Rhodesian brand of multi-racialism, allowing marginal black participation in the white-dominated political system, was, in essence, an internal settlement designed to perpetuate white control and privilege. The incorporation of Africans in the Cabinet in 1976 was indicative of the expansive potential of this option. The formation of ZUPO in late 1976 was designed to confer upon this option a measure of modernity and respectability. However, even before the Portuguese decolonization introduced a new impetus to the Rhodesian conflict system, the government was well aware of the limitations of a solution resting solely on a collaborating group devoid of nationalist legitimacy. Thus in 1973, as we have seen, Smith began negotiating an internal settlement with Muzorewa. However, what Smith offered to the Africans was not sufficient to entice even the moderate ANC. In the aftermath of the Victoria Falls bridge conference, Smith negotiated an internal settlement with Nkomo, a leader possessing both nationalist credibility and regional support. But even the radically changing regional circumstances and the opportunity to settle with a nationalist of such standing did not induce the Rhodesian government to concede sufficiently. In the wake of Kissinger's initiative and the Geneva conference, with majority rule within two years having been conceded, the scope for an internal settlement widened markedly. Thus, rejecting the Richard proposals on January 24, 1977, Smith presented the original Kissinger proposals as a basis for both international and internal settlement.[1] However, although the internal option was in the air from early 1977 and despite the fact that Smith's offer was much more attractive, the internal negotiations began in earnest only towards the end of the year. Conditions had to mature, potential partners had to make the necessary adjustments and the international effort had to be consummated before the internal option could be seriously entertained. From the perspective of an internal settlement, the Kissinger plan was devalued by changing conditions and by new plans. The Rhodesian government had to make further concessions to maintain the attractiveness of the internal option. Their ability to make these concessions must be primarily understood in the context of the unfolding guerilla war and Smith's standing in white politics.

The guerilla war continued to expand and intensify. In January 1977 Rhodesian sources estimated the number of guerillas operating inside the country at 1,500. In April and September 1977 the estimates rose to 2,500 and 3,600 respectively.[2] By September 1977 it was also estimated that there were some 8,000 guerillas ready for action in Mozambique and Zambia.[3] The number of casualties rose dramatically with almost daily reports of losses of soldiers and white civilians. In early July 1977 the death of the 360th member of the security forces since the beginning of the guerilla war in 1972 was announced.[4] In 1977, 197 Rhodesian soldiers were killed in action, only slightly below the number for the years 1972–1976.[5] In early December 1977 the 115th white civilian died in the five-year long bush war.

Although the guerillas intensified their operations and strengthened their hold on the African population, particularly in the ZANU areas, the impact of the guerilla effort had not yet decisively shifted the military balance in the guerillas' favour. Smith may have been over-optimistic when saying that his military chiefs had told him that they could go on indefinitely,[6] but the Rhodesian military and political leadership, even later in 1977, did not perceive the military situation as being desperate and uncontrollable. They did not totally lose the military initiative on either the internal or the external front. While not able to stop the guerillas' infiltration and the expansion of the guerilla war, the internal military effort was not without success. In almost daily encounters during 1977 the Rhodesians claimed to have killed 1,774 guerillas compared with 1,917 for the period between 1972 and 1976.[7] The internal military operations were backed up by an increase in the pace of resettlement of Africans in protected villages.[8] However, because of the limited effectiveness of internal operations and the defensive nature thereof, the military thrust was increasingly directed towards external operations in which the security forces could seize the initiative and give expression to their definite superiority in military skill and ingenuity. The external operations were aimed at stemming the guerilla tide by disrupting their training, supply and operations infrastructure, mainly in Mozambique. Besides the extensive use made of the outdated but highly effective air force, the Rhodesian elite units were increasingly deployed in such operations. These operations, directed mainly against ZIPA in Mozambique, culminated in November 1977 in two successive attacks on guerilla bases in Chimoio and Tembue.[9] In early 1978 Rhodesian forces began to launch across-the-border attacks on ZIPRA targets in Zambia.[10]

The guerilla offensive failed to force the hand of the Rhodesian government partly because of lack of unity and coordination in the guerilla camp. The PF had originally been formed as an alliance between two distinct political movements. However, in the wake of the Geneva conference the FLP, who had accorded the PF exclusive recognition, were keenly interested in fostering a more binding unity. ZANU and ZAPU also professed unity. Adopting the FLP rationale, Nkomo spoke of the danger of having more than one army at independence.[11] He sounded enthusiastic about the prospect of unity: "A dream since 1963 has finally come true. These reunification plans between us and ZANU are genuine because it comes from the inside."[12] Mugabe stressed the need for a strong army as the motive behind the search for military unity.[13]

As early as December 1976 Mugabe spoke of reconstituting ZIPA, or rather reabsorbing ZIPRA forces in ZIPA (ZANLA).[14] On January 17, 1977 ZANU and ZAPU set up a 10-member coordinating committee "to implement the jointly-agreed programme".[15] However, by the end of 1977, despite much deliberation and encouragement by the regional patrons,[16] military unity was still elusive. The truth of the matter was that the question of ZANU–ZAPU unity was still most problematic. When Mugabe said that the PF was not a marriage of convenience,[17] and when Nkomo was raving about "a dream since 1963" coming true,[18] they were either euphoric or speaking to the gallery. Nyerere admitted, in July 1977, that obstacles to unity were deep-seated differences between the two movements.[19] Despite fighting a common enemy for broadly the same goal of liberation, ZANU and ZAPU, Mugabe and Nkomo, were strange bedfellows. The long-standing rivalry and animosity which dated back to the early 1960s had been recently fuelled and exacerbated by the cohabitation under the ZIPA roof. Speaking to the PF military sub-committee, ZIPRA cadres attributed their opposition to unity to the killing of their comrades by ZANLA guerillas at Magagao in 1976.[20] The differences between ZANU and ZAPU were further intensified by the perceived imminence of liberation. As independence and the transfer of power were approaching, the competition was for much higher stakes. The PF was basically a tactical alliance, a platform from which both movements sought to further common as well as particular goals and interests. Neither was genuinely seeking unity in equality. Neither was prepared to relinquish ideology or to discard ambitions. For Mugabe, unity was the absorption of ZAPU and ZIPRA into ZANU. He was too devoted to ZANU and its historic mission to contemplate its dilution. For Nkomo with his ethnically limited mobilization potential, full unity would have been politically suicidal. At the time the PF was established, there was a most striking imbalance between ZIPA (ZANLA), with a large force and fighting experience, and ZIPRA, with neither. Nkomo had little interest in military unity, in which his guerillas would be submerged. It is also doubtful that he was interested, as it is argued,[21] in a genuine political unity. A loose alliance served him well in keeping his options open.

The delay in the implementation of unity generated suspicions in the uneasy alliance. ZANU's suspicions were heightened when the news of

Kaunda's secret meeting with Smith on September 25, 1977 came to light. A ZANU official claimed that a deal had been sealed to hand over power in independent Zimbabwe to Nkomo. After meeting with Kaunda to clear the matter up, Mugabe, his suspicion not having been allayed, confirmed that the Kaunda–Smith meeting created an atmosphere of mistrust within the PF.[22] In November 1977 a new controversy flared up around the Anglo-American proposal to hold the election before independence. While Nkomo insisted on holding the election after independence, Mugabe demanded that it be held during the interim period. In early December Nkomo responded to Owen's invitation to come to London for talks, while Mugabe declined.[23] On December 7–8 Mugabe and Nkomo conferred in Maputo, after almost three months during which they had not met, and papered over the differences regarding the Anglo-American proposals.

The most important issue which generated frustration, suspicion, tension and animosity within the ranks of the PF was the pursuit of the war. Already during the earlier phase of common ZIPA experience, ZANU had claimed that ZIPRA guerillas were not shouldering the burden of the struggle. This was still the case under the PF umbrella. Nkomo was painfully aware that at a time when guerilla struggle was becoming the main liberation strategy and when independence was on the horizon, his military inferiority was a very serious political handicap. Thus, from the second half of 1976, after withdrawing from ZIPA, he launched a massive recruitment and training campaign, which by early 1978 provided him with a well-trained, equipped and disciplined army of some 6,000–8,000 guerillas. ZIPRA's army was trained by Cubans, mainly in Zambia and Angola, and was generously provided with high-quality military hardware by the Soviet Union.[24] ZIPRA, however, until early 1978, committed only a small fraction of their guerilla force inside Rhodesia. At the same time that ZIPA were infiltrating badly trained fighters to step up the pressure, and paying a very high price in casualties, ZIPRA's well-trained guerillas were confined to their barracks. This gave rise to speculations that ZAPU was training its army primarily for the prospective struggle for power with ZANU.[25] Besides aggravating relations between the allies, ZAPU's policy prevented the PF from unleashing its full military potential. Large parts of Rhodesia, traditionally supporting ZAPU, remained relatively unaffected by the guerilla war. This enabled the Rhodesians to employ their limited forces more effectively against ZIPA and to entertain the belief that the military situation was manageable.

From a white Rhodesian perspective, the escalating ZIPA military pressure, even without the cooperation of ZIPRA, began to have an impact on the government attitude towards a political settlement. Brave public utterances notwithstanding, white political and military leaders came to realize that, while not facing an imminent military collapse, they were entangled in a no-win situation, and that a political solution was essential. Speaking on television in early June 1977, General Walls, the commander of the recently established Combined Operations, stressed that terrorism could be stopped only by political means.[26] On September 27 the Minister of Combined Operations linked the increased military effort to the objective of attaining a political settlement.[27] In private, General Walls warned Smith that as the guerilla pressure mounted, the government's bargaining position with respect to a settlement was weakening.[28]

The escalating guerilla war generated additional pressures which pointed to the desirability of a political settlement. The economic cost of the war was rising markedly. By mid-1977 the daily cost of the war had been as high as £500,000.[29] The estimates of defence spending for the 1977–1978 budget rose by 44 per cent to a record R$141 million. The overall projected counter-insurgency cost was estimated at R$200 million, about 26 per cent of the budget.[30] In September 1977 and February 1978, the defence allocation was supplemented by more than R$30 million.[31] The overall economic situation was deteriorating steadily. Particularly worrying was the fall of 6 per cent in the volume of manufacturing production following a 6.6 per cent fall in 1976.[32] In its October 1977 *Economic Bulletin*, the Standard Bank of Rhodesia, after detailing the effect of the war on the economy, had the following to say on the impact of 1977: "Over the past year the damage to the economy has switched from being temporary in character to permanent and structural in nature."[33] The forecasts for the future were equally gloomy. The predictions of the Rhodesian Banking Corporation in February 1978 were pessimistic all round. The Standard Bank's verdict, a month later, was unequivocally bleak: "Time is running out for the Rhodesian economy."[34] While the economy was not on the brink of collapse, the gravity of the situation must have had a significant impact on the government's political thinking. In his 1978 New Year message, while admitting the gravity of the economic situation, Smith failed to attribute it to the escalating war.[35] In early 1978, however, he confessed that the worsening economic situation was a major factor in prompting his government to seek a political settlement.

The intensifying war was also adversely affecting the morale of the white population. Besides the effect of the sharply rising casualties on the small face-to-face white society, there was a general sense of insecurity as the war zone was expanding. Convoys and curfews not only served to improve security, but also to underline the inherent insecurity. There was also a stepping up of the call-ups for military service. By mid-1977, white men under the age of thirty-eight were liable to be called up for at least 190 days a year, and those between thirty-eight and fifty could expect to serve not less than 70 days a year.[36] This severely disrupted not only the economy but also family life. The decline in morale was reflected in the emigration figures. In the first eight months of 1977, 11,685 whites left the country, while only 3,972 immigrated.[37] By the end of the year there was a net outflow of 10,908 whites, coloureds and Asians.[38] This was an alarming rate for such a small community.

It was the first time that the internal black–white conflict had generated strong pressures within white Rhodesian society for a genuine political solution. The business community was prominent among those putting pressure on the government for a settlement. Being at the sharp end of the economic struggle, they were more acutely aware of the approaching economic disaster. They also hoped that a settlement would improve the horizons of the Rhodesian siege economy. They believed that a moderate African regime could not fail to recognize the potential of the Rhodesian capitalist economy and would guarantee the conditions for the flourishing of their enterprise. In late April 1977 a new drive to achieve an early political settlement by businessmen, professionals and some farmers was reported. One of the farmers reflected the group's mood: "We have accepted majority rule and want to get on with it as soon as possible."[39] In early July more than 400 Bulawayo businessmen, at a combined meeting of the local chambers of commerce and industry, overwhelmingly approved a plan to study ways of assisting efficient transition to black majority rule.[40] On August 29 the president of the Associated Chambers of Commerce of Rhodesia (ACCOR) said that the business community wanted a settlement and was ready to capitalize on a settlement in a way which would lead to an economic explosion.[41] The multi-national corporations were certainly keen on a "neo-colonialist" transfer of power which would preserve their Rhodesian interests. It was with such a solution in mind that Lonrho's "Tiny" Rowland was instrumental in arranging the Kaunda–Smith meeting on September 25, 1977.[42] The business community was an important recruiting ground for the liberal opposition. Under its National Unifying Force guise this opposition, led by the outspoken Allan Savoury, called for an almost unconditional handing over of power to the African majority.[43] While Smith did not take Allan Savoury seriously, he had nevertheless to pay attention to pressures from more important sectors. As we have seen, army commanders were also advocating a political settlement, which at that stage could only mean majority rule. In fact Smith himself, in the aftermath of his surrender to Kissinger and in view of the rising cost of the war, recognized the desirability of a genuine settlement. However, unlike Allan Savoury, he was not prepared to entertain an unconditional hand-over. With the high rate of guerilla casualties inside Rhodesia and the resounding success of the external operations, the government could still perceive that they could negotiate a settlement from a position of relative strength and choose acceptable partners.

The government knew that more concessions to nationalist opinion were essential if they wished to attract credible moderate nationalist leaders to a settlement. On February 10, 1977 Smith threw a bait to Muzorewa offering to hold a referendum to test domestic African opinion regarding the choice of leadership. This was, however, clearly manipulative and Muzorewa gave it the cold shoulder.[44] On February 23 Smith announced a plan to modify the Land Tenure Act in a way which would open white land to African ownership.[45] The desegregation of white land which had been rejected by Smith in 1976 was a major change. In theory, at least, it eliminated the main economic pillar of the settler regime. While still rejecting political desegregation (common roll) and some elements of social desegregation (health facilities and residential areas), he announced other measures to ease racial discrimination.[46]

In legislating the amendment to the Land Tenure Act, which was constitutionally entrenched, Smith encountered opposition in the ranks of the RF. In a caucus meeting on March 2, 1977, which discussed the amendment, nine MPs expressed their objection and withdrew from the caucus.[47] When the amendment came before Parliament for its third reading on March 4, 12 RF dissidents voted against it. The government secured the required two-thirds majority only by bringing two loyal RF MPs from their sick-beds and by convincing three African MPs to vote with the government.[48] The 12 MPs were from the ranks of the conservative wing of the RF who had opposed Smith in the past. For them this amendment was far worse than the surrender to Kissinger. They still thought that provincialization of some sort could serve as a basis for a settlement.[49] For them, the elimination of territorial segregation marked the end of their dream of political segregation. This was their breaking point.

This was the first major rift in the RF since UDI and the first open challenge to Smith's leadership. He could not launch a new political initiative before securing his political base and receiving a new mandate from his people. On April 18 he called a special RF congress which gave him an overwhelming mandate to negotiate a settlement on the basis of his interpretation of majority rule.[50] This, however, did not obviate the need to deal directly with the challenge of the dissidents. The expulsion of the dissidents from the party in June and the growing signs of dissatisfaction at grass root level culminated in early July 1977 in the formation of the right wing Rhodesian Action Party.[51] The formation of RAP and the growing attacks on Smith's leadership posed a serious challenge to the Rhodesian government. The dominance of the RF and Smith's total command of the party were essential elements in post-UDI white politics. The authority of the party and its leader had to be reasserted before any determined effort towards a political settlement could be ventured. It was with this in mind that on July 18 Smith announced the holding of a general election on August 31, 1977.[52] The resounding RF victory gave Smith the mandate he sought. His party won 84 per cent of the votes cast and all the 50 white seats.[53]

It may be argued that this exercise in white politics at a time when the country was engulfed in guerilla war and when the Rhodesian problem had become a focus of keen regional and international interest was irrelevant. However, as long as white power was a reality, petty white politics remained very relevant. The exigencies of white politics considerably limited Smith's ability to make far-reaching political concessions which could be attractive to moderate nationalists. In the shadow of a general election, he was forced to remain within the confines of broadly accepted principles and policies. Thus he continued to speak of "the best majority rule" rather than black or unqualified majority rule.[54] He also continued to insist on a qualified franchise, while agreeing, without committing himself, to consider other means of protecting minorities.[55] When referring to his plan for an internal settlement, he envisaged "the creation of a broad-based government, incorporating those black Rhodesians who are prepared to work peacefully and constitutionally with government".[56] While being vague enough for the taste of the white electorate, it could hardly be attractive to moderate African nationalists at a time when even Chief Chirau was demanding universal adult franchise.[57]

If Smith had chosen to launch his internal settlement plan soon after the collapse of the Geneva conference in early 1977, he might have been able to entice ZUPO to go along with him. ZUPO, however, could not provide the domestic legitimacy and support which would have at least some potential for regional and international recognition. To achieve such a settlement, Smith had to attract African leaders with nationalist credentials. Such leaders were not yet available in early 1977. They came forward towards the end of the year not merely in

179

response to Smith's concessions. They had been groomed for their internal role primarily by the turbulent dynamic of intra-nationalist politics and by FLP attitudes. The internally-based nationalist leaders were ready to come forward only when the process of their political marginalization in the context of radicalizing nationalist politics had been completed.

These moderate nationalists did not easily give up their place in the central nationalist arena. They continued to fight for what they considered as their rightful place under the nationalist sun. It was, however, little more than rearguard action. On February 4, 1977 the position of the PF was further enhanced when the OAU Liberation Committee "endorsed the decision of the front-line states to give full political, material and diplomatic support to the Patriotic Front". It was not yet, however, a full victory for the PF. Delegates from some African countries blocked a Nigerian resolution calling for the "derecognition" of Muzorewa and Sithole factions and referring to the PF as "the sole nationalist movement in Zimbabwe".[58] The position of Muzorewa and Sithole was further eroded when in June 1977 the OAU Liberation Committee resolved to recommend to the forthcoming OAU summit conference to recognize the PF as the only legitimate representative of the Zimbabwean people.[59] At the conference itself, Kaunda, in a passionate speech, was instrumental in swaying the African heads of state towards the FLP position. Expressing satisfaction with the performance of the guerillas under the leadership of the PF, the summit called on "all Zimbabweans devoted to the struggle for the liberation of their country to do so within the Patriotic Front". The intensive efforts of Muzorewa and Sithole in lobbying moderate African heads of state came to naught.[60]

The OAU Libreville resolution was very consequential in determining the course of the Rhodesian crisis. On the one hand, it reinforced the PF in its determination to pursue the guerilla struggle to its logical conclusion. On the other hand, the Libreville resolution pushed the marginalized nationalist leaders into Smith's arms. Having already lost their regional base, they had now been excluded from the broader African arena. Since they were not prepared stoically to accept political oblivion, Rhodesia, with its African population as a political base and Ian Smith as a potential partner, was their only salvation. Sithole, in returning to Rhodesia from exile on July 10, 1977, soon after the OAU summit,[61] indicated that he had fully grasped the implications of the Libreville verdict. He was followed in September by James Chikerema, another veteran nationalist, who returned to Rhodesia after 13 years of exile.[62]

The internal leaders had to lose the international battle as well before they would be finally ready to negotiate and settle with Smith. From a broader perspective as well, the balance of the international involvement in the wake of the Geneva conference and throughout 1977 was instrumental in ushering in the internal settlement. One may have expected that the abysmal failure of the Geneva conference would discourage the international actors. As it turned out, however, the post-Geneva phase witnessed a very intensive international effort to effect a peaceful settlement in Rhodesia. The sudden death of Crosland, and the appointment of David Owen as Foreign Secretary in early 1977, were partly responsible for the British display of initiative and vigour. Young, energetic and ambitious, Owen must have seen the Rhodesian problem as a platform from which he could launch an international career. It was, however, the new Carter administration in the White House which provided the main impetus to the renewed international initiative. Commenting on Carter's victory, Smith expressed, on November 3, 1976, his confidence that the new U.S. president would be as dedicated to the cause of peace and stability and to the checking of the Soviet encroachment as his predecessor.[63] This was the misunderstanding of the year. The Carter administration infused into the Rhodesian crisis new conceptual and ideological inputs which had a definite impact on its course. These inputs stemmed from a new world view and reformulated U.S. global goals. The new global outlook of the Carter administration as such is beyond the scope of this study. However, the analysis of U.S. Rhodesian policy would be incomplete without reference to the new U.S. global strategy from which this policy was derived.

Carter introduced to the White House a global outlook and strategy which were radically different from those shared, to a smaller or greater extent, by successive U.S. administrations since the end of the Second World War. He heralded a new, constructive American involvement in the world. The conceptualizer and apostle of the new global deal was Zbigniev Brzezinski, Carter's National Security Adviser. The main thrusts of Brzezinski's globalism were broadly shared by Cyrus Vance and Andrew Young, who were responsible for Carter's southern African policy. In an article published in summer 1976, Brzezinski analysed the U.S.'s dire global position and offered a prognosis[64] which he further conceptualized after assuming office. Brzezinski believed that the U.S. was facing a potentially threatening crisis which stemmed from successive global policies which had failed to come to grips with radical world changes. He was particularly critical of the obsession with containing the Soviets. The Vietnam war was the Waterloo of this obsolete global strategy. The pursuance of such futile global policy was fraught with dangers of growing American isolationism and a corresponding increase in global hostility towards the U.S. Because of growing American dependence on a shrinking world, this dual trend could place in jeopardy not only U.S. economic welfare but also the very foundation of its socio-political system. This was a rather catastrophic outlook which envisaged not only American doom but also global chaos. However, these destructive trends were not inevitable. What America needed was a new leadership which would accept Brzezinski's diagnosis and adopt his cure. It would be a leadership which would rid itself of the conceptual shackles of the past and face constructively the challenges of a changing world. In May 1977, well established in his office, Brzezinski said:

> It is our view that we are now at a stage of history in which the United States again has to undertake a creative process of building a new world system. This must take into account the cumulative effect of all of the changes that have occurred in the past 15 to 20 years.[65]

By that time the U.S. was on the right course – the saviour and his apostle were leading their flock on the right track. On two occasions in 1977 – in October in a speech before the Trilateral Commission and in December in a briefing, or rather a lecture, to reporters – Brzezinski elaborated extensively on his analysis and global strategy.[66] Essentially, Brzezinski was the advocate of the integration of the Third World into the global system on a constructive and equal basis. He urged the decolonization of U.S. global policy. He was captured, indeed fascinated, by the emergence of the Third World in the wake of decolonization. He was impressed by the demographic explosion therein which dramatically changed the profile of the world. He was acutely aware of the impact of modernization among the new nations and the political implications inherent in a crisis of unfulfilled socio-economic expectations. He also noted the meteoric economic rise of some Third World countries such as Venezuela, Mexico, Brazil, Nigeria and Saudi Arabia. Little did he know that with the exception of the last, they would all be in economic decay or veritable bankruptcy by the early 1980s. In a sense, Brzezinski was a victim of a political mirage created by the petro-dollar boom of the 1970s.

Brzezinski's concern for the plight of most Third World countries was not primarily altruistic. Unlike Kennedy's U.S. mission in the world, it was not simply another revival of Wilsonian universal idealism. The Carter administration's global strategy rested essentially on a well articulated perception of U.S. self-interest. The world which the U.S. faced was not the bi-polar world of the past, dominated by the West and the communist bloc. It was rather a multi-polar world also shaped by the rich and poor nations of the Third World. This increasingly complex world could not be taken for granted. The U.S. was increasingly dependent on the Third World for raw materials, energy and also trade. From this perspective, the deteriorating socio-economic conditions in the Third World were becoming a matter for U.S. concern because they served as the infrastructure for the emergence of an ideological and political climate of hostility towards the West. This, in turn, could adversely affect the terms of trade between the U.S. and the Third World which would, in turn, have grave domestic consequences for U.S. society.

This profound transformation of America's global hinterland had been totally ignored by the Nixon and Ford Republican administrations which had been beset by a restricted and out-dated bi-polar conception of the world. The only viable and fruitful alternative was a positive American leadership based on a constructive engagement. This entailed a recognition of the legitimacy of global ideological and political pluralism and diversity. It also involved a positive identification with, and accommodation of, the legitimate and just aspirations of the underprivileged nations of the earth. On a socio-economic plane, it called for redistribution of global resources. In this respect, Brzezinski and his disciples were the prophets of a transition from the welfare state to global welfare. This was the only way in which the U.S. could shape a congenial world which would guarantee its well-being and prosperity.

The implications of Carter's new globalism for Africa, southern Africa and Rhodesia, in particular, were immediate and unmistakable. Referring to Carter's African policy, Vance stressed that "in no other aspect of foreign policy did our administration differ so fundamentally from that of our predecessors".[67] The appointment of Andrew Young, a black civil rights hero and a close confidant of Carter, as UN representative with full cabinet status, was indicative of the centrality of both the UN and Africa in the new administration's global policy. The UN was up-graded by Carter as an important platform for the pursuance of his policy.[68] From a hostile body dominated by an automatic anti-Western majority, the UN had to be transformed into an instrument for the shaping of a congenial world. In the UN context, black Africa, representing the biggest Third World contingent, was of particular importance. Africa, with its wealth of mineral and energy resources as well as its hunger, poverty and deprivation, was also the epitome of the Third World which Carter wanted constructively to engage. It was not incidental that Young's first important mission was a tour in Africa.[69] When defining U.S. interests in Africa, Vance conspicuously omitted the previously overriding strategic interests. He was more specific in referring to Soviet–Cuban involvement in the black continent: "The U.S. should not have negative, reactive policies opposing Cuban or Soviet involvements, but should develop alternative policies."[70] Indicative of the new African policy was also the shift in the focus of American interests from South Africa to Nigeria, the oil-rich and most populous African country. Nigeria was considered as the leading state in black Africa and Young believed that nothing could be achieved in that continent without its support.[71]

Black–White confrontation in southern Africa presented the new administration with challenges as well as opportunities. The reshaping of economic relations with Africa and improving the social conditions of its masses was at best an arduous, long-term project. In Lagos in August 1977 Young referred to the immensity of this task.[72] The issues pertaining to southern Africa, which were of great concern to Africa as a whole, were, on the other hand, of a political-ideological nature. Such issues lend themselves more easily for quick political gain. It was with this in mind that Young undertook his first trip to Africa in February 1977. It was for this purpose that he participated in the international conference in support of the African people in Rhodesia and Namibia in Maputo in May 1977,[73] and in the anti-apartheid conference in Lagos in August 1977.[74] These were ideal platforms from which he criticized past U.S. policies and propagated the new U.S. global and African gospel.[75] Southern Africa, in particular, was also a perfect arena to postulate and test Carter's doctrine of human rights which was central to his political philosophy. The human rights crusade was not a separate ideological thrust, nor did it simply emanate from Carter's religious convictions.[76] It was an integral part of the American model, of the American economic, social and political value system which the Carter administration wanted to project and use in the ideological competition between Western democracy and communist totalitarianism. Southern Africa was the testing ground for yet another component of Carter's sophisticated global strategy. In order to shift West–East competition to the level of value system and quality of life there was an urgent need to defuse regional conflicts around the world which relegated the competition to the level of violence and military struggle on which the Soviets throve. The need to resolve the southern African regional conflict was particularly urgent because it contained the potential for bitter, overlapping and mutually reinforcing East–West and North–South conflicts.[77] Thus, the U.S. administration had compelling reasons to take part actively in its resolution. The Rhodesian crisis was on the top of Carter's southern African agenda because of its fluidity and its explosive potential.

This then was the background for the revitalization of the Anglo-American Rhodesian initiative. On January 31, 1977 Vance fired the first Rhodesian shot on behalf of the new administration. Expressing regrets at the failure of the Geneva conference, he not only stated categorically that no U.S. support would be given to Rhodesia but also announced the administration's intention to repeal the Byrd Amendment, allowing U.S. purchase of Rhodesian chrome. This was meant "to re-emphasize our opposition to the maintenance of the illegal minority-imposed control of government in Rhodesia".[78] The initial Anglo-American consultations in early February 1977 were occasioned by Young's passage through London on his way to Africa. The British impressed on Young the need for a fresh peaceful initiative. They argued that only American participation could make it work because only they could influence the regional patrons to induce their clients to cooperate. According to Vance, uppermost in British thinking was their fear for their extensive economic interests in both black Africa and South Africa.[79] In February, Vance told Ivor Richard that the U.S. would work with Britain with a view to reconvening the Geneva conference.[80] In the meantime, Young had completed his African tour during which, besides projecting the new spirit of Washington, he had also discussed in Tanzania the resumption of the Rhodesian settlement efforts.[81]

On February 22 David Owen assumed Crosland's mantle. On March 11, at the end of a two-day visit to Washington, Callaghan, the British prime minister, stated that Britain, supported by the U.S., was ready to resume negotiations for a Rhodesian settlement. He indicated that Britain had a new, though unfinalized, plan for achieving a settlement.[82] At a meeting in Washington between Vance, Owen and Carter, the latter agreed to a new joint Anglo-American effort to achieve a negotiated Rhodesian settlement in 1978. The idea was still to convene a conference to settle the two central issues of constitution and transition. The transition was expected to last not more than six months, during which elections would be held under the supervision of a caretaker British administration. It was also decided to set up a development fund to assist the new independent state. Carter agreed to Owen's request that the U.S. cooperate with Britain as a full partner.[83] Having secured American support, Owen announced his intention to visit Africa to discuss the Rhodesian issue with the parties concerned.[84] On April 1 Vance discussed with Owen the latter's forthcoming

African trip. Owen's broad plan was to convene a preparatory conference with American participation, even if Smith refused to attend.[85] In the meantime, the Americans had prepared their credentials. On March 18 Carter repealed the Byrd Amendment underlining his commitment "to the concept of rapid transition to majority rule in Rhodesia under non-violent conditions".[86] On April 10 Owen left London for a week-long tour which took him to Lagos, Dar es Salaam, Maputo, Cape Town, Salisbury, Lusaka, Luanda and Gaberone, where he met the respective heads of state. He also met Mugabe and Muzorewa.[87] The results of the tour seemed to Owen positive enough to warrant the spelling out of the broad tasks of the prospective conference. This he did in Parliament on April 19. The conference, which he hoped would convene in June or July 1977 under the auspices of Britain and the U.S., would deal with the drawing up of a constitution protecting basic human rights, the working out of an "acceptable democratic process for the transfer of power and discussing the role of the international fund". Owen projected such optimism that he earned himself congratulations for the success of his "exacting and rigorous mission" from his opposition counterpart.[88] These, however, had not yet really been earned. Nkomo and Mugabe, in a joint press conference in Lusaka, stated three weighty objections to Owen's broad plan: "No American participation in the conference, the Patriotic Front must be the sole representatives of the African people ... the negotiations must be between Britain and the Front and Mr Smith must not have a separate representation."[89]

This was a definite setback which required the re-evaluation of the whole initiative. Owen was particularly upset about the objection to U.S. participation at the conference, which he considered as a vital component of his strategy. Vance, meeting Owen in London on May 6, 1977, persuaded the latter to scrap the idea of American participation "in deference to African concerns". The alternative was not a conference without the Americans but rather a substitute for a conference. This was the origin of the "consultative group" agreed on by Owen and Vance and announced by the former on May 11.[90] The idea was that the consultative group would meet the different parties to the conflict with a view to closing gaps and reaching an agreement. The alternative allowed for full and equal U.S. participation. It also circumvented the PF objection to the participation of Smith and the moderate nationalists in the conference. The resort to this alternative indicated a certain Anglo-American bias towards the PF. Smith interpreted it as "an attempt to pander to the Patriotic Front and the frontline Presidents".[91]

On May 24 John Graham, the British special envoy to the consultative group, held talks in Dar es Salaam with members of the PF coordinating committee.[92] In Salisbury he was joined by his American counterpart, Stephen Low, the U.S. ambassador to Zambia, in a meeting with the Rhodesian government delegation. Smith, according to Vance, was adamantly opposed to universal franchise unless the constitution included specific guarantees for the whites. He was prepared to accept a transitional period much shorter than two years if his demand for a qualified franchise was accepted.[93] Smith himself stated that the issues of franchise and guarantees would be the most important ones if the negotiations were to succeed.[94] On May 29 the Anglo-American group met Mugabe in Maputo.[95] The PF strongly objected to Smith's demands regarding both franchise and constitutional guarantees.[96] In early June Ted Rowlands, the British Under Secretary for Foreign and Commonwealth Affairs, was in Washington for consultation on Rhodesia.[97] On June 8, reporting in a Congress hearing, the U.S. Deputy Assistant Secretary of State for African Affairs, while not minimizing the difficulties, sounded a few optimistic notes regarding the efforts of the consultative group.[98] This optimism was rather unwarranted in view of positions expressed by other participants in the talks with the consultative group.[99]

Against this background, Vance and Owen met in Paris on June 24. Owen's concern about apparent contacts between Smith and Muzorewa gave the meeting an element of urgency. Earlier in June, on the basis of the consultative group's report, the British and the Americans concluded that special arrangements for the whites in a settlement were essential if Smith was to take part in the negotiations. At the Paris meeting, the question of the maintenance of law and order was uppermost in the minds of Owen and Vance. Owen maintained that for domestic reasons a British force was out of the question. He also believed that the whites would reject a UN peace-keeping force while they might be more receptive to the idea of a Commonwealth force. With regard to the local security forces, Owen was of the opinion that the guerilla forces should form the backbone of the army with the possibility of integrating certain units of the Rhodesian army, mainly the black battalions, into the new army.[100] On June 27 the Foreign Office confirmed that it was working with the U.S. State Department on a plan which contained three elements: an independence constitution, a development fund for independent Zimbabwe and an international peace-keeping force to maintain law and order during the transition period. The Foreign Office projected a sense of urgency regarding the Rhodesian initiative.[101]

The second shuttle of the consultative group in early July 1977 proceeded against the background of a radicalizing OAU holding its annual summit conference in Gabon. This round proved a complete fiasco. On July 7, as the group began its tour, the British government rejected any form of British military involvement in the transition period.[102] Thus, on the crucial issue of maintenance of law and order, they had nothing to offer. In Lusaka, on July 7, Nkomo refused to discuss constitutional issues with the group before finalizing the total transfer of political, military, police and judicial powers to the African majority.[103] This rebuff came from a leader they considered as moderate and whom they favoured as a successor to Smith.[104] They must have been hardly surprised when they subsequently encountered a similar response from Mugabe in Maputo.[105] Later, on July 17, the coordinating committee of the PF concluded that the Anglo-American initiative was designed to salvage rather than destroy the minority regime.[106] The group fared no better when they met in Salisbury with the Rhodesian Foreign Minister on July 10.[107] Smith himself made it clear that he was disappointed with their new settlement proposals.[108]

Owen did not give up. On July 23 he was again in Washington for talks with Carter and Vance on the final touches of a joint settlement proposal. Carter insisted on the need to base the proposals on universal franchise and free and fair elections open to all parties. He even spoke favourably of the prospect of Muzorewa emerging victorious. Owen, on the other hand, maintained that security arrangements were crucial to the acceptability of the proposals as a whole. In deference to the position of the PF and the FLP, it was agreed that the "Zimbabwe National Army" would be based on the guerilla forces, but that elements of the Rhodesian security forces would be integrated into the army in order to provide a bulwark against Marxist influences and to prevent white exodus. The main elements of the joint proposals concluded at that meeting were: "A transition based on British authority and restoration of legality; a democratic constitution; genuine majority rule with protection for the rights of all individuals; and free and impartial elections under British supervision and international observation". It was decided not to allow either party to veto the plan. It was also agreed not to block a settlement by Smith which followed the basic principles of the plan if the plan was rejected by the PF. Owen agreed that before broaching the plan, the Americans would discuss it with Nyerere during his forthcoming visit to Washington. It was also agreed to exert pressure on South Africa if it failed to deliver Smith.[109] Thus, although at that stage of the conflict resolution process the international actors were dealing directly with the Rhodesian actors more than before, they were also aware of the centrality of the respective regional patrons.

Carter and State Department officials met with Nyerere in Washington on August 4–5. State Department Africa experts were dismayed to learn from Carter that in private talks with Nyerere he had agreed that the nationalist guerilla forces would form the basis for the Zimbabwean army and that this provision would be incorporated in the Anglo-American proposals. In exchange, Nyerere agreed to endorse the proposals and to try to persuade the FLP to follow suit and to get from the PF an unequivocal commitment to the principle of fair elections.[110] No wonder that Nyerere was highly impressed with Carter's attitude towards Rhodesia.[111] While the securing of Nyerere's cooperation was an achievement, the price for it made it impossible for Smith even to consider the proposals. This private deal reflected both Carter's bias towards the African cause and his lack of understanding of the complexities of the Rhodesian conflict. Owen was upset about this deal, which was contrary to the understanding reached during his last Washington visit, because he still firmly believed in the need for some balance within the security forces.[112] Owen must have presented his views to Nyerere during his visit to London on his way back home. Indeed, Nyerere was disappointed that he did not find in London the same sense of urgency that he had encountered in Washington, and left London "a little confused".[113] This may have been the reason for his refusal to meet, in London, British and American officials and for his reference to the need to escalate the war.[114] In a brief meeting with Vance at Heathrow Airport on August 12, Nyerere, however, appeared to have agreed to Owen's idea of balancing PF dominance in the army with a role for the Rhodesian police during the transition, while maintaining his part of the deal with Carter.[115] On August 20 Nyerere announced that he had received two days earlier a joint Anglo-American message which confirmed their previous agreement that the guerillas would form the Zimbabwean army and that the Rhodesian forces must be dismantled.[116] Pik Botha, South African Foreign Minister, was also in London for discussions with the British and Americans. While saying that the Anglo-American proposals were "very serious", he remained uncommitted: "As far as Rhodesia is concerned, South Africa does not favour a specific plan."[117]

On August 25, as Owen was leaving for his crucial mission in southern Africa, Callaghan warned that it could be the last chance for a negotiated settlement in Rhodesia.[118] Indicative of Nigeria's newly acquired prominence, Owen began his shuttle in Lagos, where he met Young. They proceeded to Lusaka which they reached on August 27.

This mission, which was to crown the Anglo-American effort, proved a pitiable failure. Even before the mission started in Lusaka there were indications that elements in the Anglo-American proposals which had been leaked were unacceptable to both sides.[119] Owen and Young met the FLP in Lusaka on August 27. The Tanzanian *Daily News* reported from "sources from the meeting" that the deal proposed was unacceptable.[120] Nyerere's statement after the meeting lent credence to the *Daily News* report: "Our function is to get Smith and his army out of the way ... If we don't get it, we will continue the struggle." It was hardly surprising that the PF reacted similarly after Mugabe and Nkomo had met Owen and Young.[121] The Anglo-American team did not fare better on the white side of the dividing line. In two sessions with Vorster and Pik Botha on August 29, Owen and Young could not persuade the former to lend support to the proposals. While promising to ensure that Smith would honour any agreement he would sign, they refused to apply pressure on him to accept proposals about which they themselves had grave reservations.[122] Empty-handed, the Anglo-American team proceeded to Salisbury where they presented to the Rhodesians the final version of the proposals in writing. By then Smith's position was stronger than it had been for a long time. On August 31 he received an overwhelming mandate from his white electorate. A few days earlier he had returned full of confidence from Pretoria where he had held "cordial and constructive" discussions with Vorster. He stated publicly that Rhodesia had been given a free choice between international and internal settlement.[123] His white electorate and his white regional patron were the two pillars of his strength. Thus reinforced, Smith said two days before meeting Owen and Young that despite the new proposals, he was going to proceed with his plans for an internal settlement.[124]

The proposals which saw the light of day in Salisbury on September 1 represented a genuine attempt at compromise between conflicting interests and forces.[125] The independence constitution provided for universal franchise, but also for the election of 20 (out of 100) Specially Elected Members "to give adequate representation to minority communities". To allay the fears of the whites, the constitution also contained a Bill of Rights to protect "fundamental human rights and freedoms". The transitional arrangements were both crucial and problematic. To satisfy the PF the transitional period was to last not more than six months. To avoid the conflicting demands for a share in the transitional government, the proposals provided for a British Resident Commissioner armed with total legislative and executive powers. The maintenance of law and order, rightly a keen concern to all involved, was to be the task of the Commissioner of Police, "appointed by and responsible to the Resident Commissioner" and commanding the existing Rhodesian police force. This was part of the revised version of the deal between Carter and Nyerere. The proposals failed, however, to include the other essential part of the deal, namely the dissolution of the Rhodesian army. The Resident Commissioner was "to take command, as Commander-in-Chief, of all armed forces in Rhodesia". One of his tasks was "the formation, as soon as possible ... of a new Zimbabwe National Army which will, in due course, replace all existing armed forces ...". There was no mention of the source of recruitment. As the British were not prepared to commit their own forces, the proposals also included a role for the UN force during the transition. The UN was also to appoint "a Special Representative whose role will be to work with the Resident Commissioner and to observe that the administration of the country and the organization and the conduct of the elections are fair and impartial". The role assigned to the UN could hardly have been expected to please the whites. The proposals also included a sweetener in the guise of the "Zimbabwe Development Fund".

As often happens, the attempt to compromise two widely diverging sides ended up with the compromise being rejected by both. Smith responded to the proposals in a news conference on September 2. Tactically, he did not reject the proposals outright. This was, however, merely a diplomatic smoke-screen. Referring to the substance of the proposals he spoke of the "almost crazy idea" that his government would dissolve itself "without knowing what the replacement is going to be". A fully "crazy suggestion" was the one which emerged more from Owen's supplementary statement than from the proposals themselves, namely that the guerilla forces would form the basis for the security forces. Smith also objected to universal franchise and to UN involvement. He viewed the proposals as "a very cunning scheme to ensure that the Patriotic Front will be the next government of Rhodesia".[126]

The PF was more thorough in responding to the proposals, but not more positive. The PF Coordinating Committee met in Maputo on September 9, and after three days of deliberations came out with an elaborate response.[127] Significantly, the PF referred exclusively to the transitional arrangements. They rejected the role of the Resident Commissioner whom they viewed not as a neutral actor, but rather as a colonial officer whose government was involved in the dispute. They also strongly objected to the role of the Rhodesian police force and bureaucracy during the transition as well as to the retention of elements of the existing legislation. They claimed that under such circumstances the elections could not be impartial. They also rejected the Resident Commissioner's role as builder of the Zimbabwean army. They demanded the total dismantling of the Rhodesian army and police. Their view of the desirable transition arrangements was expressed unequivocally: "The only guarantee of the definite advent of genuine independence for Zimbabwe is the direct involvement of the patriotic liberation forces in all organs and functions of the Transitional Structures." Towards this objective, they were prepared to hold talks with the British government.

From the point of view of conflict management, the performance of Britain and the U.S. was grossly inadequate. Primarily they seem not to have fully grasped the dynamic of the intensifying conflict and the impact thereof on the respective positions of the different parties involved. They should have known before submitting their proposals that they could not serve even as a useful basis for bridging the gap between the PF and the Rhodesian government. Although Smith essentially accepted black majority rule, the gap was simply still too wide. As Smith moved towards, and perhaps beyond, possible previous middle ground, the PF, carried on the wave of a successful guerilla war, further radicalized its positions. After meeting Owen and Young, Nyerere referred to this shifting middle ground syndrome:

> If our Western friends are interested in helping us, then Smith and his army must go. ... Had it been two years back, when a peaceful solution was still possible, it would have been possible for the new government in Zimbabwe to inherit the entire structure – the army, police and other institutions.[128]

The Anglo-American effort could have resolved the conflict only if it was accompanied by sufficient political muscle either to push the two sides to the middle ground or to bring one of them to submission. However, neither the fading colonial power nor the eager super-power could produce such muscle, either directly or indirectly through the respective regional patrons. The same conflict dynamic which kept the gap between the conflicting domestic parties wide apart also brought the positions of the regional patrons closer than ever to the positions of their respective Rhodesian clients. On September 22, after a two-day meeting, the FLP stated only that the proposals "form a sufficient basis for further negotiations between the parties concerned".[129] Neither Britain nor the U.S. could pressurize the PF into accepting the plan or the FLP into prevailing on their clients.

The white component of the Rhodesian equation could have seemed more promising from the point of view of the potential for shifting positions. While the British and the Americans had no direct leverage in their relations with Rhodesia, they could hope to pressurize Smith through his regional patron. Vance believed that if "properly handled" the South Africans would support a negotiated settlement.[130] Indeed, the South African government had very good reasons for supporting a peaceful settlement in Rhodesia. In fact, they had better reasons for that during 1977 than in September 1976. Their communist onslaught nightmare was coming true with a vengeance. March 1977 was an ominous month in this respect. Fidel Castro spent much of the month travelling the length and breadth of Africa spreading the gospel of revolutionary solidarity.[131] Towards the end of March, Podgorny, the U.S.S.R. President, also made a tour of Africa, concentrating on southern Africa where he visited Tanzania, Zambia and Mozambique.[132] In South African eyes March was also, not coincidentally, the time of the invasion of Zaïre by the Katangese gendarmes, based in Angola and believed to have been trained, inspired and led by Cubans.[133] A government mouthpiece spoke of "communist moves which could eventually engulf ten states including South Africa".[134] The pro-government *Citizen* gave a very dramatic description: "Angola and Mozambique are red. Zaïre is invaded from Angola by Red-backed forces. Swapo are poised for a push from Angola with the backing of the Reds. Rhodesia is attacked by Red-trained terrorists. The capitals of Black Africa are centres of communist intrigue, payola and payoffs."[135]

Thus, a peaceful settlement in Rhodesia as part of a Western effort to stabilize the region and check communist advance was, more than ever before, a vital South African interest. However, the U.S.–South Africa understanding which brought Smith to submission in September 1976 did not last the Ford–Kissinger era. The Kissinger–Vorster understanding and cooperation rested on two main pillars: that the Rhodesian settlement formed part of a joint effort to combat communism, and that in exchange for the support in Rhodesia, and possibly Namibia, South Africa would be left alone to sort out its racial problems. The Carter administration did not wish to inherit this shady Kissingerian deal. From this perspective, the same global and African strategy which made Carter so eager to solve the Rhodesian conflict contained the seeds of failure. Carter could hardly have been expected to join South Africa in an anti-Soviet crusade. Young, in fact, repeatedly claimed that the Cubans served as a stabilizing factor in Angola.[136] In this vein, his answer to a question about the prospect of a Marxist regime in Rhodesia was: "I don't know what a Marxist

193

government means any more. If Angola is a Marxist government and its main trading partner is the United States, then that doesn't worry me."[137] Vance writes in his book: "President Carter and I were not willing to seek political advantage by presenting opposition to Soviet influence and radicalism as the foundation of American policy towards Pretoria."[138] As Vance points out, the new attitude towards South Africa was reinforced by the administration's stand on the issue of human rights. From this point of view, Carter could not make a deal on Rhodesia on the basis of absolving South Africa. This would have been not only morally inconceivable to a highly moralistic administration, but also grossly counter-productive to the whole African strategy. How could they insist on majority rule in Rhodesia and ignore it in the case of South Africa which was conceived by black Africa as the bastion of white supremacy and racialism? Brzezinski did concede that "South Africa is much more complex" than Rhodesia and Namibia and that consequently the solution to its domestic problems would take more time.[139] However, already in February 1977 it had been reported in South Africa that Young envisaged majority rule in South Africa in less than four years, probably 18 months.[140] This was hardly pleasant music to South African ears. The direct and immediate U.S. challenge to apartheid also stemmed from the administration's strategy of conflict resolution which was diametrically opposed to Kissinger's step-by-step approach. Brzezinski presented his approach when answering a question about the possibility of pressure on South Africa on the apartheid issue being self-defeating in attempting to secure majority rule in Rhodesia and Namibia:

I would say that not to do it would be self-defeating. If you pursue a policy that was pursued at one stage by this country of getting Vorster to help you get change in Rhodesia at the cost of supporting him in South Africa – all you're doing is transferring the conflict to a higher, more intense and more enduring phase.[141]

Vance described this approach similarly: "The republic itself was part of a larger problem of instability in southern Africa because of its own political repression and racial discrimination."[142] This fancy approach may have been theoretically plausible. However, as a conceptual tool for the purpose of resolving the Rhodesian conflict, it was certainly counter-productive.

The South Africans were shocked and bewildered by the new tunes emanating from Washington. The Afrikaans nationalist press reacted in amazement and rage.[143] Official South Africa soon joined in. In April

1977 Pik Botha, the new Foreign Minister, reacted vehemently to Young's reference to South Africa as illegitimate.[144] Speaking in Parliament in mid-April, Dr Mulder said that South Africa was becoming tired of being slapped in the face by the Western world and that it might look for friends elsewhere.[145] During the first few months of the new administration, there were also a few comforts such as the affirmation that South Africa was, after all, legitimate, or Carter's statement that South Africa was a "stabilizing force".[146] There may have been some hopes that the young administration was still finding its feet, and that matters might be resolved. Pik Botha attributed the administration's attitude to American ignorance of the complexities of Africa and southern Africa in particular. There were some hopes that the U.S. would rise to the reality of international relations. Thus, in early May 1977 an SABC commentary suggested that recent Soviet encroachments throughout Africa would bring the U.S. back to its traditional anti-communist stance. It saw the prospective Vorster–Mondale meeting as an opportunity to re-establish U.S.–South Africa cooperation.[147] The meeting which took place in Vienna on May 19–20 was of considerable importance in the evolution of the Rhodesian conflict. The Americans did not treat the prospective meeting lightly. Since March, the U.S. vice-president, Vance, Brzezinski and Owen had prepared an "authoritative statement" of U.S. southern Africa policy which would enable Mondale to convey to Vorster the full thrust of the new policy.[148] The crucial part of the Vienna meeting was that relating not to Rhodesia or Namibia, but to South Africa itself and the prospect of U.S.–South Africa relations. Mondale made it absolutely clear that when the administration spoke of full African participation in South Africa they meant one man one vote and that if progress towards that end was not initiated, the relations between the two countries would be adversely affected. Mondale emphasized that U.S. policy, far from being ephemeral, stemmed from the depth of experience of a transformed American society.[149] Reporting on the meeting to Parliament on May 27, Vorster admitted: "We may not like it, but there is this gulf between the U.S.A. and South Africa. Their standpoint is 'one man one vote' and we in this Parliament reject it."[150]

American attempts, in the wake of the Vorster–Mondale meeting, to sweeten the bitter pill in order not to push the South Africans into the laager, failed to mask the main thrust of their policy. Although there was no wish to precipitate an open and irreparable crisis with the Western super-power, the Afrikaner nationalist reaction to Carter's policy was characterized by defiance and determination. *Die Burger* concluded on June 17 that "as far as South Africa is concerned, we believe there is no salvation whatsoever in trying to appease America."[151] There was also a sense of moral indignation which was expressed by Pik Botha: "What have we done to the black people here? We have not hated them. We have not eradicated them as the Americans did their Indians. Russia is getting better treatment than we are. Where is the morality in that?"[152] Under the prevailing circumstances, there was no basis for South African support for U.S. designs. Pretoria was not likely to cooperate in implementing a strategy whose ultimate goal was the destruction of white South Africa. They could hardly have been expected to collaborate with those whom they perceived as giving in to the communists instead of fighting them. Connie Mulder went as far as saying that he was more perturbed by the West's response to the Marxist challenge than by the challenge itself.[153] Joining the British and the Americans in implementing the proposed Rhodesian settlement, which was bound to enthrone the PF "Marxists", was contrary to South Africa's perceived vital regional interests. South Africa was concurrently facing another diplomatic offensive in southern Africa. In April 1977 the five Western members of the UN Security Council formed the so-called Contact Group to negotiate with South Africa and SWAPO an internationally accepted settlement for Namibia.[154] In view of the prevailing mood in Washington, there was a definite possibility that within the framework of such a settlement "Marxist" SWAPO would be a serious contender.

Facing such a bleak prospect, the South African government, interested as it was in an international settlement, began to see merit in a moderate internal settlement. In Namibia, since 1976, they had begun to implement such a settlement through the Turnhalle constitutional conference.[155] At best, the internal settlements in Namibia and Rhodesia could eventually acquire international recognition. At worst, they could provide South Africa with room to manoeuvre, with a temporary military and diplomatic buffer to ward off, or to postpone, the perceived onslaught against the republic itself. These were the considerations which determined South African attitudes towards the Anglo-American Rhodesian initiative. Since they did not want to precipitate a head-on confrontation with the U.S., they exhibited apparent willingness to cooperate. Thus, despite his basic disagreement with Mondale, Vorster undertook at the Vienna meeting to "support British and American efforts to get the directly interested parties to agree to an independence constitution".[156] Pik Botha, who went to meet Owen and Vance in August, was even prepared to say that the Anglo-American proposals merited close consideration by the parties concerned.[157] At the same time, the South African government persistently refused to commit itself to any specific plan or to exert pressure on Rhodesia.

Since South Africa's cooperation was vital in making Smith amenable to the Anglo-American proposals, the U.S. was not inclined equanimously to accept Pretoria's aloofness. Thus, pressure on South Africa to secure its collaboration figured prominently in U.S. thinking on Rhodesia. At the end of the Mondale–Vorster meeting, the former warned about the consequences of a failure to achieve progress on all fronts.[158] Vance writes that Mondale warned that in such a case the U.S. "would have to change its position of opposing mandatory sanctions against South Africa".[159] In their July meeting in Washington, Carter, Vance and Owen agreed that if Vorster failed to get Smith to accept their proposals, the U.S. "would put strong pressure on South Africa".[160] In his meeting with Nyerere in early August and in subsequent letters to other front-line presidents, Carter stated that if the PF accepted the Anglo-American proposals and Smith declined, the U.S. would support sanctions against South Africa to induce them to exert pressure on Smith.[161] In early August Vorster blamed the U.S. for backing an international pressure campaign against South Africa.[162] Coming back from his August 12 London meeting with Owen and Vance, Pik Botha clearly indicated that strong pressures were exerted on him.[163] Of course, these were only threats to exert pressure. Until the failure of the Owen–Young shuttle in September 1977, no actual pressure was exerted. Few countries will yield to threats of pressure when perceived vital national interests are at stake. This was certainly true in a country like South Africa, afflicted by siege mentality and used to being threatened. These threats were, in fact, counter-productive, serving only to reinforce Pretoria's defiance. Returning from his London meeting, Pik Botha said that he had told Vance and Owen that they were mistaken if they thought that South Africa would yield to pressure. He added that since they were pushing South Africa towards "destruction" his government saw no advantage in cooperating with them in solving the problems of southern Africa.[164]

In fact, one of the main "achievements" of the threats and the Anglo-American effort as a whole was to throw Vorster into Smith's arms. As the crucial Owen–Young shuttle was approaching, South Africa's attitude towards Rhodesia became more favourable. On August 4, 1977 Pik Botha said at the end of a visit to Salisbury: "We are not going to let outsiders dictate their solutions to our part of the world." On that occasion, Smith said that he got from South Africa full backing for his internal settlement plans.[165] After meeting Vorster on the eve of his crucial encounter with Owen and Young, Smith said that he was confident that he would continue to enjoy South Africa's backing if he rejected the Anglo-American proposals and that he was given by South Africa freedom to choose between international and internal settlement.[166] Indeed, all that Vorster was prepared to undertake in his meeting with Owen and Young was that Smith would abide by any agreement he signed.[167]

Thus, in sum, the Anglo-American initiative failed due to a mutually reinforcing combination of a faulty comprehension of the complexities and dynamics of the conflict, a choice of inappropriate strategy, and a failure to mobilize sufficient diplomatic resources. Although the settlement proposals were rebuffed by all the parties involved, the British and the Americans did not give up easily. For the Americans, southern Africa was one of the major thrusts in their new global policy and they were not likely to take the first "no" for an answer, especially when they had not yet played out their cards. Since they had exhausted all the reasoning, any ray of hope could rest only on the application of actual pressures. As their scope for exerting pressure on the PF, directly or indirectly, was very limited, their only option was to turn the screws on South Africa. They had to move from threats to positive action. It may not have been entirely coincidental that on September 2, the day Smith effectively rejected the Anglo-American proposals, the *Star* reported from Washington that the U.S. had prepared "a set of contingency options" against South Africa.[168] In the Johannesburg *Sunday Times*, on September 11, there was reference to Young's threat to "squeeze" South Africa until it forced Smith to surrender.[169]

South Africa could hardly afford to treat lightly the prospect of a Western and international onslaught in addition to the perceived communist one. It would have been a grave error to precipitate such an eventuality. Thus, while not forgoing the essence of their attitude towards the Anglo-American proposals, the deflection, or at least the delay, of Western and/or international pressure became a major South African foreign policy goal. In this endeavour, South Africa needed the cooperation of its client. Indeed, cooperation and coordination of policy between the white patron and his client throughout the Anglo-American initiative were far greater than ever before. There is little doubt that the essence of Smith's response to the Anglo-American proposals, namely accepting them as a basis for further negotiations while rejecting their essence, formed part of a coordinated strategy worked out at the Vorster–Smith meeting in late August 1977. The main thrust of this strategy found expression in the Afrikaans press. The *Oggenblad* wrote on September 3: "Mr Smith's best strategy now would be to continue talking with the British and Americans, but in between, get his own internal settlement off the ground."[170] Pik Botha, in an interview, reflected more authoritatively government thinking. While arguing that sanctions against South Africa would be counter-productive, and condemning the security arrangements contained in the Anglo-American proposals, he also made it clear that his government did not favour an internal settlement and had committed itself to an internationally recognized settlement.[171] Smith gave expression to his cooperative mood on September 18 by suspending his plans for an internal settlement.[172] Earlier, on September 12, Smith had been in Pretoria for consultations with Vorster and some of his senior ministers.[173] The Kaunda–Smith meeting on September 25, the preparations for which had been known to the British and the Americans, fitted nicely into the patron–client positive tactic.[174] This tactic was rewarded when on September 20 the U.S. National Security Council Policy Review Committee concluded that since Smith was willing to negotiate, the time had not yet come to apply sanctions against South Africa.[175]

Encouraged by signs of responsiveness and flexibility on the part of South Africa and Rhodesia and by the fact that the PF and FLP had left the door slightly open, the Americans and the British proceeded with their initiative on the basis of the rejected proposals. In terms of the proposals, the UN Security Council proceeded on September 29, 1977 to appoint a special UN representative to work with Field Marshal Lord Carver, the British Resident Commissioner for Rhodesia.[176] Under the Security Council mandate, the UN special representative was to hold discussions on a cease-fire with all the Rhodesian parties and the UN Secretary General was to report on the results of the discussions as soon as possible.[177] On October 21 the British government announced that Carver would begin his mission to negotiate a cease-fire at the end of the month, assisted by Lieutenant-General Prem Chand, the UN special representative.[178] The Carver–Chand Mission was stillborn, worthy of its Owen–Young parentage. It represented a grave error of judgement, strongly suggesting that the initiators had learnt very little from their previous failure. Smith was absolutely correct saying on October 23 that Carver had been given an "impossible task" and that the British had "put the cart before the horse".[179] Indeed, what point was there to discuss a cease-fire when there had been no previous agreement on the constitution and the transition arrangements? Owen exhibited a gross ignorance of the relevant circumstances and of the true state of his initiative when he spoke on October 17 on its prospect: "There is no obvious obstacle to having serious discussions at present. If our demands were totally unacceptable we would have to look at it,

but all the parties have shown a willingness to discuss the proposals."[180]
No sound policy could stem from an unsound assessment of the reality.

Carver and Chand's first stop was Dar es Salaam where they met Nkomo and Mugabe. The Mugabe section of the PF had already voiced, on October 25, strong opposition to the role of the UN peace-keeping force and to Carver's role as builder of the new army. They repeated their insistence on the total dismantling of Rhodesia's military and para-military forces and on ZIPA's policing the transition period.[181] Nkomo also said that he wanted to talk about the transfer of power to the PF and only then would he be prepared to discuss the cease-fire.[182] Thus, the meeting which was supposed to last two days was finished in about an hour.[183]

Carver and Chand did not fare better in Salisbury, which they reached on November 2. Smith had already taken strong exception to the British plan to disband the Rhodesian security forces.[184] There had to be good new reasons for Smith to be forthcoming. Expressing optimism on October 17, Owen pinned his hopes also on the application of pressure on South Africa.[185] These were still mere threats. Towards the end of October the Americans and the British were beginning to move from threats to action.[186] Around the time Carver and Chand were on their tour, the Security Council was discussing anti-South African actions. While rejecting a resolution calling for economic sanctions, the Western bloc supported a mandatory arms embargo which was subsequently imposed on November 4, 1977.[187]

If the British and Americans believed in the effectiveness of such pressure, they had grossly miscalculated. They should have taken more seriously what South African leaders had been saying. In mid-September, Vorster insisted that he would not compel Smith to accept the Anglo-American plan even in the face of U.S. pressure.[188] In reaction to Carter's announcement that the U.S. would support an arms embargo against South Africa, Pik Botha threatened that it would "make it more difficult to find possible solutions for southern Africa".[189] South Africa's defiance was further reinforced, at that particular juncture, by the impact of two interlinked domestic developments which the British and the Americans, from their global vantage point, seem to have failed to consider. In August and September Vorster outlined his proposals for a new constitutional dispensation which proposed to integrate the coloureds and the Indians in a unitary three-tier system.[190] Seeking a fresh mandate for the new constitution, he announced on September 21 that parliamentary and provincial elections would be held on November 30, 1977.[191] The combination of domestic reform which touched at the root of Afrikaner nationalist ideology and a policy of regional appeasement was the worst possible recipe for a Nationalist electoral campaign.

Thus, by the time Carver and Chand reached Salisbury on November 2, Smith's position vis-à-vis his regional patron was even stronger than it had been at the time of his meeting with Owen and Young on September 1, 1977. Smith not only rejected Carver's plan without much ado, but also demonstrated his indignation at the British for coming with the same "insane" proposals by treating the distinguished lord insultingly. Under the prevailing favourable circumstances, Smith could hardly have been expected to agree to disband most white army units, to restrict his black battalions to the barracks and to approve the formation of six new battalions from the guerilla forces as a basis for a new national army.[192] As this plan suggests, the U.S. and Britain sought to close the gap between the PF and the Rhodesian government by making their proposals more attractive to the former and putting pressure on the latter. However, the attraction was not sufficient and the pressure proved counter-productive. Much more attraction and much more pressure were required to give their initiative a fair chance.

The failure of the Anglo-American initiative allowed Smith at last to launch his favoured internal option. There remained the question of partners. The obvious candidates were Chief Chirau and his ZUPO, Muzorewa and his UANC and Sithole with his private ZANU. These shared two very serious shortcomings. Firstly, they controlled no guerilla armies. This meant that the internal regime with the existing limited military potential would have to face an escalating guerilla war. Secondly, they lacked regional and broader African support. This meant that the chances of such internal settlement to secure African and international legitimacy and recognition were rather scant.

This was the background of the meeting between Kaunda and Smith which was expedited by Lonrho's chief. Denial by both Kaunda and Smith notwithstanding, the most obvious and relevant common denominator of Kaunda, Smith and Rowland was their preference for Nkomo as the leader of independent Zimbabwe. From a white perspective, Nkomo had what the other internal candidates sorely lacked − a well-trained, effective and disciplined army, a limited but solid regional support and extensive African and international connections. He was also perceived, despite his Soviet connections, as a Rhodesian Kenyatta in the making. There is evidence that the Rhodesians continued to maintain fairly regular secret contacts with Nkomo after the collapse of the Smith–Nkomo negotiations in March 1976.[193] When news about the Kaunda–Smith meeting leaked out, a Zambian spokesman confirmed the information on 1 October, but minimized its significance.[194] If this was the case, it would be very difficult to account for a second trip by a Rhodesian delegation to Zambia three weeks later to negotiate "on all points concerning pensions, concerning certain rights for minorities and representation in parliament and so on".[195] In the end, no breakthrough resulted from these meetings. The leakage of the news of the first meeting was certainly not helpful. Beyond that, however, it seems that both Kaunda and Nkomo were too caught up in the dynamic of the escalating liberation war to be able to disengage and make a separate deal with Smith. The Zambians were quick to reaffirm their commitment to the guerilla war.[196] Nkomo, despite difficulties within the uneasy PF alliance and his anxieties resulting from his weakness therein, must have been very hesitant about the whole exercise. He was aware of the high price in terms of nationalist legitimacy that he would have to pay for striking a separate deal with Smith. Rhodesian officials who were involved in the secret contacts with Nkomo said that while preferring a peaceful settlement, he always stressed that it had to include Mugabe.[197] On November 14, in a dire need to reconfirm his belligerent credibility, Nkomo declared that the guerilla forces would fight a "war to the end".[198]

With the failure of the Kaunda–Smith contacts, the only candidates for an internal settlement were the non-PF moderate African leaders and parties. Of these, ZUPO was eager from the outset. On March 3, 1977 Smith formally met ZUPO's leadership to discuss the prospect of internal settlement.[199] The moderate nationalists, having no guerilla armies to back them, knew, after the Geneva conference, that the internal settlement was one of their options. They were, however, also aware of the high price that such an option entailed. Consequently, they did not intend to plunge into it light-heartedly. As long as the process of their marginalization in the nationalist camp had not been completed, they persistently and determinedly rejected it. However, by early July the rejection of the non-PF nationalists by the FLP and the OAU considerably narrowed their options. The return of Sithole to Rhodesia on July 10 was indicative of their drift towards the internal solution. However, they had to lose the international battle as well before they would come forward. The original insistence of the British and Americans on the participation of all the nationalist factions who had taken part in the Geneva conference in their settlement plan, despite PF objections,[200] gave the moderates some hope. Muzorewa, in particular, hoped to win an internationally supervised free and fair election. Thus, on May 24, 1977 the UANC lent support to the Anglo-

American initiative.[201] However, by August, when Owen and Young toured southern Africa with their proposals, the moderates realized that there was no international salvation for them either. The Anglo-American team ignored Muzorewa's demand for a referendum to decide who would negotiate on behalf of the nationalists, and the transition arrangements gave a clear advantage to the PF.

By early September, the prospects for an internal settlement looked better. As seen above, however, Smith himself shelved the expected internal initiative on September 18, and a week later he met Kaunda. By September the moderate nationalists were almost ripe for the picking. Already on July 28 Sithole had pledged that under majority rule the Rhodesian security forces would not be dismantled.[202] Clearly, he saw the Rhodesian security forces as an alternative military power base. On September 20 Chikerema, Muzorewa's first vice-president, said much the same.[203] Although Muzorewa saw fit the next day to repeat his party's official view that the new national army should be based on the guerilla forces,[204] it is very doubtful that he either meant it or wished it.

For the moderate nationalists to come forward, they also needed an offer of a credible settlement that would offset the loss of credibility through negotiating with Smith. The crucial issue was the franchise. They could not afford to accept Smith's demand for a qualified franchise. On May 24 Muzorewa said that it was too late for a qualified franchise.[205] In late July 1977 Muzorewa announced a plan consisting of universal franchise and independence by March 1978.[206] By then, even ZUPO was demanding universal franchise. A ZUPO spokesman, in fact, blamed Muzorewa for "stealing" this demand from his party.[207] In early September Sithole stated: "The African people regard the franchise as the key to the present problem."[208] Beyond that, the moderates were prepared to reassure the whites with respect to vital issues like the security forces, the economy, white participation in the politics of independent Zimbabwe and individual rights.[209]

After the general election of August 31, and the presentation of the Owen–Young plan the following day, Smith began gradually to gravitate towards his potential partners. On September 2, carried by the momentum of the election campaign, he still rejected universal franchise. It was, however, a somewhat diluted, vague and qualified rejection.[210] Asked on September 25 if he was on the verge of conceding one man one vote, he replied: "Yes, with the proviso that I would like to know what the alternative ideas are for preserving the kind of standards that I have referred to and I have been assured that there are ways and means of doing this."[211] Smith, however, was still vacillating, giving a negative answer to the same question on another occasion the same day.[212]

By mid-November Smith was ready to make a definite move in the direction of the internal settlement. He began by engaging in secret contacts with the three potential partners. Muzorewa, in his auto-biography, gives a detailed account of these initial contacts. In mid-November he was invited to meet Smith, Sithole and Chirau. Having refused to take part in a joint meeting with his African counterparts, Smith agreed to meet him separately. Smith urged Muzorewa and his UANC colleagues to negotiate a settlement. At their first meeting, in response to Muzorewa's inquiry Smith committed himself to universal franchise provided he would receive, in return, guarantees for the whites under black rule. At their second meeting, the following day, Smith agreed to announce publicly his commitment to one man one vote.[213] On November 24 Smith announced his intention to negotiate an internal settlement on the basis of adult suffrage.[214] Sithole and Chirau responded positively. Muzorewa tried to make extra gain from the occasion and reinforce his nationalist credibility. Addressing a youth rally on November 27 he declared that Smith had capitulated and given in to the demand of majority rule. He wanted the British to chair the prospective conference but did not present this as a condition for UANC participation. He set September 12, 1978 as the date for independence and demanded that the conference be over by the end of 1977. He did not seek to exclude the PF leaders but delivered a scathing attack on them for causing so much misery by inciting the war from their luxurious hotels.[215]

The internal settlement talks were conducted on a totally different basis compared with previous negotiations such as the Victoria Falls bridge conference or the Smith–Nkomo talks. Firstly, majority rule on the basis of universal adult suffrage, which had immense symbolic as well as political significance for both whites and blacks, had been publicly and genuinely conceded. Secondly, all the participating parties had a very keen interest in the success of the talks since an internal settlement was for them perhaps the last chance to assert themselves and avoid political oblivion. On this basis, the belief of the parties involved that it was possible to effect a rapid progress[216] was not unwarranted. On December 9, 1977 the negotiating parties agreed to conclude the negotiations within two to three weeks.[217] Yet it took some 11 weeks to reach an agreement on the basic constitutional arrange-ments and guarantees and a further two and a half weeks to agree on the transition arrangements. Three interlinked and mutually reinforcing factors may account for this long and often arduous process. Firstly, there was the dynamic of an intensifying and evidently successful nationalist struggle with its concomitant syndrome of rising expectations and targets. Secondly, there was among the African parties a major preoccupation with nationalist legitimacy and credibility. Thirdly, there was the group dynamic of a divided moderate African camp. Under such circumstances, the internal African leaders, and particularly Muzorewa and Sithole who laid claims to nationalist leadership, were not simply negotiating with Smith. Concurrently, they were looking over their shoulders with a view to scoring points and enhancing political support within and without Rhodesia. In addition, there was crafty Ian Smith, who exploited African division and the group dynamic stemming thereof to what he considered his advantage.

The first hurdle appeared at the very beginning of the talks. Muzorewa failed to participate in the first meeting on December 2, 1977, because he declared a week of mourning for those killed by the Rhodesian forces on November 28 in Mozambique.[218] Muzorewa demanded from Smith an explanation for the massacre and an assurance not to repeat it. In spite of the unsatisfactory reply from Smith, Muzorewa decided to attend the second meeting on December 9. This behaviour was indicative of the basic dilemma facing the internal nationalist leaders, torn as they were between the exigencies of nationalist legitimacy and the requisites of political survival. In the words of Muzorewa: "I was not going to be small and risk the UANC's pragmatism."[219] It was indicative of the balance between the two conflicting considerations that pragmatism prevailed. The December 9 meeting centred on the two main issues of adult suffrage and constitutional guarantees. Some progress was apparently made.[220] Muzorewa, keen to keep up his pseudo-militant posture in an inherently moderate political reality, warned on December 11 that he would call a general strike "to bring the whites down within two weeks", if the talks failed to produce a settlement.[221] Troubles began in the following meeting on December 12. Smith, having conceded universal adult suffrage, expected the Africans to reciprocate by conceding to the eight-point list of constitutional guarantees for whites which he had submitted on December 9. Only the last point concerning one-third of the seats in Parliament for whites was controversial.[222] Times had changed with a vengeance: some three years earlier Smith himself had refused to concede a blocking third to the African majority as a basis for a settlement. The issue of white representation in Parliament was not resolved until mid-February 1978. On December 12 Muzorewa accepted one-third whites in Parliament, provided they were elected on a common roll. Sithole, on the other hand, accepted the principle of separate rolls, but agreed to only one-fifth white representation. On December 21 Muzorewa accepted Sithole's proposal. On December 28 Smith still insisted on one-third. He agreed to their election on a common roll provided they would have gone through white primary elections.[223] By early January 1978 Smith still demanded his one-third.[224] The conference had been by then transformed into meetings of the heads of delegations and their deputies. On January 11 the Africans, having agreed on a common stand, convinced Smith to accept 28 whites in a Parliament of 100. The African leaders agreed that this arrangement would last 10 years or the life of two Parliaments, whichever was the longer.[225] This time it was Sithole's turn to act the tough nationalist. Pressed by his rebellious central committee, Sithole demanded that the reserved white representation be limited to only five years. Smith, on his part, conditioned his acceptance of the 28-seats offer on it being in force for 15 years and on evolving a blocking mechanism which would not make it possible for black MPs to change the constitution on their own.[226] On January 22 Sithole was still adamant,[227] and by January 24 Smith was apparently prepared to leave him out. Sithole's aides were rather pleased, believing that it would earn him points in his domestic leadership struggle with Muzorewa.[228] On January 25 the deadlock seemed over when Sithole, bowing in his turn to the call of *realpolitik*, accepted the 10-year period, and a blocking mechanism was agreed on. It was also agreed as to which issues would be dealt with by the interim government.[229] However, before the agreement was formally signed, Muzorewa took over from Sithole the role of the nationalist trouble-maker, demanding the renegotiation of the method of electing the white MPs. Muzorewa insisted that only 20 white MPs be elected on a separate roll, the rest being subject to election on the common roll.[230] The constitutional controversy developed into a bitter struggle between the two claimants for the domestic nationalist mantle.[231] This deadlock came to an end on February 15, 1978. However, the protracted negotiations offered the opponents of the internal settlement an opportunity to regroup and act.

The prospect of an internal settlement reactivated the Anglo-American initiative. In early December 1977, immediately following the formal opening of internal talks, Owen invited the leaders of the PF for further talks in Malta in the middle of the month.[232] This he did despite the fact that the Anglo-American proposals had been essentially rejected by all concerned parties only a short while earlier. Owen and Vance feared that an internal settlement containing a formal commitment to majority rule would present them with an unenviable dilemma. Owen warned the Americans that it would be difficult for his government to reject it or to maintain the sanctions against the regime that would emerge therefrom. Vance, on his part, feared that changing mood in Capitol Hill in the wake of Soviet–Cuban aggression in the Horn of Africa would precipitate pressures on the President to support a pro-Western internal regime in Rhodesia. He hoped that by keeping the Anglo-American initiative alive, they would at least prevent the PF from intensifying the war and slow the momentum towards an internal settlement.[233] Originally, Owen and Vance had intended the Malta talks to include all the Rhodesian parties who had been represented in Geneva. However, when Smith declined they decided to go along only with the PF.[234] Owen regarded the Malta talks as the last attempt to convince Nkomo and Mugabe to accept the moderate nationalists as parties to a settlement.[235]

On December 4, 1977 Mugabe rejected the British invitation out of hand, claiming that they were not serious about the talks and reiterating his determination to achieve liberation through armed struggle. A day later, the PF issued a statement claiming that the recent Rhodesian attacks on guerilla camps in Mozambique completely shattered the prospects of the Anglo-American proposals.[236] On December 8, following a meeting in Maputo, Mugabe and Nkomo wrote a letter to Owen declining his invitation to come to London on December 13 to discuss the transition arrangements. The PF, they wrote, was put off by Owen's equivocal reaction to the Rhodesian raids and to the internal talks, and by his apparent downgrading of the prospective talks as a result of Smith's refusal to take part.[237]

The British and the Americans, however, were not distracted by this response. Having been rebuffed by both the domestic parties and the PF, they pursued their revitalized initiative through the African regional patrons. They made their approach through Machel, ZANU's patron. On January 6, 1978 Carver and Chand came to Maputo where they held three-day talks with the Mozambican President. Machel's previous belligerency and militancy had been mellowed by the considerable cumulative economic losses incurred by his country as a result of Rhodesian retaliations. Carver said that his visit to Maputo left him "with a very strong feeling that there was a strong support for the Anglo-American proposals there". Machel himself said that the "time was ripe" for alternative negotiations that would include the PF. A senior Machel aide made it even clearer that Mozambique supported the Anglo-American proposals as a basis for negotiations. He added, significantly, that the PF insistence that it should control the armed

207

forces during the transition was "unrealistic".[238] This attitude was much more moderate and forthcoming than that of moderate Kaunda, who on December 6, 1977 had stated plainly: "We will not discuss the Anglo-American initiative."[239] On January 19, 1978, following a four-day meeting in Maputo, Nkomo and Mugabe toed their host's line, offering to meet Owen in Malta on January 26.[240]

On January 29, departing from London for Malta, both Owen and Young sharply criticized the internal settlement talks.[241] The proposals presented at Malta modified the original Anglo-American ones in providing for a governing Council which the Resident Commissioner would be obliged to consult. Below the level of this Council, the Commissioner was to establish committees to deal with different spheres of government responsibility. The Commissioner was also to chair two military committees, one dealing with the implementation of the cease-fire and the other charged with the formation of the Zimbabwe national army. The proposals also defined the Commissioner's functions.[242]

Despite the modifications designed to meet the PF taste, the gap in Malta between the proposals and the PF position was still considerable. The PF strongly objected to what they considered the Commissioner's "dictatorial powers". They proposed the Mozambique model of genuine power-sharing during the transition period. They also objected to the role of the UN peace-keeping force under Carver's command and to the inclusion of the African internal parties in the transitional government.[243] Although the gap between the sides narrowed only marginally, the talks did not end in a breakdown. The British and the Americans believed that any solution without the PF was doomed to failure and would only exacerbate violence and regional instability. The PF hoped that the talks would prevent the former supporting the internal settlement.

From an Anglo-American point of view, the Malta talks were counter-productive in that they provided extra incentive for the internal parties to bring their negotiations to a positive conclusion. As mentioned above, the crucial breakthrough came about on February 15, 1978. The full internal agreement was signed on March 3, 1978.[244] The agreement provided for a 100-seat Parliament of which 28 were whites. Twenty of the latter were to be elected on a separate white roll, while the rest were to be elected on the common roll from a list of 16 candidates nominated by the 20 white MPs. The entrenchment of white representation was to last 10 years or the life of two parliaments, whichever was the longer. The agreement also provided for a declaration of rights, independent judiciary, independent public service board and for public service, police, prison and defence forces free from political interference. It guaranteed pensions and allowed dual citizenship. All these provisions were constitutionally entrenched and could be amended only by a vote of at least 78 MPs. The agreement also set up an interim government and defined its duties and functions. The interim government consisted of an Executive Council, composed of the four heads of delegations, and of a Ministerial Council with a white and black minister for each portfolio or group of portfolios, functioning as a Cabinet. The existing Parliament was to continue to function during the transition with defined functions among which was the enacting of the new constitution. It was agreed that independence day would be December 31, 1978.

Smith achieved for the whites most of what they could have expected under the guise of transfer of power to black majority rule. The Africans were granted majority rule through an overwhelming preponderance in Parliament. However, through the entrenched constitutional provisions, the majority rule government was turned into a guarantor and protector of white interests. In particular, these provisions made it impossible for the black government to effect meaningful changes in the bureaucratic instruments of power. The maintenance of the public service, police force, defence force and prison service "in a high state of efficiency and free from political control" was merely a euphemism for white control. The new government was to be a prisoner of the colonial state's apparatus of power.

African disunity and Smith's manipulation of it may partly account for his success. Beyond that, however, the internal parties, having no military power base of their own and no effective, committed and well-organized political structures, and having to face a raging guerilla war, were forced to rely on the existing control and coercion structures. They had no option other than to accept the strings attached, too. Smith's victory was, however, illusory. The whites proved short-sighted and exhibited a lack of proper appreciation of the political dynamic of the historical process of which they were part. Introvert, paranoiac and lacking in confidence, they pinned their hopes on tight constitutional guarantees instead of the goodwill of the majority, on tight control of the vital instruments of power instead of a viable and legitimate political force. This was a heavy burden for a political dispensation which had to pass the test of internal as well as external legitimacy.

CHAPTER EIGHT

From Salisbury to Lancaster House: the Failure of the Internal Settlement,

March 1978 – August 1979

With the signing of the internal settlement, the Rhodesian crisis entered a new stage which culminated in the Lancaster House conference, the ultimate act of decolonization. At the level of goals, the internal settlement represented a death blow to white-settler political supremacy and a victory to the principle of African majority rule. Smith signed away white minority rule and set in motion a constitutional process at the end of which an African-dominated Parliament was elected and Bishop Muzorewa became prime minister. Yet the signing of the internal settlement served only to intensify and escalate the armed conflict between the internal regime and the nationalist guerillas. This apparent incongruity between goals and strategy can be at least partly explained by the growing internalization of the conflict. The struggle between the proponents and opponents of the internal settlement was so fierce because at stake was not only the political-ideological profile of the emerging state, but also the political survival of movements and leaders.

For the internal parties the signing of the settlement agreement signified only the beginning of a struggle. They had to secure wide domestic, particularly African, support; they had to win the guerilla war or at least to contain it within manageable limits; they had also to win the battle for regional, African and international recognition. For the internal settlement to have any chance at all, the parties involved had to maximize the potential of the agreement and of the alliance of political forces which staked their future on it. It was in their failure to achieve it that lay one of the main causes of their ultimate failure. From this perspective, an analysis of the performance of the internal parties, individually and collectively, would be an appropriate point of departure.

210

Among the internal partners, a major share of the blame lay at the door of the whites. This was so because at least in the crucial period leading to the internal elections in April 1979, they were the dominant partner. In the Ministerial Council every black minister had a white counterpart. In the more consequential Executive Council, the ultimate decision-making body in the interim period, Smith's supporters were only one in four. This numerical ratio, however, did not reflect the balance of power and influence in that body. The lack of unity and harmony among the African partners offered Smith a convenient space for manoeuvring and manipulation. Above all, Smith represented the incumbent regime which continued firmly to control the civil administration, responsible for the day-to-day running of the country, and the security forces which carried the burden of the intensifying guerilla war. This gave Smith considerable leverage. His undoing was that he used his influence in a counter-productive manner.

From a white perspective, the internal settlement had a very promising potential. It was based on the widely accepted principle of majority rule and was signed by moderate African leaders who undertook to guarantee the vital interests of the white settlers in an African-governed state. However, in implementing the settlement agreement, Smith and his colleagues continued to betray a narrow, parochial approach. While going a long way in further guaranteeing white interests, they exhibited little understanding of the requisites of the broader foundations on which the whole settlement had to rest, namely domestic African support. Thus, they pursued a strategy of effecting as little change as possible. By following such a narrow path, they seriously undermined the chances of the whole settlement.

The inadequacy of Smith's approach was amply demonstrated in his handling of the abolition of racial discrimination, a task specifically undertaken by the signatories of the settlement. A prompt eradication of racial discrimination could have earned much credit to the internal parties. To have the desirable effect, it had to be done speedily and gracefully. It was, however, completed only in February 1979[1] without any grace. By June 1978 black MPs were complaining of lack of full commitment by the government to the abolition of racial discrimination.[2] On July 5 a government spokesman said that "the transitional government had accepted in principle that discrimination should be abolished except where its retention was necessary or desirable in the national interest". The government also announced the appointment of a committee of ministers to investigate ways and means of removing racial discrimination. It was to consist of four white and only two black ministers. Muzorewa said that the committee would start working

211

within a few weeks, hardly a show of seriousness and determination.[3] Reacting to the formation of the committee, the UANC stated that it was "fed up with the Government's dilly-dallying and the use of delaying tactics" regarding the removal of race laws. In a similar vein, Sithole's ZANU stated that the race laws should have already been removed.[4] Only on August 8, more than five months after the signing of the internal settlement, did the interim government announce the opening of public facilities to members of all races. This was still in the realm of petty racial discrimination. While Muzorewa was raving, Sithole's ZANU criticized the government for its "half-measures" in abolishing segregation in relatively unimportant fields. Only two months later, on October 10, the government agreed to end racial discrimination in the more crucial fields of land tenure, education and health. Even then it showed much more consideration for the sensitivities of the whites than for the aspirations of the blacks. Substituting economic and other barriers for legal ones,[5] the government effectively ensured that there would be as little racial mixing as possible. Minister Cronje reassured the whites regarding the upholding of "standards" in the sensitive field of education. White parents could rest assured; very few black children could have filtered through the tight net.[6] As late as December 1978 Smith still found it necessary to persuade the whites of the need to remove racial discrimination.[7] At the beginning of 1979 African children living in white suburbs were refused entry to white schools on the grounds that the appropriate law had not yet come into effect.[8] This was not only a manifestation of bad taste and pettiness; it also highlighted the tight control the white bureaucracy still exercised. The behaviour of the departing white oligarchy could hardly have instilled faith among the Africans in the internal settlement. The process of removing racial discrimination was finally concluded on February 1, 1979, when the acting President signed orders which sanctioned eight new laws abolishing all forms of racial discrimination.

The handling by the whites of the more substantial interlinked issues of constitution, elections and transition to internal majority rule was not more impressive. The internal agreement was specific on these issues. Independence day was to be on December 31, 1978, after the constitution would have been drafted and enacted and elections been held.[9] However, by early May 1978 doubts regarding the date of independence had begun to creep in.[10] The UANC responded bitterly. Its spokesman viewed the issue as a test for the Executive Council's sense of urgency, claiming that a failure to meet the target date for independence would make the whole internal agreement a "gigantic fraud".[11] By the end of May it seemed as if the government was beginning to respond to the pressure of time. To save time it decided on May 31, to hold the elections on a party list system which obviated the need to undertake the time-consuming delimitation process.[12] On July 25 the government announced a tight timetable leading to independence by December 31, 1978.[13] However, on September 14, speaking in the name of "practicalities of life", Smith hinted that the target date might not be met.[14] On September 20 Muzorewa rejected calls to postpone the elections "pending a decrease in the war and the lifting of sanctions".[15] On September 27 the white co-Minister of Internal Affairs indicated that the plans were more than a month behind schedule.[16] A day later, Smith attributed the delay to the fact that "it's a pretty difficult and complex operation".[17] Muzorewa responded by stating that a delay would destroy the goodwill generated by the internal agreement and would render it null and void.[18] Finally, on October 29 Smith made a definite statement that because of "mechanical problems" the timetable for majority rule would be postponed by a few months. Muzorewa dismissed Smith's statement as his private opinion, stressing that the Executive Council would have to be convinced before it approved such postponement. Sithole went further, asserting that only the original conference could sanction a change in the target date.[19] However, it was Smith's "private opinion" which prevailed when on November 15 the Executive Council agreed on a new timetable leading to elections on April 20, 1979.[20] Muzorewa's subdued reaction could hardly conceal his deep disappointment: "I have no choice but to say that I am satisfied."[21] Government officials conveniently blamed a Shona–Ndebele dispute over Ndebele parliamentary representation for the delay.[22] It was a poor excuse.

The more plausible cause for the delay emerged on January 2, 1979, with the publication of the new constitution. If Muzorewa was disappointed by the delay, it must have taken a lot of time to convince him to swallow this bitter constitutional pill. Like the case of removal of discrimination, it reflected the white strategy of minimizing change. The verdict of the Commonwealth Secretariat was sharp and unequivocal: "a most extraordinary one-sided racist and anti-democratic document."[23] Such a harshly worded assessment could have been expected from a body representing Third World opinion. However, even the objective observer can find little fault in the unflattering analysis of the Secretariat. It was not the kind of document to which even a moderate African nationalist, in his good senses and exercising free choice, would add his signature. The pro-white bias was already entrenched in the internal agreement of March 3, 1978. However, the constitution went much further in guaranteeing white interests. In the legislature, the internal agreement guaranteed the whites 28 seats, in a House of Assembly of 100, for at least 10 years. The new constitution instituted also the Senate, an upper house consisting of 30 senators. The composition of the Senate betrayed the bias of the constitution. Ten Senators were to be elected by the white MPs; 10 were to be nominated by the Council of Chiefs, and 10 were to be elected by the African MPs.[24] It was a distinctly conservative body designed to moderate an already potentially moderate House of Assembly. The government was to be headed by a prime minister[25] rather than by an executive president. This ensured greater control of the executive by a Parliament in which the whites could expect to be influential. Beyond that, the constitution also provided for a government of national unity, in which each party would be represented in the same proportions as their representation in the House of Assembly, for at least five years. This gave the whites, representing some 3 per cent of the population, a considerable say in the government. According to one report, the Africans agreed to that only after being warned, by their white counterparts, that white army officers would be unwilling to fight for a purely black government. George Nyandoro of the UANC gave expression to the African sentiment: "We have been sold down the river. This is a fundamental departure from the March 3 agreement."[26]

The power of the prospective African majority government was further restricted by being effectively prevented, by the constitution, from making changes in the higher echelons of the bureaucracy. They were forced to operate through the incumbent white officialdom. This was achieved through the institution of four commissions which were to control appointments in government service. The qualifications for membership in these commissions ensured that for the foreseeable future, they would be dominated by whites. The independence of the commissions was entrenched in the constitution. As if this was not sufficient, the qualifications for appointment to vital top positions in the public service made them virtually inaccessible to Africans for a long time.[27] This was a shrewd adjustment of the principle of qualification of which the whites had been so fond. White landed interests were also firmly entrenched by the constitution. The legislature and executive branches were denied the power to acquire land compulsorily. This power was reserved to a court of law under strictly defined conditions. In the case of a compulsory acquisition, a handsome compensation was guaranteed to the owner.[28] The government was effectively prevented from redressing the economic inequalities in this vital sector of the economy. If all these guarantees were not enough, the whites also scored a symbolic victory in that the future state was to be named Zimbabwe/Rhodesia, rather than Zimbabwe as the Africans had wished.

It is difficult to account for Sithole's statement that the people of Rhodesia could not get a better constitution.[29] In opening his election campaign, Muzorewa ventured to give vent to his disappointment and frustration. After saying that the UANC had been too generous in making concessions to the whites he added: "When we have political power in our hands, all else, even the things that are bothering you in the constitution, will be added unto us."[30] However, in the face of a public storm, Muzorewa said that he was misinterpreted.[31] Dr Ahren Palley, a white liberal who had been legal advisor to Muzorewa, had resigned from the committee drafting the constitution because he believed that the Bishop had made too many concessions to the whites.[32]

What made African leaders like Muzorewa, with an indisputable nationalist record, accept an independence constitution with which even a white liberal could not associate himself? Basically, in their dealings with Smith, the internal African leaders continued to suffer from the same weaknesses and handicaps which had beset them during the negotiations leading up to the signing of the internal agreement. The only difference was that after signing the agreement, their vulnerability markedly increased. From the perspective of nationalist politics, the signing of the agreement was, for the internal leaders, the crossing of the Rubicon. Individuals could still disengage and cross back to the militant nationalist camp. However, the bridge was too light to carry the prominent internal leaders and their movements. For these the internal option was the only hope. The rivalry between the moderate leaders which had increased after the signing of the internal agreement[33] made them easy prey for Smith. Furthermore, as the guerilla war, rather than receding as hoped, in fact intensified, the future of the internal settlement as a whole, and of the internal African leaders in particular, became more heavily dependent on the white-controlled security forces. Finally, there was a failure of leadership, especially on the part of Muzorewa who led the most organized, credible and popular internal party. Muzorewa failed to use his power resources in the negotiating process. Power in such a process is not an objectively measurable resource. It exists in the perception of the participants, as a potential which can be measured only when put to the test. Muzorewa must have been too impressed with Smith's bargaining position. African vulnerability was all too apparent, whereas white control of the power structures could hardly have been ignored. However, this imbalance may have been more apparent than real. Essentially, Muzorewa was not powerless. In a situation in which the whole internal effort hinged largely on the test of domestic African acceptability, the power of Muzorewa to withhold his consent was a formidable negotiating asset. An internal settlement with only Sithole and Chirau would have been an utter farce. Muzorewa's weakness stemmed from his failure to exploit this potentially very effective asset.

To make it worse, Muzorewa revealed his weakness and indecisiveness very early, soon after the Executive Council had been set up. This came to light in the crisis which flared up around the dismissal of Byron Hove. Hove was Muzorewa's nominee as co-Minister of Justice, Law and Order. He was dismissed on April 28, 1978, after having refused to withdraw his accusations regarding the negative attitude of the judiciary, the police and the public service towards Africans and his call for the Africanization of the police.[34] Hove certainly reflected the views of the party and the majority of Africans and his demands were not outrageous in the context of transition to majority rule. The whites, however, decided to blow the matter up. For Muzorewa, it was a crucial test of leadership. His management of the crisis was utterly poor. On May 7, 1978 the UANC executive decided to allow the Executive Council a week to reconsider its dismissal of Hove. The party's publicity secretary made it clear that if Hove was not reinstated the UANC would withdraw from the Council.[35] Subsequently, Muzorewa agreed to the setting up of an all-party committee to investigate the issue. The committee found that Muzorewa was present in the two meetings at which the Hove issue was discussed and resolved. On the basis of this "revelation", the Executive Council decided to uphold his original decision.[36] A lot of steam was let out at the following meeting of the UANC executive. However, the decision was not to leave the government for the noble reason that "it would be inconsistent with the integrity of the UANC for us to fail to honour an agreement of which we were a party."[37] The damage to Muzorewa's standing within the internal settlement was severe. Smith had no reason to take Muzorewa's subsequent complaints and threats seriously. Muzorewa's handling of the independence timetable issue was even more abysmal. In early May 1978 the UANC issued a timetable leading to independence on the original date – December 31, 1978. However, in October, after three of the four deadlines set by the party had elapsed, Muzorewa was still complaining and demanding independence by the end of the year.[38] In mid-November he accepted the delay with humiliating resignation.[39] It is hardly surprising that Smith had it all his way in the final version of the constitution.

Smith had his way because he was able to use his partners' weaknesses to what he considered his advantage. As a political manipulator, as distinct from a statesman, he preferred not to deal with a common African front. He knew that the UANC was the only internal party which enjoyed wide grassroots support. He was well aware that Muzorewa was by far the most popular internal leader. He could have settled with Muzorewa and the UANC alone. Such a settlement would have been at least as credible without Sithole and Chirau, probably more so. Smith, however, must have figured that in negotiating with a unified, popular UANC, he would not be able to secure a minimum change, maximum safeguards settlement. He needed Sithole and Chirau not to enhance legitimacy, but rather to widen his manoeuvring space. Judging by the constitution, manipulation paid handsome dividends. This, however, was achieved at the cost of credibility and legitimacy. At a time when white Rhodesia was on the way out and black majority rule on the way in, when the test of domestic African acceptability was crucial in itself and as a means for securing external recognition, the price was very heavy. Dialectically, white success contained the seeds of their failure.

How can one account for Smith's failure to adjust strategy to changing circumstances? How did he not realize that, in the new era his country was heading for, nationalist legitimacy was a resource of prime importance for the building of the socio-political basis for the internal regime? How did he not understand that Muzorewa and his party were assets to be nurtured and promoted rather than undermined and discredited? The RF self-defeating strategy may be explained by the nature of the settler interests it represented, by the white-settler ruling tradition it embodied, by the Rhodesian settler-rootedness it professed and by the negotiating pattern it had experienced. These were mutually reinforcing. As reflected clearly in the constitution and in the handling of the removal of racial discrimination, the RF represented three broad socio-economic groups. Primarily it represented the vulnerable, largely conservative, white farming community. In a country in which land redistribution had become a nationalist battle cry, white farmers were very concerned about the security of their assets. The tight constitutional guarantees gave them that security. The second group, which was well protected by the constitution, was the bureaucratic elite. The positions held by members of this group were obvious targets of nationalist parties which wanted effectively to rule the country and had to compensate and satisfy their leadership. The third was an assorted group which included numerous whites employed in the lower echelons of the state bureaucracy, small businessmen and semi-skilled workers. These shared in the exceptionally comfortable and congenial Rhodesian-settler way of life not so much because of their contribution to the wealth of the colony as because they were well provided for and protected by a system based on white domination and privilege. These were apprehensive about the future because they knew that they would be among the first victims of the inevitable African clamour for Africanization. The entrenchment of the position of the white bureaucratic elite could protect them against brutal Africanization. The guarantees for pensions provided those employed by the government with an economic safety net. Members of this group were particularly concerned by the prospect of declining "standards", especially in the fields of housing, health and education. They were protected by the qualified way in which racial discrimination was removed.

The RF strategy also reflected the long tradition of white-settler self-rule of which it was the inheritor. In declaring UDI, the RF consummated this tradition. The Rhodesian settlers since 1923 had cultivated their interests and protected their privileges through direct control of the colonial state's political and bureaucratic structures. When they were finally forced to relinquish minority rule, it was difficult for them to rely only on constitutional guarantees and on being a white pressure group in a black-dominated state. Thus, they sought to safeguard their future mainly through direct participation in the political process and through control over the state bureaucracy. The RF insistence on tight constitutional guarantees may be related to the constitution-making practice to which they had been exposed as a formal British colony. Since the late 1950s, the British had made the negotiations for a constitution the centrepiece of their decolonization effort in Rhodesia. The British sought to use the constitution to safeguard the interests of the African majority and to guarantee unimpeded progress to majority rule in the context of a settler-dominated colonial state. In the context of Zimbabwe/Rhodesia, the RF sought to use the same constitutional mechanism to safeguard white interests, privileges and influence under black majority rule. Lastly, one has to take into account the feeling widely shared by white Rhodesian settlers that they were not merely birds of passage, but part and parcel of the Rhodesian landscape. Thus, even when the dream of a white-dominated Rhodesia was irrevocably shattered, the white farmers did not act like their Kenyan counterparts who sought compensation for their land so that they could leave the country. Rather, the RF, representing the white farmers, sought constitutional safeguards and political influence which would enable them to stay.

Loaded with deficiencies and weaknesses which were increasingly evident since the signing of the internal agreement, the internal parties faced the enormous task of achieving domestic legitimacy and external recognition. In their anguish and frustration, internal leaders, particularly whites, blamed Britain and the U.S. for their domestic failure. Besides the natural inclination to externalize blame, this reflected a lack of understanding of the requisites of the unfolding situation. The domestic front was strictly their own responsibility and only success therein could have served as a launching pad for securing external legitimacy. It is not argued that had the whites been wiser and had the internal team as a whole functioned better, domestic success would have been guaranteed. However, by minimizing the potential of the settlement, the RF seriously undermined whatever chances it may have had.

For the externally based guerilla movements, the prospect of internal majority rule was a definite threat. Responding to the formal signing of the agreement, Nkomo and Mugabe stated on behalf of the PF: "The agreement is completely bogus and leaves both political and military power in the hands of the settler minority."[40] For the militant nationalists in the PF a naked, undisguised settler regime was preferable because it kept the line of division clear. The prospect of an internal regime with an African majority in Parliament and an African prime minister posed a threat because it had a potential for domestic and external support. This prompted the PF to sharpen their political-ideological stances. Thus, on February 25, 1978 the co-leaders of the PF declared their resolve to continue the struggle "for the attainment of true freedom and genuine independence",[41] true and genuine becoming essential adjectives. The PF also spoke of the transfer of "total power"[42] and of "total independence".[43]

In ZANU, in particular, the advent of the internal regime enhanced the ideological radicalization along anti-imperialist revolutionary lines. In early 1978 the *Zimbabwe News* published an abridged version of lectures on political education for ZANU cadres which contained a class analysis of the Rhodesian society and which set the goal of crushing the "capitalist state". It also stated that "the major means of production will be nationalized in the interests of the workers and the peasants."[44] Later in the year, the ZANU organ published an article which reported the following: "ZANU has already embarked on a campaign to build a Marxist–Leninist vanguard party. ... A special ZANU committee has been established to refine the ideological line of the party and to provide long-term direction that will be required in the course of the Zimbabwe socialist revolution."[45] ZANU's socialist zeal seemed to have rubbed off on their ZAPU partners whose leadership, despite very strong communist links, was rather mute on the issue of a socialist revolution.[46]

The sharpened ideological message had to be propagated among the masses to prevent the erosion of support for militant nationalism.[47] In ZANU, the education of the masses was nothing new; it was at the root of their Chinese-oriented guerilla strategy. The advent of the internal regime only added a sense of urgency resulting from the apparent narrowing of the gap between internal majority rule and the goals of the guerilla movements. ZANU propaganda campaigns included the distribution of pamphlets, one of which read as follows: "ZANU warns all Zimbabweans against the traitors of the people's struggle. These puppets are being used by Smith and his imperialist masters ... to mislead you into accepting a puppet regime."[48] The internal leaders were singled out for vicious attacks. Thus, Mugabe depicted them as "renegade and quisling Sithole, stooge Muzorewa and puppet Chirau".[49]

The PF, which had little faith in the intentions of the British and the Americans, viewed the guerilla struggle as their strategy for thwarting the internal settlement. On the eve of the signing of the internal agreement, the co-leaders of the PF stated: "It is our common bond to ensure the immediate intensification of the war effort to defeat fascist Smith, the collaborator gang of four, and the evil Anglo-American machinations."[50] For ZANU, the armed struggle was the only appropriate strategic option. This was restated by Mugabe on June 21, 1978: "this only underlines the importance of our continuing our armed struggle, because only through it can we actually overthrow the present system and ensure that power has been transferred to the masses."[51]

A common PF stand notwithstanding, ZAPU continued, in the wake of the signing of the internal agreement, to vacillate between the strategic options. Nkomo's meeting with Smith in August 1978, which will be disussed below, indicated that he did not forgo the peaceful option. However, the failure of the meeting and the subsequent shooting down of a Rhodesian civilian aircraft by ZIPRA guerillas proved that the dynamic of the conflict was pushing Nkomo further towards the armed struggle option. Nkomo was apparently under pressure from his radicalized troops over his meeting with Smith. Subsequently, Rhodesian massive raids on ZIPRA camps in late 1978 pushed Nkomo and ZAPU towards a more militant, belligerent stance.[52]

In their rejection of the internal settlement and their determination to pursue the guerilla war to its successful conclusion, the PF enjoyed the solid support of their regional patrons. While not totally discarding the option of an internationally sponsored negotiated settlement, the failure of the Anglo-American initiative and the signing of the internal agreement further pushed them towards a militant stance. On March 26, 1978, at the end of a summit meeting convened to discuss the signing of the internal agreement, the FLP stated their position:

> The present circumstances demand an intensification of the just armed struggle for the liberation of Zimbabwe. The Front line states, therefore, reaffirm their total and unswerving support to the armed struggle being waged by the people of Zimbabwe under the leadership of the Patriotic Front for the attainment of *complete* independence and the establishment of a *genuine* democratic government [my italics].[53]

In July 1978, the OAU Council of Ministers, meeting in Khartoum, lent support to the FLP and the PF. It condemned the internal settlement and encouraged "the appreciable prosecution of the armed struggle being waged by the Patriotic Front, the sole liberation movement of Zimbabwe".[54] The Nkomo–Smith meeting in Lusaka in August 1978 threatened to cause a rift in the FLP. However, an emergency FLP meeting, convened to sort out the confusion, ended in a declaration supporting the intensification of the armed struggle. According to Kaunda's aide, the meeting restored unanimity to the ranks of the FLP.[55]

The regional patrons' support for the armed struggle was not limited to verbal encouragement. Tanzania continued to offer training facilities to ZIPA (ZANLA) while Angola provided the same for ZIPRA. Botswana was the conduit for ZIPRA recruits en route from Matabeleland to the training camps. Mozambique and Zambia continued to carry the main brunt of the guerilla war, even in the face of massive Rhodesian retaliation. On September 15, 1978 Machel reaffirmed his country's dedication to the liberation of Zimbabwe despite the heavy toll it was paying.[56] Kaunda's preference for a peaceful settlement did not diminish his dedication to the cause of liberation. Even when for dire economic reasons Zambia decided to make use of the Rhodesian railway system,[57] it was not matched by a decline in the support for ZIPRA. Zambia remained committed even when, from October 1978, its territory was subjected to retaliatory actions by the Rhodesian forces. Zambia offered ZIPRA training camps deep inside its territory and operational bases along the Zambesi.[58]

In their military endeavour, the PF also received increasingly generous support from their traditional communist backers. Unlike the British and the Americans, whose involvement in the Rhodesian crisis was diplomatic and aimed at achieving a negotiated, peaceful settlement, the communist countries involved played their part by rendering military assistance to the nationalist guerillas and promoting a violent take-over by them. To signify their increasing interest in the area, the Soviets sent a delegation of the Supreme Soviet to Zambia where they were complimented by Kaunda for their support for the liberation of southern Africa.[59] In Rhodesia, however, ZANU, the dominant liberation movement, had been traditionally supported by the Chinese and had pro-Chinese sentiments and ideological inclinations. The Soviets remained steadfast in their support for ZAPU even when it became increasingly apparent that ZANU was the major partner in the PF. In the past the Russians had demanded from Mugabe to recognize Nkomo's leadership in exchange for arms supply.[60] During 1978, with the escalation of the war, Mugabe renewed his efforts to gain access to the superior Soviet arsenal. At the end of July 1978 Mugabe travelled to Cuba to "strengthen the alliance between ourselves and those countries with which we share revolutionary interests".[61] He asked for arms and training facilities "which Cuba is affording our counterpart in the Patriotic Front".[62] Shortly after, on August 15, Mugabe led a high-level delegation on a visit to Angola, the most loyal Soviet client among the FLP. The ZANU organ reported that the discussions held by the delegation "led to a better understanding of our respective policy and establishment of closer ties of friendship and solidarity".[63] Mugabe himself visited the Soviet Union, and ZANU delegations visited the Soviet Union and other Eastern European countries.[64] Yet in early October 1978 Mugabe stated that he had not received much support from either Russia or Cuba.[65]

The Soviets and their allies were heavily involved in preparing the ZIPRA war machine. They supplied them with heavy, modern and sophisticated weapons including armoured vehicles and anti-aircraft missiles. The training of ZIPRA forces in camps in Angola and Zambia was done mainly by Cuban and East German instructors. ZIPRA cadres were also trained in Cuba.[66] As the war escalated in 1978 and 1979, Soviet and Cuban involvement in planning and supervising ZIPRA's strategy and operations increased considerably. Cuban advisers commuted daily from their embassy in Lusaka to the ZAPU War Council.[67] The Soviet ambassador to Zambia appointed Colonel Vladimir Buchiyev, a fellow KGB agent, as the head of a 12-man Soviet advisory team of military specialists whose task was to assist ZIPRA.[68] At the ZIPRA military headquarters the Soviets installed a communication centre which directed and supervised operations.[69]

Unity within the PF, which was more crucial than before as it was poised for a showdown with the internal settlement, remained as elusive as ever. ZANU's attitude towards ZAPU had not changed.

Addressing the OAU summit conference, Mugabe spoke of the PF and ZIPA, not mentioning ZANU and ZANLA at all.[70] However, beyond this tactical facade ZANU continued to view itself as the sole legitimate expression of the liberation struggle. This was the dominant theme emanating from the educational and propaganda messages relayed by the ZANU leadership to party members and fighters.[71] Lip service to unity efforts was still paid. Thus, on October 7, 1978 Mugabe dismissed the possibility of a civil war between the two movements and presented an impressive agenda for unity which had already been covered, including plans for a joint military command and joint operations. He admitted, however, that "this is the theoretical basis that we have accepted but the practice is yet to come."[72] In fact, disunity and mutual hostility and suspicion were actually exacerbated as the struggle for liberation was nearing its climax. On April 11, 1979 Mugabe stated that ZANU and ZAPU could not unite because of ideological differences, him being a committed Marxist while Nkomo was still in the middle of the road.[73] Mugabe also claimed that ZAPU's insistence on Nkomo as the leader of the nationalist movement was another obstacle on the way to unity.[74] ZANU also envied and resented the support ZAPU was receiving from socialist countries and organizations: "All diplomatic, material and financial aid from these international bodies went to ZAPU and our efforts were sabotaged. The intention was very clear; it was to strangle ZANU and destroy it."[75] Mugabe himself alleged that Nkomo tried to dissuade Fidel Castro from inviting him to Havana for the Youth Festival, adding that "even after I had come he spent 2 hours with Fidel Castro protesting about the invitation."[76] More disturbing for ZANU was ZAPU's objection to military cooperation. On October 7, 1978 Mugabe divulged what appears to have been the main cause for lack of progress on the road to unity. Whereas ZANU wanted military unity first and political unity after the victory, ZAPU insisted on the reverse order.[77] When the Ethiopians offered to train PF forces, Nkomo was willing to accept the offer only if the two armies would be trained in two separate camps.[78] The division within the PF was very deep indeed.

ZAPU insisted on political unity first because of their much smaller popular ethnic base compared with the Shona-based ZANU. Their only hope of playing a meaningful role in what seemed an imminent transition of power was by controlling their own military power base. With their demand for seniority for their movement and their leader in the united party, the chances of unity were nil. This position enabled them to maintain their army without paying the political price involved in appearing as opponents of unity. Since 1977 ZAPU had been engaged in a massive recruitment drive. By September 1977 Nkomo had some 3,000 trained guerillas and 10,000 recruits undergoing military training. By February 1978 ZIPRA could claim some 8,000 trained guerillas[79] and by mid-September its fighting forces were estimated between 10,000 and 12,000 strong.[80] This remarkable increase was a cause for anxiety for ZANU, which suspected ZAPU's political designs. The Nkomo–Smith meeting in August 1978 must have caused alarm in ZANU. The failure of the meeting was hardly a consolation. The fact that Nkomo kept his allies ignorant of his scheme could only confirm their suspicion that Nkomo had not relinquished the idea of fulfilling his political ambitions through negotiating a separate deal with Smith. Earlier, in April 1978, Mugabe had told Western diplomats that he believed that Nkomo would join the internal settlement.[81] ZANU's suspicions were reinforced by the nature of ZAPU's forces' deployment. Most of Nkomo's well-trained and heavily armed troops were deployed in barracks in Zambia. In mid-September 1978 it was estimated that Nkomo had committed only some 1,000 of his guerillas inside Rhodesia. Furthermore, ZIPRA's army was trained and organized for a conventional rather than a guerilla war. The assessment in the Rhodesian army was that Nkomo would deploy his army to give their forces a *coup de grace*, after having been worn by ZIPA, and to smash the latter, collecting the "victor's spoils".[82] The possibility of Nkomo using his troops in an eventual showdown with ZANU was openly discussed by the press,[83] and it is highly unlikely that such an eventuality was not considered in ZANU. Over and above their mutual suspicion and rivalry, the PF partners were intent on a showdown with the internal settlement regime.

The internal parties also pinned their hopes on a showdown with the PF. In planning and preparing for this they could count on the support of their regional patron. South Africa, which had welcomed the signing of the internal agreement, continued to support this option. While they had to pay lip service to the international option[84] in order to pre-empt international pressure, the South Africans had a keen interest in the success of the internal settlement. In a speech in Graaf Reinet on May 27, 1978, Vorster went a long way in expressing support for the internal regime. He made a passionate appeal to the British and the Americans to recognize it and to remove the economic sanctions in the name of peace and anti-communism.[85] In December 1978 South Africa refused to support an effort to convene an internationally sponsored conference before the internal elections.[86] The South African government believed, or hoped, that the internal regime would stand a better chance after a successful test of domestic legitimacy. As long as the transitional government operated within the terms of the agreement, it could rely on South Africa. Their economic lifeline remained open, they received economic support and were provided with military supplies for the pursuit of the war.

In staking their political future on the internal option, the signatories of the agreement sought to rely not only on their regional patron's support. Foremostly, they believed that they could secure popular African support inside the country. Among the African internal leaders there were those with a nationalist record and a claim for nationalist legitimacy. Soon after signing the agreement, Muzorewa boasted that the internal settlement enjoyed the support of 85 per cent of the population.[87] The crowd of more than 200,000 Africans who came to greet him on his return from the U.S. some 10 days later[88] could render credence to this claim. A spot survey which gave the internal leaders 76 per cent support, against a support of only some 24 per cent to Mugabe and Nkomo,[89] could also be seen as a good omen. This assumed popularity was expected to be instrumental in the achievement of the most immediate and crucial goal, namely the termination of, or at least a considerable reduction in, the guerilla war. In April 1978 Sithole said: "Free elections will follow the cease-fire and then will come international recognition."[90] Indeed, the cease-fire was a top priority and a crucial test for the internal settlement.

The onus of delivering the goods was, of course, on the African partners. These exhibited optimism which generated great expectations. Less than a week after signing the agreement, Muzorewa said: "Now that they are attaining their cherished goal, majority rule, the people of Zimbabwe will lay down their arms."[91] In April 1978 Sithole said that once the programme for the safe return of the guerillas was finalized, he would call them to lay down their arms and return home. He was confident that they would respond positively.[92] This optimism rubbed off on General Walls, who said that the cease-fire plans which were being worked out had the potential for a "vast success".[93] Only on May 2, two months after the signing of the internal agreement, did the Executive Council announce its cease-fire package. It included the release of political detainees, the removal of the ban on ZANU and ZAPU and a guarantee of safe return. It also contained a promise to dismantle the protected villages "as the fighting dies and peace is restored".[94] Even when the announcement failed to have an impact, the internal leaders continued to disseminate hopes and illusions.[95] Smith was more modest, being confident that by the end of the year there would be a major reduction in violence.[96] This was echoed by Muzorewa in early July.[97] His confidence notwithstanding, a week later Muzorewa issued a passionate call to the guerillas. He tried to drive a wedge between the fighters and their leaders who "wine and dine and strut around in the luxurious hotels of Lusaka and Maputo and other parts of the world".[98]

The leaders of the internal settlement actually claimed success in their endeavour. On June 15, 1978 Smith said that there were definite signs of de-escalation in the guerilla war.[99] On July 1 Muzorewa claimed that in certain areas the security forces and the guerillas were observing the cease-fire.[100] In early August Sithole spoke of real progress: "We are winning daily more and more of the guerillas to our side."[101] In November General Walls was more specific, claiming that 2,000 former guerillas had come over to the government side.[102] For the sake of credibility "returning guerillas" were soon put on display. On August 13 Rhodesian television showed Muzorewa meeting with ex-guerillas and a certain Comrade Max describing himself as the District Commissioner of the area.[103] The truth about the "returned guerillas" emerges from the account of a Selous Scouts commander: "The more we had to do with the whole pathetic set-up, the more we came to realize that the Government ... and through them the people of Rhodesia ... were being taken for a long and bumpy ride."[104]

The so-called returned guerillas, who were also known as auxiliaries, were, in fact, members of the private armies built by Muzorewa and Sithole. By the end of 1978 these party auxiliaries controlled certain tribal areas which were termed, not altogether appropriately, "free zones".[105] These private armies, particularly Sithole's, soon reverted to terrorizing the rural communities. They certainly added little to the prestige and popularity of the internal regime. The congress of the African Farmers' Union heard detailed accusations about ill-treatment of African peasants by these armies.[106] The auxiliaries contributed little to the anti-guerilla effort. Their function was mainly political. When a recruit was asked about his activities, he replied candidly: "We're teaching people how to vote."[107]

Hopes, illusions and pretences notwithstanding, the internal government soon realised that the guerilla war had escalated rather than de-escalated. In fact, the guerilla war reached such proportions that it became the main determinant in the evolution of the Rhodesian crisis. Since militarily and politically the auxiliaries were a liability rather than an asset, the burden of the war rested on the shoulders of the security forces. Since the highly effective but small army could not cope with the expanding war, the internal government tried to expand its military mobilization potential. In mid-September 1978 it announced the application of compulsory conscription for blacks. Military sources were sceptical about the scheme: "We simply have not got the training facilities, let alone the arms to equip a black conscript army."[108] A survey recorded unanimous black opposition to the idea.[109] Of the first call-up of 1,500 on January 10, 1979, only 300 turned up.[110]

The PF was also not in a position to maximize its potential military strength. As before, the main burden of the war fell on the shoulders of ZANU and its military wing ZIPA. As ZANU was entering this crucial stage of the liberation struggle, the position of Mugabe at the head of the party and of the Mugabe–Tongogara alliance in ZIPA was further enhanced and consolidated. This was not, however, before another challenge to Mugabe's leadership had been thwarted. Details of this challenge, which coincided with the launching of the internal settlement, came to light in early July 1978, when reports of the escape of 15 ZANU leaders from FRELIMO detention made the headlines.[111] The challengers included some very high-ranking political and military leaders. They apparently wanted to topple Mugabe. According to an accomplice who had fled to Zambia, the motive was ideological: "Most of them are, at heart, basic socialists and can't stomach the hard Marxist–Leninist line being pursued by Mugabe."[112] Most of them were also members of the Karanga sub-Shona group. This episode did not have a serious effect on ZANU and the pursuit of the war. Within the party, the position of the Mugabe generation seems to have been enhanced. Mugabe, well in control of the political and military structures, reaffirmed the supremacy of the party.[113]

Having consolidated the party leadership, ZANU responded to the challenge of the internal settlement by unleashing all its military potential. This was manifested in the sharp increase in ZIPA guerillas operating inside Rhodesia. From February 1978 to January 1979 their numbers doubled from 4,500 to 9,000. These guerillas were spread throughout the eastern half of Rhodesia from Zambia in the north to South Africa in the south.[114] The volume of guerilla action also rose considerably. The number of officially reported monthly incidents increased from 600 in late 1978 to 1,000 in April 1979.[115] These remarkable advances were attributable to the persistent and successful pursuit of their Chinese-inspired guerilla strategy designed to entrench and expand control of the countryside.[116] Justin Nyoka, a black Rhodesian journalist who had joined ZANU, spent some three and a half months in the latter part of 1978 with ZIPA forces in different parts of Rhodesia. Even if he was guilty of some revolutionary exaggeration, his detailed account of the extent and degree of ZANU's control and activities is most impressive. There were many areas in Mashonaland which were *de facto* liberated or semi-liberated. While the Rhodesian security forces could operate in these areas, the civil administration totally collapsed. ZANU provided alternative structures and services and launched a political education campaign. This also enabled ZANU to mobilize the rural population to support the guerilla offensive. They set up local militias, intelligence services and a logistic support system. In this way, the guerillas could move in the rural areas like "fish in the water".[117]

From this solid base, the guerillas carried their offensive further afield. Their immediate targets beyond their rural African strongholds were the white farms and farmers. Their aim was to undermine the agricultural economic backbone of the regime and the morale of this vital segment of the white population. They sought to achieve it by directly attacking white farms and by disrupting the rural road communication system through mining and ambushing. They also attacked the African labour force. In some areas, the guerillas were very successful. In Chipinga area, from March to December 1978, 10 whites were killed.[118] In Melsetter area, in 1978, 14 whites were killed by guerillas operating from the surrounding African reserve in addition to 11 killed in the previous year. In 1978 alone 24 homesteads were destroyed. Consequently, most of the whites left the area. In 1976 there had been in this area 150 white families living on timber estates and 45 families living on farms. By 1978 their numbers were reduced to 62 and eight respectively.[119] In a meeting in Umtali in January 1979, a desperate farmer from the same district begged Smith: "Please sir, come out and do something for these people before there is nobody left."[120]

In intensifying their activities in the rural areas and spreading their effective control, ZANU followed Mao's strategy of surrounding the urban-industrial areas from the countryside. During that period ZIPA forces, in fact, began to attack the urban centres. In December 1978 Rex Nhongo, ZANU's Deputy Defence Secretary, disclosed that ZIPA had launched a new campaign to disrupt the remaining communication lines in order to isolate completely the towns and cities.[121] On October 15, 1978 the guerillas underlined this new strategy by launching a rocket and mortar attack on Umtali.[122] The biggest and most daring urban guerilla operation was the destruction of the oil depot in Salisbury's industrial area in December 1978.[123] These, however, were isolated actions rather than an urban offensive. Neither did ZIPA forces really encircle the urban centres in the military sense of the word. As part of its urban-industrial thrust, ZANU called on the black workers to join in the struggle by sabotaging the economy.[124] There was, however, no meaningful response to this call and the urban-industrial sectors were only very marginally disrupted. ZANU also failed to get a positive response to its call to the black soldiers to lay down their arms.[125] Another thrust of the ZANU offensive was directed against leaders and supporters of the internal African nationalist parties. In June 1978, Muzorewa alleged that special terror squads had been sent from Mozambique to eliminate UANC officials who tried to make contact with the guerillas.[126] On November 13 ZANU broadcast a long list of "traitors", "puppets", "opportunists", "buffoons", etc. from the different internal parties, calling on them to resign or face elimination.[127] In late May 1978 four Sithole supporters were murdered in the Wedza area. In early July four UANC officials were murdered in the north-east. Later in July 39 unarmed members of Sithole's ZANU were massacred in the eastern operation area.[128] Judging by the attendance at meetings addressed by internal ministers in rural areas, ZANU's campaign was remarkably successful.[129] In sum, with all their success, ZANU alone could not yet bring the internal regime to its knees. From this perspective the attitude of its ZAPU ally was crucially important.

ZAPU, which had about 10,000 well-trained ZIPRA guerillas, could not afford to sit back while ZANU was making all the running. At a time when the armed struggle was nearing a climax, abstention was potentially very costly. It could have been costly in terms of legitimacy and claim to the spoils of liberation. There was a more immediate threat of the dynamic and aggressive ZIPA advancing into areas to which ZAPU laid claim. There were, indeed, areas which were contested by both guerilla armies.[130] ZAPU evolved a strategy designed to give answers both to the requisites of the escalating liberation war and to its anxieties regarding ZANU's advances. Thus, ZAPU increased their contribution to the guerilla war. According to one account, the number of ZIPRA guerillas inside Rhodesia rose from 953 in February 1978 to 1906 in January 1979.[131] By Easter 1979 their numbers had grown to around 2,500.[132] This new infusion was reflected in an increase of guerilla actions in the ZAPU-controlled areas in Matabeleland. They were mainly active in ambushing vehicles and attacking mission stations, schools and medical clinics. Many of these had to close down.[133] The main contribution of ZIPRA to the guerilla war was qualitative rather than quantitative. On September 3, 1978 an Air Rhodesia Viscount civilian aircraft was shot down by ZIPRA fighters using a Russian Sam 7 ground-to-air missile. Thirty-eight of the passengers died in the crash and of the 18 survivors, 10 were killed by ZIPRA guerillas.[134] The death of so many whites in one action and in such a manner was undoubtedly the greatest shock the whites had experienced since the beginning of the war. On February 19, 1979 ZIPRA guerillas shot down another Viscount, killing all 59 crew and passengers.[135] Thus, without committing many men, ZAPU had made a most dramatic contribution to the escalation of the war. Nkomo, however, had much more far-reaching plans. Inspired and guided by its Soviet patrons, ZIPRA was planning, training and preparing for a full-scale conventional invasion, the centrepiece of which was the deployment of an armoured column. The aim of the invasion was apparently to crush both the Rhodesian army and ZIPA.[136] Had ZAPU committed the bulk of its well-trained troops inside Rhodesia, a combined PF military effort could have had the potential for precipitating a military collapse of the internal regime.

As it was, the new ZAPU input combined with ZIPA's increasing aggressiveness posed the Rhodesian security forces a serious military challenge. This much greater challenge was met with the same forces and essentially the same strategy that had been used before. These forces were far too small for the task. The following was the assessment of the Selous Scouts commander: "The Rhodesian war machine, minuscule by world standards, was by the beginning of 1978 stretched to its full limits, and Com-Ops [Combined Operations], although alive to the pressure points, could do very little to bring the internal situation under control." He stressed, in particular, the shortage in helicopters which were essential for both internal and external operations.[137] Because of this shortage, the Rhodesians could not even make full use of their elite troops. The military command's initial reaction to the increase in the volume of guerilla infiltration was to try to maintain control throughout the country. The result was that the security forces stretched themselves too thinly to be effective. In the second half of 1978, after analysing this adverse development, the military planners made strategic adjustments. Firstly, they defined what they considered as vital areas – the most productive agricultural areas, the industrial areas and the vital routes to South Africa. These were defended by the security forces. Most of the African rural areas, considered as nonvital, were abandoned by the military. Although the police did not withdraw, they could not, without regular support from the army, hope to maintain control.[138] Under these new conditions, it was not particularly difficult for ZIPA to set up liberated and semi-liberated zones. The idea behind this strategic adjustment was to relieve the army from low-effective, defensive duties, deploying it centrally in high-effectivity operations.

The high-effectivity strategy was not new, consisting of internal counter-insurgency operations and pre-emptive external strikes. The large numbers of guerilla casualties were proof of the success of internal operations. However, because ZIPA had little difficulty in infiltrating fresh guerillas, the pre-emptive external operations became even more vital than before in the eyes of Rhodesian strategists. Small-scale pre-emptive operations were carried out more or less on a regular basis. Large-scale operations were also carried out. Two major attacks on ZIPA camps in Tembue and Chimoio were carried out at the end of July and on September 20, 1978, respectively.[139] The dramatic successes of 1977 were, however, difficult to achieve in 1978. The guerillas in Mozambique had learnt the lessons of past experience. The targets were too scattered and well defended for the small Rhodesian force to have any impact.[140] Subsequently, the emphasis was on disruption of military supplies through Mozambique.[141]

Lack of success in the Mozambique front must have been at least partly responsible for the shift of the pre-emptive strikes to Zambia against ZIPRA build-up. Small-scale, low-key operations against ZIPRA forward bases were carried out early in 1978. Despite the increasing ZIPRA involvement in the guerilla war in 1978, the decision to attack their camps deep inside Zambia was not easy. Firstly, the white partners were still toying with the idea of enticing Nkomo into joining the internal settlement. From this perspective, ZIPRA's conventional army could be construed as a potential asset rather than a threat. Secondly, dramatic, large-scale violation of Zambia's territorial sovereignty was more problematic than in the case of Mozambique. The failure of the Smith–Nkomo meeting in August 1978, and the shooting down of the first Viscount in early September, relieved the Rhodesians from all inhibitions. ZIPRA's large, conventional military camps deep inside Zambia offered a considerable scope for Rhodesia's accomplished pre-emptive strikers. With a view to maximizing the benefit of surprise, the Rhodesians unleashed their airforce and their airborne and heliborne elite troops in a massive attack against three major ZIPRA bases housing some 9,000 guerillas. The results, according to Rhodesian count, were devastating.[142] On December 22, 1978 the Selous Scouts attacked the Moromba camp in a remote corner of Zambia where ZAPU kept its prisoners.[143] On February 26, 1979 Rhodesian planes attacked ZIPRA's main training base in Angola.[144] By March 1979 the Rhodesians were aware of ZAPU's offensive plans. It was then that they activated their plan to assassinate Nkomo. The shooting down of the first Viscount turned Nkomo from a potential ally into a military target. The Central Intelligence Organization (CIO) began to plan his assassination in late December 1978. On the night of April 12–13, 1979 the SAS, assisted by a top CIO agent, struck deep in the heart of Lusaka. The idea was to disrupt ZIPRA's invasion plans by eliminating Nkomo and destroying ZAPU's headquarters in Lusaka. The Rhodesians were apparently afraid that the invasion would take place before the elections, due to be held a week later. At the end of Operation Bastille, ZAPU HQ and Nkomo's residence in the heart of Lusaka lay in ruins. Nkomo, however, was not at home.[145] The same night, the Selous Scouts abducted the entire ZIPRA southern front command from their headquarters in Francistown, Botswana.[146] The following morning the SAS sank the ferry which served as a link between Zambia and Botswana across the Zambesi.[147]

In the period under consideration, the Rhodesians introduced a new element in their offensive strategy. In April 1978 a decision was taken to launch a campaign of economic sabotage against the guerillas' host countries. That particular decision was related to Zambia: "The government," said a senior CIO officer to an operative, "has decided the time is ripe to start waging limited economic warfare against Zambia. Let us discourage them from supporting ZIPRA so strongly. Hit them where it hurts ... sabotage installations that will savage the Zambian economy."[148] The first assignment was to put the Mufulira copper mine permanently out of operation. The attempt ended in a failure. A plan to blow up a Zambian Airways plane in retaliation for the shooting down of the Viscount also failed. In late October two trains were blown up. At the end of that month, a Shell/BP fuel depot was sabotaged without much damage.[149] The economic sabotage campaign against Mozambique achieved much more spectacular results, because unlike in Zambia it was not entrusted to CIO operatives operating covertly. In carrying it out the Rhodesians made use of a new counter-insurgency agent. In the manner of "an eye for an eye", the CIO established in 1976 the Mozambique National Resistance (MNR), alias RENAMO. Only by mid-1978 was there a big enough MNR military group to be used against the FRELIMO government. The MNR forces operated in collaboration with the SAS. Their first operation in early 1979 was the destruction of the Mavuze hydro-electric power station on Chicamba Real Dam. On March 23, 1979 an SAS–MNR force carried out the biggest and most successful economic sabotage of the war on the Beira fuel depot.[150]

The highly professional, daring and resourceful Rhodesian security forces could still hit hard when they could identify their targets. To be effective in their external operations they needed concentrated, "sitting duck", high-damage targets. As the raid in Mozambique in 1978 showed, once the guerillas learnt the lessons, the Rhodesians were running out of such targets. Internally, as perfected as the counter-insurgency tactic was, the Rhodesian army was far too small to stem the fast-growing guerilla tide. Although the Rhodesian security forces were not entirely helpless, and while the government had not yet been brought to submission by the guerilla pressure, the military balance during 1978 and early 1979 was definitely tilting towards the guerillas. Whereas the security forces had reached the limits of their potential power, the guerillas had a lot in reserve. The Selous Scouts commander figured that from around the end of 1978, Rhodesia was crumbling.[151] For the first time a military victory by the guerillas was definitely in the realm of the possible. Even Smith conceded publicly in January 1979 that Rhodesia could not win the guerilla war.[152] The cost of the war was exorbitant. By April 1979 the security bill was 1.3m rand a day.[153] Ordinary Rhodesians voted with their feet. In 1978, 18,000 white Rhodesians left the country, a record in Rhodesia's history.[154]

It was against the background of a guerilla war escalating towards a climax that the international diplomatic initiative designed to facilitate a peaceful settlement continued to unfold. The failure of the Malta meeting in February 1978, and the signing of the internal settlement on March 3, were essentially a vote of no confidence in the Anglo-American initiative. The internal agreement posed a severe dilemma to the Americans and the British. Despite its shortcomings, it contained definite elements of transfer of power to the black majority. It was also a distinctly moderate, pro-Western settlement, and particularly agreeable to Western electorates and their representatives. Thus, Andrew Young's negative reaction to Smith and Muzorewa's announcement with regard to the agreement, on February 15, 1978, caused Carter problems in Congress.[155] Soon after the agreement was signed, four prominent American senators introduced a resolution urging the administration to give it "serious and impartial consideration".[156] Vance writes that "public opinion in the United States and Britain welcomed the Salisbury agreement." According to Vance, the British government was also under growing pressure to extricate itself from its Rhodesian responsibility. The government anticipated strong pressure from Parliament to recognize the internal regime once an elected black majority government took office.[157]

At the same time, the internal settlement harboured grave dangers for the West. It was clear that a settlement which was rejected by the FLP and the PF would precipitate considerable escalation in the guerilla war. Reacting to the February 15, 1978 announcement of the internal agreement, Andrew Young articulated only what was in the minds of British and American policy makers: "I could see another Angola-type situation. It is not addressing itself to the issues for which some 40,000 guerillas are fighting." There was, as Young pointed out,

233

a danger of internationalization of the Rhodesian conflict: "The problem is that we have evidence there would be a massive commitment of Russian weapons as there was in Angola."[158] The fear of a direct Soviet–Cuban involvement, which had already hung in the air, was exacerbated by their more recent performance in the Horn of Africa, which reached a climax in early 1978, and by the news about a large build-up of Soviet heavy weapons in Mozambique.[159] The prospect of such involvement engulfing the whole sub-continent in a mini, racial Armageddon was the nightmare of the Western partners. In such an eventuality they would face the unenviable choice between abstaining and seeing the communists gaining the upper hand or supporting the cause of white supremacy.

The agonizing dilemmas and conflicting pressures were responsible for the inconsistent, and at times contradicting messages which emanated from London and Washington. Whereas Young predicted an escalating civil war, Owen responded differently to the February 15 announcement: "I believe this is a significant move towards majority rule and it should be welcomed." He also told Parliament that the quicker Rhodesia could be brought to independence on the basis of the agreement, the more likely they were to get a satisfactory solution.[160] Vance writes that Owen "was increasingly drawn towards the idea of building upon the internal settlement". His idea was to broaden the scope of the settlement by including Nkomo.[161] In February Owen told Sithole: "The world must see a sincere and genuine offer to Joshua Nkomo to join and take part in the interim administration. The earlier Nkomo is involved the easier we can legalize."[162] In early March 1978 Owen refused to give assurances that Britain would not recognize the agreement without the involvement of the PF.[163] This was not a policy Carter could support. While there were congressional pressures to give a favourable, or at least impartial consideration to the internal settlement, there were also countervailing pressures. Thus, the 16 members of the Congressional black caucus urged Carter to reject the internal settlement.[164] While the black caucus, as such, may not have been a powerful pressure group, the black voters they represented were of prime domestic and electoral importance to Carter. Beyond and above considerations of intra-systemic pressures, Carter, in 1978, despite setbacks related to the unyielding nature of regional and international realities, was still firmly committed to the global outlook from which his African policy derived. In terms of this policy, support for the internal settlement was inconceivable. Vance added a touch of *realpolitik* when writing of the danger of associating the U.S. with the internal regime: "Our African policy would be shattered, with the Soviets and the

Cubans picking the pieces."[165] The U.S. could adopt only a policy which would be endorsed by the FLP and Africa as a whole. At the same time, they could not appear to be partisans of the PF and the FLP. In this respect, the balance of domestic pressures was reinforced by the administration's belief that, as in the Middle East, the accessibility to both sides of the conflict offered them a clear advantage over the Soviets. It was in line with these considerations that the Americans and the British, together with other Western members of the UN Security Council, abstained on March 14, 1978 in a vote on an African-sponsored resolution calling for the rejection of the internal settlement.[166] Likewise, Carter instructed Young and Vance neither to support the settlement nor to reject it outright.[167] Such a passive, reactive posture in a situation of escalating armed conflict was fraught with dangers.

This was the main motive behind the decision to keep the Anglo-American initiative alive. At best, it could bring about the desired peaceful settlement. Alternatively, the mere active pursuit of a settlement could discourage the guerillas from intensifying, or at least from internationalizing, the armed conflict. The Anglo-American plan, which had just failed so badly, seems to have been the only viable basis for the revitalization of the diplomatic option. This was primarily so not only because the Americans and the British could not agree on a new plan, but also because the FLP and the PF regarded it as the only basis for further negotiations.[168] The FLP feared that the British and the Americans would gravitate towards the internal settlement.[169] This would not only improve the chances of the internal settlement, but also considerably escalate the armed struggle with a possibility of foreign intervention. Despite their commitment to the armed struggle, which was amply demonstrated, this was a bleak prospect, especially to Mozambique and Zambia. Mozambique had already paid an enormous economic price for its devotion to the PF cause, while Zambia, with its faltering economy, badly needed the use of its traditional southern outlet to the sea. Thus, in their Dar es Salaam meeting in March 1978, the FLP called on the British and the Americans to make their position on their plan clear. The PF was also aware of the dangers inherent in Western flirtation with the internal regime. Thus, while preferring to achieve their goal through the barrel of the gun, they were prepared to go along with the Anglo-American proposals to prevent Anglo-American support for the internal settlement. After meeting Owen in London in mid-March 1978, Mugabe and Nkomo insisted that while "the war still goes on" the Anglo-American proposals should form a basis for negotiation.[170]

Earlier, in the second half of February 1978, before the internal agreement was signed, the Carter administration's Policy Review Committee had concluded "that we must build a bridge between the Patriotic Front and the Salisbury parties, drawing the former into a settlement while reducing the danger of a protracted civil war". They also asserted that "the Anglo-American proposals should remain on the table as a vehicle for negotiations, but above all, as a standard against which the fairness of a final settlement could be measured."[171] Meeting on March 9, 1978 Carter, Vance and Owen agreed that the Anglo-American plan was the best basis from which to proceed. The following day, Carter spoke in favour of closing the gap between the internal settlement and the Anglo-American plan.[172] Soon the British and the Americans moved from words to diplomatic action. On March 17 British and American representatives met in Pretoria representatives of the Rhodesian government to enlighten them on their governments' thinking.[173] A few days later, on March 21, Young visited Dar es Salaam assuring Nyerere of Carter's commitment to the Anglo-American plan and seeking his advice on how to reactivate it.[174] By the time Carter was in Lagos in late March and early April, the Anglo-American diplomatic drive had taken shape. According to Brzezinski, Carter envisioned a meeting with the PF and their patrons in April which would be followed, possibly in May, by a second meeting which would also include the internal parties.[175] This coincided with the position of the PF, who earlier, in mid-March, had conditioned their participation in a full-scale conference on the holding of a Malta-type meeting first.[176] Soon after, on April 5, John Graham from the British Foreign Office left for a southern African shuttle. He was joined by Stephen Low, the U.S. ambassador to Zambia, and together they set out to expedite the Anglo-American initiative. They visited Lusaka, and in Maputo they met the PF leaders.[177] While they were visiting these capitals, the U.S. announced that a meeting between Owen and Vance and the PF would be held in Tanzania on April 15.[178] In Salisbury the Anglo-American emissaries and their idea of an all-party conference did not receive a hearty welcome.[179] This should not have surprised them. Their proposed conference, on the basis of the Anglo-American plan, held no promise for the still euphoric internal partners. Earlier, in March, Smith had accepted the idea of a new conference provided it did not entail the renegotiation of the internal agreement.[180] About a week later, Muzorewa, returning from a visit to Britain and the U.S. with a belief that he had found support for the internal settlement, predicted that within a year the country would be a member of the OAU.[181] On April 14 Chikerema said: "We are the government; they have nothing to tell us about how to run this country."[182] Hardly a compromising mood.

The "Malta-Two" conference took place in Dar es Salaam on April 14–15. To indicate their commitment to the Anglo-American plan, Vance and Owen brought with them Lord Carver and Prem Chand. On the African side, the PF, the FLP and Nigeria were represented. For Vance and Owen, the conference was very disappointing. The PF not only insisted on their dominance in the transition but also backed away "from the principle of internationally supervised elections open to all parties".[183] The communique issued at the end of the meeting stated that the British and the Americans regarded the PF proposals as a fundamental deviation from the Anglo-American plan which would have to be negotiated.[184] The PF was clearly not in a compromising mood either. They seemed more interested in the diplomatic process which tied the British and the Americans to a neutral position than in the successful conclusion of their effort. Carter was enraged upon reading the report of the meeting and instructed Vance to protest sharply to the FLP about PF intransigence.[185] Indeed, what emerges clearly from the report on the meeting is that as the guerilla war was increasingly becoming the dominant feature of the conflict, the PF came into its own and was directly and largely independently involved at all levels in defence of their interests.

The failure in Dar es Salaam did not augur well for the subsequent discussions in Pretoria and Salisbury. While being still interested in an internationally recognized settlement, South Africa did not want to jeopardize the chances of the internal settlement. As before, all they were prepared to undertake was that the Rhodesians would abide by whatever they agreed to.[186] In Salisbury, the members of the Executive Council showed little interest in what Vance and Owen had to offer. Instead, they tried to persuade them to support the internal settlement. They were evasive regarding an all-party conference, promising only to consider it.[187] Back in London, Owen admitted in Parliament that there were faint signs of progress.[188] U.S. officials blamed the PF for the failure of the mission.[189]

Thus, another major Anglo-American effort came to naught. The British and the Americans were desperately groping for a viable Rhodesian policy. The second Shaba invasion in May 1978, and Castro's message to the U.S. Congress that he would be prepared to assist the PF,[190] added a new element of urgency especially among U.S. policy makers with their wider global concerns. In June 1978 one of the assumptions affecting their policy on Rhodesia was that "Soviet and Cuban intervention is a strong possibility if the conflict continues, and

U.S. interests would suffer." This sense of urgency was not reflected, however, in any new policy.[191] For want of innovative ideas, the British and the Americans sought to maintain a diplomatic momentum by continuing to peddle their inadequate, rejected plan. In the second week of June, Graham and Low were again on their trail. They went first to Salisbury trying to persuade the internal parties to accept the idea of an all-party conference. The latter, however, were in no mood for compromise. The recent Shaba invasion had apparently led them to believe that the West would wake up to the challenge of Soviet expansionism and adopt a more realistic attitude towards it.[192] They were also still optimistic about their domestic support.[193] In Maputo the Anglo-American emissaries tried to sell Mugabe the idea of direct talks between the PF and the internal leaders. Mugabe rejected this outright while agreeing to attend a constitutional conference to discuss the independence constitution.[194] In a meeting with U.S. State Department officials in Washington on June 19, 1978, Nkomo rejected altogether the idea of an all-party settlement: "The U.S. is failing in this. We are winning the war, so why should we talk when we are soon going to get there anyway."[195] The British and the Americans were evidently flogging a dead horse.

Successive failures produced increasing pressures on policy makers in London and Washington. This was partly the background against which a new initiative was launched, namely the covert attempts to use Nkomo as a bridge between the internal settlement and external acceptability. In England, the massacre of 12 British missionaries and dependants in the Elim Mission on June 23, allegedly by ZIPA guerillas, precipitated a severe Conservative attack on the government's Rhodesian policy. Conservative MPs demanded from Owen to rule out further talks with the PF and to recognize the internal settlement.[196] On June 29 Margaret Thatcher, the leader of the opposition, asked the government to hold another debate on Rhodesia in the Commons.[197] However, more significant domestic pressures had been building up in the U.S. Congress. The pressures, which focused on an effort to lift the economic sanctions against Rhodesia, had begun in spring 1978.[198] The Rhodesian issue also became entangled in the web of American electoral politics. With the mid-term elections for the Senate and the House of Representatives, due to be held on November 7, 1978, approaching, the efforts of the conservative pro-Rhodesian pressure group headed by Senator Jesse Helms were reinforced by timid centrists and liberals who were facing conservative challengers.[199] On June 29 a resolution in the Senate calling for the lifting of sanctions by September 1979 was narrowly defeated in a 48–42 vote. The conservative Senators made it known that they would have another try at the very first opportunity.[200] Carter's Rhodesian policy was evidently resting on a shaky domestic basis. During the first half of July, the anti-sanction campaign gathered momentum.[201] The Rhodesian Executive Council, smelling a kill, despatched Muzorewa to Washington to assist the pro-Rhodesians.[202] The administration, sensing defeat, directed its efforts towards toning down the prospective Congressional resolution. After much discussion, Senators Javitz and Case offered a compromise which would have lifted sanctions by December 31, 1978, "if the president determined that the Rhodesian government had demonstrated its willingness to attend an all-parties conference and a new government had been installed following free, internationally supervised elections".[203] The Case–Javitz amendment was approved by the Senate in a 59–36 vote.[204] It was subsequently ratified by the House of Representatives on August 3.[205] The administration warded off the more extreme Helmes amendment at the cost of watering down its policy. As Vance put it, it "illustrated the growing difficulty of holding to a balanced African policy". He attributed it to the prevailing public mood as Carter's presidency was approaching mid-term. According to Vance, there was also "a perceptible hardening of attitudes" within the administration.[206] Meanwhile, on August 2 the House of Commons narrowly defeated a Conservative attempt to force the government to lift sanctions in a 171–165 vote.[207]

While the U.S. administration still put on a brave face, insisting that it would persist in its Rhodesian policy,[208] the alternative strategy – the Nkomo covert option – was nearing its climax. Owen favoured the inclusion of Nkomo in the internal settlement soon after the signing of the internal agreement. However, only in response to the subsequent failure of the Anglo-American efforts and to mounting domestic pressure, Vance agreed to secret British attempts to arrange an exploratory meeting between Smith and Nkomo, on condition that it would include the possibility of Mugabe's subsequent participation.[209] According to Martin and Johnson, secret contacts aimed at bringing Nkomo in began as early as April 1978. Smith's security adviser, Derrick Robinson, Brigadier Joseph Garba, the former Nigerian Commissioner for External Affairs, Lonrho's "Tiny" Rowland, Nkomo, Sithole, Chief Chirau and Chief Ndiweni were apparently involved in these contacts.[210] By the end of June when the British got the green light from Washington, Smith was much keener on the Nkomo option. In mid-June he had already expressed disappointment with the efforts to bring about a cease-fire.[211] In the third week of July he openly blamed his black partners for failing to deliver the goods.[212] Bringing in a nationalist leader with effective control over a growing guerilla army and regional and international support made very good political sense. The secret contacts, which received new impetus in late June 1978 following U.S. consent, were handled by Owen. Smith, Nkomo and Kaunda showed interest in a meeting between the first two. Subsequently Owen conducted secret discussions in which the Nigerians also were involved, with a view to holding the meeting in August. The other presidents were not aware of these contacts.[213]

The meeting between Nkomo and Smith was held on August 14, 1978 at the State Lodge outside Lusaka. The Zambian venue and involvement is explainable not only in terms of Kaunda's special relations with Nkomo; it also reflected Zambia's growing economic difficulties, which caused Kaunda some two months later to decide on opening the Rhodesian border in order to avail his country of the southern outlet to the sea. In addition to Nkomo, Smith and Kaunda's representative, Brigadier Garba of Nigeria was also present at the meeting.[214] Since Carter's visit to Nigeria earlier in 1978, the Nigerians had become actively involved in the efforts to resolve the Rhodesian conflict. The centrality of Nigeria in African and world politics in the U.S. global outlook was apparently matched by Nigerian self-perception. Riding the wave of the oil boom, they began to view themselves as the great African power. The meeting was held in great secrecy. Smith apparently promised to cede "full power" to Nkomo before the elections. Nkomo, however, responded that Mugabe had to be involved. He asked the Nigerians to try to arrange that Mugabe would attend a subsequent meeting.[215] The second meeting was never held. On August 31 Sithole publicly accused Smith of secretly negotiating with Nkomo and gave information about the content of the meeting.[216] At first, Nkomo and Smith denied having met, but on September 2 the former chose to reveal the details of the meeting.[217] On the same day, the FLP ended a two-day emergency meeting to discuss the Nkomo–Smith talks. They papered over their differences and reaffirmed their support for the Anglo-American plan.[218] The shooting down of the Air Rhodesia Viscount on September 3 by ZIPRA guerillas put an end to the Nkomo option.

A meeting between Callaghan and Kaunda on September 21–22 failed to produce a new impetus to the efforts to resolve the Rhodesian impasse.[219] In October 1978 the centre stage moved to Washington. It was forced on the Americans by the Rhodesian Executive Council which requested visas to the U.S. for its members in order to capture American public opinion and to boost the campaign for the lifting of sanctions. On October 4, in the face of African protest, the State

Department reluctantly granted Smith and his colleagues visas. The administration feared that a refusal to grant Smith a visa and a fair hearing would provide valuable ammunition to the legislators who were fighting for the lifting of sanctions.[220] The State Department presented the visit as an opportunity to promote a peaceful settlement.[221] In a meeting between Vance, the British ambassador to the U.S., Smith and Sithole, Smith still refused to attend an all-party conference. However, on October 12, in compliance with the terms of the Case–Javitz amendment, and in spite of Muzorewa's objections, Smith conceded in the Senate's Foreign Relations Committee that the Executive Council would attend an "adequately prepared" all-party conference.[222] On October 20 the Executive Council conferred with American and British officials at the State Department. At the end of the meeting Smith announced: "We have agreed at this meeting to five basic points with which the conference will be associated and we will now go forward from there."[223] A senior U.S. official subsequently enunciated the five points: (1) provision for holding free and fair elections; (2) cease-fire; (3) transitional administration; (4) formation of armed forces to serve the independent government; (5) basic principles to be included in the independence constitution, including guarantees of individual rights.[224]

Having succeeded in persuading the internal parties to take part in a conference, the British and the Americans did not really advance the cause of peace in Rhodesia. They were soon faced again with the unyielding nature of the Rhodesian reality. While Smith and his colleagues were still in the U.S., the Rhodesian security forces launched their massive attacks on ZIPRA bases in Zambia. Understandably, Nkomo, in particular, was hardly in a mood for compromise. His rejection on October 22 of the plan for an all-party conference was endorsed by his patron, Kaunda. The Zambians interpreted the grant of visas to the internal leaders and the understanding reached with them in Washington as a definite shift in the Anglo-American approach: "Under the original proposals, Britain and America were on our side – but not any longer."[225] Another Anglo-American initiative came to naught. It seems that what kept them going was, as Owen said on October 25, the fear that if the negotiations stopped, it would be very difficult to revive them.[226] It was a minimalistic expectation which stemmed from a year and a half of continuous frustrations. From that point on, the Americans took a back seat, and the British undertook the thankless task of keeping the dying embers alive.[227] In early November 1978 Lord Carver and a Foreign Office team took again to the southern African trail in another vain attempt to narrow the gap between the PF and the internal parties.[228] The resignation of Lord Carver on November 23, after he and Owen had concluded that it was no longer appropriate to maintain his post of Resident Commissioner designate,[229] provided a strong indication that the original Anglo-American plan was, in fact, dead. A week earlier, Callaghan, after consulting Carter, had already announced another initiative. He planned to send Cledwyn Hughes, to be accompanied by Stephen Low, to southern Africa and Nigeria to find out whether the conditions were right for convening an all-party conference along the lines of Camp David.[230] Judging by the reactions of the domestic parties, Hughes was heading for another exercise in futility. Whereas Smith reiterated the interim government's agreement to participate in a conference without preconditions, the PF also stuck to their guns stating that they would attend only if handing over of power was on the agenda.[231] Hughes was asked by Callaghan to answer two questions: (1) Would all parties to the Rhodesian conflict be prepared to attend a meeting to consider a negotiated settlement? (2) If so, would there be a reasonable chance of such a meeting producing a successful outcome?[232] Hughes' answer was affirmative to the first question and unequivocally negative to the second. Assessing that the gap between the parties was too wide to be bridged, he recommended against holding a conference.[233] He concluded that there was no point in making another attempt to secure a negotiated settlement before April 20, 1979. At the same time, he recommended that the U.S. and British governments remain committed to a negotiated settlement, and viewed the Anglo-American plan as the best basis for an eventual settlement.[234] On January 17, 1979 Callaghan informed the House of Commons that he accepted Hughes' view that no useful purpose would be served by convening an all-party conference in the immediate future.[235]

As emerged clearly from Hughes' report, any fresh international initiative was rendered premature pending the outcome of the approaching internal elections. It was not that the British and the Americans were committed to accepting the verdict of the elections. In refusing to send official observers to monitor the elections both governments expressed their unwillingness to be associated with them. Meeting members of the Executive Council on March 22, U.S. and British officials, while conceding that the elections could not be scrapped, insisted that the elected leaders would have to accommodate the PF.[236] Earlier in March Owen had gone further, stating in advance that the elections could not be "free and fair" because of the exclusion of the PF.[237] However, the British Rhodesian policy, in general, was to be subject to the outcome of the British general elections due to be held on May 3, a fortnight after the Rhodesian internal elections. The Carter administration was no more in a position to chart a clear Rhodesian policy. With the Congress breathing heavily down its neck, it had no choice but to await the results of the two general elections.[238]

Thus, the Rhodesian conflict system was focused in early 1979 on the approaching internal elections. These were a major test and challenge to the contending camps. For the internal parties, the elections were the consummation of the whole internal exercise. A large turnout of black voters could be construed as indicating popular support, and pave the way for external recognition. On April 18 Muzorewa predicted that the OAU would split over the question of recognition.[239] Sithole promised that the war would be over a few months after the election.[240] For the PF also, the internal election was a crucial test. At stake was their claim for control of liberated and semi-liberated areas. Furthermore, a failure of the elections could very well be the last nail in the internal settlement's coffin. On April 16, 1979 Mugabe broadcast a special appeal to his fellow Africans to abstain from voting. He also gave last-minute instructions to his forces to thwart the elections.[241] Nkomo, not having many guerillas inside Rhodesia, revoked his pledge to prevent the elections from taking place by force of arms.[242] The government, on its part, mobilized all its potential military manpower to give the elections an effective security screen.[243] By mid-April the government had nearly 100,000 men under its command.[244] The government also carried out a large-scale campaign to persuade and encourage the Africans to vote.[245]

The most significant element in the elections was the turnout of 64.45 per cent of the electorate.[246] The views of the observers who had monitored the elections about their being "free and fair" were conflicting.[247] A lot depended on the bias of the observers and on the rigidity of the criteria against which the elections were evaluated. The guerilla war situation throughout much of the African areas was, at best, not one in which free democratic elections could be held. There was certainly intimidation by both the guerillas and the security forces. On the whole, there is little doubt that the turnout represented a great achievement for the government. It was, however, more a reflection of the balance of power between the government bureaucratic machinery and security forces and the guerillas at the given time than of the will of the African people. The government could maintain this balance of power only at the cost of bringing the economy to a standstill.

Leaders of the internal settlement grossly misinterpreted the significance of the elections and the consequences thereof. On April 23, 1979 Smith expected at least the lifting of sanctions by the U.S. and estimated that recognition could be secured within two months.[248] Muzorewa got carried away by the electoral success and his personal victory, expecting recognition and predicting a victory over PF guerillas.[249] As emerges from the casualty figures among the guerillas, the security forces and black and white civilians during May 1979, as reported by the Combined Operations Headquarters,[250] Muzorewa had little understanding of the dynamic of the unfolding guerilla war. As the figures for June show, the guerillas were not impressed either by the formation of a black government on May 30, 1979[251] or by the establishment on June 7 of an Amnesty Directorate whose task was to persuade them to lay down their arms.[252] As soon as the government demobilized those recruited for providing the security screen during the elections, the balance of power reverted to its former dimensions. The guerillas, who had chosen to lie low in the face of the government's massive show of force, continued to operate quite freely across much of the country. The assumption of power by a black government did not remove the cause of the war. In fact, it served only to exacerbate the conflict. The stakes were higher and the war assumed the ugly and brutal nature of a fraternal strife. One of the expressions of the sense of urgency in the nationalist guerilla camp was their decision to step up the effort to strengthen unity within the PF.[253] While old animosities did not disappear and the mere agreement proved far easier than its implementation, PF leaders were acutely aware that the successful pursuit of the war at that critical stage required greater unity and greater effort.

Thus, Muzorewa faced a more determined enemy challenging his new kingdom. The internal parties, worthy of their transitional government parentage, proved unable to meet the challenge and give Muzorewa a fair chance. Unlike their enemies, who at least attempted to forge unity, the internal parties were unable to forgo sectarian and personal interests in order to promote the option on which their own future depended. Sithole, upset that his grandiose fantasies were not matched by electoral realities, not only attacked the conduct of the elections, appealed to the high court to have them annulled and called for a judicial inquiry, but also boycotted Parliament.[254] In July 1979 the tension between Sithole and the Muzorewa government reached a climax. On July 20 the security forces launched a disciplinary action against auxiliary forces operating in "Mafia type gangs", killing 183 auxiliaries. Although the Combined Operations Headquarters tried to cover it up, the operation was directed against Sithole's men. On the same day, Sithole's ZANU headquarters in Salisbury was searched, as were homes of party officials, including Sithole. A number of officials and 100 auxiliaries were detained. On July 23 another six of Sithole's officials were detained.[255] Only on July 31 did Sithole decide to end his boycott and to join the House of Assembly with his 11 colleagues.[256] Even then, he issued demands which hardly enhanced the prestige of the regime.[257] Under these circumstances, it is hardly surprising that the tension between Muzorewa and Sithole did not subside.[258] In Muzorewa's own party, sub-Shona tribalism reared its ugly head. Chikerema, the UANC vice-president, denounced Muzorewa for surrounding himself with a "tribal mafia". Chikerema, a member of the Zezuru ethnic group, alleged that Muzorewa intended to allocate most ministries to his Manyika co-ethnics. Another Zezuru demanded half the ministries for his group.[259] On June 20 Chikerema broke away from the UANC and formed the Zezuru-based Zimbabwe Democratic Party (ZDP) which controlled eight parliamentary seats.[260] This cut Muzorewa's parliamentary representation from an absolute majority of 51 to 43.[261] The UANC, on its part, made continuous efforts to have the Chikerema faction ejected from the House of Assembly.[262]

With so much energy and bitterness invested in political struggles between its components, the internal regime could not hope to instill confidence and enthusiasm among the country's citizens or to mobilize all its political resources to fight the military challenge. The guerilla war continued unabated. In fact, inside the country, the war became more brutal with increasing numbers of white and black civilians, particularly the latter, becoming targets for the guerillas.[263] In their external operations, the security forces continued to concentrate their efforts against ZIPRA with a view to disrupting Nkomo's invasion plans.[264]

Essentially, the guerilla war was still in a state of stalemate. The security forces, while definitely not being in a position to win the war, were not on the verge of defeat either. They had not lost their combative spirit and the will to fight. They were still able to operate offensively both internally and externally, inflicting heavy losses on the guerillas. They were unable, however, to stamp out the tide of the guerillas' infiltration and the increasing tempo of guerilla actions. The guerillas, with much military potential yet untapped, were riding the wave of victory. Military victory was not, however, an imminent prospect. From this perspective, the war in itself, in the months following the internal elections, did not provide an impetus which could dramatically change the course of the Rhodesian conflict. Such new impetus was to be provided by a renewed, more determined international involvement which launched the conflict on a course of diplomatic and peaceful, rather than military and violent, solution.

In the wake of the elections, it seemed for a short while that the god of history was smiling at the internal partners at last. Within two weeks of their great domestic electoral success, there appeared a shining star in the international horizon. On May 3, 1979 the British electorate voted in a Conservative government to be headed by Margaret Thatcher. Smith, seasoned in the vacillations of British politics, was not euphoric. However, while not believing that it would solve all the regime's problems, he did think that the British general election results were "good news". The less experienced Muzorewa was more jubilant: "Our victory would not have been complete without Mrs Thatcher's victory."[265]

These expectations were fed by the attitudes the Conservatives had exhibited towards the internal settlement while in opposition. In February 1978 John Davies, the Conservative shadow foreign secretary, had welcomed the prospect of an internal settlement provided it complied with the six principles forming the basis of the bi-partisan approach to rendering legitimacy and recognition to Rhodesia.[266] The internal settlement constitution clearly fulfilled five of them. The sixth, the test of acceptability, was to be taken care of by the elections. The Conservative election manifesto, issued on February 6, 1979, was even more positive: "If the six principles ... are fully satisfied following the present Rhodesian elections, the next Government will have the duty to return Rhodesia to a state of legality, move to lift sanctions, and do its utmost to ensure that the new independent state gains international recognition."[267] On March 24, in a major speech, Mrs Thatcher stated that the party would judge the election on the basis of a report by a team of party observers.[268] Thus, the hopes and expectations raised in Salisbury by the Conservatives' electoral victory were not altogether misplaced. The internal leaders could also rejoice at what Lord Carrington, the new Foreign Secretary, had to say on May 6: "I do not think anyone can ignore an election in which 65 per cent of the people voted." From his criticism of his predecessor, a definite change of course could be inferred. He said that the government was waiting for the report of the party's team of observers and that it was committed to restoring Rhodesia to legality if the elections were found to have been free and fair.[269] On May 23 Carrington told a deputation of the Commonwealth High Commissioners in London that the government believed that the Rhodesian elections had transformed the situation in that country.[270] A day earlier, Mrs Thatcher and Lord Carrington had addressed the House of Commons and the House of Lords respectively on the Rhodesian question. Mrs Thatcher had repeated her pre-election undertakings.

246

Having informed the House of Lords that Lord Boyd and his team of observers had come to the conclusion that with certain reservations the elections were fairly conducted, Carrington said: "The government will be guided by his conclusions in seeking to build on the progress which had already been made in Rhodesia. They reinforce our aim and our determination to return Rhodesia to legality in conditions of peace and of wide recognition."[271]

Yet the Zimbabwe/Rhodesian government was realistic enough to assess that they could not expect a fresh British initiative before the Commonwealth conference, due to be held in August 1979. They expected that the impetus for recognition and lifting of sanctions would come from Washington. They pinned their hopes on the U.S. Congress, which had already demonstrated its sympathy towards the internal settlement. They could derive particular satisfaction from a 75 to 19 vote in the Senate on May 14 calling on Carter to lift sanctions within 10 days of the formation of a black-dominated government in Salisbury.[272] With a view to exploiting this avenue of pressure on the U.S. administration, Muzorewa sent a message to the U.S. Congress asking for recognition on the ground of compliance with the requirements of the Case–Javitz amendment. He also accused Carter of trying to stifle democracy by maintaining sanctions.[273] On June 7 Carter announced that the U.S. would continue to apply sanctions because in terms of the amendment "I cannot conclude that the elections were either free or fair."[274] Muzorewa was still optimistic, viewing Carter's decision as a temporary setback.[275] His optimism fed on the Senate's persistent and increasing pressure on the president. On June 12 the Senate voted 52 to 41 against a compromise forwarded by the administration which would delay the lifting of sanctions until December 1, 1979. The following day the Senate adopted, in an 89 to 7 vote, a rider on a military bill ordering Carter to lift sanctions immediately.[276] Thomas O'Neil, the Speaker of the House of Representatives, was confident that the House would follow in the Senate's footsteps. When Carter threatened to veto the bill, he was bitterly attacked by Muzorewa for his "bankrupt policy". To boost his Congress strategy, Muzorewa sent, on June 13, envoys to prepare his own visit to Washington.[277]

Muzorewa, in fact, dived into the deep water of American politics without possessing a realistic appreciation of the complexities thereof. Whereas the support for Muzorewa centred mainly in the Senate, the administration had sufficient room to manoeuvre in the House of Representatives.[278] This Muzorewa was soon to discover. On June 15 the Foreign Affairs Committee of the House of Representatives sent, to the full House, a bill which would have lifted sanctions by December 15, 1979, "unless the President determined that it would not be in the interests of the U.S. to do so".[279] This compromise would have given Carter a large measure of discretion. It had conveniently split the Congress in the middle. At the end of June the House of Representatives defeated an amendment which would have forced Carter to make a special application to Congress to extend the sanctions beyond December 1, 1979. The House, in a 350 to 37 vote, passed the Foreign Affairs Committee's bill.[280] This setback did not deter Muzorewa from proceeding with his planned visit to the U.S. On his departure on July 8 he said he hoped "to be able to knock some sense into the heads of those who are emotionally charged as far as the situation here is concerned".[281] Returning to Salisbury, he declared that sanctions would be lifted and his country recognized in three months' time.[282] His optimism definitely indicated that he had come back as ignorant of the nature of the U.S. government and politics as he had been upon leaving Salisbury. The truth was that Carter was not in the least inclined to change the course of his Rhodesian policy, even under stronger congressional pressure. The change hoped for by Muzorewa would have entailed a serious setback to U.S. African and global policy. Carter certainly could not have been expected to change course radically when he had comfortable room to manoeuvre between the Senate and the House of Representatives. In remaining committed to his Rhodesian policy, Carter was also motivated by the prospect of a black backlash. Reacting to the Senate initiative, black American groups mounted a large-scale campaign against lifting sanctions. Thus, mutually reinforcing global and domestic considerations kept U.S. Rhodesian policy well on course. Carter, in fact, was not totally hostile to the internal settlement. He recognized that the elections significantly changed the Rhodesian scene. He believed, however, that the elections were a significant step in the right direction, rather than the final destination. He was prepared to lift sanctions, but only if conditions had been fulfilled which would have undone the internal settlement – the revision of the constitution, progress towards an all-party conference and internationally recognized elections.[283]

Muzorewa equally misread the mood of Margaret Thatcher when visiting London on the way back from the U.S. He was very impressed by her sincerity and honesty, adding that "I feel certain that she is about to lead us to the promised land."[284] In fact, Mrs Thatcher was about to make a *volte face* which would push Muzorewa into the political wilderness and his Zimbabwe/Rhodesia to the graveyard of history. She soon discovered that an election manifesto of an opposition party could not easily be transformed into government policy. In the wake of the British elections, pressures on the Conservative government to modify its attitude towards the Rhodesian question were mounting. Meeting Vance on May 21, 1979, Lord Carrington was "dismayed" by U.S. conditions for the lifting of sanctions.[285] It was clear that Carter would have nothing to do with a British policy based on the Conservatives' election promises. The prospect of lifting sanctions was also challenged by NATO members.[286] Expectedly, strong opposition to lifting sanctions and recognition came from black Africa. On May 25 the OAU Liberation Committee warned the U.S. and Britain against recognition of the "new puppet regime".[287] In June, after meeting in Dar es Salaam, the foreign ministers of the FLP and Nigeria warned the U.S. and Britain that recognition of the Muzorewa regime would endanger their relations with black Africa.[288] Of particular importance was the tough attitude adopted by Nigeria, Britain's main African trading partner. On May 24 the Nigerian government turned down British tenders for a very lucrative contract, indicating that this policy would be upheld until Britain clarified its position towards Rhodesia.[289] African pressures were also very relevant in the broader context of the Commonwealth. Indeed, the shaping of an appropriate Rhodesian policy became a top British priority in view of the Commonwealth conference due to be held in early August 1979. Significantly, and indeed symbolically, the conference was to be held in Lusaka. On May 18, the Commonwealth High Commissioners in London produced a consensus condemning the Rhodesian elections. They also decided to send a delegation to Mrs Thatcher to warn her against recognition of the Muzorewa government or the lifting of sanctions.[290] Kaunda said that if Britain recognized Rhodesia, the Queen would address an empty hall at the opening of the Commonwealth conference.[291] On July 22 Nyerere warned that Tanzania would withdraw from the Commonwealth if Rhodesia were to become a member.[292]

It was, thus, becoming increasingly evident that the implementation of the Conservatives' pre-election policy would be very costly to Britain. Furthermore, Thatcher could expect a veritable fiasco in her international debut in Lusaka. Following the logic of its policy, Britain might find itself, together with South Africa, supporting an internationally ostracized regime involved in a war it could not hope to win. This was a suicidal policy which a pragmatic Conservative government could not entertain. As the implications of this option unfolded, the British government began to make the necessary adjustments for a change of course. On May 21, when Carrington told the House of Lords that the government was seeking "to build on the progress which has

249

already been made in Rhodesia" and was determined "to return Rhodesia to legality in conditions of peace and international recognition",[293] the British government was beginning to climb down. Speaking in the House of Commons on July 25, Mrs Thatcher said that, Boyd's positive conclusions notwithstanding, the government had not yet determined if the principle of acceptability had been fulfilled. In rationalizing her indecision, she further revealed the change in her thinking: "and if we go along that consultation route, it will be to the benefit of Rhodesia. It is a way in which we can gain this country's acceptance to legal independence."[294] Since the Commonwealth conference, due to open within a week, was obviously the immediate consultation forum, the new British policy spelled doom for the Muzorewa regime.

As the process of consultation and shaping of a new policy unfolded, the departure from the Labour Rhodesian strategy became increasingly striking. Since Kissinger had dragged Britain into the Rhodesian crisis in late 1976, the main international impetus had been generated in Washington. Mrs Thatcher was clearly determined to re-establish British primacy. In her speech in the Commons on May 22, she stressed: "We accept that responsibility for Rhodesia rests with this House."[295] Vance, from his Washington perspective, noticed that the new government was assuming the role of senior partner regarding Rhodesia.[296] In mid-May, less than two weeks after the election, the new government indicated the importance it attached to Rhodesia by sending a Foreign Office envoy, Sir Anthony Duff, to Salisbury to sound out local politicians and officials.[297] In her May 22 speech Thatcher announced her intention to send a senior Foreign Office official to Salisbury to establish close contact with the Muzorewa government, and another emissary to explain British views to leaders of African and Commonwealth states.[298] On June 25 the two envoys were back in London to discuss with Lord Carrington Britain's Rhodesian policy.[299] The process of consultation, which also included the U.S. and Britain's European Community partners, reached a climax in early August in the Commonwealth conference in Lusaka. Declaring on her arrival in Lusaka on July 31 that Britain would not recognize Zimbabwe/Rhodesia without the approval of other Commonwealth states,[300] Mrs Thatcher gave the conference a veto power.

On August 1, the opening day of the Commonwealth conference, Nigeria announced the nationalization of British Petroleum (BP) interests. Although the direct reason for that act was BP's supply of oil to South Africa, the Nigerians made it clear that it was also aimed at putting pressure on Britain over the Rhodesian policy.[301] This was a grim reminder to Britain as to what it could expect if it failed to satisfy the conference. Margaret Thatcher came to Lusaka not only prepared for a climb down, but also intent on turning a defeat into a victory. In her opening speech on August 1 Mrs Thatcher, though speaking in general terms, further underlined the shift in British policy: "The aim is to bring Rhodesia to legal independence on a basis which the Commonwealth and the international community as a whole will find acceptable."[302] In her second speech, which was wholly dedicated to Rhodesia, she tried to maintain a balance between taking cognizance of the progress achieved by the internal settlement and criticizing it. Of the four points she made in clarifying the British position, only one was new: "We accept that our objective must be to establish that independence on the basis of a constitution comparable with the constitution we have agreed with other countries."[303] These general outlines were sufficient for the right-wing *Daily Express* to write, on August 4, that "Mrs Thatcher looked set last night to do a Charles de Gaulle on Rhodesia." The Nigerians, on the other hand, were still not satisfied. They demanded a timetable and assurances that Thatcher would go "a good deal further". They also threatened to leave the Commonwealth.[304] The gap between the generalities enunciated by Thatcher and the more specific demands of the African members, as outlined by Nyerere,[305] could not be bridged in an open debate. This task was assigned to delegation leaders from Britain, Australia, Tanzania, Zambia and Jamaica and Mr Rampal, the Secretary General, over the weekend of August 4–5.[306] The compromise plan included elements from Thatcher's statements and a more specific application thereof to satisfy the Africans. These included "the adoption of a democratic constitution, including safeguards for minorities", the holding of "free and fair elections properly supervised under British Government authority and with Commonwealth observers", the holding of a constitutional conference to which all parties would be invited, and the cessation of hostilities and the lifting of sanctions. The plan was subsequently endorsed by a specially arranged meeting of all the delegations.[307] In this plan Britain went all the way, rendering the internal settlement null and void. In return, it received the full backing of the Commonwealth in general and of the FLP in particular, in discharging its decolonizing task. The FLP also relinquished its demand that the PF be the sole legitimate representative of Rhodesian Africans.

Muzorewa's reaction to the deliberation and to the plan of the Commonwealth was astonishing. Following Mrs Thatcher's August 3 speech, he observed that the British position did not seem to have changed.[308] Then he found in the Commonwealth plan "some positive elements and some which will require clarification".[309] There were, however, some more sober souls in Salisbury. The ZRBC reported that "observers in Salisbury say that Mrs Thatcher's new proposals are merely a watered-down version of the Anglo-American plan."[310] Even South Africa reacted more bitterly. Pik Botha said that his government was "deeply disturbed" by the new plan, adding that events had "suddenly, virtually overnight, taken a very serious course".[311] This sudden turn of events was a serious blow to the idea of a constellation of southern African states, the new South African regional grand design enunciated by President P.W. Botha in April 1979.[312] A moderate Zimbabwe/Rhodesia, well disposed towards its patron, was expected to play a major role in this constellation revolving around South Africa. South Africa, however, could do nothing against such a wide international consensus which supported the new Rhodesian plan.

Although the Commonwealth plan signed the death warrant of the internal settlement, the initial reaction of the PF was not favourable. A ZANU broadcast on August 6 viewed the plan as nothing more than another imperialist manipulation designed to deny the liberation movement the fruits of the imminent victory and to safeguard the imperialist, settler interests in Rhodesia.[313] Mugabe presented three principles from which ZANU could not deviate:

(1) That the people of Zimbabwe become sovereign in and over their country through the transference of total and unfettered power to them from Britain;
(2) That the present Smith regime be completely disbanded so as to create a clear and irreversible process towards genuine independence;
(3) That the combined armed forces of the illegal regime be dismantled and our liberation forces be constituted as a national army of Zimbabwe.[314]

Nkomo, on his part, rejected the idea of elections supervised by Britain.[315] The PF's initial reaction to the Commonwealth plan revived optimism in Salisbury. It was expected that the PF would wreck the conference and leave Muzorewa and his government as the only partners in terms of the plan.[316] It was, however, premature. Once Tanzania and Zambia actively participated in drawing up the plan and they were supported by Mozambique, the manoeuvring space of the PF disappeared. The initial rejection of the plan indicated that the PF failed to understand that without the firm support of their regional partners they had lost their veto power. On August 10 Nyerere over-ruled the PF: "The Patriotic Front is not rejecting the idea of election or a new constitution." He also shrugged off their preconditions: "Smith would like to have his army and I suppose the Patriotic Front would like to have theirs, but the agreement says 'properly supervised elections under British authority'."[317] Kaunda and Nyerere said that they could persuade the PF to come to the negotiating table.[318]

On August 6 Mrs Thatcher told the Lusaka Press Club: "We mean to move swiftly towards our immediate objective of working with the parties to draw up an independence constitution."[319] The British government, indeed, did not waste any time. On August 14 it sent invitations to the Muzorewa government and the PF to attend a constitutional conference at Lancaster House on September 10, 1979. Attached to the invitations was an 11-point outline of proposals for the independence constitution. These proposals considerably diminished the privileges of the white minority.[320] The opposing domestic parties had little choice. The Commonwealth plan dramatically changed the rules of the game. In view of the new broad regional and international consensus, the domestic parties lost their autonomy within the conflict system. The Thatcher government, with a new sense of mission and with newly discovered power stemming from the Commonwealth backing, was becoming a dominant factor and actor in the process of conflict resolution in Rhodesia. On August 15 the Muzorewa government accepted the British invitation.[321] On the same day, ZAPU also accepted the invitation while rejecting a British plea for a cease-fire during the conference.[322] Mugabe dragged his feet for a while, saying that "there were points the British government had to clarify."[323] On August 20 Nkomo and Mugabe accepted the invitation on behalf of the PF, while rejecting the constitutional framework proposed by the British government and the call for a cease-fire.[324]

CHAPTER NINE

Lancaster House Conference –
a Victory for Diplomacy at Last

From the perspective of the unfolding conflict dynamics, the Lancaster House conference was, in a sense, an anti-climax. Since 1974 successive attempts by powerful regional and international actors to bring about a peaceful settlement in Rhodesia had all failed. Diplomacy, operating through patron–client networks, proved inadequate in harnessing the destructive domestic conflict energy and transforming it into a constructive energy for peace, reconciliation and reconstruction. In the first half of 1979, the conflict seemed to be heading for an almost inevitable violent climax. The internal parties, having attained what they perceived as a resounding electoral success, were in no mood for abdication. They were strongly supported, morally, materially and militarily, by a powerful regional patron. The Muzorewa government seemed determined to try and win the guerilla war and achieve international recognition. The guerilla movements, on their part, were prompted by the emergence of the internal regime to escalate the guerilla war. And yet, by the close of 1979, at the end of the Lancaster House conference, Rhodesia was set on a course which resulted within a few months in a peaceful transition of power coupled with wide domestic, regional and international recognition.

How can we account for this turn about in what had seemed as the natural, almost inevitable, course of the Rhodesian conflict? Gary Wasserman, writing in late 1978, ruled out an effective British de-colonizing role.[1] And yet, in the last quarter of 1979, Lancaster House hosted yet another grand constitutional conference and the British government performed an effective, crucial decolonizing role. In his very comprehensive and competent study of the Lancaster House conference, Davidow attributes the conference's success to what he terms "situational elements – clarity of goals, absence of superpower involvement, British diplomatic heritage, the Conservative party tradition, Carrington as a symbol, Carrington's qualities, the setting, the Press and intelligence – and to Carrington's tactics".[2] While not ignoring the favourable broader circumstances,[3] he does give

254

prominence to intra-conference factors and performance. While this may be plausible from the narrow perspective of conference management study, it is inadequate from the perspective of the broader and longer conflict resolution process. This is not to ignore or underestimate the highly competent role played by the British government and Lord Carrington, in particular. It is doubtful, however, that similar situational elements and tactics would have produced similar results at the Geneva conference some three years earlier. The crucial determinants, which may account for the success of the Lancaster House conference, must be sought in the dynamics of the escalating conflict, generated by the inter-action in and between the different levels of the Rhodesian conflict system. These dynamics, and the impact thereof on the attitudes of the different actors, shaped the uniquely favourable circumstances at the time of the conference. The greatness of Thatcher and Carrington lay in their excellent grasp of these dynamics, and in their being able to evolve a highly appropriate and effective conference management strategy and tactics which maximized the benefit of the favourable circumstances.

At the level of goals, the gap between the opposing domestic parties was much narrower than at the time of the Geneva conference, for example. Black majority rule, on the basis of one man-one-vote had not only been conceded in principle. Zimbabwe/Rhodesia was actually governed by a black majority government. This in itself, as we have seen, had had no impact at the level of strategy pursued by the domestic parties. In fact, the violent struggle intensified because vital questions related to power and ideology remained unresolved. However, the narrowing of the gap was not insignificant in its potential for conflict resolution. At the level of conflict strategy, the suggestion that the circumstances surrounding the conference were propitious because the war reached a stalemate which brought both sides to near exhaustion,[4] is not wholly plausible. While the intensification of the guerilla war was undoubtedly of crucial importance, its impact on the different parties and actors was uneven. It is true that the escalation of the war made the internal partners well disposed to British mediation. The whites, in particular, were disillusioned with the performance of their black partners. Having made what they considered the ultimate political sacrifice, they expected to be rewarded with peace and stability. The idea of fighting to the bitter end to defend a black majority government was not particularly appealing. As demonstrated during the conference, most of them were prepared to forgo political gains for the sake of ending the war. Muzorewa and his partners hoped that the Conservative government would recognize the internal regime and lift sanctions. Realizing that recognition could come only at the end of a mediating process in which all parties would take part, the Muzorewa government was prepared to take the risks involved. South Africa, Muzorewa's faithful and indispensable regional patron was similarly motivated. P.W. Botha, the new premier, supported Muzorewa wholeheartedly. However, Zimbabwe/Rhodesia, engulfed in an escalating guerilla war which could attract foreign intervention, was a grossly counter-productive prospect. The end of the war and international recognition without changing the moderate nature of the regime was the prize South Africa was after. South Africa believed that this could be achieved through British mediation. Thus, the impact of the war was conducive to the British diplomatic effort as far as the white regional patron and its domestic clients were concerned.

The war had a different and uneven impact on the nationalist guerillas and their regional patrons. The arguments that the former were well disposed toward British mediation as a result of the casualties they had suffered,[5] or because they realized that the road to victory would not be short enough,[6] are unconvincing. The nationalist guerilla movements, and ZANU in particular, had not been deterred by high casualty figures even when prospects were bleak. In 1979, the number of casualties was still very high, but the horizon was much brighter. The guerillas were certainly not exhausted. ZANU perceived a protracted guerilla war as the best means to achieve genuine decolonization. Nkomo, who had built a formidable conventional army, viewed the war path also as the best road to Salisbury. Thus, the logic of the war did not dictate a change of course to the guerilla movements; had they had their way, they would not have come to Lancaster House. They would certainly not have put their signature on the outcome of the conference. Paradoxically, the nationalist guerilla movements were induced to come to Lancaster House and to make considerable sacrifices by their successes rather than by their failures. Dialectically their success on the guerilla front was their undoing. The increasing tempo of the guerilla war inside Rhodesia undermined the vital regional base of both ZANU and ZAPU. As the Rhodesian security forces failed to stem the guerilla tide inside the country, they turned to a pre-emptive strategy of hitting the guerillas in their bases in their regional host countries. In 1978, when the pre-emptive strategy proved ineffective, they launched, in addition, a campaign of economic sabotage against Zambia and Mozambique. The Muzorewa government stepped up this economic war during the conference.

Against Zambia, Zimbabwe/Rhodesia unleashed a total economic onslaught. The aim was to cut off landlocked Zambia from all its outlets

256

to the sea, with the exception of the southern route running through Rhodesia. By November this onslaught had almost totally isolated Zambia from the outside world.[7] On November 5 the Zimbabwe/ Rhodesian government suspended the traffic of maize to Zambia through its territory because of the latter's persisting support for ZIPRA guerillas.[8] As a result of the sharp drop in the domestic maize production in the 1978–1979 season, Zambia was crucially dependent on massive supplies of maize from the south to avert famine. It was expected that Zambia would run out of maize by the end of 1979. Since some 40 per cent of the country's population was urban, severe maize shortage could be expected to have serious political repercussions.[9] In Zambia, there was growing unease about the cost of the war. In early October, before the unleashing of the economic offensive, the state-owned television ran a series of discussions on the prospect of a settlement in Rhodesia. Most participants, including a number of MPs, stressed the need for a settlement if the faltering Zambian economy was to be given a chance to recover. One MP even threatened that unless a settlement was reached, the PF could not expect Zambian support.[10] Kaunda himself responded bravely to the mounting economic pressures.[11] Brave public pronouncements notwithstanding, there is little doubt that Kaunda was painfully aware of the urgent need for a settlement. Even in a personalized regime like that of Zambia, there was a limit to the ability of the leader to pursue a policy of an essentially external nature against the balance of domestic opinion. Kaunda undoubtedly remained faithful to the core and essence of liberation. He was not, however, in a mood to give the PF *carte blanche* and incur the devastating cost.

Mozambique, which had suffered in the past from attacks on its economic infrastructure, was not spared either. In fact, an attack on Gaza Province on the eve of the Lancaster House conference signalled the beginning of the new wave of economic onslaught. In this large-scale operation in the Limpopo valley, the "rice basket" of Mozambique, military as well as economic targets were hit.[12] Throughout the conference, the Zimbabwe/Rhodesian forces, assisted by the MNR, attacked economic targets throughout the country.[13] The prospect of an escalating guerilla war in Rhodesia clearly spelled doom for Mozambique's already badly shattered economy. In a letter to Mugabe during the conference, Machel wrote that he expected the Rhodesians to concentrate their attacks on Mozambique, adding that "we will not be in a position to resist." He even predicted the fall of his regime in about July 1980.[14]

Thus, the situation in which the guerillas escalated the war inside

257

Rhodesia without affecting the retaliatory capability of the Rhodesian security forces seriously undermined their regional bases. The Rhodesians, having lost the initiative inside the country, turned Zambia and Mozambique into whipping-boys – with devastating effects. A protracted war which was favoured by ZANU as the surest way to pursue their revolution could not be entertained by the regional patrons. The goals and interests of patrons and clients were indeed very clearly contradictory. The predicament of the two vital regional patrons considerably limited the manoeuvring space of the guerilla movements. They could expect unqualified support only for the very core of the liberation goal. Thus, when negotiating the constitution, excesses like total political power or total socio-economic transformation were out of the question. Having effectively lost the military option, the PF was forced to concede and compromise all the way. Much of the frustration and rage exhibited by PF leaders during the conference stemmed from the tension between their sense of power in the battlefield and their sense of political powerlessness at the conference table.

The stage of evolution of the Rhodesian conflict was beneficial in yet another way. All the major participants in the conference believed that although the conference could not guarantee the achievement of their optimal goals, they had a good chance of outdoing their opponents. In any event, even modest gains derived from the conference far outweighed the cost expected to be incurred by those responsible for its collapse. Muzorewa believed, or hoped, that at best the PF would withdraw from the conference and he would get a "second-class solution" which would grant him recognition and end the sanctions. At worst, he believed that he stood a good chance of winning a free and fair election. Mugabe, with his broad ethnic base and with his guerillas controlling much of the Shona countryside, had good reasons to believe that ZANU could win the independence elections. Nkomo's electoral prospects were not particularly bright because of his narrow ethnic base. He could hope, however, to be part of a winning PF party or to become a marginal, yet essential, figure in a coalition headed by either Mugabe or Muzorewa. The regional patrons broadly shared their client's perception of their political prospects. The South Africans shared with Muzorewa both his preference for a "second-class solution" and his confidence regarding his electoral prospects in the context of a "first-class solution".[15] Machel, who in 1978 had sent teams to ZANLA-controlled areas, was convinced of ZANU's popular support.[16] Kaunda had little hesitation in choosing between his own power base and the electoral prospects of his protégé.

Then there was the changing of the guards in London which brought the Conservatives to power. While it would be wrong to attribute the success of the conference and the peaceful resolution of the Rhodesian conflict solely or predominantly to the diplomatic skills of Mrs Thatcher's government, it is equally wrong to attribute it solely to the favourable circumstances prevailing in southern Africa. Favourable circumstances on their own, especially in the context of such a bitter and complex conflict, are no guarantee of success. Favourable circumstances could be used, or wasted, by the actors participating in the conflict resolution process. The mere change in the identity of one of the two main international actors opened new horizons. A re-elected Labour government could be expected to pursue, with more or less vigour, the Anglo-American plan and to maintain the Anglo-American partnership. These had proved grossly inadequate as a strategic concept and as agents of conflict resolution. A new British government could afford to take a fresh look at the Rhodesian problem and its role therein. Learning from past mistakes of an opposing party is an asset to any new government. While the Conservatives were bound by the bipartisan Rhodesian policy embodied in the six principles, there was scope for conceptual, strategic and tactical variations. The change of government in London also served as an opportunity for the domestic and regional actors to rethink and reshape their goals and strategies. Within the context of a Labour government pursuing the Anglo-American option, the likelihood was that the diplomatic stalemate would have persisted and the armed struggle would have remained the dominant strategic feature.

The emergence of Mrs Thatcher's government was more than an opportunity for a fresh look. A fresh look is no guarantee for success either. A reassessment can result in a worse policy. The Conservative government's vital contribution rested primarily on a proper grasp of the structure and dynamics of the conflict system, on the conception of an appropriate strategy and on an outstanding demonstration of diplomatic skills in bringing about the conference and managing it. The most important result of the Conservatives' reassessment was the abandonment of the Anglo-American linkage. One of the main faults of the Anglo-American approach was that, although they tried to carve a middle ground, they exhibited a definite PF–FLP bias. The bias which stemmed from the basic orientation of the Labour government and the Carter Administration was reinforced by the belief that at the crucial regional level a friendly understanding with the FLP could be effectively complemented with pressures on South Africa. This proved a gross error of judgement because the attempts to put pressure on South

Africa were counter-productive, serving only to strengthen the alliance between Pretoria and Salisbury. From this perspective, a Thatcher–Carter partnership held little promise. The Conservative government was determined to take full responsibility for the decolonization of Rhodesia. Examining the conflict system, the British realized that the weak link in the regional chain, in the second half of 1979, was the FLP rather than South Africa. They understood that to achieve a peaceful settlement, the good will of South Africa must be courted and culti-vated through understanding and positive inducements rather than threats and pressures. The Conservatives were well placed to cultivate South Africa's good will, if only because they were far more acceptable to Pretoria than Labour, or a Labour–Carter combination. A well-disposed South Africa could be expected to lead Muzorewa along the desired path because the latter was in no position to resist his regional benefactor. The nationalist guerillas, because of their perceived military successes and the radicalization in their ranks were expected to be the harder nuts to crack. Britain could hope to influence them only through their regional patrons. The cooperation of the FLP was secured through a combination of understanding and pressure. Understanding was secured in the context of the Commonwealth, of which Tanzania, Zambia and Botswana were members. In this respect, Thatcher transformed the Commonwealth from the most serious constraint on her original Rhodesian policy into a major asset in her pursuit of a peaceful settlement. In Lusaka, in August 1979, a Commonwealth consensus was achieved regarding Britain's role and the broad principles of the prospective settlement. This provided the British government with a useful safety net. Although the Common-wealth acted as a pressure group on behalf of the PF, it also exercised a moderating influence on them. The pressure on the FLP was provided by circumstances, namely the sliding of Zambia and Mozambique towards economic chaos. Although Britain did not produce these pressures, they could certainly rely on them.

The Conservatives' grasp of the requisites of an appropriate conflict resolution strategy was matched by their outstanding performance as conference managers. After receiving the Commonwealth mandate, Thatcher acted with promptness and determination. With the invita-tions to the parties attending the conference, the British issued an 11-point outline of the independence constitution. The outline followed the Westminster model with a titular head of state and an executive prime minister responsible to a Parliament composed of two houses. While providing for reserved white seats, it scrapped the vast veto power the whites had under the internal constitution. While the independence of the judiciary was guaranteed, the large measure of independence of the civil administration and the security forces was eliminated. A declaration of rights was also included.[17]

The negotiating tactic pursued by Carrington during the conference was simple and effective. With regard to the issues on the conference's agenda, he adopted a step-by-step approach: first the constitution, followed by the transition arrangements, and then the cease-fire. The conference unfolded in such a way that the conclusion of each issue provided Carrington with growing leverage and correspondingly reduced the manoeuvring space of the participants and the PF, in particular. Once the constitution embodying the model of the independent state was agreed upon, it was more difficult for the contending parties to oppose the transition arrangements and when this issue was concluded, the finalizing of the cease-fire was more easily secured. This negotiating tactic, in itself, could not bridge the gap between the Muzorewa team and the PF. Had Carrington acted as neutral chairman trying to pull the opposing sides to the middle ground between them, it is doubtful that agreement would have been reached. For Carrington, the middle ground was not simply a half-way house between the conflicting positions. He articulated this element in his approach when relating to the gap on the transition arrangements:

> Because one side has accepted them does not mean that the bargaining should now start once more to shift the balance to a point halfway between the proposals now on the table and the position taken by the Patriotic Front. That would represent a very fundamental miscalculation of these negotiations.[18]

Carrington, himself, produced drafts of proposals for each of the issues which represented the British view of the desirable and practical middle ground. These proposals were designed to enable Britain to execute effectively its decolonizing responsibility. Carrington made only marginal changes to allow the recalcitrants to save face. When his marginal concessions failed to bring about agreement, he presented deadlines, hoping that the balance of pressures would do the trick. Carrington's deadlines were shifting deadlines, designed to produce extra efforts and pressures, rather than rigid ultimatums which could wreck the conference.

The pattern throughout the conference was that Muzorewa's team accepted British proposals without much ado and then the tough bargaining with the PF would begin. Muzorewa's agreement was used by Carrington as a lever in his negotiations with the PF. To make his deadlines credible, he used the threat, stated or implied, of a "second-class solution" with Muzorewa. In fact, the "second-class solution" served Carrington in his dealings with both sides. For Muzorewa, this solution was in fact a first-class one. It made him more amenable even to the less appealing British proposals, hoping that they would be rejected by the PF, thus expediting his favoured solution. The prospect of such a solution also kept the South Africans in a positive frame of mind. Some writers suggest that the British seriously entertained the prospect of a "second-class solution".[19] It seems very doubtful that the Conservative government contemplated such a solution with all the expected adverse consequences which they had rejected in the wake of their assumption of power. To be effective, the threat had to be credible. The fact that it was taken at its face value is a proof of its effectiveness rather than its seriousness.

In his opening address on September 10, Carrington presented the outline of the constitution as the basis for negotiations and argued for the conclusion of the constitutional issue before proceeding further.[20] Responding for the PF, Nkomo stated that the "British proposals were too vague for us to judge whether they are adequate to our comprehensive task." Arguing against the precedence of the constitution, he said that "the critical period leading to independence is as vital as the independence constitution itself."[21] Muzorewa, for his part, stressed that his regime satisfied the six principles and expressed the hope that Carrington would not insist on making changes in the March 1978 constitution.[22] Before the conference could settle down to discuss substance, Carrington had to deal with two PF procedural challenges. Before the opening, the PF tested Carrington by challenging the seating arrangements around the conference table. This merely provided him with an opportunity to demonstrate his no-nonsense approach to the management of the conference.[23] Following the opening session, the PF objected to the conference agenda, proposing their own, which gave precedence to the transition arrangements.[24] On September 12 Carrington, assisted by the FLP, forced a face-saving compromise which preserved the essence of the original British agenda.[25]

Carrington then presented a summary of the British constitutional proposals elaborating on the outline of principles which had been attached to the invitations.[26] On September 14 the PF presented its own constitutional proposals, which bore little resemblance to the British ones. It did not provide for reserved white seats or for special protection for minority rights.[27] Carrington insisted that only the British proposals would serve as a basis for negotiations.[28] At that stage, he began to apply his "Muzorewa first" negotiating tactics, working on an

262

agreement with his team which could serve as a credible "second-best solution" option. He had little problem persuading the African members of the Muzorewa delegation to rid themselves of the informal white domination entrenched in the internal constitution. Smith, however, urged on by British right wingers, refused to part with the whites' veto power. On September 21, after much deliberation, all the Muzorewa delegation including three out of four whites voted for accepting in principle the British draft.[29]

Carrington could now concentrate his efforts on the more arduous task of convincing the PF. The FLP, who had their observers in London, played an important supportive role. With Nyerere having accepted the British draft before it had been tabled,[30] the manoeuvring space of the PF shrank considerably. Indeed, strong pressure from their regional patrons made them accept, on September 24, the reservation of 20 per cent of the lower house seats for whites.[31] It was not easy for the PF to accept provisions they considered "racist". This was a major breakthrough. The PF had crossed an ideological Rubicon. They still had a long list of reservations regarding the entrenchment of white rights and privileges. However, they essentially fought a rearguard battle. They could hardly have expected the FLP to support them in breaking the conference over these essentially marginal issues. Without the backing of their patrons, Mugabe's threat that "we can achieve peace and justice for our people through the barrel of the gun"[32] sounded hollow. Yet, the PF had to be dragged screaming and kicking.

On October 3, 1979 Carrington delivered his first deadline. He wanted a firm yes or no by October 8.[33] The firm yes, delivered by Muzorewa on October 5,[34] put extra pressure on the PF. As the negotiations dragged on, the PF objections focused on the land issue. They strongly objected to the guarantees and compensation for white lands which would considerably restrict the government's ability to redistribute this vital national resource. Probably in response to FLP and Commonwealth advice or pressure, the PF did not give in the October 8 plenary meeting a firm no answer. A flexible no was their response to Carrington's flexible deadlines. They proposed to move on to the next item on the conference's agenda without sorting out the outstanding constitutional issues. In a short plenary session on October 9, Carrington rejected their proposal which ran against the essence of his step-by-step negotiating strategy. Instead, he presented them with another deadline – October 11.[35] On October 11 the PF stuck to their guns. At that stage, Carrington turned to representatives of the FLP and the Commonwealth to assist him in breaking the deadlock. On

263

October 11 and 12, he met with these representatives. British officials said that they would welcome any FLP assistance towards the successful conclusion of the conference.[36] The PF did not neglect the FLP front either. On October 13 the vice-presidents of ZANU and ZAPU flew to southern Africa to explain the PF stand to their regional patrons. Kaunda and Nyerere reportedly informed the British of their broad support for the constitution, but upheld the PF objections on the land issue.[37] The deadlock also prompted South Africa to add its voice and weight to the balance of pressures. They made it known that their army would counter any take over attempt by the PF if the conference collapsed. They informed Carrington of their support for the British proposals, but strongly opposed futher concessions to the PF.[38]

By October 15, when the PF did not come forward, Carrington used, for the first time, his "second-class solution" weapon. He suspended the PF from the negotiations until they accepted the constitutional proposals and stated his intention to proceed with bilateral talks with the Muzorewa delegation. He did this in order to maximize the effect of the threat. Shridath Ramphal, the Commonwealth secretary, who followed the negotiations very closely and was very active in the background, was quick to criticize Carrington for acting against the spirit of the Commonwealth Lusaka accord. He stated that only an all-party settlement was envisaged by the Commonwealth.[39] A meeting between Carrington and Ramphal resulted in both softening their tone and in the latter increasing his efforts to find a common ground.[40] Perhaps as a result of this meeting, the British appeared more accommodating. The British conference spokesman said that the British were ready to meet the PF at any time and that they could rejoin the conference as soon as they accepted the constitution.[41] Pik Botha, sensing a possibility of a "second-class solution" rushed to London to convey his government's views on "the situation in Southern Africa, and, in particular, in Zimbabwe/Rhodesia". He was apparently satisfied with what he had heard from Thatcher and Carrington.[42]

The future of the conference depended, at that stage, on an emergency meeting of the FLP scheduled in Dar es Salaam for October 17. By then, the only outstanding issue was compensation for land. The PF itself had begun to climb down. On October 16 they said that they would rejoin the conference as soon as they had received clarifications on the land issue. On the same day, Nyerere minimized the dimensions of the crisis claiming that the question of compensation was "not a constitutional matter", but rather "a policy matter". He said that both the British and the PF had agreed on the principle of compensation and that the only question was who would pay it.[43] The FLP meeting, in which the vice-presidents of ZANU and ZAPU took part, publicly supported the PF on the compensation issue and rejected any solution without the PF. The FLP congratulated their clients on the constructive spirit they had displayed at the conference. According to Jaster, however, the PF got the following message from the FLP: "Since you have already publicly accepted the really major provisions of the constitution, you cannot threaten to break up the conference over a minor issue like compensation. The Front-Line will not back you."[44] The FLP also stated that they were satisfied that the British government understood the need for clarification on the question of land compensation. Stating that that would be done, the FLP communique actually indicated that a compromise had already been agreed. It was essentially a question of a financial burden the British were not keen to shoulder on their own. By that time, rich Uncle Sam had already come to the rescue, offering to share the cost.[45] From a position of co-drivers, the Americans were relegated to the role of lubricating the negotiating machine. The position taken by the FLP left the PF little choice. They only needed a face-saving rationale. The fig leaf was provided by the U.S. financial commitment, the only recent development that could justify a climb down. They also saved face by loosely linking their acceptance to the outcome of the negotiations on the transition.[46] Face-saving notwithstanding, Carrington had it all his way and the PF accepted without changes the British constitutional proposals.

With the agreement on the constitution, the gap between the parties regarding the essence of the solution was finally bridged. This gave an element of inevitability to the conflict resolution process. On November 13, 1979 Carrington referred to this new perspective: "With an agreement already reached on genuine majority rule and an end to the rebellion against Britain's authority, there can be no turning back."[47] And yet, the negotiations on the transition arrangements were at least as stormy as the ones on the constitution. Mugabe accounted for that on November 10: "We are facing a very critical moment because we have now come to the stage where we are discussing the areas of physical power, the areas which matter to any government if that government is to have sovereignty in terms of physical control of the country."[48] The struggle for power, in this context, should not be simplistically construed as a naked opportunistic struggle for the colonial spoils. Although the constitution sketched the economic, social and political outlines of the independent state, the struggle for the character of Zimbabwe had not yet been settled. It was believed that the rulers of independent Zimbabwe would still be in a position to shape it in their ideological image. As Mugabe said: "It is, therefore,

265

necessary that we ensure that the transition will lead to genuine independence rather than to a neo-colonialist state."[49]

On October 22 Carrington submitted to the conference the British proposals for the transitional period which was to last two months. The country was to be run by a British governor exercising his powers through the incumbent bureaucracy and relying on the existing security forces. He was to supervise the elections which were to be internationally observed.[50] This was the essence of the vague document Carrington presented. The proposals included a very bitter pill for Muzorewa – he had to step down and hand over to the British governor. Carrington, true to his tactical plan, first concentrated his effort in getting Muzorewa to agree. On October 27, 1979 Muzorewa conceded. In his address to the nation on October 30 he explained his decision to his people, trying to save face and to make political profit: "I repeat: Country first and I and my delegation's interests last."[51] The truth is, of course, that he had no option. His white partners who controlled his civil and military instruments of power, and who had already conceded so much in accepting the constitution, were not willing to fight a hopeless war to keep Muzorewa in power for an additional two months. Muzorewa could have also believed or hoped that the PF would reject the proposals and that he would then get the "second-class solution".

From Carrington's point of view, this prospect provided him again with a stick for his tougher negotiations with the PF. The PF had very strong objections to the main elements of the British transition proposals. Firstly, they objected to the role of a British governor claiming that he could not be impartial and demanding instead transitional control structures based on power-sharing. They also rejected the exercise of power through the existing civil administration and security forces. Instead, they proposed the establishment of transitional security forces composed of PF forces and of the Rhodesian army and police which would operate alongside a UN peacekeeping force and a UN police force. They also demanded that the transitional period be extended to six months.[52] These proposals were totally unacceptable to the British. It meant a long transitional period in which they would have authority without control. Britain was prepared to fulfil its decolonizing responsibility, but on condition that this was done effectively and honourably. Britain believed it could be done only by exercising absolute power through the existing power structures. Thus Carrington insisted on the PF accepting his proposals.

On October 26 the PF clashed angrily with Carrington over his "dictatorial attitude". Claiming that Britain, in trying to impose a solution, did not honour the spirit of the Commonwealth mandate, the

PF sought to enlist the Commonwealth support against Carrington. On the night of October 26, Nkomo and Mugabe met Ramphal to discuss their complaint. A PF spokesman said that they expected the Commonwealth leaders to state their views on the matter: "If one member distorts the Lusaka Agreement, the others must speak up."[53] The hopes of the PF of enlisting the Commonwealth against Carrington were dashed on October 30, when the Commonwealth Southern Africa Committee failed to come out openly in favour of the PF demand to involve the UN or to produce any major criticism of the British proposals. Their only unanimous objection related to the brevity of the transitional period.[54] Just the same, the Commonwealth efforts to mediate between Carrington and the PF resulted in some marginal modifications in the British proposals. However, none of the major reservations of the PF had been addressed in the "detailed proposals for implementing the independence constitution" submitted by the British to the conference on November 2, 1979.[55]

The PF were angry and frustrated. Already on November 1, in the face of Carrington's determination, they threatened to pack their bags and go back to war.[56] Later, on November 10, in a message to his people and the ZANLA forces, Mugabe said: "And so we must continue to look, not to Lancaster ... if anything, the struggle must now be intensified."[57] Threats of war, however, could only be effective if supported by the FLP. The FLP support was particularly needed because from November 5, when Muzorewa accepted the detailed transition proposals, the threat of a "second-class solution" was again in the air.[58] Public pronouncements notwithstanding,[59] the FLP support was at best qualified. On November 4 Nyerere indicated that he would not support the PF call for a UN peacekeeping force, saying that Carrington "may be right" in rejecting it. He also said that Britain was probably right in relying on the existing structures during the transition. He thought, however, that the two-month period was too short.[60] The PF had obviously not coordinated its positions and tactics with its patrons. Britain, with its flanks protected, could increase the pressure on the PF. On November 5, the day Muzorewa accepted the detailed transition proposals, it was made known that the British government was preparing enabling legislation for the transition. The bill in question was to cover the powers of the governor, the new constitution and the elections.[61] On November 8 Kaunda flew to London to prevent the collapse of the conference. By then his country's outlet to the Tanzanian coast was severed and he faced a maize blockade by Zimbabwe/Rhodesia. A senior Foreign Office official said that Kaunda knew that peace was his only salvation.[62] On his arrival, he met

Nkomo and Mugabe in his London hotel. Mugabe raised his objection to the Rhodesian bureaucracy and police force running the country during the transition. Kaunda warned that the FLP were tired of the war and could not contemplate its continuation. He said that while this did not mean peace at any price, it meant more concessions.[63] This amounted to a veto on the war option. Kaunda urged the British to extend the transitional period and to use a Commonwealth force to monitor the cease-fire.[64] A Commonwealth monitoring force had been suggested earlier in November by Nyerere.[65] On the length of the transition, a Nigerian minister formally warned Britain that six months was the absolute minimum required for transition and fair elections.[66] The British government agreed to set up a fairly strong Commonwealth Force of military observers equipped with light personal arms.[67] While insisting on a two-month transition, they agreed to add 10–14 days for the cease-fire to consolidate.[68] On November 12 Carrington demanded from the PF that they accept the transition plan "within the next day or two". The PF responded, saying that they did not see it as an ultimatum and that the existing differences should be resolved through further negotiations. The Foreign Office tried to exert pressure on the PF by playing both on the Muzorewa option and on the supposed differences between Mugabe and Nkomo.[69] On November 13 Carrington offered the PF a face-saver in the following insertion: "The forces on both sides would be equally responsible to the governor for the observance of the cease-fire and would come under his authority."[70] This symbolic recognition of their armies and the theoretical equality with the Rhodesian forces facilitated the acceptance of the transition plan by the PF on November 15.[71]

The following morning, Carrington submitted the cease-fire plan, and the Lancaster House conference entered its third and final stage. With the issues concerning the constitution and the transition settled, the negotiations regarding the technicalities of the cease-fire were expected to be short and easy. Presenting the proposals, Carrington said: "I envisage a matter of days."[72] And yet, it took more than a month to clinch a cease-fire agreement which consummated the conference. These negotiations witnessed some of the most bitter encounters between the British and the PF. On December 3 Carrington said: "I do not despair of reaching an agreement, but I am as close to despair as I have been in the whole three months of these negotiations."[73] The British kept on threatening a "second-class solution",[74] while the PF threatened "an all-out war with the British Governor in charge of Rhodesia",[75] before an agreement was reached. Viewed from the perspective of the dynamic of conflict resolution, these were storms in a tea cup. The British had not gone so far to forgo the real prize and face a hostile world with a "second-class solution." From the point of view of their relations with their regional patrons, the PF had no option of wrecking the conference and pursuing the war. The success of the conference at that stage was in fact a foregone conclusion.

How then can we account for the great difficulties encountered on the road to the ultimate success? At the root of it lay the genuine fear of the PF that its forces would be exposed and endangered during the delicate and uncertain phase of implementing the cease-fire and the election campaign. This fear was exacerbated by the fact that despite the symbolic equality, the security forces would have a clear advantage over the guerillas, both in terms of their actual status and their fire power. They feared that in case of a collapse of the transition exercise, its forces would be easy prey to the Rhodesian airforce and superior conventional army. The British suspected that the PF dragged their feet because they needed time to reinforce their guerillas inside the country.[76] There was also a residue of frustration and rage among the PF leaders at the way the conference had progressed. It resulted from the tension stemming from their inability to translate their success in the Rhodesian battlefield to negotiating resources at Lancaster House. This was exacerbated by the way Carrington, representing their obsolete colonial master, had it all his way. Letting off steam provided some emotional compensation. More importantly, it must be understood in terms of the relations between the PF and their regional patrons during the conference. In the case of the cease-fire, in particular, the FLP sympathized with the anxieties of their clients and wanted to support them in their efforts to improve their position. However, since a peaceful settlement was a vital interest for key regional patrons, they could not allow the PF to wreck the conference. As a result of these contradictory interests and inclinations, the FLP played a passive role during this phase of the negotiations. This gave the PF a convenient space to pursue their aggressive negotiating tactics. They were, however, constrained by the strict red lines drawn by their patrons. Finally, a tough performance could be useful as an opening step in the forthcoming election campaign.

The British cease-fire plan, which was submitted on November 16, included the following main points:

(1) The cease-fire would be implemented as quickly as possible and would not be more than seven to ten days.
(2) Movement of all forces would cease and military operations would be limited to self-defence.

(3) Commanders of the forces involved would be responsible to the British governor aided by a military adviser and a team of British liaison officers.
(4) A joint commission would assess and supervise the observance of the cease-fire.
(5) A cease-fire monitoring group would be established under the authority of the governor to observe the cease-fire.[77]

The PF counter-proposals, presented on November 19, differed markedly from the British ones, demanding a substantial Commonwealth peacekeeping force and the disbandment of certain Rhodesian military and paramilitary units.[78] It is doubtful that the PF seriously expected their proposals to serve even as a basis for negotiations. Most of the demands of the PF ran against the core and essence of the British transition plan. As a negotiating tactic, the presentation of extreme counter-proposals had twice proved grossly counter-productive. On November 22 the British presented both sides with an ultimatum to accept or reject their proposals. This precipitated an angry PF response against the high-handed British negotiating style. Mugabe said, rather undiplomatically, that Carrington could "go to hell."[79]

On November 23 Ramphal, through the Southern African Committee, forced on Britain a resolution regarding an independent team of Commonwealth observers.[80] The main arena, however, shifted to Dar es Salaam, where on November 24, Nkomo and Mugabe were to meet the FLP to seek support for their negotiating strategy. On November 23 Mrs Thatcher issued a statement expressing anxiety that the achievements of the conference would be jeopardized by "ill judged actions and decisions". Earlier, she had also sent a personal message to Nyerere.[81] On November 25, after the Dar es Salaam meeting, Mugabe and Nkomo said that they had received full backing for their position.[82] Nyerere himself, accusing Carrington of "playing tricks" to secure power for Muzorewa, gave credence to this assertion.[83] This was, however, only a negotiating posture designed to give the PF some leverage. In the meeting itself the story was different. Nyerere and Machel urged accommodation. According to Smith and Simpson, Machel told them thus: "We hear what you are saying, but we know you will hear us when we say the war must end." In private, Nyerere expressed optimism saying that "they both have too much to lose for the conference to fail."[84] Acting as crisis managers, the FLP defined, clearly and narrowly, the parameters within which the PF could manoeuvre. Mugabe and Nkomo went back to London determined to use this limited space to the best of their ability.

On November 26 the Muzorewa delegation dutifully accepted the cease-fire proposals. The PF was still not forthcoming, ignoring again the ultimatum: "Our document and the British one must be examined in minute detail, however long it takes."[85] This, of course, the British were not prepared to do, insisting on their proposals as the only basis for negotiations. Into these stormy waters jumped Pik Botha, who came to London for the second time since the opening of the conference. Arriving in London on November 28, he urged the British government to bring the conference to a successful conclusion without delay, warning against the danger of a general escalation of violence in southern Africa.[86] In view of PF intransigence, he could have hoped to encourage the British to clinch the "second-class solution". On November 30 Prime Minister P.W. Botha disclosed that South African forces had been operating inside Zimbabwe/Rhodesia "for some time" providing protection for the trade routes leading to South Africa.[87] This added another controversial item to the cease-fire agenda. In the meantime, the PF stuck to its guns. Even a British concession regarding the size of the Commonwealth monitoring force[88] did not produce a breakthrough. Thus, for example, the PF insisted on the need for two months to get the cease-fire instructions to their forces.[89] At the end of November, instead of relating to the British proposals, the PF produced another set of counter-proposals. Carrington, on his part, issued another deadline – December 3, 1979. The PF did not budge. The British were frustrated: "There is deep disappointment in the Foreign Office tonight. We have tried – God knows how we have tried – to meet the concerns of the Patriotic Front. But the Patriotic Front has now come to Lord Carrington with new and quite plainly non-negotiable demands."[90] By the deadline of December 3, when Mugabe failed to provide an answer, Carrington cancelled the plenary session scheduled for that day.[91]

In a cabinet meeting held on that day, Carrington obtained an Order in Council authorizing the prime minister to select a governor for the colony of Southern Rhodesia. He also set in motion a discussion on another Order in Council which would authorize the government to promulgate the new constitution.[92] The "second-class solution" weapon had to be sharpened if it was to serve its purpose. On November 30 Ramphal launched a new Commonwealth mediating effort. At that stage, Mugabe seems to have been the main stumbling block. A ZAPU spokesman said: "A settlement is in sight and only a stupid person would jeopardize it."[93] Mugabe's intransigence focused on the South African military presence in Rhodesia. Ramphal offered the following declaration to be included in the cease-fire plan: "There will be no external involvement in Rhodesia under the British governor. The position has been made clear to all Governments concerned." Mugabe demanded that South Africa be specifically mentioned. Carrington refused, fearing the reaction of General Walls and the South Africans. After the December 3 cabinet meeting, Ramphal appealed to Carrington to reconsider his objection. After discussing it with Walls and the South Africans, he conceded.[94] The British cease-fire plan was agreed on by the PF in a plenary session held on December 5. An agreement on the implementation of the plan was still to be reached.[95] As a perceptive African diplomat observed "Mugabe won that argument, but lost the war."[96] Indeed, Mugabe had little to show for his zeal and determination. As in the case of the constitution and the transition, the British had it virtually all their own way.

Eager to force the pace of the conference and to signal that the process had reached a point of no return, the British began to implement the transition plan. On December 7 Lord Soames was formally appointed as governor and the Zimbabwe bill, which was to grant the country independence status as a republic, was published. On December 11 the Zimbabwe/Rhodesia Parliament resolved un-animously to dissolve itself and to revert to colonial rule. The following day, Lord Soames arrived in Salisbury and assumed the supreme authority on behalf of the British Crown. On that day, the sanctions were removed.[97] PF rage resulting from these acts was exacerbated by the final plan for the cease-fire which they viewed as discriminatory against them. They were further infuriated by Carrington's final ultimatum issued on December 14, demanding a firm reply by the next day. In response, Zvobgo threatened war against the British governor. The PF was particularly critical of the distribution of assembly points which, they thought, greatly favoured the security forces. Zvobgo's reply on behalf of the PF was: "The answer, Lord Carrington, is No ... No ... No ..."[98] This, however, reflected frustration rather than determination. In fact, at that time, the PF was in no position to say no. At that critical juncture, Machel stepped in. He sent an urgent message to Mugabe with Fernando Howana, one of his closest advisers, and his representative at Lancaster House. He told Mugabe unequivocally that the war was over and that he had to take the risks and fight the elections. He also told him that should the conference fail, he would be granted asylum, but no bases to pursue the war. This was the ultimate FLP dictate which could not be ignored. On December 16 Mugabe explained to his central committee that they had no option but to accept the British proposals.[99] On December 17, 1979 the PF leaders initialled

272

the cease-fire agreement.[100] The agreement was formally and ceremonially signed by all the parties on December 21.[101] This signalled the successful conclusion of a conference which had witnessed an exceptional performance in conflict and conference management. It was a triumph for diplomatic skill, wisdom and common sense.

NOTES

CHAPTER ONE

1. *Rhodesian Herald (RH)*, 27–4–1974.
2. *Rhodesian Financial Gazette (RFG)*, 24–5–1974.
3. *RH*, 27–4–1974.
4. *RH*, 31–5–1974.
5. *RH*, 27–4–1974.
6. *RH*, 26–4–1974; *RFG*, 24–5–1974.
7. Middlemas, *Cabora Bassa: Engineering and Politics in Southern Africa*, London 1975, pp.322–323.
8. *African Contemporary Record (ACR)*, 1974–1975, p.B387.
9. *Sunday Times (ST)* (Jhb), 28–4–1974.
10. *ACR*, 1974–1975, p.B387.
11. *ACR*, 1974–1975, pp.B387, 390.
12. Middlemas, *Cabora Bassa*, p.327.
13. *ACR*, 1974–1975, p.B392.
14. *ACR*, 1974–1975, p.B393; Middlemas, *Cabora Bassa*, p.332.
15. *The Star (St.)*, Johannesburg, 15–6–1974.
16. *Survey of World Broadcast (SWB)*, 12–6–1974, Radio Salisbury (R. Sby), 11–6–1974.
17. *Rand Daily Mail (RDM)*, 3–8–1974.
18. Guy Arnold, "Rhodesia Under Pressure", *Africa Report*, July–August 1974, p.20.
19. *RH*, 29–5–1974.
20. *St.*, 23–7–1974.
21. *ACR*, 1974–1975, p.B520.
22. *ACR*, 1974–1975, pp.B512–514.
23. *Rhodesia: Mid-1974*, South African Institute for International Affairs (SAIIA), "Statement by the Rhodesian Prime Minister on June 19, 1974".
24. *SWB*, 12–6–1974, R. Sby, 11–6–1974.
25. *RH*, 20–6–1974; A. Chambati, "The African National Council and the Rhodesian Solution", p.12.
26. *RH*, 16–5–1974; 23–5–1974; 1–6–1974; *RDM*, 27–5–1974.
27. A. Chambati, "The African National Council and the Rhodesian Solution", p.13.
28. *Rhodesia: Mid-1974*, SAIIA, "A Statement by the Rhodesian Prime Minister, June 19, 1974", p.22.
29. A. Muzorewa, *Rise Up and Walk*, London, 1979, p.133.
30. T. Kirk and C. Sherwell, "The Rhodesian General Election of 1974", *Journal of Commonwealth and Comparative Studies*, 13, 1 March 1975.
31. *Rhodesia: Mid-1974*, SAIIA, "A Statement by the Rhodesian Prime Minister, June 19, 1974", pp.23–24.
32. *Rhodesia: Mid-1974*, SAIIA, "A Statement by the Rhodesian Prime Minister, June 19, 1974", p.25.
33. *Rhodesia: Mid-1974*, SAIIA, "A Statement by the Rhodesian Prime Minister, June 19, 1974", p.25.
34. Kirk and Sherwell, "The Rhodesian General Election of 1974", p.18.
35. *Rhodesia: Mid-1974*, SAIIA, "A Statement by the Rhodesian Prime Minister, June 19, 1974", pp.21, 25, 26.
36. *St.*, 22–6–1974, 11–7–1974; *SWB*, 18–7–1974, R. Sby, 16–7–1974; 25–7–1974, R. Sby, 23–7–1974.

NOTES

37. *RH*, 11–7–1974.
38. *RH*, 21–9–1974.
39. *RH*, 11–10–1974.
40. *SWB*, 23–9–1974, R. Sby, 20–9–1974.
41. *RDM*, 3–8–1974; *St.*, 21–9–1974, 7–10–1974.
42. *RFG*, 9–8–1974; *ACR*, 1974–1975, p.B508.
43. *RH*, 4–5–1974.
44. *Times of Zambia (TOZ)*, 30–4–1974.
45. *RH*, 4–5–1974.
46. *RDM*, 17–5–1974.
47. A. Chambati, "The African National Council and the Rhodesian Solution", p.13.
48. *RH*, 26–6–1974.
49. *RH*, 11–6–1974.
50. *RDM*, 26–6–1974.
51. *RH*, 21–6–1974.
52. *RH*, 25–6–1974, 26–6–1974.
53. *RDM*, 30–7–1974.
54. *RDM*, 1–8–1974.
55. *RDM*, 5–8–1974.
56. *ACR*, 1974–1975, pp.B393–394.
57. *St.*, 26–9–1974.
58. *ACR*, 1974–1975, p.B514; *TT*, 17–10–1974; *RDM*, 27–9–1974; *RH*, 27–9–1974, 28–9–1974.
59. *TOZ*, 18–9–1974.
60. *RFG*, 4–10–1974.
61. *RDM*, 17–10–1974.
62. *SWB*, 7–6–1974, R. Lusaka (R. Lus), 4–6–1974; 20–6–1974, R. Lus, 17–6–1974; *St.*, 1–7–1974.
63. *RH*, 20–6–1974.
64. *RH*, 2–7–1974.
65. *RDM*, 30–8–1974, 27–9–1974, 9–10–1974; *RH*, 25–9–1974, 8–10–1974, 9–10–1974.
66. *RH*, 23–10–1974.
67. *ST* (Jhb), 9–6–1974.
68. *St.*, 16–10–1974.
69. *ARB*, September 1974, p.3377.
70. *RH*, 11–6–1974.
71. *St.*, 24–8–1974.
72. *St.*, 24–8–1974.
73. *Guardian (Gdn)*, 7–6–74; *St.*, 8–6–1974; *ST*, (Jhb) 9–6–1974.
74. *RH*, 31–8–1974.
75. Middlemas, *Cabora Bassa*, p.331.
76. *ARB*, August 1974, p.3347.
77. *ACR*, 1974–1975, p.A4.
78. *St.*, 4–9–1974.
79. *RH*, 30–10–1974.
80. *RH*, 8–10–1974.

CHAPTER TWO

1. C. Legum, *Southern Africa, The Secret Diplomacy of Detente*, London, 1975, p.4.
2. *RH*, 30–5–1974.
3. "Vorster Speech in Parliament, 30–8–1974", *Southern Africa Record (SAR)*, SAIIA, Johannesburg, 2, June 1975, p.11.
4. Legum, *Southern Africa, The Secret Diplomacy of Detente*, p.6.

275

5. *SAR*, 2, June 1975, pp.11–12.
6. M.M. Burdette "The Mines, Class Power, and Foreign Policy in Zambia", *Journal of Southern African Studies*, (10, 2, April 1980), pp.207–08; *ACR*, 1974–1975, p.B336.
7. *ACR*, 1974–1975, pp.B336–337.
8. "Lusaka Manifesto, 1969", *SAR*, 2, June 1975, p.3.
9. "Lusaka Manifesto, 1969", *SAR*, 2, June 1975, pp.6–7.
10. D.G. Anglin, "Zambia and the Southern African Detente", *International Journal* (XXX,3/Summer 1975) p.493.
11. Martin and Johnson, *The Struggle For Zimbabwe*, pp.138–42.
12. Martin and Johnson, *The Struggle For Zimbabwe*, p.144.
13. D.G. Anglin and T.M. Shaw, *Zambia's Foreign Policy: Studies in Diplomacy and Dependence*, Boulder, 1979, pp.279–284, 288–289.
14. *Africa* (London), May 1974, p.12.
15. *Africa* (London), May 1974, p.9.
16. *Africa* (London), May 1974, p.13.
17. *TOZ*, 12–11–1974.
18. Martin and Johnson, *The Struggle For Zimbabwe*, p.134.
19. Martin and Johnson, *The Struggle For Zimbabwe*, p.145.
20. Martin and Johnson, *The Struggle For Zimbabwe*, pp.134–135.
21. Legum, *Southern Africa, The Secret Diplomacy of Detente*, p.6; Martin and Johnson, *The Struggle For Zimbabwe*, p.136; "Hilgard Muller Speech 11–9–1974", in F.R. Metrowich, *Towards Dialogue and Detente*, Sandton 1975, p.49.
22. Martin and Johnson, *The Struggle For Zimbabwe*, p.138.
23. Martin and Johnson, *The Struggle For Zimbabwe*, pp.138–143.
24. *SAR*, 1, March 1975, pp.4–5.
25. *SAR*, 2, June 1975, p.17.
26. *RH*, 29–10–1974.
27. Metrowich, *Towards Dialogue and Detente*, p.31.
28. *ARB*, October 1974, pp.3421–3422.
29. *Comment and Opinion (C&O): A Weekly Survey of the South African Press and Radio*, Pretoria, Department of Information, 15–11–1974, p.6.
30. *C&O*, 15–11–1974, p.8.
31. *SWB*, 18–12–1974, R. Jhb 16–12–1974.
32. *SAR*, 1, March 1975, pp.1–4.
33. *SAR*, 1, March 1975, p.6.
34. *SAR*, 1, March 1975, p.8.
35. *SAR*, 1, March 1975, p.8.
36. *SAR*, 2, June 1975, pp.17–19.
37. *SAR*, 2, June 1975, p.20.
38. *SAR*, 2, June 1975, p.19.
39. *SAR*, 2, June 1975, p.20.
40. *RH*, 25–3–1975.
41. Interview: E. Sutton-Pryce, August 1983.
42. *RH*, 2–11–1974.
43. Martin and Johnson, *The Struggle For Zimbabwe*, p.151.
44. Martin and Johnson, *The Struggle For Zimbabwe*, p.144.
45. Martin and Johnson, *The Struggle For Zimbabwe*, pp.70–71.
46. Meredith, *The Past Is Another Country*, pp.72–73.
47. This account is based on Martin and Johnson, *The Struggle For Zimbabwe*, pp.147–151; M. Nyagumbo, *With the People*, London 1980 pp.216–221; Muzorewa, *Rise Up and Walk*, pp.139–141.
48. *RH*, 25–2–1975, Interview of Mugabe with the Executive of the Catholic Commission.
49. *Gdn*, 5–12–1974.

NOTES

50. Martin and Johnson, *The Struggle For Zimbabwe*, p.154; *RDM*, 27–3–1975, a report about a ZANU memorandum.
51. Nyagumbo, *With the People*, pp.217–218.
52. *RH*, 25–2–1975.
53. Meredith, *The Past Is Another Country*, pp.162–163.
54. Martin and Johnson, *The Struggle For Zimbabwe*, p.155.
55. *RH*, 25–2–1975.
56. Edison Zvobgo, "Report of a Special Trip to Zambia During the Period 3, August to 19, August 1975", Confidential: Restricted Circulation; Appendix III, p.4.
57. Muzorewa, *Rise Up and Walk*, Appendix C, pp.275–276.
58. Zvobgo, "Report of a Special Trip to Zambia", Appendix III, p.4.
59. Muzorewa, *Rise Up and Walk*, Appendix III, p.275.
60. "No lowering of standards" was a Rhodesian government euphemism for maintaining the government in white hands.
61. Martin and Johnson, *The Struggle For Zimbabwe*, pp.152–153.
62. *SAR*, 4, February 1976, p.1; "Statement by Ian Smith 7–12–1974".
63. Muzorewa, *Rise Up and Walk*, p.144.
64. *RH*, 10–12–1974.
65. *SAR*, 4, February 1976, p.1, "Ian Smith – Statement 7–12–1974"; Meredith, *The Past Is Another Country*, p.163.
66. The discussions between the Rhodesian officials and the FLP on December 6.
67. *ARB*, December 1974, p.3467.
68. Martin and Johnson, *The Struggle For Zimbabwe*, p.153.
69. *RH*, 12–12–1974.
70. Muzorewa, *Rise Up and Walk*, pp.277–278.

CHAPTER THREE

1. *Daily News (DN)*, Dar es Salaam, 20–12–1974.
2. *St.*, 17–12–1974; *RDM*, 18–12–1974; *RH*, 25–2–1975.
3. *RH*, 16–1–1975.
4. *For the Record*, "Prime Minister's Interview with Richard Kershaw, BBC 'Panorama' ", Salisbury 8–5–1975.
5. *RH*, 16–1–1975.
6. *SWB*, 28–5–1975, R. Sby, 26–5–1975.
7. *Financial Mail (FM)* (Jhb), 13–6–1975.
8. *RH*, 31–7–1975.
9. *RH*, 15–1–1975, 31–7–1975; *ST* (Jhb), 27–7–1975; *SWB*, 31–5–1875, R. Sby, 29–5–1975; 27–8–1975, R. Sby 22–8–1975.
10. *RH*, 17–5–1975.
11. *RH*, 5–4–1975.
12. *Gdn.* 14–5–1975.
13. *RH*, 13–5–1975.
14. *RH*, 17–5–1975; Interview: Wickus de Kock, Karino, South Africa, August 1983.
15. *ACR*, 1972–1973, p.B447.
16. Interview: Wickus de Kock.
17. *SWB*, 1–7–1975, R. Sby, 27–6–1975.
18. *RH*, 16–1–1975.
19. *St.*, 23–8–1975.
20. *RH*, 9–5–1975, 17–5–1975; *Gdn*, 14–5–1975.
21. Andre Holland, MP, *RH*, 9–5–1975.
22. Muzorewa, *Rise Up and Walk*, p.276.
23. *RH*, 25–2–1975.
24. *RDM*, 20–3–1975.

25. *St.*, 24–3–1975.
26. *RH*, 7–1–1975.
27. *The Times (TT)*, 22–1–1975.
28. *Southern Africa (Sn.A)* (New York, Southern African Committee), April 1975, p.12.
29. *RH*, 3–5–1975.
30. *RDM*, 16–5–1975.
31. *SWB*, 18–1–1975, R. Sby, 17–1–1975.
32. *St.*, 23–8–1975.
33. *SWB*, 8–1–1975, Radio Johannesburg (R. Jhb), 6–1–1973.
34. *RH*, 2–5–1975.
35. *St.*, 17–2–1975.
36. *Sn.A*, April 1975, p.17.
37. Zvobgo, "Report of a Special Trip to Zambia" p.23.
38. *RH*, 23–12–1974.
39. *ACR*, 1974–1975, p.B701.
40. *C&O*, 28–2–1975.
41. *C&O*, 16–5–1975, p.1.
42. *C&O*, 10–1–1975, p.4.
43. *C&O*, 28–2–1975, p.6.
44. *C&O*, 21–2–1975, p.5.
45. *C&O*, 28–2–1975.
46. *C&O*, 22–2–1975, p.4.
47. *C&O*, 25–4–1975, p.6.
48. *C&O*, 23–5–1975, p.6.
49. *C&O*, 29–8–1975, p.2.
50. *C&O*, 29–8–1975, p.3.
51. *Observer (Obs)*, London, 19–1–1975; *ST* (Jhb), 19–1–1975.
52. *C&O*, 17–1–1975, p.3.
53. *C&O*, 17–1–1975, p.6.
54. *C&O*, 24–1–1975, p.6.
55. *RH*, 18–12–1975.
56. *SWB*, 3–1–1975, R. Jhb, 31–12–1974.
57. *RH*, 21–1–1975.
58. *RH*, 12–2–1975.
59. *ST* (Jhb), 19–1–1975.
60. *C&O*, 31–1–1975, pp.8–9.
61. *C&O*, 31–1–1975, p.9.
62. Interview: Wickus de Kock.
63. Interview: Wickus de Kock.
64. *RH*, 19–3–1975.
65. Interview: Wickus de Kock.
66. *C&O*, 4–4–1975, p.1.
67. *RH*, 2–7–1975.
68. *RH*, 13–1–1975.
69. *RH*, 18–1–1975.
70. *RH*, 24–4–1975. The confidential report which was reported to have been written by the farmer was publicized by Dr Edson Sithole. Kaunda claimed that the report was forged. In my view, there is more than a grain of truth in it.
71. *RH*, 25–6–1975.
72. Interview: Wickus de Kock.
73. *RH*, 24–4–1975.
74. Martin and Johnson, *The Struggle For Zimbabwe*, p.153.
75. *ARB*, January 1975, p.3483.
76. *RDM*, 10–2–1975.

77. *DN*, 2–5–1975.
78. *SAR*, 2, June 1975, p.27.
79. *ARB*, January 1975, p.3483.
80. *ARB*, February 1975, pp.3519–3520; Anglin, "Zambia and South African Detente", pp.496–497.
81. Nyangoni and Nyandoro, *Selected Documents*, p.297.
82. *ARB*, April 1975, p.3583.
83. *SAR*, 2, June 1975, pp.31–34.
84. *ARB*, April 1975, p.3583.
85. "Dar es Salaam Declaration on Southern Africa", Adopted by the OAU Council of Ministers on April 10, 1975, *SAR*, 2, June 1976, p.40.
86. *SAR*, 2, June 1976, pp.41–43.
87. Martin and Johnson, *The Struggle For Zimbabwe*, p.137.
88. *RH*, 13–12–1974.
89. *RH*, 4–12–1974.
90. *RH*, 4–12–1974, 5–12–1974.
91. *RH*, 4–1–1975.
92. *ARB*, January 1975, p.3505.
93. *SWB*, 15–1–1975, R. Sby, 13–1–1975.
94. *ARB*, January 1975, p.3505.
95. *RH*, 15–1–1975.
96. *RH*, 17–1–1975; *SWB*, 18–1–1975; R. Sby, 16–1–1975.
97. *RH*, 29–1–1975.
98. *ARB*, February 1975, p.3539.
99. See beginning of this chapter.
100. *RH*, 13–1–1975; *ARB*, January 1975, p.3507.
101. *TT*, 18–1–1975.
102. See above pp.34–34.
103. *DN*, 18–12–1974.
104. *RH*, 12–12–1974, 31–12–1974.
105. *RH*, 13–12–1974.
106. *RH*, 13–1–1975.
107. *Africa*, 42, February 1975, p.13.
108. *RH*, 7–1–1975.
109. Martin and Johnson, *The Struggle For Zimbabwe*, p.171.
110. Meredith, *The Past Is Another Country*, p.169.
111. Meredith, *The Past Is Another Country*, p.171; *RH*, 31–12–1974, 23–1–1975; *ARB*, January 1975, p.3507.
112. *SWB*, 19–12–1974 R. Sby, 18–12–1974.
113. *SWB*, 13–1–1975, R. Jhb, 10–1–1975.
114. *RH*, 14–1–1975.
115. *SWB*, 15–1–1975, R. Sby, 13–1–1975; 7–2–1975, R. Sby, 5–2–1975; *RH*, 31–1–1975.
116. *RH*, 17–1–1975; *SWB*, 7–2–1975, R. Sby 5–6–1975.
117. *Africa*, 42, February 1975, p.15.
118. *RH*, 3–1–1975, 4–1–1975; *St.*, 4–1–1975.
119. *SWB*, 18–1–1975, R. Sby 15–1–1975.
120. *RH*, 3–1–1975.
121. Muzorewa, *Rise Up and Walk*, p.146; *Africa*, 42, February 1975, p.15.
122. *Sn.A*, 8, 4, April 1975, p.17.
123. *DN*, 8–1–1975, 11–1–1975; Martin and Johnson, *The Struggle For Zimbabwe*, p.172.
124. *St.*, 13–1–1975.
125. Meredith, *The Past Is Another Country*, p.173.
126. *St.*, 17–2–1975.

127. Martin and Johnson, *The Struggle For Zimbabwe*, p.172.
128. *ARB*, January 1975, p.3505.
129. *DT*, 22–1–1975.
130. *SWB*, 23–1–1975, R. Lus, 21–1–1975.
131. *RH*, 21–1–1975.
132. *RH*, 21–1–1975.
133. *TT*, 22–1–1975.
134. *RH*, 6–2–1975; *SWB*, 7–2–1975, R. Sby, 5–2–1975.
135. *SWB*, 14–2–1975, R. Sby, 12–2–1975.
136. *RH*, 25–2–1975, 26–2–1975; *St.*, 14–2–1975 Meredith, *The Past Is Another Country*, p.174.
137. Meredith, *The Past Is Another Country*, p.172.
138. *TT*, 11–2–1975.
139. *RH*, 12–2–1975.
140. *RH*, 4–3–1975.
141. Muzorewa, *Rise Up and Walk*, p.148; *RH*, 5–3–1975; Interview: Wickus de Kock.
142. *DT*, 27–3–1975.
143. *RH*, 5–3–1975.
144. *ARB*, March 1975, p.3569.
145. *RH*, 18–3–1975.
146. *SWB*, 19–3–1975, R. Lus, 17–3–1975.
147. *C&O*, 14–3–1975, pp.2,4; 21–3–1975, pp.2–3; *RH*, 15–3–1975.
148. *RH*, 8–3–1975.
149. *ARB*, March 1975, p.3569.
150. *RH*, 19–3–1975; Interview: Wickus de Kock.
151. *RH*, 3–4–1975.
152. Meredith, *The Past Is Another Country*, p.181.
153. *RH*, 5–4–1975.
154. *For The Record*, 'Prime Minister's Interview in Panorama, BBC 8–5–1975'.
155. P. Stiff, *See You in November*, Alberton, 1985, pp.124–143.
156. Martin and Johnson, *The Struggle For Zimbabwe*, p.174.
157. Meredith, *The Past Is Another Country*, pp.176–178.
158. See a reply of ZANU detainees in Zambian prisons to the report of the Chitepo Commission, 10–4–1976 in *The Price of Detente* printed for ZANU by Workers Publishing House, London, undated.
159. Martin and Johnson, *The Struggle For Zimbabwe*, pp.185–186.
160. Martin and Johnson, *The Struggle For Zimbabwe*, pp.183–184.
161. Nyangoni and Nyandoro, *Selected Documents*, pp.308–314.
162. *The Price of Detente* printed for ZANU by Workers Publishing House, London, undated, p.2.
163. Zvobgo, "Report of a Special Trip to Zambia", pp.3, 26.
164. Martin and Johnson, *The Struggle For Zimbabwe*, pp.177–180.
165. *ARB*, March 1975, p.3572.
166. Martin and Johnson, *The Struggle For Zimbabwe*, p.179.
167. *ARB*, April 1975, p.3604.
168. Zvobgo, "Report of a Special Trip to Zambia", p.18.
169. *DN*, 21–5–1975.
170. Zvobgo, "Report of a Special Trip to Zambia", p.11.
171. Martin and Johnson, *The Struggle For Zimbabwe*, p.196.
172. *RH*, 17–4–1975.
173. *For The Record*, "Prime Minister's Speech at the Opening of Trade Fair Rhodesia 1975, 28–4–1975", p.8.
174. *RH*, 17–4–1975, 19–4–1975.
175. *RH*, 28–4–1975.
176. *RH*, 28–4–1975.

NOTES

177. *For The Record*, "Prime Minister's Speech at the Opening of Trade Fair Rhodesia, 28–4–1975", pp.7,11.
178. *For The Record*, "Interview with Richard Kershaw, BBC, Panorama", 8–5–1975.
179. *DN*, 16–5–1975.
180. *RH*, 23–5–1975; Meredith, *The Past Is Another Country*, p.186.
181. *ARB*, May 1975, p.3635.
182. *ARB*, May 1975, p.3636.
183. *RH*, 27–5–1975.
184. *RH*, 2–6–1975.
185. *RH*, 4–6–1975; *Gdn*, 5–6–1975.
186. *Gdn*, 9–6–1975.
187. *TT*, 13–6–1975.
188. *RH*, 9–7–1975.
189. Muzorewa, *Rise Up and Walk*, p.158; Martin and Johnson, *The Struggle For Zimbabwe*, p.216.
190. *St.*, 15–7–1975.
191. *ARB*, July 1975, p.3710.
192. Meredith, *The Past Is Another Country*, p.187; *ARB*, July 1975, p.3710, August 1975, p.3738.
193. *ARB*, July 1975, pp.3709–3710.
194. *RDM*, 8–8–1975.
195. *ARB*, August 1975, p.3738.
196. Interview: Wickus de Kock.
197. *ARB*, August 1975, p.3738.
198. Interview: Wickus de Kock; *ST* (Jhb), 17–8–1975.
199. Muzorewa, *Rise Up and Walk*, pp.160,162.
200. Interview: Wickus de Kock, based on minutes taken at the Pretoria meeting.
201. *ARB*, August 1975, pp.3738–3739.
202. *ST* (Jhb), 17–8–1975.
203. Interview: Wickus de Kock.
204. Muzorewa, *Rise Up and Walk*, p.165.
205. Text of declaration, *RDM*, 27–8–1975; Meredith, *The Past Is Another Country*, p.193.
206. *SWB*, 26–8–1975, R. Sby, 25–8–1975.
207. *RDM*, 27–8–1975.
208. *RH*, 27–8–1975.
209. *RDM*, 27–8–1975.
210. *St.*, 2–9–1975.
211. *ARB*, August 1975, p.3740.
212. *ARB*, August 1975, pp.3740–3741; *TT*, 27–8–1975.
213. *SWB*, 18–8–1975, R. Jhb, 15–8–1975.
214. *SWB*, 28–8–1975, R. Lus, 27–8–1975.
215. *SWB*, 28–8–1975, R. Sby, 26–8–1975.
216. *C&O*, 11–8–1975.
217. Interview: Wickus de Kock.
218. *ST* (Jhb), 9–2–1975, 13–4–1975, 13–4–1975; *Property and Finance* – (Sby) June 1975, July 1975.
219. *ST* (Jhb), 9–3–1975.
220. *St.*, 9–3–1975.
221. *For The Record*, "Prime Minister's Speech at the Opening of Trade Fair Rhodesia, 1975, 28–4–1975".
222. *St.*, 11–6–1975.
223. J. D'Oliveira, *Vorster – The Man*, Johannesburg 1977, pp.57, 64, 109–112.
224. D'Oliveira, *Vorster*, p.244.
225. Interview: Harold Pakendorf (editor, *Die Vaderland*), August 1983.

226. *RH*, 21–2–1975, 9–4–1975; *SWB*, 23–4–1975, R. Jhb, 21–4–1975; *C&O*, 20–6–1975, p.8.
227. Martin and Johnson, *The Struggle For Zimbabwe*, p.157.
228. *For The Record*, "P.M. Interview with Richard Kershaw, BBC Panorama, 8–5–1975".
229. *TT*, 10–4–1975.

CHAPTER FOUR

1. *ACR*, 1975–1976, pp.B421–432.
2. *C&O*, 19–9–1975.
3. *ACR*, 1975–1976, p.B610.
4. *St.*, 4–9–1975.
5. *St.*, 21–10–1975; *ST* (Jhb), 26–10–1975.
6. *RFG*, 21–11–1975.
7. *ACR*, 1975–1976, pp.B391–392.
8. *ARB*, Economic, Financial and Technological Series (ec.) September 15 – October 14, 1975, p.3652, October 15 – November 14, 1975, p.3685.
9. *ARB* (ec.), July 15 – August 14, 1975, pp.3584–85.
10. *ARB* (ec.), 1975–1976, pp.B392–395; *ARB* (ec.), August 15 – September 14, 1975, pp.3611–3612.
11. Anglin and Shaw, *Zambia's Foreign Policy*, pp.300, 337.
12. Anglin and Shaw, *Zambia's Foreign Policy*, p.334.
13. W. Tordoff, "Zambia: The Politics of Disengagement" *African Affairs*, 76,30, January 1977, p.66.
14. *ARB* (ec.), August 15 – September 14, 1975, p.3611.
15. *ARB* (ec.), November 15 – December 14, 1975, p.3711.
16. *ACR*, 1975–1976, p.B394.
17. *RH*, 13–11–1975; *St.*, 13–11–1975.
18. *Obs.* 23–11–1975.
19. *RH*, 3–12–1975.
20. Martin and Johnson, *The Struggle For Zimbabwe*, p.216.
21. *African Recorder*, July 30 – August 12, 1975, p.4033.
22. *St.*, 22–11–1975.
23. *DN*, 20–11–1975.
24. T. Hodges, "Mozambique: The Politics of Liberation" in G.M. Carter and P. O'Mera, *Southern Africa: The Continuing Crisis*, Bloomington 1979, pp.79–83; *ACR*, 1975–1976, pp.B282–284.
25. T. Hodges, "Mozambique: The Politics of Liberation" p.86.
26. *ACR*, 1975–1976, pp.B284–286.
27. *ACR*, 1975–1976, p.B283.
28. *ACR*, 1975–1976, p.B283.
29. *SWB*, 27–9–1975, R. Lourenço Marques (LM) 25–9–1975.
30. Martin and Johnson, *The Struggle For Zimbabwe*, p.216; Muzorewa, *Rise Up and Walk*, p.172; *Obs.* 23–11–1975, 7–12–1975.
31. *St.*, 1–10–1975; *RH*, 6–9–1975, 26–11–1975.
32. T. Ranger, "The Changing of the Old Guard: Robert Mugabe and the Revival of ZANU", *Journal of Southern African Studies*, 7, 1, October 1980, p.80.
33. The only active operational zone in the north-east.
34. Meredith, *The Past Is Another Country*, p.204.
35. Martin and Johnson, *The Struggle For Zimbabwe*, p.216.
36. Muzorewa, *Rise Up and Walk*, p.172.
37. *Obs*, 23–11–1975.
38. *For The Record*, "Prime Minister's Statement to Parliament on 26–8–1975".

39. *ACR*, 1975–1976, pp.659–661; *ST* (Jhb), 9–11–1975.
40. *ARB*, September 1975, p.3767.
41. *RDM*, 27–9–1975.
42. *RDM*, 9–9–1975; see also *St.*, 18–9–1975.
43. *RDM*, 9–9–1975.
44. *RH*, 20–9–1975; *RDM*, 20–9–1975.
45. *RDM*, 26–9–1975.
46. *RH*, 25–9–1975; *RDM*, 19–9–1975, 26–9–1975; *ST* (Jhb), 28–9–1975.
47. *St.*, 26–9–1975; *ST* (Jhb), 28–9–1975.
48. Interview: E. Sutton-Pryce, August 1983.
49. *RH*, 6–9–1975.
50. *RH*, 13–10–1975.
51. *St.*, 2–9–1975.
52. Muzorewa, *Rise Up and Walk*, pp.166–167.
53. *RH*, 29–9–1975.
54. J. Nkomo, *The Story of My Life* (London, 1984), p.156.
55. *St.*, 2–9–1975.
56. *Revolution* (Official organ of the ANC), October 1975, p.4.
57. This was so according to Enos Nkala of ZANU, *SWB*, 5–6–1975, R. Sby, 2–6–1975.
58. Muzorewa, *Rise Up and Walk*, p.153; RH, 2–6–1975, 3–6–1975, 4–6–1975.
59. *SWB*, 18–6–1975, R. Sby, 16–6–1975.
60. *RH*, 7–7–1975.
61. Muzorewa, *Rise Up and Walk*, pp.166–167.
62. *The Zimbabwe Review* (ZR) 5, 1/1976, pp.6–7.
63. *RH*, 3–9–1975.
64. *RH*, 8–9–1975.
65. *RH*, 29–9–1975.
66. Nkomo, *The Story of My Life*, p.156.
67. *RH*, 13–9–1975.
68. *RH*, 29–9–1975.
69. *RH*, 27–10–1975.
70. *SWB*, 21–6–1975, R Sby 18 6 1975.
71. *RDM*, 1–7–1975.
72. *African Recorder* July 16–29, 1975, p.4024; Muzorewa, *Rise Up and Walk*, p.167.
73. *ZR*, 4, 4/1975, July – August 1975, pp.8–9; *RH*, 1–7–1975.
74. *St.*, 2–9–1975.
75. *St.*, 23–9–1975.
76. *RH*, 8–9–1975.
77. *ZR*, 5, 34/1976, p.15.
78. *RDM*, 2–10–1975.
79. *RH*, 2–10–1975.
80. Muzorewa, *Rise Up and Walk*, p.169.
81. Interview: Wickus de Kock.
82. *SWB*, 11–7–1975, R. Lus, 8–7–1975.
83. *SWB*, 21–7–1975, R. Lus, 18–7–1975.
84. *St.*, 30–9–1975.
85. *SWB*, 29–10–1975, R. Lus, 27–10–1975.
86. *Obs*, 23–11–1975.
87. *SWB*, 29–10–1975, R. Jhb, 27–10–1975; *RH*, 28–10–1975.
88. *RH*, 13–9–1975; Muzorewa, *Rise Up and Walk*, p.169; Meredith, *The Past Is Another Country*, p.200.
89. *RDM*, 17–9–1975.
90. *SWB*, 19–9–1975, R. Lus, 16–9–1975.
91. Meredith, *The Past Is Another Country*, p.200.
92. *St.*, 10–12–1975, 16–12–1975; *RH*, 11–12–1975.

93. *St.*, 16–12–1975.
94. *RH*, 4–12–1975.
95. *RDM*, 14–11–1975; *ARB*, November 1975, p.3835; *ZR*, 5, 1/1976, p.11.
96. *African Recorder*, December 3–16, 1975, p.4132.
97. *St.*, 7–10–1975.
98. *DN*, 3–12–1975.
99. *St.*, 1–11–1975.
100. *ZR*, 5, 1/1976, p.11.
101. *Obs*, 23–11–1975.
102. *RDM*, 2–12–1975.
103. Nkomo, *The Story of My Life*, pp.254–255, "Declaration of Intention to Negotiate a Settlement".
104. *St.*, 2–12–1975.
105. Nkomo, *The Story of My Life*, p.156.
106. *RDM*, 20–9–1975; see also *RDM*, 27–9–1975; *ARB*, November 1975, p.3834.
107. *SWB*, 11–12–1975, R. Lus, 9–12–1975.
108. *St.*, 3–9–1975.
109. *RFG*, 24–10–1975.
110. *St.*, 29–9–1975.
111. *RDM*, 28–11–1975.
112. *ARB*, December 1975, p.3870.
113. *C&O*, 28–11–1975, p.3.
114. *RDM*, 9–2–1976.
115. *SWB*, 3–3–1976, R. Jhb, 1–3–1976.
116. *St.*, 23–2–1976.
117. *ST*, (Jhb), 7–3–1976.
118. *ARB*, (ec.) 15–2–1976 – 14–3–1976, p.3803.
119. *ST* (Jhb), 7–3–1976.
120. *ST* (Jhb), 14–3–1976.
121. *St.*, 10–3–1976.
122. *RDM*, 22–3–1976.
123. *For The Record*, "Press Interview with Smith 20–3–1976".
124. *ACR*, 1975–1976, p.Λ52.
125. *SWB*, 30–1–1976, R. Lus, 29–1–1976.
126. *ACR*, 1975–1976, p.A55.
127. *SWB*, 3–3–1976, R. Lus, 2–3–1976.
128. *SWB*, 6–3–1976, R. Lus, 5–3–1976.
129. *SWB*, 4–2–1976, R. Lus, 2–2–1976.
130. *SWB*, 17–2–1976, Radio Dar es Salaam (R. Dar) 14–2–1976.
131. *ST* (Jhb), 7–3–1976.
132. *SWB*, 9–3–1976, R. Dar, 7–3–1976.
133. *ARB*, January 1976, p.3887.
134. *SWB*, 10–2–1976, R. Jhb, 8–2–1976.
135. *SWB*, 4–3–1976, Radio Maputo (R. Map), 3–3–1976.
136. *ARB*, January 1976, pp.3887–3888.
137. Martin and Johnson, *The Struggle For Zimbabwe*, p.224.
138. *TT*, 18–12–1975.
139. *RDM*, 23–12–1975.
140. *St.*, 30–1–1976.
141. *SWB*, 3–1–1976, R. Sby, 31–12–1975.
142. *RDM*, 8–3–1976.
143. *RDM*, 5–1–1976.
144. *St.*, 18–2–1976.
145. *SWB*, 17–2–1976, R. Lus, 13–2–1976.
146. *St.*, 2–3–1976.

147. *St.*, 8–3–1976.
148. *St.*, 8–3–1976.
149. *Gdn*, 11–3–1976.
150. *RDM*, 12–3–1976.
151. *FT*, 16–3–1976.
152. *St.*, 17–3–1976.
153. *Gdn*, 18–3–1976, 19–3–1976.
154. See text, Nyangoni and Nyandoro, *Selected Documents*, pp.389–398; RDM, 20–3–1976.
155. *Gdn*, 20–3–1976.
156. *FT*, 20–3–1976.
157. *For The Record*, "Press Interview with P.M. Smith 20–3–1976", p.1.
158. *RDM*, 30–3–1976.
159. *ARB*, December 1975, p.3868.
160. *RDM*, 21–2–1976.
161. *RH*, 27–2–1976.
162. *ARB*, March 1976, p.3971.
163. *For The Record*, "Press Interview with P.M. Smith 20–3–1976", p.5.
164. *St.*, 5–4–1976.
165. *ST* (Jhb), 4–4–1976.
166. *RDM*, 27–3–1976.
167. *St.*, 24–3–1976.
168. *ST* (Jhb), 28–3–1976.
169. *ARB*, March 1976, p.3973.
170. *St.*, 26–3–1976.
171. *St.*, 26–3–1976.
172. *Zimbabwe News* (*ZN*), January/May 1976, pp.21–22.
173. Martin and Johnson, *The Struggle For Zimbabwe*, pp.197–199.
174. Martin and Johnson, *The Struggle For Zimbabwe*, p.200; *ZN*, January/May 1976, pp.11–14.
175. *ZN*, January/May 1976, p.12.
176. *ZN*, January/May 1976, pp.12 13.
177. D. Smith and C. Simpson with I. Davies, *Mugabe*, London 1981, p.74.
178. Martin and Johnson, *The Struggle For Zimbabwe*, pp.204, 206.
179. T. Rangers, "Politicians and Soldiers: The Re-emergence of the Zimbabwe African National Union" Conference on Zimbabwe, Department of Politics, University of Leeds, 21–22, 6, 1980, p.9.
180. Rangers, "Politicians and Soldiers", p.10.
181. Zvobgo, "Report of a Special Trip to Zambia", pp.25, 56, 57.
182. *ZN*, January/May 1976, p.12.
183. Rangers, "Politicians and Soldiers", p.11–12.
184. Martin and Johnson, *The Struggle For Zimbabwe*, p.210.
185. Martin and Johnson, *The Struggle For Zimbabwe*, pp.211–213.
186. Martin and Johnson, *The Struggle For Zimbabwe*, p.219.
187. Zvobgo, "Report of a Special Trip to Zambia", p.53.
188. Martin and Johnson, *The Struggle For Zimbabwe*, p.220.
189. *ZN*, January/May 1976, pp.33–34.
190. Martin and Johnson, *The Struggle For Zimbabwe*, p.217.
191. For an excellent account of the formation of ZIPA, see Martin and Johnson, *The Struggle For Zimbabwe*, pp.217–222.
192. Martin and Johnson, *The Struggle For Zimbabwe*, pp.223–224; Lt Colonel Ron Reid Daly as told to P. Stiff, *Selous Scouts Top Secret War*, Alberton, South Africa 1982, pp.281–282.
193. Muzorewa, *Rise Up and Walk*, pp.186–187.
194. Muzorewa, *Rise Up and Walk*, pp.194–195.

CHAPTER FIVE

1. *Gdn*, 12–4–1976.
2. *RDM*, 27–3–1976.
3. *ARB*, July 1976, p.4080.
4. *Gdn*, 12–4–1976.
5. *SWB*, 3–7–1976, R. Map, 1–7–1976.
6. *SWB*, 16–8–1976, R. Map, 14–8–1976.
7. *St.*, 18–6–1976, 21–6–1976; *Gdn*, 1–7–1976. Reid Daly, *Selous Scouts*, pp.311–312.
8. *Gdn*, 12–4–1976; *TT*, 31–5–1976.
9. *St.*, 10–6–1976.
10. *ARB*, June 1976, p.4066.
11. *ARB*, June 1976, p.4067.
12. *ARB*, January 1976, p.3908.
13. Martin and Johnson, *The Struggle for Zimbabwe*, p.223; see also Reid Daly, *Selous Scouts*, pp.281–282.
14. Martin and Johnson, *The Struggle for Zimbabwe*, pp.223–224.
15. Martin and Johnson, *The Struggle for Zimbabwe*, p.222.
16. *ARB*, March 1976, p.3969.
17. *ARB*, May 1976, p.4035.
18. *ST* (Jhb), 16–5–1976.
19. *St.*, 10–6–1976.
20. *ARB*, March 1976, p.3969.
21. *ARB*, September 1976, p.4171.
22. Martin and Johnson, *The Struggle for Zimbabwe*, p.224.
23. *Gdn*, 11–6–1976.
24. *ARB*, June 1976, p.4066.
25. Martin and Johnson, *The Struggle for Zimbabwe*, p.223.
26. *SWB*, 7–6–1976, R. Jhb, 4–6–1976.
27. *St.*, 9–4–1976, 25–5–1976; *ARB*, April 1976, p.4001; *RDM*, 22–5–1976.
28. *SWB*, R. Sby, 7–6–1976; 18–6–1976, R. Sby, 5–6–1976; 8–7–1976, R. Sby, 6–7–1976; 17–7–1976, R. Sby, 14–7–1976; *ARB*, July 1976, p.4097; *RDM*, 21–4–1976.
29. *RDM*, 15–5–1976; *St.*, 25–5–1976; *SWB*, 16–6–1976, R. Sby, 14–6–1976; 14–6–1976, R. Sby, 12–6–1976; 10–6–1976, R. Sby, 8–7–1976.
30. *SWB*, 23–7–1976, R. Sby, 21–7–1976; *FT*, 12–8–1976.
31. *SWB*, 10–6–1976, R. Sby, 8–6–1976; 14–7–1976, R. Sby, 12–7–1976; 22–7–1976, R. Sby, 19–7–1976; *RDM*, 22–7–1976.
32. See for example, *SWB*, 23–6–1976, R. Sby, 18–6–1976; 28–6–1976, R. Sby, 26–6–1976; 8–7–1976, R. Sby, 6–7–1976.
33. *RDM*, 14–5–1976.
34. *SWB*, 14–6–1976, R. Sby, 12–6–1976.
35. *SWB*, 11–8–1976, R. Sby, 9–8–1976.
36. *SWB*, 23–9–1976, R. Map., 22–9–1976.
37. "Zimbabwe People's Army (ZIPA): Interview with Dzinashe Machingura", *Journal of Southern African Affairs* (JSAA), 1, October 1976.
38. *RDM*, 27–3–1976.
39. Nyagoni and Nyandoro, *Selected Documents*, p.399, "ANC: press statement by Bishop Abel Muzorewa, 20–4–1976".
40. Nyagoni and Nyandoro, *Selected Documents*, p.415.
41. *RDM*, 7–7–1976.
42. *RDM*, 27–3–1976.

43. *St.*, 26–4–1976.
44. *St.*, 10–9–1976.
45. *RH*, 21–4–1976.
46. Nyagoni and Nyandoro, *Selected Documents*, p.423.
47. Nyagoni and Nyandoro, *Selected Documents*, pp.401–402, "ANC: report of a special plenary meeting of the ZLC, Lusaka, 17–20, April 1976".
48. *Gdn*, 17–4–1976.
49. Nyagoni and Nyandoro, *Selected Documents*, pp.403–409.
50. *TT*, 31–5–1976.
51. *TT*, 31–5–1976.
52. Nyagoni and Nyandoro, *Selected Documents*, pp.413, 417, "ANC: address by Bishop Muzorewa, President, to the 27th regular session of the co-ordinating committee of the OAU Liberation Committee meeting", Dar es Salaam, Tanzania, May 31 – June 4 1976.
53. *RH*, 5–6–1976; *St.*, 9–6–1976.
54. Muzorewa, *Rise Up and Walk*, p.200.
55. Nyagoni and Nyandoro, *Selected Documents*, p.417.
56. Nyagoni and Nyandoro, *Selected Documents*, p.418.
57. *St.*, 7–6–1976.
58. *ARB*, July 1976, pp.4079, 4080.
59. Martin and Johnson, *The Struggle for Zimbabwe*, pp.240, 242–243.
60. *ARB*, August 1976, p.4132; Muzorewa, *Rise Up and Walk*, pp.201–206.
61. See below, pp.120.
62. See below, pp.130–41.
63. *St.*, 10–9–1976.
64. Muzorewa, *Rise Up and Walk*, p.206.
65. *St.*, 10–9–1976.
66. *RDM*, 10–9–1976.
67. *St.*, 10–9–1976.
68. Martin and Johnson, *The Struggle for Zimbabwe*, p.243; Smith and Simpson, *Mugabe*, p.91.
69. Smith and Simpson, *Mugabe*, pp.85–87.
70. Smith and Simpson, *Mugabe*, p.89.
71. Ranger, "Politicians and soldiers", p.13.
72. Martin and Johnson, *The Struggle for Zimbabwe*, p.242.
73. Martin and Johnson, *The Struggle for Zimbabwe*, pp.243, 245.
74. Ranger, "Politicians and Soldiers", p.13.
75. *The Zimbabwe Review* (ZR), Vol.5, 2/76, pp.13–14.
76. *ARB*, July 1976, p.4080.
77. Martin and Johnson, *The Struggle for Zimbabwe*, pp.243–244.
78. *St.*, 28–9–1976; *RDM*, 30–9–1976.
79. *Obs.*, 26–9–1976.
80. *SWB*, 24–6–1976, R. Sby, 22–6–1976.
81. *SWB*, 9–6–1976, R. Sby, 7–6–1976.
82. See also *SWB*, 10–7–1976, R. Sby, 8–7–1976; 17–7–1976, R. Sby, 14–7–1976; 29–7–1976, R. Sby, 27–7–1976; 6–8–1976, R. Sby, 3–8–1976.
83. *RDM*, 14–5–1976.
84. *TT*, 28–5–1976; *FT*, 16–8–1976; *SWB*, 4–5–1976, R. Sby, 1–5–1976; 12–5–1976, R. Sby, 10–5–1976; 26–5–1976, R. Sby, 24–5–1976.
85. *SWB*, 7–5–1976, R. Sby, 5–5–1976.
86. *ARB*, May 1976, p.4032.
87. *ARB* (ec.), April 14 – May 15, 1976, p.3869.
88. *DT*, 16–7–1976.
89. *RFG*, 7–5–1976.
90. *ACR*, 1976–1977, p.917.

91. *SWB*, 17–5–1976; R. Sby, 13–5–1976.
92. *FT*, 3–8–1976.
93. *FT*, 3–8–1976; *St.*, 20–8–1976; *ARB* (ec.), March 15 – April 14, 1976, p.3834.
94. *ARC*, 1976–1977, p.B918.
95. *TT*, 31–5–1976.
96. *TT*, 29–4–1976.
97. *ARB*, May 1976, p.4033.
98. *RH*, 4–9–1976.
99. *ST* (Jhb), 5–9–1976.
100. *RH*, 26–7–1976; *Obs.*, 22–8–1976.
101. *SWB*, 17–9–1976, R. Sby, 15–9–1976.
102. Interview: J. Mussett, Jhb, September 1983.
103. *SWB*, 17–9–1976, R. Sby, 15–9–1976.
104. *St.*, 28–4–1976.
105. *Gdn*, 11–6–1976.
106. *St.*, 28–8–1976.
107. *RDM*, 9–9–1976.
108. *St.*, 22–5–1976.
109. *St.*, 4–5–1976.
110. *St.*, 14–6–1976.
111. *St.*, 23–8–1976.
112. *SWB*, 7–8–1976, R. Sby, 5–8–1976.
113. *ACR*, 1976–1977, p.B911; Reid Daly, *Selous Scouts*, pp.280–422.
114. *ACR*, 1976–1977, p.B914.
115. See, for example, Reid Daly, *Selous Scouts*, pp.280–290.
116. *SWB*, 21–8–1976, R. Sby, 18–8–1976.
117. *St.*, 14–6–1976; see also *St.*, 2–6–1976.
118. *SWB*, 6–7–1976, R. Sby, 2–7–1976.
119. *SWB*, 8–6–1976, R. Sby, 6–6–1976.
120. *St.*, 18–6–1976.
121. Reid Daly, *Selous Scouts*, p.320.
122. Reid Daly, *Selous Scouts*, pp.280–281, 285–288, 291–293.
123. Reid Daly, *Selous Scouts*, pp.296–299.
124. Reid Daly, *Selous Scouts*, pp.303–320.
125. *SWB*, 1–7–1976, R. Map., 30–6–1976.
126. *SWB*, 2–7–1976, R. Sby, 30–6–1976; 5–7–1976, R. Sby, 3–7–1976.
127. *ST* (Jhb), 15–8–1976.
128. *FT*, 12–8–1976.
129. *FT*, 12–8–1976.
130. See, for example, the reaction of *Die Burger*, *C&O*, 20–8–1976, p.14.
131. *FT*, 12–8–1976.
132. *ARB*, August 1976, p.4132.
133. Reid Daly, *Selous Scouts*, pp.321–405.
134. Interview: E. Sutton-Pryce; P. Walls, September 1983.
135. *St.*, 22–5–1976.
136. *St.*, 22–5–1976.
137. *Gdn*, 11–6–1976.
138. *SWB*, 27–8–1976, R. Sby, 25–8–1976.
139. *ARB*, March 1976, p.3971.
140. *TT*, 29–4–1976.
141. *St.*, 28–4–1976.
142. *St.*, 28–4–1976.
143. *RDM*, 1–5–1976.
144. *SWB*, 4–5–1976, R. Sby, 1–5–1976.
145. *St.*, 29–4–1976.

146. *ADM*, 9–9–1976.
147. *SWB*, 18–9–1976, R. Sby, 16–9–1976.
148. *ARB*, May 1976, p.4033; June 1976, p.4067.
149. *St.*, 16–6–1976.
150. *RH*, 17–6–1976; see also *St.*, 16–6–1976.
151. *RII*, 24–7–1976.
152. *ARB*, March 1976, p.3971.
153. *ARB*, March 1976, p.3972.
154. M.A. El-Khawas and B. Cohen (eds.), *NSSM 39 – the Kissinger Study of Southern Africa*, Westport CT, 1976.
155. *ACR*, 1975–1976, pp.A19–21.
156. H.G. Zeidenstein, "The Reassertion of Congressional Power: New Curbs on the President", *Political Science Quarterly*, 93, 3, Fall 1978, pp.393–409; T.E. Cronin, "An Imperiled Presidency", *Society*, November/December 1978, pp.57–59.
157. Meredith, *The Past is Another Country*, p.220.
158. *SAR*, July 1976, p.10.
159. Meredith, *The Past is Another Country*, pp.218–219.
160. *RDM*, 21–4–1976.
161. *ARB*, April 1976, p.4004; *RDM*, 28–4–1976.
162. *SWB*, 1–5–1976, R. Map, 29–4–1976.
163. *SWB*, 19–5–1976, R. Jhb, 17–5–1976.
164. *C&O*, 7–5–1976, pp.3–5.
165. *C&O*, 7–5–1976, p.4.
166. *C&O*, 21–5–1976, p.5.
167. *C&O*, 9–4–1976, p.11.
168. *SWB*, 20–5–1976, R. Jhb, 18–5–1976.
169. *RDM*, 18–5–1976.
170. *ARB*, June 1976, pp.4062–4063.
171. Martin and Johnson, *The Struggle for Zimbabwe*, p.239.
172. *ARB*, June 1976, p.4071; *RH*, 30–6–1976.
173. *RDM*, 18–5–1976.
174. *RII*, 18–8–1976, 19–8–1976; *St.*, 16 8 1976, 19–8–1976.
175. Martin and Johnson, *The Struggle for Zimbabwe*, p.239.
176. *ARB*, August 1976, p.4131.
177. *ACR*, 1976–1977, pp.A30–31.
178. *ARB*, August 1976, p.4131.
179. *RII*, 7–9–1976.
180. *RH*, 8–9–1976.
181. *SWB*, 10–9–1976, R. Jhb, 8–9–1976.
182. *ACR*, 1976–1977, p.A32.
183. *RII*, 13–9–1976.
184. *RII*, 15–9–1976.
185. *ARB*, September 1976, p.4166.
186. *RII*, 15–9–1976.
187. *ARB*, September 1976, p.4166.
188. Martin and Johnson, *The Struggle for Zimbabwe*, p.249.
189. *SWB*, 18–9–1976, R. Lus., 16–9–1976.
190. *ARB*, September 1976, p.4166.
191. *ARB*, September 1976, p.4166.
192. *ACR*, 1976–1977, p.A33.
193. Meredith, *The Past is Another Country*, p.249.
194. *RH*, 13–9–1976.
195. *ARB*, September 1976, p.4163.
196. *SWB*, 15–9–1976, R. Jhb, 13–9–1976.
197. Martin and Johnson, *The Struggle for Zimbabwe*, p.248.

198. Interview: P. Walls; E. Sutton-Pryce; J. Mussett Meredith, *The Past is Another Country*, pp.242, 249; *ACR*, 1976–1977, p.A32.
199. *ARB*, September 1976, p.4164.
200. *ARB*, September 1976, p.4164.
201. *ARB*, September 1976, p.4165.
202. *RH*, 18–9–1976.
203. Meredith, *The Past is Another Country*, p.253.
204. Martin and Johnson, *The Struggle for Zimbabwe*, p.249.
205. *ACR*, 1976–1977, p.A34.
206. *ACR*, 1976–1977, p.A36.
207. *St.*, 24–9–1976.
208. *SWB*, 27–9–1976, R. Sby, 24–9–1976.
209. Interview: J. Mussett.
210. Interview: J. Mussett.
211. Interview: J. Mussett.
212. *SWB*, 30–9–1976, R. Sby, 28–9–1976; Meredith, *The Past is Another Country*, p.259; Smith version was approved by Vorster, see *ARB*, January 1977, p.4300.
213. *SWB*, 27–9–1976, R. Sby, 24–9–1976.
214. Meredith, *The Past is Another Country*, pp.254–255.
215. Meredith, *The Past is Another Country*, p.254.
216. Martin and Johnson, *The Struggle for Zimbabwe*, p.252.
217. Interview: E. Sutton-Pryce.
218. *St.*, 24–9–1976.
219. *RH*, 23–9–1976.
220. *ARB*, September 1976, p.4167.
221. *SWB*, 22–9–1976, R. Lus. 20–9–1976.
222. *SWB*, 23–9–1976, R. Lus. 22–9–1976.
223. *ACR*, 1976–1977, p.A36.
224. *RH*, 23–9–1976.
225. *SWB*, 27–9–1976, R. Map. 23–9–1976.
226. *RH*, 24–9–1976.
227. *ARB*, September 1976, p.4171.
228. *ARB*, September 1976, p.4170.
229. Meredith, *The Past is Another Country*, p.263.
230. *ARB*, September 1976, p.4170.
231. *ARB*, September 1976, p.4170.
232. *SWB*, 29–9–1976, R. Lus, 27–9–1976.
233. *SWB*, 30–9–1976, R. Jhb, 29–9–1976.
234. *ARB*, September 1976, p.4172.
235. *RH*, 29–9–1976.
236. Martin and Johnson, *The Struggle for Zimbabwe*, p.256.
237. *SWB*, 30–9–1976, R. Sby, 28–9–1976.
238. *St.*, 28–9–1976.
239. *RDM*, 19–10–1976.
240. Meredith, *The Past is Another Country*, p.257.
241. *St.*, 28–9–1976.
242. *SWB*, 30–9–1976, R. Sby, 28–9–1976.
243. *C&O*, 1–10–1976, p.8.
244. *St.*, 29–9–1976.

CHAPTER SIX

1. *ARB*, October 1976, p.4197.
2. *St.*, 27–9–1976.

NOTES

3. *RH*, 28–9–1976.
4. *RDM*, 30–9–1976.
5. *RH*, 5–10–1976.
6. *RH*, 29–9–1976.
7. *RH*, 28–9–1976.
8. *RDM*, 30–9–1976.
9. *RH*, 2–10–1976.
10. *RH*, 23–10–1976.
11. *RH*, 21–10–1976.
12. *RH*, 4–10–1976.
13. *ST* (Jhb), 26–9–1976.
14. *St.*, 23–9–1976.
15. *ST* (Jhb), 26–9–1976.
16. *St.*, 28–9–1976.
17. *RDM*, 30–9–1976; Martin and Johnson, *The Struggle For Zimbabwe*, p.257.
18. *RDM*, 1–10–1976; Muzorewa, *Rise Up and Walk*, pp.209–210.
19. *ARB*, October 1976, p.4198.
20. *RH*, 5–10–1976; Muzorewa, *Rise Up and Walk*, p.213.
21. *RDM*, 7–10–1976; *ARB*, October 1976, p.4198.
22. Ranger, "Politicians and Soldiers", p.13.
23. Martin and Johnson, *The Struggle For Zimbabwe*, pp.257–258, 260–262.
24. "Interview with Dzinashe Machingura, 22–9–1976", *Journal of Southern African Affairs* (JSAA) 1, October 1976, p.12.
25. *SWB*, 19–10–1976, R. Map, 17–10–1976.
26. *SWB*, 2–10–1976, R. Map, 30–9–1976.
27. *SWB*, 18–10–1976, R. Sby, 15–10–2976.
28. Martin and Johnson, *The Struggle For Zimbabwe*, p.258; *SWB*, 21–10–1976, R. Tanjug, 19–10–1976.
29. *SWB*, 2–10–1976, R. Map, 30–9–1976.
30. *SWB*, 6–10–1976, R. Map, 4–10–1976.
31. *SWB*, 21–10–1976, R. Map, 19–10–1976.
32. *St.*, 28–9–1976.
33. *FT*, 25–10–1976.
34. *SWB*, 27–10–1976, R. Sby, 25–10–1976.
35. *SWB*, 11–10–1976, R. Dar, 9–10–1976.
36. *St.*, 26–9–1976; *SWB*, 27–10–1976, R. Sby, 25–10–1976.
37. *St.*, 1–10–1976.
38. *SWB*, 16–10–1976, R. Map, 14–10–1976.
39. *SWB*, 2–10–1976, R. Dar, 30–9–1976.
40. *SWB*, 1–10–1976, R. Jhb, 29–9–1976.
41. *SWB*, 11–10–1976, R. Lus, 8–10–1976.
42. *ARB*, October 1976, p.4197.
43. *SWB*, 19–10–1976, R. Lus, 17–10–1976; *ARB*, October 1976, pp.4199–4200.
44. *SWB*, 19–10–1976, R. Lus, 17–10–1976.
45. *RH*, 13–10–1976.
46. *RH*, 21–10–1976.
47. *RH*, 21–10–1976.
48. *RH*, 22–10–1976.
49. *RH*, 23–10–1976.
50. *SWB*, 8–10–1976, R. Sby, 6–10–1976.
51. *SWB*, 25–10–1976, R. Sby, 23–10–1976.
52. *RH*, 23–10–1976.
53. *St.*, 15–10–1976.
54. *RH*, 20–10–1976.
55. *SWB*, 28–10–1976, R. Jhb, 26–10–1976.

56. *SWB*, 1–11–1976, R. Sby, 29–10–1976.
57. *ARB*, October 1976, p.4202; *ZR*, 6, January 1977, p.3; "Muzorewa at Zimbabwe Conference in Geneva", The United African National Council of Zimbabwe, London, p.4.
58. *ARB*, October 1976, p.4202.
59. *St.*, 9–11–1976.
60. *RDM*, 6–11–1976.
61. *St.*, 11–11–1976.
62. *RH*, 25–11–1976.
63. *St.*, 1–11–1976.
64. *RH*, 27–10–1976.
65. *ARB*, November 1976, p.4237.
66. *St.*, 9–11–1976.
67. Muzorewa, *Rise Up and Walk*, p.220.
68. *RH*, 5–11–1976, *SWB*, 6–11–1976, R. Sby, 5–11–1976.
69. *RH*, 5–11–1976.
70. Meredith, *The Past Is Another Country*, p.284.
71. See text of statement *ZR*, 6, January 1977, pp.12–13.
72. Meredith, *The Past Is Another Country*, p.284; Smith and Simpson, *Mugabe*, p.96.
73. *SWB*, 9–1–1977, R. Sby, 7–1–1977.
74. Martin and Johnson, *The Struggle For Zimbabwe*, p.261.
75. *SWB*, 1–12–1976; R. Map, 29–11–1976.
76. *St.*, 13–12–1976, Muzorewa, *Rise Up and Walk*, pp.222–223.
77. *RH*, 16–12–1976.
78. *RH*, 10–12–1976.
79. Text of proposals in *ZR*, 6, January 1977, pp.5–6; The *ZR* wrongly dates the text November 2, see *SWB*, 3–12–1976, R. Lus, 2–12–1976.
80. *ARB*, October 1976, p.4199.
81. *SWB*, 3–12–1976, R. Lus, 2–12–1976.
82. *SWB*, 4–12–1976, R. Sby, 3–12–1976.
83. *SWB*, 14–12–1976, R. Sby, 13–12–1976.
84. *Obs.*, 12–12–1976.
85. *SWB*, 13–12–1976, R. Sby, 11–12–1976; 14–12–1976, R. Sby, 13–12–1976.
86. Meredith, *The Past Is Another Country*, p.286.
87. *SWB*, 17–12–1976, R. Sby, 14–12–1976.
88. *RH*, 16–12–1976.
89. *RDM*, 29–11–1976; *SWB*, 21–12–1976, R. Lus, 19–12–1976.
90. *ZR*, 6, February 1977, p.10; *ARB*, January 1977, p.4295.
91. *St.*, 12–1–1977; *ARB*, January 1977, p.4296.
92. *RH*, 11–12–1976.
93. *ST* (Jhb), 2–1–1977.
94. *SWB*, 17–1–1977, R. Sby, 16–1–1977.
95. *SWB*, 29–12–1976, R. Dar, 26–12–1976.
96. *ZR*, 6, February 1977, p.9; *SWB*, 19–1–1977, R. Map, 17–1–1977.
97. Martin and Johnson, *The Struggle For Zimbabwe*, p.261.
98. *St.*, 27–1–1977.
99. Martin and Johnson, *The Struggle For Zimbabwe*, p.261.
100. Martin and Johnson, *The Struggle For Zimbabwe*, p.262; *SWB*, 21–1–1977, R. Dar, 19–1–1977; 27–1–1977, R. Map, 25–1–1977.
101. *SWB*, 19–1–1977, R. Map, 17–1–1977.
102. *RH*, 23–12–1976.
103. *DN*, 1–1–1977.
104. *SWB*, 18–12–1976, R. Sby, 16–12–1976.
105. *SWB*, 6–1–1977, R. Jhb, 4–1–1977.
106. *ACR*, 1976/1977, p.A47.

107. *SWB*, 6–1–1977, R. Jhb, 4–1–1977.
108. Meredith, *The Past Is Another Country*, p.288.
109. *ARB*, January 1977, p.4295.
110. *SWB*, 8–1–1977, R. Map, 6–1–1977.
111. *ACR*, 1976–1977, p.A46.
112. *ACR*, 1976–1977, pp.A46–47.
113. *SWB*, 10–1–1977, R. Dar, 7–1–1977.
114. *ARB*, January 1977, p.4295.
115. *ARB*, January 1977, p.4297.
116. See Text *ACR*, 1976/1977, pp.A47–50.
117. *SWB*, 24–1–1977, R. Sby, 21–1–1977.
118. *SWB*, 26–1–1977, R. Sby, 24–1–1977.
119. *ARB*, January 1976, p.4297.
120. *SWB*, 15–1–1977, R. Sby, 13–1–1977.
121. See also Reid Daly, *Selous Scouts*, p.444; *ACR*, 1976/1977, p.A41; Meredith, *The Past Is Another Country*, pp.280–281.
122. Reid Daly, *Selous Scouts*, pp.451–452.
123. *SWB*, 21–1–1977, R. Sby, 19–1–1977.
124. *SWB*, 27–1–1977, R. Sby, 25–1–1977.
125. Reid Daly, *Selous Scouts*, pp.452–453.
126. Reid Daly, *Selous Scouts*, pp.444–448, 460–466.
127. *SWB*, 2–12–1976, R. Sby, 30–11–1976; *RH*, 31–12–1976.
128. Reid Daly, *Selous Scouts*, pp.422–438, 454–459; B. Cole, *The Elite: The Story of the Rhodesian Special Air Service*, Transkei, 1984, pp.111–112, 114–129; Meredith, *The Past Is Another Country*, p.282.
129. *St.*, 15–10–1976, 2–11–1976; *RH*, 8–11–1976, *TT*, 29–1–1977.
130. *C&O*, 15–10–1976, p.5, 22–10–1976, p.14.
131. *SWB*, 3–11–1976, R. Jhb, 1–11–1976.
132. *SWB*, 5–1–1977, R. Jhb, 3–1–1977.
133. *SWB*, 14–10–1976, R. Jhb, 12–10–1976.
134. *SWB*, 26–11–1976, R. Map, 24–11–1976; 1–12–1976, R. Havana, 29–11–1976, R. Prensa Latina, 29–11–1976.
135. *ACR*, 1976–1977, p.B416.
136. *SWB*, 21–12–1976, R. Jhb, 19–12–1976.
137. *SWB*, 31–12–1976, R. Jhb, 30–12–1976.
138. See, for example, *C&O*, 15–10–1976, p.4, 22–10–1976, p.14, 12–11–1976, p.13.
139. *SWB*, 13–11–1976, R. Luanda, 11–11–1976.
140. *SWB*, 17–1–1977, R. Jhb, 14–1–1977.
141. *C&O*, 19–11–1976, pp.1–6.
142. *C&O*, 12–11–1976, p.1.
143. *ARB*, January 1977, p.4304.
144. *St.*, 6–1–1977.
145. *FT*, 14–1–1977.
146. *RFG*, 15–10–1976.
147. Interview: Sutton-Pryce.
148. *SWB*, 20–12–1976, R. Sby, 17–12–1976.
149. *SWB*, 26–1–1977, R. Sby, 24–1–1977.
150. *SWB*, 9–12–1976, R. Sby, 6–12–1976.
151. *SWB*, 29–12–1976, R. Sby, 23–12–1976.
152. *SWB*, 17–12–1976, R. Sby, 14–12–1976.
153. *St.*, 30–11–1976.
154. Meredith, *The Past Is Another Country*, p.291; *FT*, 14–1–1977.
155. *SWB*, 17–1–1977, R. Sby, 15–1–1977.
156. *SWB*, 31–1–1977, R. Sby, 27–1–1977.
157. *SWB*, 26–1–1977, R. Sby, 24–1–1977.

158. *RH*, 31–12–1976, *SWB*, 31–12–1976, R. Sby, 29–12–1976.
159. *SWB*, 1–1–1977, R. Sby 30–12–1976.
160. *RDM*, 14–12–1976.
161. *SWB*, 22–11–1976, R. Sby, 19–11–1976.
162. *RDM*, 14–12–1976.
163. *SWB*, 17–12–1976, R. Sby, 14–12–1976.
164. *FT*, 21–1–1977.
165. *SWB*, 17–1–1977, R. Jhb, 16–1–1977.
166. *ARB*, January 1977, p.4297.

CHAPTER SEVEN

1. *SWB*, 26–1–1977, R. Sby 24–1–1977.
2. *ACR*, 1976–1977, p.B909; 1977–1978, p.B1041.
3. *ACR*, 1977–1978, p.1041.
4. *RDM*, 4–7–1977.
5. Martin and Johnson, *The Struggle For Zimbabwe*, p.279.
6. *TT*, 5–2–1977.
7. Martin and Johnson, *The Struggle For Zimbabwe*, pp.279–280.
8. *ACR*, 1977–1978, pp.B1042–1043.
9. Cole, *The Elite*, pp.129–189; Reid Daly, *Selous Scouts*, pp.489–501, 505–531.
10. Cole, *The Elite*, pp.190–198; Reid Daly, *Selous Scouts*, pp.532–540.
11. *SWB*, 26–3–1977, R. Map 24–3–1977.
12. *RDM*, 26–4–1977.
13. *SWB*, 14–7–1977, R. Dar 12–7–1977.
14. *SWB*, 29–12–1976, R. Dar 26–12–1976.
15. *SWB*, 19–1–1977, R. Map 17–7–1977.
16. *SWB*, 16–4–1977, R. Map 14–4–1977; 22–4–1977, R. Lus 19–4–1977, R. Dar 19–4–1977; 3–5–1977, R. Map 1–5–1977; 4–5–1977, R. Dar 2–5–1977, 3–5–1977; 14–7–1977, R. Dar 12–7–1977; 19–7–1977, R. Dar 18–7–1977; 27–7–1977, R. Lus 25–7–1977; 15–9–1977, R. Map 13–9–1977; 15–10–1977, R. Sby 13–10–1977; Martin and Johnson, *The Struggle For Zimbabwe*, p.279; *Obs.* 8–5–1977.
17. *SWB*, 29–12–1976, R. Dar 26–12–1976.
18. *RDM*, 26–4–1977.
19. *SWB*, 27–7–1977, R. Lus 25–7–1977.
20. Martin and Johnson, *The Struggle For Zimbabwe*, p.279.
21. Meredith, *The Past Is Another Country*, p.318.
22. *ARB*, October 1977, p.4614.
23. *FT*, 21–11–1977, *St.*, 30–11–1977; *DN*, 26–11–1977; *SWB*, 23–11–1977, R. Dar 22–11–1977; 24–11–1977, R. Lus 23–11–1977; *St.*, 7–12–1977, 8–12–1977.
24. *St.*, 21–11–1977, 3–3–1978; *ARB*, January 1977, p.4721; Meredith, *The Past Is Another Country*, p.304.
25. *St.*, 3–3–1978.
26. *SWB*, 3–6–1977, R. Sby 2–6–1977.
27. *ARB*, September 1977, p.4581.
28. *Interview*: P. Walls.
29. Meredith, *The Past Is Another Country*, p.305.
30. *SWB*, 2–7–1977, R. Sby 30–6–1977. R$1.28 = £1.
31. *ACR*, 1977–1978, pp.B1043–1044; at the beginning of the war in 1972, defence spending was as low as some R$20m a year.
32. *ACR*, 1977–1978, p.1047.
33. *St.*, 14–11–1977.
34. *ACR*, 1977–1978, pp.B1047–1048.

35. *ARB* (Ec.), 1978, p.4531.
36. *ACR*, 1977–1978, p.B1042.
37. *ARB*, September 1977, p.4581.
38. *ACR*, 1977–1978, p.1047.
39. *RDM*, 29–4–1977.
40. *St.*, 2–7–1977.
41. *SWB*, 1–9–1977, R. Sby 29–8–1977.
42. Meredith, *The Past Is Another Country*, p.315.
43. *TT*, 18–8–1977; *St.*, 18–8–1977.
44. *RH*, 11–2–1977.
45. *RH*, 24–2–1977.
46. *RH*, 24–2–1977.
47. *SWB*, 4–3–1977, R. Sby 2–3–1977.
48. *SWB*, 8–3–1977, R. Sby 4–3–1977.
49. *SWB*, 17–3–1977, R. Sby 15–3–1977.
50. *SWB*, 20–4–1977, R. Sby 18–19–4–1977.
51. *RH*, 2–5–1977; *SWB*, 3–5–1977, R. Sby 29–4–1977; 25–6–1977, R. Sby 23–6–1977; 8–7–1977, R. Sby 5–7–1977; *St.*, 4–7–1977; *FT*, 20–6–1977, 5–7–1977.
52. *SWB*, 20–7–1977, R. Sby 18–7–1977.
53. *SWB*, 2–9–1977, R. Sby 1–9–1977.
54. *SWB*, 8–7–1977, R. Sby 6–7–1977.
55. *SWB*, 9–7–1977, R. Sby 6–7–1977; *IHT*, 11–7–1977.
56. *SWB*, 20–7–1977, R. Sby 18–7–1977.
57. *IHT*, 11–7–1977.
58. *ARB*, February 1977, p.4310.
59. *SWB*, 25–6–1977, R. Map 22–7–1977.
60. *ARB*, July 1977, p.4487.
61. *ARB*, July 1977, p.4512.
62. *ARB*, September 1977, p.4577.
63. *SWB*, 5–11–1976, R. Sby 3–11–1976.
64. Z. Brzezinski, "America in a hostile world", *Foreign Policy*, Summer 1976, pp.65–95. For a critical appraisal of the evolution of Brzezinski's global outlook, see S. Serfaty, "Brzezinski: Play it again Zbig", *Foreign Policy*, Fall 1978, pp.3–21.
65. *U.S. News and World Report*, 30–5–1977.
66. USIS, Tel-Aviv, *American Foreign Policy Series* "Text of remarks by Z. Brzezinski before the Trilateral Commission in Bonn, 25–10–1977"; *The Nairobi Times* 1–1–1978; The main elements of Brzezinski's thought appear in Carter's famous speech at Notre Dame University on May 24, 1977, see "Carter calls for new expanded policy"; South Bend, Indiana, 22–5–1977, Official Text, USIS, Tel-Aviv.
67. Vance, *Hard Choices*, New York, 1983, p.256.
68. *Newsweek*, 28–3–1977.
69. *ARB*, February 1977, p.4418.
70. H. Bienen, "U.S. foreign policy in changing Africa", *Political Science Quarterly*, Fall 1978, pp.454–455.
71. *ARB*, August 1977, p.4522.
72. *ARB*, August 1977, p.4522.
73. *ARB*, February 1977, p.4334.
74. *ARB*, August 1977, p.4522.
75. *Commentary*, August 1978, p.18.
76. *Newsweek*, 28–3–1977, pp.18–19.
77. *U.S. News and World Report*, 30–5–1977, p.38.
78. *SAR*, 8, March 1977, p.49.
79. Vance, *Hard Choices*, pp.261–262.
80. Vance, *Hard Choices*, p.262.

81. *ARB*, February 1977, p.4334.
82. *SWB*, 15–3–1977, R. Sby 12–3–1977.
83. Vance, *Hard Choices*, pp.263–264.
84. *SWB*, 16–3–1977, R. Sby 14–3–1977.
85. Vance, *Hard Choices*, p.264.
86. *SAR*, 9, July 1977, p.6.
87. *ARB*, April 1977, pp.4403–4404; *SWB*, 16–4–1977, R. Sby 13–4–1977; 14–4–1977, R. Gaberone 14–4–1977.
88. *ARB*, April 1977, p.4405.
89. *DT*, 21–4–1977.
90. Vance, *Hard Choices*, pp.264–165; *ARB*, May 1977, p.4437.
91. *SWB*, 14–5–1977, R. Sby 12–5–1977.
92. *SWB*, 26–5–1977, R. Dar 24–5–1977.
93. Vance, *Hard Choices*, p.266.
94. *SWB*, 31–5–1977, R. Jhb 29–5–1977.
95. *SWB*, 31–5–1977, R. Map 29–5–1977.
96. Vance, *Hard Choices*, p.266.
97. *New York Times (NYT)*, 2–6–1977.
98. *St.*, 9–6–1977.
99. *SWB*, 11–6–1977, R. Sby 9–6–1977; *DN*, 11–6–1977; *ARB*, June 1977, p.4452.
100. Vance, *Hard Choices*, pp.266–267.
101. *ARB*, June 1977, p.4471.
102. *ARB*, July 1977, p.4513.
103. *SWB*, 11–7–1977, R. Lus 7–7–1977.
104. Vance, *Hard Choices*, pp.268–269.
105. Martin and Johnson, *The Struggle For Zimbabwe*, p.268.
106. *DN*, 18–7–1977.
107. *SWB*, 12–7–1977, R. Sby 10–7–1977.
108. "Rhodesia and the Anglo-American Proposals, Part II", Government Printer, Salisbury, August 1977.
109. Vance, *Hard Choices*, pp.267–268.
110. Vance, *Hard Choices*, p.269.
111. *DN*, 16–8–1977.
112. Vance, *Hard Choices*, p.269.
113. *DN*, 16–8–1977.
114. *DN*, 9–8–1977.
115. Vance, *Hard Choices*, p.269.
116. *DN*, 21–8–1977.
117. *RDM*, 15–8–1977.
118. *ARB*, August 1977, p.4538.
119. *ARB*, August 1977, p.4538.
120. *DN*, 28–8–1977.
121. *ARB*, August 1977, p.4539.
122. Vance, *Hard Choices*, p.270; *ARB*, August 1977, p.4539.
123. *Gdn*, 29–8–1977.
124. *SWB*, 1–9–1977, R. Sby 30–8–1977.
125. See text of proposals and Owen's explanation thereof, *SAR*, 12, May 1978, pp.4–12.
126. *SWB*, 5–9–1977, R. Sby 2–9–1977.
127. See text *ZR*, 6–9–1977, pp.2–3, 46.
128. *SWB*, 31–8–1977, R. Lus 28–8–1977.
129. *ARB*, September 1977, p.4578.
130. Vance, *Hard Choices*, pp.261–262.
131. *ACR*, 1977–1978, p.A110.
132. *ACR*, 1977–1978, p.A95.

133. *ACR*, 1977–1978, pp.A111–112, B591–594; *SAD*, 25–3–1977, p.3.
134. *SAD*, 25–3–1977, p.1.
135. *The Citizen*, 21–3–1977.
136. *Christian Science Monitor*, 14–10–1977; *SAD*, 11–2–1977.
137. *ARB*, February 1977, p.4334.
138. Vance, *Hard Choices*, p.263.
139. USIS, Tel-Aviv, *American Foreign Series*, "Text of remarks by Z. Brzezinski before the Trilateral Commission in Bonn, 25–10–1977".
140. *SAD*, 11–2–1977, p.19.
141. *U.S. News and World Report*, 30–5–1977, p.38.
142. Vance, *Hard Choices*, p.263.
143. *SAD*, 25–2–1977, p.9; 4–3–1977, p.7; 22–4–1977, pp.26–27.
144. *SAD*, 22–4–1977, p.22.
145. *SAD*, 22–4–1977, p.4.
146. *SAD*, 22–4–1977, p.5.
147. *SWB*, 7–5–1977, R. Jhb 5–5–1977.
148. Vance, *Hard Choices*, p.263.
149. *SAR*, 9, July 1977, pp.1–20, Mondale's statement at the end of the meeting, 20–5–1977.
150. *SAR*, 9, July 1977, p.28.
151. *SAD*, 24–6–1977, p.22.
152. *SAD*, 24–6–1977, p.4.
153. *SAD*, 27–5–1977.
154. *ACR*, 1977–1978, pp.B843–844.
155. *ACR*, 1976–1977, pp.B769–770.
156. *SAR*, 9, July 1977, p.22.
157. *RDM*, 15–8–1977.
158. *SAR*, 9, July 1977, p.17.
159. Vance, *Hard Choices*, p.265.
160. Vance, *Hard Choices*, p.268.
161. Vance, *Hard Choices*, p.271.
162. *SAD*, 12–8–1977, p.1.
163. *SAD*, 19–8–1977, p.1.
164. *SAD*, 19–8–1977, p.1.
165. *RDM*, 5–8–1977.
166. *Gdn*, 29–8–1977.
167. Vance, *Hard Choices*, p.270.
168. *St.*, 2–9–1977.
169. *ST* (Jhb), 11–9–1977.
170. *SAD*, 9–9–1977, p.24.
171. *FT*, 20–9–1977.
172. *ARB*, September 1977, p.4577.
173. *ARB*, September 1977, p.4576.
174. *ARB*, October 1977, p.4614.
175. Vance, *Hard Choices*, p.271.
176. *ARB*, September 1977, p.4578; *TT*, 2–9–1977.
177. *ARB*, September 1977, p.4578.
178. *ARB*, October 1977, p.4614.
179. *FT*, 24–10–1977.
180. *RDM*, 18–10–1977.
181. *SWB*, 27–10–1977, R. Map 25–10–1977.
182. *St.*, 1–11–1977.
183. Meredith, *The Past Is Another Country*, p.320.
184. *FT*, 24–10–1977; *TT*, 29–9–1977; Meredith, *The Past Is Another Country*, p.319.
185. *RDM*, 18–10–1977.

186. Vance, *Hard Choices*, p.272.
187. *ARB*, November 1977, p.4655; *SAD*, 4–11–1977, p.1.
188. *St.*, 17–9–1977.
189. *SAD*, 4–11–1977, p.2.
190. *ACR*, 1977–1978, pp.B879–885.
191. *ACR*, 1977–1978, p.B895.
192. *SAD*, 18–11–1977; Meredith, *The Past Is Another Country*, p.320.
193. Martin and Johnson, *The Struggle For Zimbabwe*, p.287; Vance, *Hard Choices*, p.271.
194. *ARB*, October 1977, p.4614.
195. Martin and Johnson, *The Struggle For Zimbabwe*, p.284.
196. *SWB*, 6–10–1977, R. Lus 4–10–1977.
197. Martin and Johnson, *The Struggle For Zimbabwe*, p.287.
198. *St.*, 15–11–1977.
199. *SWB*, 5–3–1977, R. Sby 3–3–1977.
200. *ARB*, April 1977, pp.4403–4404.
201. *ARB*, May 1977, p.4438.
202. *DT*, 29–7–1977.
203. *SWB*, 22–9–1977, R. Sby 20–9–1977.
204. *SWB*, 23–9–1977, R. Sby 21–9–1977.
205. *ARB*, May 1977, p.4438.
206. *DT*, 27–7–1977.
207. *SWB*, 29–7–1977, R. Sby 27–7–1977; *RDM*, 3–8–1977.
208. *RDM*, 8–9–1977.
209. *RFG*, 23–9–1977; *TT*, 5–11–1977.
210. *SWB*, 5–9–1977, R. Sby 2–9–1977.
211. *St.*, 26–9–1977.
212. *TT*, 28–9–1977.
213. Muzorewa, *Rise Up and Walk*, pp.225–230.
214. *SWB*, 26–11–1977, R. Sby 25–11–1977.
215. *ARB*, November 1977, p.4641.
216. *ARB*, December 1977, p.4679.
217. Muzorewa, *Rise Up and Walk*, p.232.
218. *TT*, 2–12–1977; *Gdn*, 3–12–1977.
219. Muzorewa, *Rise Up and Walk*, p.231; *DT*, 3–12–1977.
220. *DT*, 10–12–1977.
221. *TT*, 12–12–1977.
222. Muzorewa, *Rise Up and Walk*, pp.233–234.
223. Muzorewa, *Rise Up and Walk*, pp.234–235.
224. *ARB*, January 1978, p.4717.
225. Muzorewa, *Rise Up and Walk*, pp.235–236; *Gdn*, 12–1–1978; *TT*, 12–1–1978.
226. *Gdn*, 12–1–1978.
227. *The Citizen*, 23–1–1978.
228. *Gdn*, 24–1–1978.
229. *RDM*, 26–1–1978; *ARB*, January 1978, p.4717.
230. *St.*, 7–2–1978; Muzorewa, *Rise Up and Walk*, p.236.
231. *St.*, 14–2–1978.
232. *SWB*, 5–12–1977, R. Map 3–12–1977.
233. Vance, *Hard Choices*, pp.284–285.
234. *DN*, 9–12–1977.
235. Vance, *Hard Choices*, p.284.
236. *SWB*, 7–12–1977, R. Dar 5–12–1977.
237. *DN*, 9–12–1977.
238. *ARB*, January 1978, pp.4718–4719.
239. *DN*, 7–12–1977.

240. *Gdn*, 20–1–1978.
241. *FT*, 30–1–1978.
242. *ARB*, January 1978, pp.4755–4756.
243. *SWB*, 1–2–1978, R. Map 31–1–1978; 3–2–1978, R. Map 1–2–1978; 4–2–1978, R. Map 1–2–1978; Vance, *Hard Choices*, p.285.
244. See full text of the internal agreement, Muzorewa, *Rise Up and Walk*, pp.278–282.

CHAPTER EIGHT

1. *ARB*, February 1979, p.5167.
2. *FT*, 28–6–1978.
3. *SWB*, 7–7–1978, R. Sby 5–7–1978, R. Jhb 7–7–1978.
4. *SWB*, 8–7–1978, R. Sby 6–7–1978.
5. *SWB*, 12–10–1978, R. Sby 10–10–1978.
6. *SWB*, 13–10–1978, R. Sby 10–10–1978.
7. *SWB*, 5–12–1978, R. Sby 3–12–1978.
8. *SWB*, 24–1–1979, R. Sby 21–1–1979.
9. Muzorewa, *Rise Up and Walk*, pp.278–282.
10. *RDM*, 5–5–1978.
11. *RDM*, 5–5–1978, *SWB*, 8–5–1978, R. Sby 5–5–1978.
12. *ARB*, May 1978, p.4864.
13. *ARB*, July 1978, pp.4933–4934.
14. *SWB*, 16–9–1978, R. Sby 14–9–1978.
15. *SWB*, 23–9–1978, R. Sby 21–9–1978.
16. *ARB*, September 1978, pp.4998–4999.
17. *SWB*, 30–9–1978, R. Sby 28–9–1978.
18. *SWB*, 3–10–1978, R. Sby 1–10–1978.
19. *ARB*, October 1978, p.5035.
20. *ARB*, November 1978, p.5069.
21. *DT*, 17–11–1978.
22. *ARB*, November 1978, pp.5068–5069.
23. Commonwealth Secretariat, "An analysis of the illegal regime's constitution for 'Zimbabwe–Rhodesia'" London 22–3–1979, p.1.
24. "Zimbabwe–Rhodesia Constitution" in *Rhodesia Statutes 1979*, Government Printer, Salisbury, 1979.
25. "Zimbabwe–Rhodesia Constitution" pp.275–282.
26. *RDM*, 2–12–1978.
27. "Zimbabwe–Rhodesia Constitution" pp.287–311.
28. "Zimbabwe–Rhodesia Constitution" pp.319–327.
29. *SWB*, 12–1–1979, R. Sby 10–1–1979.
30. *SWB*, 17–1–1979, R. Sby 16–1–1979.
31. *SWB*, 17–1–1979, R. Sby 16–1–1979.
32. *St.*, 25–1–1979.
33. See, for example, *RDM* 22–5–1978, 23–5–1978; *SWB*, 24–5–1978, R. Sby 22–5–1978.
34. *SWB*, 21–4–1978, R. Sby 19–4–1978; 11–5–1978, R. Sby 9–5–1978; *Financial Mail* (Jhb), 12–5–1978, p.443; *St.*, 11–5–1978; C.J. Zvobgo, "Rhodesia's Internal Settlement 1977–1979", *JSAS*, V, 1, January 1980, p.30.
35. *Gdn*, 8–5–1978; *SWB*, 9–5–1978, R. Sby 8–5–1978.
36. *SWB*, 11–5–1978, R. Sby 9–5–1978.
37. *RDM*, 15–5–1978.
38. *SWB*, 3–10–1978, R. Sby 1–10–1978; *ARB*, October 1978, p.5035.
39. *DT*, 17–11–1978.

40. *DN*, 6–3–1978.
41. *ZN*, 10,1,1978, p.29.
42. *ZN*, 10,1,1978, p.7.
43. *St.*, 13–6–1978.
44. *ZN*, 10,1,1978, pp.53–59.
45. *ZN*, 10,4,1978, pp.14–22.
46. *SWB*, 4–1–1979, R. Addis Ababa 2–1–1979.
47. *ZN*, 10,5,1978, p.4.
48. *St.*, 13–6–1978.
49. *ZN*, 10–1–1978, p.55.
50. *ZN*, 10–1–1978, p.29.
51. *SWB*, 23–6–1978; R. Map 21–6–1978.
52. R.T. Libby, "Anglo–American Diplomacy and the Rhodesian Settlement: a loss of impetus" *Orbis*, Spring 1979, p.194.
53. *DN*, 27–3–1978.
54. *ACR*, 1978–1979, p.C31.
55. *SWB*, 4–9–1978; R. Lus 2–9–1978.
56. *ZN*, 10–5–1975, p.49.
57. *Africa*, November 1978, p.40; *SWB*, 9–10–1978, R. Jhb 7–10–1978.
58. E. Evans, "Fighting Against Chimurenga: An Analysis of Counter-Insurgency in Rhodesia 1972–1979", Historical Association of Zimbabwe, Local Series 37, p.22; *St.*, 20–10–1978.
59. *ACR*, 1978–1979, p.A74.
60. Smith and Simpson, *Mugabe*, p.88.
61. *ZN*, 10–4–1978, p.56.
62. *St.*, 7–8–1978.
63. *ZN*, 10–5–1978, p.40.
64. *RDM*, 24–11–1978.
65. D.S. Papp, "Soviet Union and Southern Africa" in R.H. Donaldson (ed.) *The Soviet Union in the Third World: Success and Failure*, Boulder and London 1981, pp.81–82; on Soviet–ZANU relations see also P. Vanneman and W. Martin James III, *Soviet Foreign Policy in Southern Africa: Problems and Prospects*, Pretoria, 1982, pp.10–11.
66. *St.*, 8–5–1978, 18–7–1978; *RDM*, 14–9–1978; Cillier, *Counter-Insurgency in Rhodesia*, p.196; Evans, "Fighting Against Chimurenga", pp.7–8.
67. Reid Daly, *Selous Scouts*, pp.707–708.
68. Evans, "Fighting Against Chimurenga", pp.7–8.
69. Reid Daly, *Selous Scouts*, p.707.
70. *ZN*, 10–4–1978, pp.44–45.
71. *ZN*, 10–1–1978, p.55, 10–4–1978, p.7, 10–6–1978, p.22; *St.* 30–8–1978.
72. *ZN*, 10–6–1978, pp.6–7; see also *ZN*, 10–5–1978, p.5.
73. *SWB*, 13–4–1979, R. Sby 11–4–1979.
74. *ACR*, 1978–1979, p.B993.
75. *ZN*, 10–6–1978, p.13.
76. *ACR*, 1978–1979, p.B993.
77. *ZN*, 10–6–1978, p.7; *ACR*, 1978–1979, p.B995.
78. *ACR*, 1978–1979, p.B993.
79. Evans, "Fighting Against Chimurenga", p.7; Cillier, *Counter-Insurgency in Rhodesia*, p.46.
80. *RDM*, 14–9–1978; *ST* (Jhb), 17–9–1978.
81. *St.*, 18–4–1978.
82. Reid Daly, *Selous Scouts*, p.592.
83. See, for example, *ST* (Jhb), 17–9–1978.
84. *ARB*, April 1978, p.4827.
85. *SAR*, 13, September 1978, pp.49–50.

86. *SAR*, 16, August 1979, p.48, Cledwyn Hughes Report 17–1–1979; Vance, *Hard Choices*, p.293; *SWB*, 24–1–1979, R. Sby 21–1–1979.
87. *St.*, 10–3–1978.
88. *RDM*, 20–3–1978.
89. *RDM*, 6–4–1978.
90. *St.*, 19–4–1978.
91. *St.*, 10–3–1978.
92. *St.*, 19–4–1978.
93. *St.*, 21–4–1978.
94. *SWB*, 4–5–1978, R. Sby 2–5–1978.
95. *SWB*, 7–6–1978, R. Sby 5–6–1978; 9–6–1978, R. Sby 8–6–1978.
96. *SWB*, 17–6–1978, R. Sby 15–6–1978.
97. *SWB*, 6–7–1978, R. Sby 5–7–1978.
98. *SWB*, 17–7–1978, R. Sby 13–7–1978.
99. *SWB*, 17–6–1978, R. Sby 15–6–1978.
100. *SWB*, 3–7–1978, R. Sby 1–7–1978.
101. *SWB*, 4–8–1978, R. Sby 2–8–1978.
102. D. Caute, *Under the Skin*, Penguin Books, 1983, p.270.
103. Caute, *Under the Skin*, p.269.
104. Reid Daly, *Selous Scouts*, pp.566–567.
105. Caute, *Under the Skin*, p.270.
106. Caute, *Under the Skin*, pp.270–271; Meredith, *The Past Is Another Country*, p.352.
107. Meredith, *The Past Is Another Country*, p.352.
108. *ARB*, September 1978, p.5002.
109. *ARB*, September 1978, p.5002.
110. *SWB*, 12–1–1979, R. Jhb 11–1–1979.
111. *RDM*, 5–7–1978, 6–7–1978; *St.*, 5–7–1978; Martin and Johnson, *The Struggle For Zimbabwe*, p.291.
112. *St.*, 6–7–1978.
113. *SWB*, 11–8–1978, R. Map 8–8–1978.
114. Cillier, *Counter-Insurgency in Rhodesia*, pp.45, 50; Martin and Johnson, *The Struggle For Zimbabwe*, p.292; Martin and Johnson claim that their numbers in mid-1978 reached 13,000.
115. Cillier, *Counter-Insurgency in Rhodesia*, p.55.
116. *ZN*, 10–1–1978, p.14.
117. *ZN*, 10–6–1978, pp.18–28; see also Gann and Henriksen, *The Struggle For Zimbabwe*, pp.90–91; Reid Daly, *Selous Scouts*, pp.553–563, 576–584.
118. Caute, *Under the Skin*, p.233.
119. Caute, *Under the Skin*, p.272; J. McBruce, *When the Going was Rough: A Rhodesian Story*, Goodwood, 1983; See also Caute, *Under the Skin*, pp.244, 258–262, 284–285, 293–294, 305; Meredith, *The Past Is Another Country*, p.341.
120. *RDM*, 12–1–1979.
121. *SWB*, 22–12–1978, R. Map 20–12–1978.
122. *SWB*, 18–10–1978, R. Sby 16–10–1978.
123. *ACR*, 1978–1979, p.B1002.
124. *SWB*, 8–11–1978, R. Map 3–11–1978.
125. *SWB*, 26–3–1979, R. Map 23–3–1979.
126. *SWB*, 30–6–1978, R. Sby 28–6–1978.
127. *ZN*, 10–5–1978, pp.57–58.
128. *St.*, 25–7–1978.
129. See, for example, Caute, *Under the Skin*, p.247; *FT*, 23–8–1978; *St.*, 23–8–1978.
130. Cillier, *Counter-Insurgency in Rhodesia*, pp.129–130; Reid Daly, *Selous Scouts*, pp.571–572; Cole, *The Elite*, p.273.
131. Cillier, *Counter-Insurgency in Rhodesia*, pp.45, 51.

132. Cole, *The Elite*, p.274.
133. Caute, *Under the Skin*, pp.249–253, 259; *ARB*, June 1978, p.4900.
134. Caute, *Under the Skin*, pp.273–277.
135. Caute, *Under the Skin*, pp.309–310.
136. Reid Daly, *Selous Scouts*, pp.708–709.
137. Reid Daly, *Selous Scouts*, p.542; See also Cole, *The Elite*, p.252.
138. Reid Daly, *Selous Scouts*, pp.589–591.
139. *ACR*, 1978–1979, p.A1002; *ARB*, September 1978, p.5002; Reid Daly, *Selous Scouts*, pp.584–588.
140. Cole, *The Elite*, pp.223–224.
141. Cole, *The Elite*, pp.233–238.
142. Cole, *The Elite*, pp.224–232.
143. Reid Daly, *Selous Scouts*, pp.591–597.
144. *SWB*, 28–2–1979, R. Sby 26–2–1979.
145. Cole, *The Elite*, pp.270–296; Stiff, *See You in November*, pp.266–299.
146. Reid Daly, *Selous Scouts*, pp.666–671.
147. Cole, *The Elite*, pp.296–304.
148. Stiff, *See You in November*, p.199.
149. Stiff, *See You in November*, pp.191–203, 217–220, 230–235.
150. Cole, *The Elite*, pp.246, 260–270.
151. Reid Daly, *Selous Scouts*, p.736.
152. *ARB*, January 1979, p.5134.
153. *St.*, 12–4–1979.
154. *ARB*, January 1979, p.5135.
155. *RDM*, 16–2–1978; Vance, *Hard Choices*, pp.285–286.
156. *ST* (Jhb), 19–3–1978; Vance, *Hard Choices*, p.286.
157. Vance, *Hard Choices*, pp.286–287.
158. *ARB*, February 1978, p.4757.
159. *RDM*, 20–3–1978, 22–3–1978; *U.S. News and World Report*, 13–3–1978, p.28.
160. *ARB*, February 1978, p.4757.
161. Vance, *Hard Choices*, p.287.
162. *St.*, 17–3–1978.
163. *DN*, 6–3–1978; see also *DN*, 11–3–1978.
164. *DN*, 11–3–1978.
165. Vance, *Hard Choices*, p.286.
166. *ARB*, March 1978, p.4790.
167. Vance, *Hard Choices*, p.285.
168. *DN*, 22–3–1978, 27–3–1978.
169. *St.*, 25–3–1978.
170. *Weekly Review (WR)* (Nairobi), 20–3–1978.
171. Vance, *Hard Choices*, p.287.
172. *DN*, 11–3–1978.
173. *RDM*, 18–3–1978.
174. *RDM*, 22–3–1978.
175. *HIT*, 4–4–1978.
176. *RDM*, 16–3–1978.
177. *RDM*, 10–4–1978.
178. *RDM*, 8–4–1978.
179. *RDM*, 15–4–1978.
180. *RDM*, 13–3–1978.
181. *RDM*, 20–3–1978.
182. *RDM*, 15–4–1978.
183. Vance, *Hard Choices*, pp.288–289; *RDM*, 19–4–1978; *SWB*, 18–4–1978, R. Map 16–4–1978.
184. *SWB*, 18–4–1978, R. Dar 16–4–1978.

NOTES

185. Vance, *Hard Choices*, p.289.
186. Vance, *Hard Choices*, p.289.
187. Vance, *Hard Choices*, p.289; *DN*, 18–4–1978.
188. *RDM*, 19–4–1978.
189. *RDM*, 24–4–1978.
190. *RDM*, 15–6–1978.
191. *Gist*, Bureau of Public Affairs, U.S. Department of State, June 1978.
192. *TT*, 27–5–1978.
193. *St.*, 12–6–1978.
194. *RDM*, 16–6–1978.
195. *St.*, 20–6–1978.
196. *ARB*, June 1978, pp.4897–4898.
197. *ST* (Jhb), 30–6–1978.
198. Vance, *Hard Choices*, p.290.
199. Vance, *Hard Choices*, p.290; *St.*, 30–6–1978.
200. *St.*, 30–6–1978.
201. *RDM*, 13–7–1978.
202. *RDM*, 15–7–1978.
203. Vance, *Hard Choices*, pp.290–291.
204. *Gdn*, 28–7–1978.
205. *St.*, 4–8–1978; *ARB*, August 1978, p.4965.
206. Vance, *Hard Choices*, p.291.
207. *TT*, 3–8–1978.
208. *St.*, 4–8–1978.
209. Vance, *Hard Choices*, p.287.
210. Martin and Johnson, *The Struggle For Zimbabwe*, pp.294–295.
211. *RDM*, 16–6–1978.
212. *Obs*, 23–7–1978.
213. Vance, *Hard Choices*, p.291.
214. Martin and Johnson, *The Struggle For Zimbabwe*, p.295.
215. *TT*, 1–9–1978; Vance, *Hard Choices*, pp.291–292.
216. *TT*, 1–9–1978.
217. *SWB*, 5–9–1978, R. Lus 2–9–1978.
218. *SWB*, 4–9–1978, R. Lus 2–9–1978.
219. *ARB*, September 1978, p.4998.
220. Vance, *Hard Choices*, p.292.
221. *TT*, 5–10–1978.
222. Vance, *Hard Choices*, pp.292–293.
223. *DT*, 21–10–1978.
224. *DT*, 21–10–1978; *FT*, 23–10–1978.
225. *FT*, 24–10–1978.
226. *FT*, 26–10–1978.
227. Z. Brzezinski, *Power and Principle: Memoirs of the National Security Adviser, 1977–1981*, London, 1983, p.142.
228. *TT*, 8–11–1978.
229. *ACR*, 1978–1979, p.B983.
230. *DT*, 24–11–1978; *SAR*, 16, August 1979, pp.34–35, "Statement by Callaghan in the House of Commons, 23–11–1978".
231. *RDM*, 29–11–1978.
232. *SAR*, 16, August 9, "Report by Cledwyn Hughes to James Callaghan on his mission to Southern Africa, 17–1–1979", p.45.
233. "Report by Cledwyn Hughes 17–1–1979", pp.45–49.
234. "Report by Cledwyn Hughes 17–1–1979", p.49.
235. *Gdn*, 18–1–1979.
236. *Gdn*, 23–3–1979.

237. *ARB*, March 1979, p.5201.
238. Vance, *Hard Choices*, p.294.
239. *RDM*, 19–4–1979.
240. *SWB*, 18–4–1979, R. Sby 16–4–1979.
241. *SWB*, 19–4–1979, R. Map 16–4–1979.
242. *SWB*, 2–4–1979, R. Sby 31–3–1979.
243. *St.*, 12–4–1979.
244. Meredith, *The Past Is Another Country*, p.359.
245. *ACR*, 1978–1979, p.B966–967.
246. *ACR*, 1978–1979, p.B977.
247. *ACR*, 1978–1979, pp.998–999; Caute, *Under the Skin*, pp.336–338; Meredith, *The Past Is Another Country*, pp.363–364.
248. *SWB*, 25–4–1979, R. Sby 23–4–1979.
249. *SWB*, 27–4–1979, R. Sby 24–4–1979.
250. See, for example, *SWB*, 12–5–1979, R. Sby 10–5–1979; 16–5–1979, R. Sby 12–5–1979; 21–5–1979, R. Sby 18–5–1979; 23–5–1979, R. Sby 21–5–1979; 25–5–1979, R. Sby 23–5–1979; 28–5–1979, R. Sby 25–5–1979; 30–5–1979, R. Sby 26–5–1979; 1–6–1979, R. Sby 30–5–1979.
251. *ARB*, May 1979, p.5278.
252. *DT*, 8–6–1979.
253. *SWB*, 17–5–1979, R. Addis 15–5–1979.
254. *SWB*, 25–4–1979, R. Sby 24–4–1979; 4–5–1979, R. Sby 2–5–1979.
255. *SWB*, 23–7–1979, R. Sby 20–7–1979; 25–7–1979, R. Sby 23–7–1979; *St.*, 25–7–1979.
256. *SWB*, 2–8–1979, R. Sby 31–7–1979.
257. *Gdn*, 1–8–1979.
258. *SWB*, 20–8–1979, R. Sby 17–8–1979.
259. *St.*, 3–5–1979.
260. *Gdn*, 28–6–1979.
261. *RDM*, 24–6–1979.
262. *SWB*, 23–7–1979, R. Sby 20–7–1979.
263. See, for example, *SWB*, 9–7–1979, R. Sby 4–7–1979; 10–7–1979, R. Sby 7–7–1979; 22–8–1979, R. Sby 18–8–1979, 20–8–1979; 23–8–1979, R. Sby 21–8–1979; 27–8–1979, R. Sby 24–8–1979; Caute, *Under the Skin*, pp.365–367.
264. *DT*, 27–6–1979; Cole, *The Elite*, pp.305–326.
265. *DT*, 5–5–1979.
266. Miles, *Triumph or Tragedy*, pp.45–46, 147.
267. Miles, *Triumph or Tragedy*, p.148.
268. Miles, *Triumph or Tragedy*, p.149.
269. *RDM*, 7–5–1979.
270. *RDM*, 24–5–1979.
271. *DT*, 23–5–1979; on Lord Boyd's report, see *Gdn*, 25–5–1979.
272. *Gdn*, 17–5–1979; *RDM*, 16–5–1979.
273. *SWB*, 17–5–1979, R. Sby 15–5–1979.
274. *ARB*, June 1979, p.5314.
275. *SWB*, 12–6–1979, R. Sby 10–6–1979.
276. *WR*, 15–6–1979.
277. *RDM*, 14–6–1979; *SWB*, 15–6–1979; R. Sby 13–6–1979.
278. Vance, *Hard Choices*, p.296.
279. *RDM*, 16–6–1979.
280. *St.*, 29–6–1979.
281. *SWB*, 10–7–1979, R. Sby 8–7–1979.
282. *SWB*, 17–7–1979, R. Jhb 15–7–1979.
283. Vance, *Hard Choices*, pp.295–296.
284. *SWB*, 17–7–1979, R. Sby 16–7–1979.

NOTES

285. Vance, *Hard Choices*, pp.295–296.
286. *RDM*, 1–6–1979; Miles, *Triumph or Tragedy*, p.160.
287. *ARB*, May 1979, p.5276.
288. *ARB*, June 1979, p.5314.
289. Martin and Johnson, *The Struggle For Zimbabwe*, pp.302–303.
290. *Obs*, 20–5–1979; Miles, *Triumph or Tragedy*, pp.159–160.
291. *ST* (Jhb), 20–5–1979.
292. *SWB*, 24–7–1979, R. Dar 22–7–1979.
293. *DT*, 23–5–1979.
294. *Verbatim Service*, London Press Service, 25–7–1979 – Text of speech by Mrs Margaret Thatcher opening the adjournment debate on Southern Africa in the House of Commons, on 25 July 1979.
295. *DT*, 23–5–1979.
296. Vance, *Hard Choices*, p.297.
297. *Gdn*, 16–5–1979.
298. *DT*, 23–5–1979.
299. *FT*, 26–6–1979.
300. *SWB*, 1–8–1979, R. Lus 31–7–1979.
301. *TOZ*, 3–8–1979; Miles, *Triumph or Tragedy*, pp.164–165.
302. Copy in author's possession.
303. Copy in author's possession.
304. *Daily Express*, 4–8–1979.
305. Copy of Nyerere's speech in author's possession.
306. Martin and Johnson, *The Struggle For Zimbabwe*, pp.313–314; "Plan for Zimbabwe, Lusaka Highlights", from the Commonwealth Secretariat.
307. "Plan for Zimbabwe, Lusaka Highlights", from the Commonwealth Secretariat.
308. *SWB*, 8–8–1979, R. Sby 4–8–1979.
309. *SWB*, 8–8–1979, R. Sby 6–8–1979.
310. *SWB*, 8–8–1979, R. Sby 6–8–1979.
311. *FT*, 8–8–1979.
312. *SAD*, 27–4–1979, p.1.
313. *SWB*, 8–8–1979, R. Map 6–8–1979.
314. *SWB*, 10–8–1979, R. Map 8–8–1979.
315. *SWB*, 10–8–1979, R. Cairo 9–8–1979.
316. *DT*, 13–8–1979.
317. *DT*, 11–8–1979.
318. *Obs*, 12–8–1979.
319. *TOZ*, 8–8–1979.
320. *Gdn*, 14–8–1979; *DT*, 15–8–1979.
321. *FT*, 16–8–1979.
322. *SWB*, 17–8–1979, R. Lus 15–8–1979.
323. *SWB*, 17–8–1979, R. Luanda 15–8–1979.
324. *SWB*, 22–8–1979, R. Dar 20–8–1979; 23–8–1979, R. Map 20–8–1979.

CHAPTER NINE

1. G. Wasserman, "Rhodesia is not Kenya", *Foreign Policy*, 33, Winter 1978–1979, p.40.
2. J. Davidow, *A Peace in Southern Africa – The Lancaster House Conference on Rhodesia*, Boulder and London, 1979, pp.101–114.
3. Davidow, *Peace in Southern Africa*, pp.100–101.
4. Xan Smiley, "Zimbabwe, Southern Africa and the Rise of Robert Mugabe", *Foreign Affairs*, 58,5, Summer 1980, p.1064; see also Davidow, *Peace in Southern Africa*, p.100.

305

5. Smiley, "Zimbabwe, Southern Africa", p.1064.
6. Davidow, *Peace in Southern Africa*, p.100.
7. *SWB*, 15–10–1979, R. Sby 12–10–1979; 18–10–1979, R. Map. 12–10–1979; 21–10–1979, R. Lus 20–11–1979; *ARB*, October 1979, pp.5453–5454; *FT*, 24–10–1979.
8. *SWB*, 7–11–1979, R. Jhb 5–11–1979.
9. *FT*, 24–10–1979.
10. *St.*, 3–10–1979.
11. *SWB*, 8–11–1979, R. Jhb 7–11–1979; 21–11–1979, R. Lus 20–11–1979.
12. Meredith, *The Past Is Another Country*, p.377; *St.*, 12–11–1979; *SWB*, 8–9–1979, R. Sby 5–9–1979; 6–9–1979, R. Map 6–9–1979; 10–9–1979, R. Sby 8–9–1979.
13. See for example *SWB* 1–10–1979, *Voice of Free Africa* (*VFA*) 29–9–1979; 23–10–1979, R. Map 21–10–1979, *VFA* 21–10–1979; 25–10–1979, *VFA* 23–10–1979; 29–10–1979, *VFA* 26–10–1979; 6–11–1979, *VFA* 2–11–1979; 20–11–1979, *VFA* 16–11–1979; 26–11–1979, *VFA* 23–11–1979.
14. Smith and Simpson, *Mugabe*, p.151.
15. Interview: H. Pakendorf (editor of *Die Vaderland*), August 1983.
16. Martin and Johnson, *The Struggle For Zimbabwe*, pp.316–317.
17. *ARB*, August 1979, pp.5389–5390.
18. *FT*, 14–11–1979.
19. Meredith, *The Past Is Another Country*, pp.375–376; R.S. Jaster, "A Regional Security Role for Africa's Front-Line States: Experience and Prospects" *Adelphi Papers*, 180, The International Institute for Strategic Studies, London, 1983, p.13.
20. Zimbabwe–Rhodesia, "Report of the Constitutional Conference", Lancaster House September–December 1979, p.10.
21. Zimbabwe–Rhodesia, "Report of the Constitutional Conference", pp.15,17.
22. Zimbabwe–Rhodesia, "Report of the Constitutional Conference", pp.18–22.
23. Davidow, *Peace in Southern Africa*, pp.53–54.
24. *SWB*, 14–9–1979, R. Map 12–9–1979.
25. Davidow, *Peace in Southern Africa*, p.55; Jaster, "A Regional Security Role", p.14.
26. Conference spokesman, "Summary of an Independence Constitution for Rhodesia, circulated to the delegates by the chairman on September 12".
27. Patriotic Front, "Brief summary of proposals for an independence constitution".
28. Davidow, *Peace in Southern Africa*, p.56.
29. *SWB*, 24–9–1979, R. Sby 21–9–1979.
30. Davidow, *Peace in Southern Africa*, p.59.
31. PF, "The Legislature"; Davidow, *Peace in Southern Africa*, p.59.
32. *Gdn*, 10–10–1979.
33. Davidow, *Peace in Southern Africa*, p.60.
34. *Gdn*, 6–10–1979.
35. Davidow, *Peace in Southern Africa*, pp.61–62.
36. *SWB*, 15–10–1979, R. Map 12–10–1979, R. Sby 13–10–1979.
37. *Obs*, 14–10–1979; *SWB*, 17–10–1979, R. Dar 15–10–1979.
38. *Obs*, 14–10–1979.
39. *FT*, 16–10–1979.
40. Davidow, *Peace in Southern Africa*, p.64.
41. *Gdn*, 17–10–1979.
42. *FT*, 17–10–1979; Davidow, *Peace in Southern Africa*, p.64.
43. *DN*, 17–10–1979.
44. Jaster, "A Regional Security Role", p.15.
45. *Gdn*, 17–10–1979; Davidow, *Peace in Southern Africa*, p.65.
46. *FT*, 19–10–1979.
47. *FT*, 14–11–1979.
48. *SWB*, 12–11–1979, R. Addis Ababa 10–11–1979.
49. *SWB*, 12–11–1979, R. Addis Ababa 10–11–1979.

50. *ARB*, October 1979, p.5452.
51. *SWB*, 1–11–1979, R. Sby 30–10–1979.
52. *SWB*, 29–10–1979, R. Map 26–10–1979.
53. *Daily Mail* (London), 27–10–1979.
54. *DT*, 31–10–1979, 1–11–1979.
55. *FT*, 3–11–1979.
56. *DT*, 2–11–1979.
57. *SWB*, 14–11–1979, R. Map 10–11–1979.
58. *FT*, 3–11–1979.
59. Smith and Simpson, *Mugabe*, pp.130–131.
60. *DT*, 5–11–1979.
61. *DT*, 6–11–1979.
62. Smith and Simpson, *Mugabe*, p.135.
63. Smith and Simpson, *Mugabe*, p.135; *DT*, 12–11–1979; *Gdn*, 9–11–1979.
64. *Gdn*, 9–11–1979.
65. *RDM*, 5–11–1979.
66. *Gdn*, 10–11–1979.
67. *DT*, 10–11–1979.
68. *DT*, 12–11–1979.
69. *FT*, 13–11–1979, 14–11–1979.
70. *FT*, 14–11–1979.
71. *TT*, 16–11–1979.
72. *FT*, 17–11–1979.
73. *Gdn*, 4–12–1979.
74. *Gdn*, 4–12–1979.
75. Davidow, *Peace in Southern Africa*, p.86.
76. Vance, *Hard Choices*, p.301.
77. *FT*, 17–11–1979.
78. *FT*, 20–11–1979.
79. *Gdn*, 23–11–1979; See also *SWB*, 26–11–1979, R. Map 23–11–1979, R. Addis Ababa 24–11–1979.
80. *DT*, 24–11–1979; *Obs*, 25–11–1979.
81. *DT*, 24–11–1979.
82. *ARB*, November 1979, p.5489.
83. Smith and Simpson, *Mugabe*, p.141.
84. Smith and Simpson, *Mugabe*, pp.140–141; see also *RDM*, 26–11–1979.
85. *TT*, 27–11–1979.
86. *RDM*, 29–11–1979.
87. Davidow, *Peace in Southern Africa*, p.81.
88. Davidow, *Peace in Southern Africa*, p.81.
89. *RDM*, 29–11–1979.
90. *Gdn*, 1–12–1979.
91. Smith and Simpson, *Mugabe*, p.144.
92. Davidow, *Peace in Southern Africa*, p.82.
93. *Obs*, 2–12–1979.
94. Smith and Simpson, *Mugabe*, pp.143–145.
95. *TT*, 6–12–1979.
96. Smith and Simpson, *Mugabe*, p.145.
97. *ARB*, December 1979, pp.5511–5513.
98. Smith and Simpson, *Mugabe*, p.150.
99. Smith and Simpson, *Mugabe*, pp.148–152; Davidow, *Peace in Southern Africa*, pp.84–90.
100. *SWB*, 19–12–1979, R. Sby 18–12–1979.
101. *TT*, 22–12–1979.

BIBLIOGRAPHY

PRIMARY SOURCES

"Carter's call for new expanded global policy", official text, USIS, Tel-Aviv
Commonwealth Secretariat, "An analysis of the illegal regime's constitution for Zimbabwe–Rhodesia", London, 22–3–1979
For the record, Ministry of Information, Immigration and Tourism, Salisbury
Gist, Bureau of Public Affairs, U.S. Department of State
Miscellaneous press releases pertaining to the Lancaster House Conference, issued by the Conference Spokesman and the Patriotic Front
Nyangoni, C. and Nyandoro, G. *Zimbabwe independence movements, selected documents*, London, 1979
Revolution, organ of the ANC
"Rhodesia and the Anglo-American Proposals", Government Printer, Salisbury, August 1977
Southern African Record (*SAR*)
Summary of an independent constitution circulated to the delegates by the chairman on September 12, 1979, by the conference spokesman
"Text of remarks by Z. Brzezinski before the Trilateral Commission in Bonn, 25–10–1977", in *American Foreign Policy Series*, United States Information Service (USIS), Tel-Aviv
"Text of speech by Mrs Margaret Thatcher opening the adjournment debate on southern Africa in the House of Commons, on 25 July 1979", Verbatim Service, London Press Service, 25–7–1979
"The price of detente", printed for ZANU by Workers Publishing House, London, undated
United African National Council in Zimbabwe, "Muzorewa at Zimbabwe conference in Geneva"
Zimbabwe Review (ZR), organ of ZAPU
"Zimbabwe–Rhodesia Constitution", *The Rhodesian Statutes, 1979*, Government Printer, Salisbury, 1979
Zimbabwe–Rhodesia, "Report of the constitutional conference", Lancaster House, September–December, 1979
Zimbabwe News (ZN), organ of ZANU
Zvobgo, Edison, "Report of a special trip to Zambia during the period 3, August to 19, August 1975". Confidential, for restricted circulation

INTERVIEWS

Cowper, Reg, Johannesburg, September 1983
Cronje, Rowan, Johannesburg, September 1983
de Kock, Wickus, Karino, September 1983
Mussett, Jack, Johannesburg, September 1983

BIBLIOGRAPHY

Pakendorf, Harold, Johannesburg, September 1983
Sutton-Pryce, Edward, Pretoria, August 1983

NEWSPAPERS, MAGAZINES AND RADIO TRANSMISSIONS

Africa, London
African Recorder, New Delhi
Africa Research Bulletin (ARB), Exeter
Christian Science Monitor
The Citizen (Johannesburg)
Comment and Opinion (C&O), a weekly survey of the South African Press and Radio, Pretoria
Daily Mail, London
Daily News (DN), Dar es Salaam
Daily Telegraph (DT), London
Financial Mail (Johannesburg)
Financial Times (FT), London
Guardian (Gdn), London
International Herald Tribune (IHT)
The Nairobi Times
Newsweek, New York
New African, London
New York Times (NYT)
Observer (Obs), London
Property and Finance (Salisbury)
Rand Daily Mail (RDM) Johannesburg
Rhodesian Financial Gazette (RFG), Salisbury
The Rhodesian Herald (RH), Salisbury
South African Digest (SAD), Johannesburg
South African Financial Gazette (SAFG), Johannesburg
Southern Africa (Sn.A.), New York
The Star (St.), Johannesburg
Sunday Times (ST), Johannesburg
Survey of World Broadcast (SWB), BBC, London
The Times (TT), London
Times of Zambia (TOZ), Lusaka
U.S. News and World Report
Weekly Review (WR), Nairobi

BOOKS

Anglin, D.G. and Shaw, T.M. *Zambia's Foreign Policy: studies in diplomacy and dependence*, Boulder, 1979
Bauman, L.W. *Politics in Rhodesia: White Power in an African State*, Cambridge, Mass., 1973.
Bruce, J.M. *When the Going was Rough*, Goodwood, 1983
Brzezinski, Z. *Power and Principle: memoirs of the National Security Adviser 1977–1981*, London, 1983
Burchett, W. *Southern Africa Stands Up: the revolution in Angola,*

309

Mozambique, Zimbabwe, Namibia and South Africa, New York, 1978
Carter, J. *Keeping faith*, New York, 1983
Caute, D. *Under the Skin*, Penguin Books, 1983
Cilliers, J.K. *Counter Insurgency in Rhodesia*, London, 1985
Cole, B. *The Elite: the story of the Rhodesian Special Air Service*, Transkei, 1984
Davidow, J. *Peace in Southern Africa – the Lancaster House Conference on Rhodesia*, Boulder and London, 1979
D'Oliveira, J. *Vorster – the Man*, Johannesburg, 1977
El-Khawas, M. and Cohen, B. (eds), *MSSM 39 – The Kissinger Study of Southern Africa*, Washington, 1976
Gann, L.H. and Henriksen, J.H. *The struggle for Zimbabwe*, New York, 1981
Hancock, I. *White Liberals, Moderates and Radicals in Rhodesia 1953–1980*, New York, 1984
Hill, D. *The Last Days of White Rhodesia*, London, 1981
Hudson, M. *Triumph or Tragedy*, London, 1981
Joyce, P. *Anatomy of a rebel: Smith of Rhodesia*, Salisbury, 1974
Lake, A. *The "Tar Baby Option" – American policy towards southern Rhodesia*, New York, 1976
Legum, C. *Southern Africa: the secret diplomacy of detente*, London, 1975
Legum, C. *Southern Africa: the year of the whirlwind*, London, 1977
Legum, C. (ed.), *Africa Contemporary Record (ACR)*, London
Lemarchand, R. *American Policy in Southern Africa: the stakes and the stance*, University Press of America, 1979
Martin, M. and Johnson, P. *The Struggle for Zimbabwe*, London and Boston, 1981
Maxey, K. *The Fight for Zimbabwe*, London 1975
Meredith, M. *The Past is another Country – Rhodesia UDI to Zimbabwe*, London, 1980
Metrowitch, F.R. *Toward Dialogue and detente*, Sandton, 1975
Middlemas, K. *Cabora Bassa: engineering and politics in southern Africa*, London, 1975
Mitchell, D. *African Nationalist Leaders in Zimbabwe: who's who*, Salisbury, 1980
Muzorewa, A. *Rise Up and Walk*, London, 1979
Nkomo, J. *The Story of my Life*, London, 1984
Nyagumbo, M. *With the People*, London, 1980
Reid Daly, R. *Selous Scouts Top Secret War*, Alberton, 1982
Shaw, T.A. and Heard, A.K. *Cooperation and Conflict in Southern Africa*, Washington, 1977
Smith, D. and Simpson, C. *Mugabe*, London, 1981
Stiff, P. *See You in November*, Alberton, 1985
Thompson, C.B. *Challenge to Imperialism: The Front Line States in the liberation of Zimbabwe*, Harare, 1985
Vance, C. *Hard Choices*, New York, 1983
Vanneman, P. and Martin James III, W. *Soviet Foreign Policy in Southern Africa: problems and prospects*, Pretoria, 1982
Windrich, E. *Britain and the Politics of Rhodesian Independence*, New York, 1978

BIBLIOGRAPHY

ARTICLES

Anglin, D.G. "Zimbabwe and the Southern African Detente", *International Journal* (Toronto) 30, 3, Summer 1975

Arnold, G. "Rhodesia under pressure", *African Report* (Washington) July – August 1974

Baker, D.J. "Rhodesia, settlement and Southern Africa", Occasional Paper, South Africa Institute of International Affairs (SAIIA) (Johannesburg), September 1976

Barber, J. "Zimbabwe's Southern African setting", *Journal of Commonwealth and Comparative Politics (JCCP)* (London) 18,1, March 1980

Barrat, J. "Detente in Southern Africa", *The World Today* (London) 33,3, March 1975

Barrat, J. "The internal agreement in Rhodesia and the outlook for an international settlement", *International Affairs Bulletin* (Johannesburg) 2,1, 1978

Bienen, H. "U.S. foreign policy in changing Africa", *Political Science Quarterly* (New York), Fall 1978

Brzezinski, Z. "America in a hostile world", *Foreign Policy*, 23, Summer 1976

Burdette, M.M. "The mines, class, power and foreign policy in Zambia", *The Journal of Southern African Studies (JSAS)* 10,2, April 1980

Chambati, A.M. "Rhodesia mid-1974: The African National Council and the Rhodesian solution", Occasional Paper, South African Institute for International Affairs (Johannesburg), July 1974

Cohen, B. "The war in Rhodesia: a dissenter's view", *African Affairs* (London), 76, 305, October 1977

Crocker, C.A. "The quest for an African policy", *The Washington Review of Strategic and International Studies*, April 1978

Day, J. "The insignificance of tribe in African politics of Zimbabwe Rhodesia", *JCCP* 18,1 March 1980

Eriksen, K. "Zambia: class formation and detente", *Review of African Political Economy*, 10, September–December 1977

Evans, E. "Fighting Cimurenga: an analysis of counter-insurgency in Rhodesia 1972–1979", Historical Association of Zimbabwe Local Series 37

Eze, O.C. "OAU faces Rhodesia", *African Review* (Dar es Salaam) 5,1, 1975

Gann, L.H. "American policy towards Zimbabwe–Rhodesia: a reappraisal", *South Africa International* (Johannesburg), January 1980

Geldenhuis, D. "Some foreign policy implications of South Africa's 'Total National Strategy'", Special Study, South African Institute of International Affairs, March 1981

Gersham, C. "The world according to Andrew Young", *Commentary*, August 1978

Geyser, O. "Detente in Southern Africa", *African Affairs* 75, 299, April 1976

Hancock, I. "The survival of the doomed: Rhodesia since UDI", *World Review*, Australian Institute of International Affairs, 17, 2, June 1978

Hendriques, J. "The struggle of the Zimbabweans: conflict between the nationalists and the Rhodesian regime", *African Affairs* 76, 305, October 1977

311

THE MAKING OF ZIMBABWE

Herskowits, J. "Dateline Nigeria: a Black power", *Foreign Policy*, 29, Winter 1977–1978

Hirschman, D. "Southern Africa: détente?" *Journal of Modern African Studies (JMAS)* (London), 14, 1, March 1976

Hodges, T. "Mozambique: the politics of liberation" in G.M. Carter and P. O'Mera, *Southern Africa: the continuing crisis*, Bloomington, 1979

Howe, R.W. "United States' policy in Africa", *Current History*, 76, 445, March 1979

Hugins, W.E. "Moralism in American foreign policy: from Jefferson to Jimmy Carter", *Issues and Studies: a Journal of Chinese Studies and International Affairs*, 14, 9, September 1978

Jaster, R.S. "A regional security role for Africa's Front-Line States: experience and prospects", *Adelphi Papers*, 180, London 1983

Kirk, T. and Sherwell, C. "The Rhodesian general election of 1974", *JCCP*, 13, 1, March 1975

Klinghoffer, A.J. "The Soviet Union and Angola", in R.H. Donaldson (ed.) *The Soviet Union in the Third World: success and failure*, Boulder and London, 1981

Legum, C. "The Soviet Union, China and the West in southern Africa", *Foreign Affairs*, 54, 4, July 1976

Libby, R.T. "Anglo-American diplomacy and the Rhodesian settlement: a loss of impetus", *Orbis* (Philadelphia), 23, 1, Spring 1979

Low, S. "The Zimbabwe settlement 1976–1979", S. Tuval and I.W. Zartman (eds.), *International mediation in theory and practice*, Boulder and London, 1985

Mick, D. "The April 1976 elections in Zimbabwe–Rhodesia", *African Affairs*, 78, 313, October 1979

Mubako, S. "The quest for unity in Zimbabwe liberation movement", *Issue*, Waltham, Mass., 5, 1, Spring 1975

Nyerere, J.K. "America and southern Africa", *Foreign Affairs*, 55, 4, July 1977

O'Mera, P. "Rhodesia/Zimbabwe: Guerilla warfare or political settlement?", in G.M. Carter and P. O'Mera (eds) *Southern Africa: The Continuing Crisis*, Bloomington and London 1979

O'Leary, J.P. "Envisioning interdependence: perspectives on future world order", *Orbis*, 22, 3, Fall 1978

Papp, D.S. "Soviet Union and southern Africa", in R.H. Donaldson (ed.), *The Soviet Union in the Third World: success and failure*, Boulder and London, 1981

Ranger, T. "Politicians and soliders: the re-emergence of the Zimbabwe African National Union", Conference on Zimbabwe, Department of Politics, University of Leeds, June 21–22, 1980

Ranger, T. "The changing of the old guard: Robert Mugabe and the revival of ZANU", *JSAS*, 7, 1, October 1980

Rees, D. "Soviet strategic penetration in Africa", *Conflict Studies*, November 1976

Serfaty, S. "Brzezinski: Play it again Zbig", *Foreign Policy*, 32, Fall 1978

Shaw, T.M. "The foreign policy of Zambia: ideology and interest", *JMAS*, 14, 1, March 1976

Shaw, T.M. "The international politics of southern Africa: change or continuity?" *Issue*, 7, 1, 1977

Shepherd, G.W, Jr. "The struggle for a new southern African policy: the Carter task", *Journal of Southern African Affairs*, 2, January 1977

Somerville, K. "The U.S.S.R. and southern Africa since 1976", *JMAS* 22, 1, 1984

Tordoff, W. "Zambia: the politics of disengagement", *African Affairs*, 76, 302, January 1977

Ullman, R.H. "Trilateralism: partnership for what?" *Foreign Affairs*, 55, 1, October 1976

Ullman, R.H. "Salvaging America's Rhodesian policy", *Foreign Affairs*, 55, 5, Summer 1977

Wasserman, G. "Rhodesia is not Kenya", *Foreign Policy*, 33, Winter 1978–1979

Wilkinson, A.R. "The impact of the war", *JCCP*, 18, 1, March 1980

Windrich, E. "Resolving the Rhodesian Conflict: Détente or Confrontation", *Ufahamu* (Los Angeles) 5, 3, 1975

Zvobgo, C.J. "Rhodesia's internal settlement 1977–1979", *JSAS*, 5, 1, January 1980

Index

314